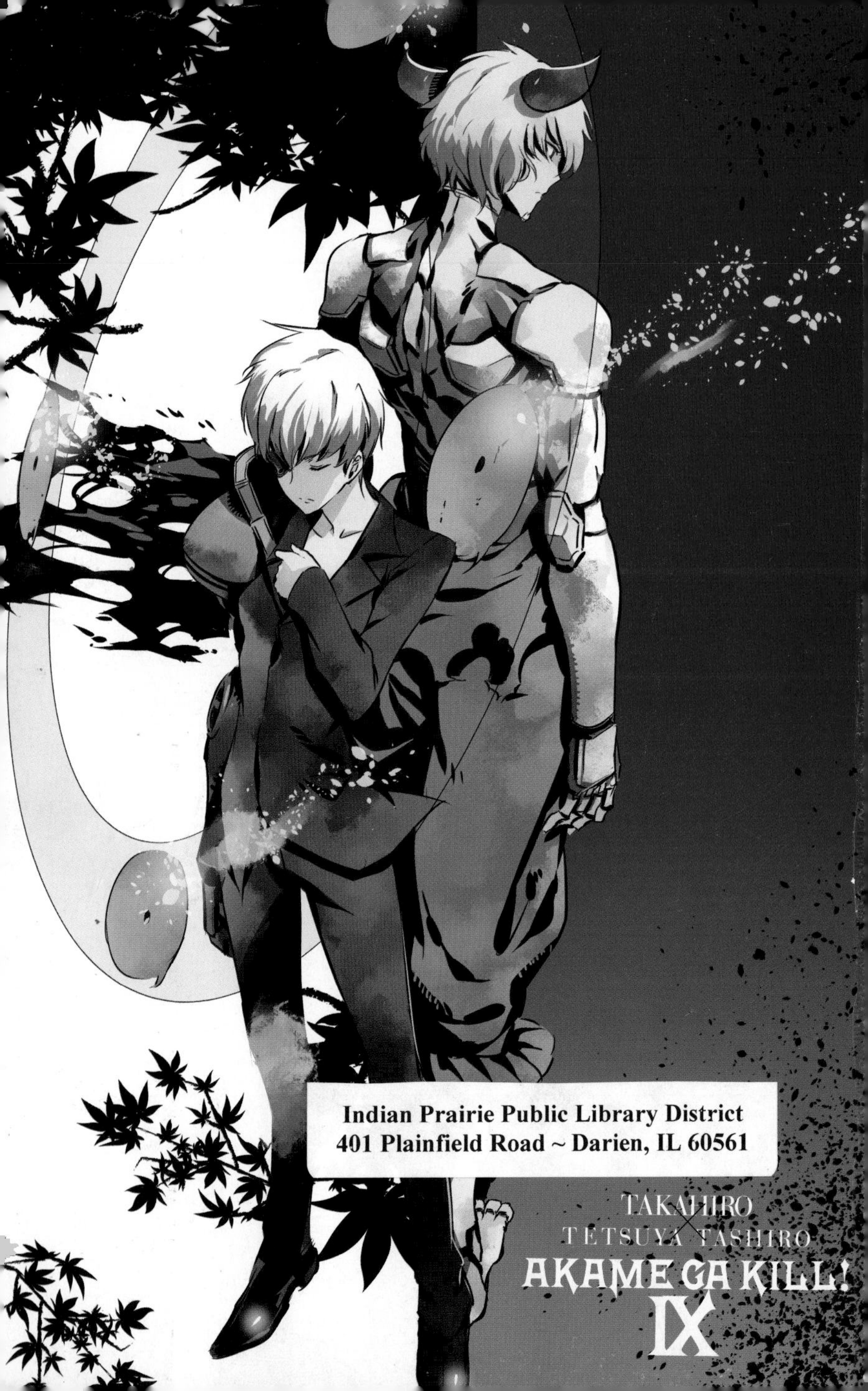
TAKAHIRO × TETSUYA TASHIRO
AKAME GA KILL!
IX

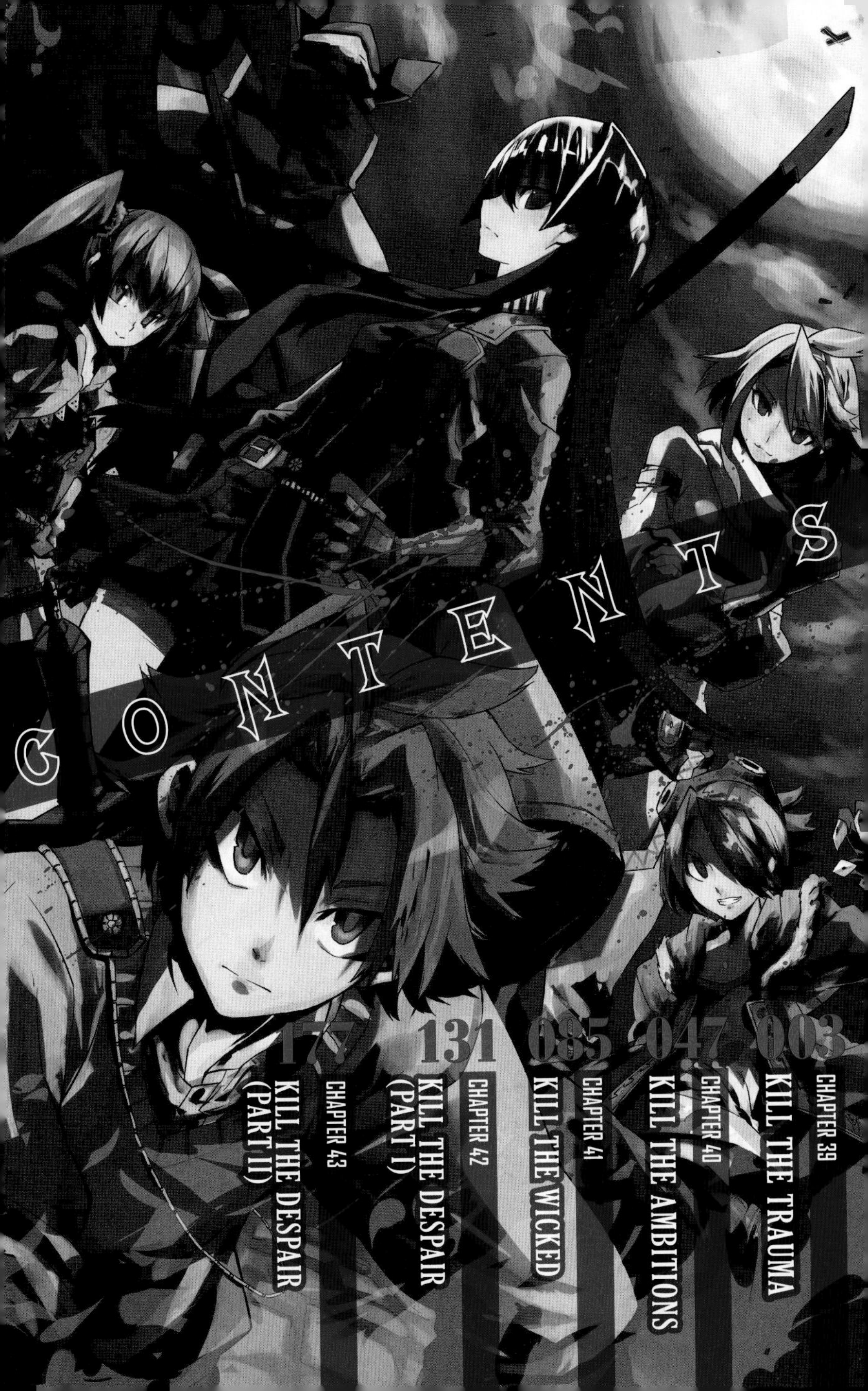

CONTENTS

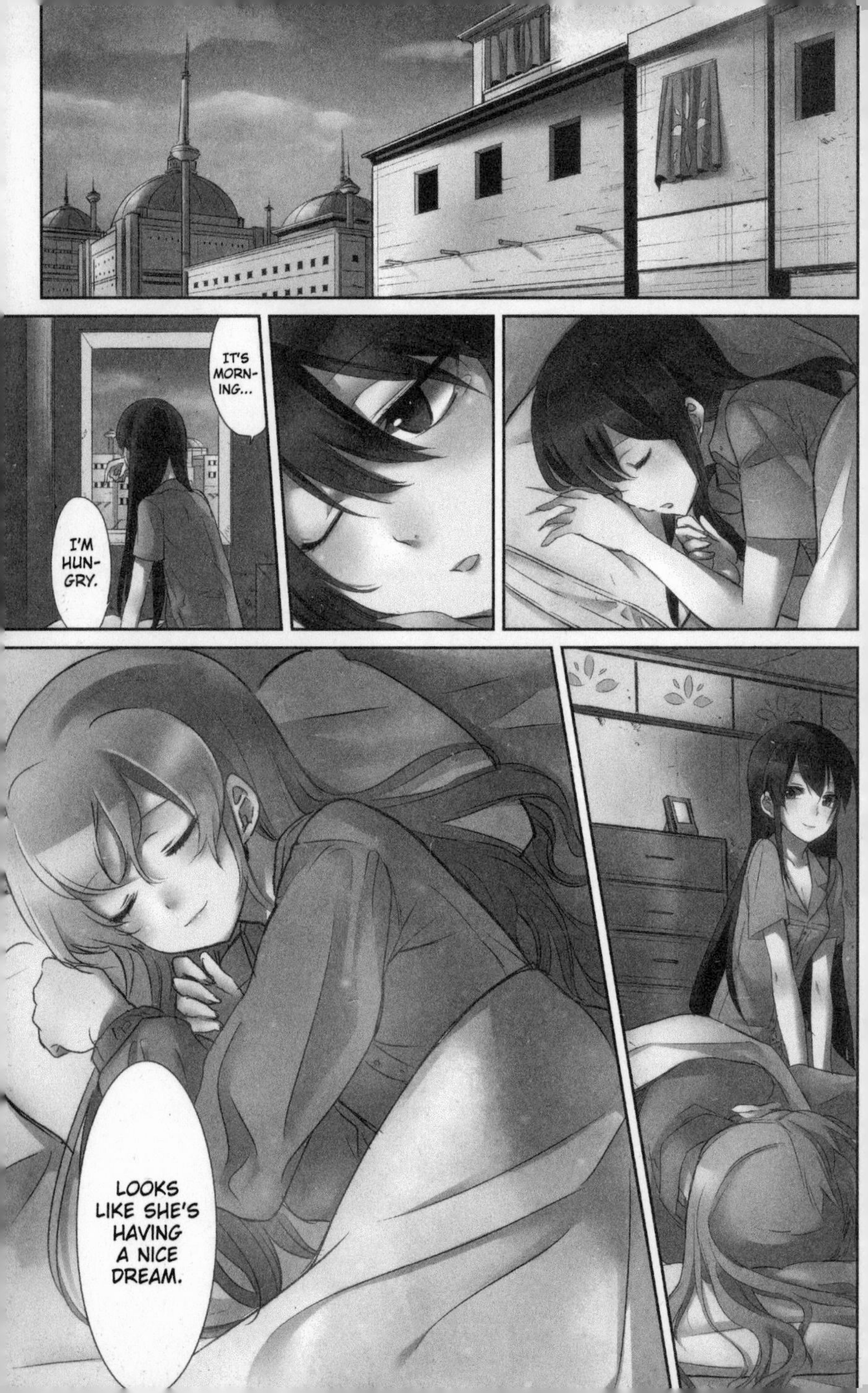
IT'S MORNING...
I'M HUNGRY.
LOOKS LIKE SHE'S HAVING A NICE DREAM.

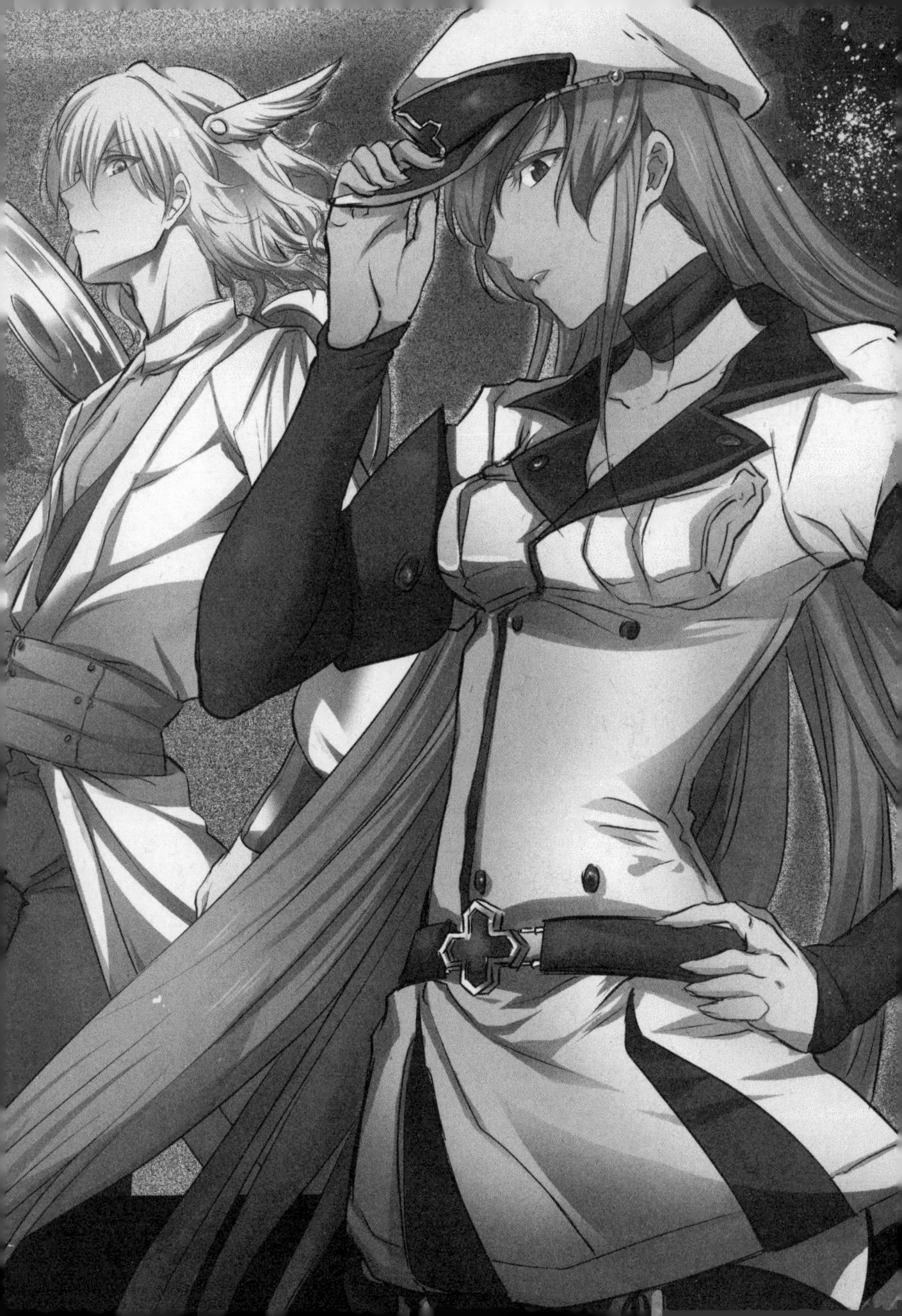

Chapter 39 - Kill the Trauma

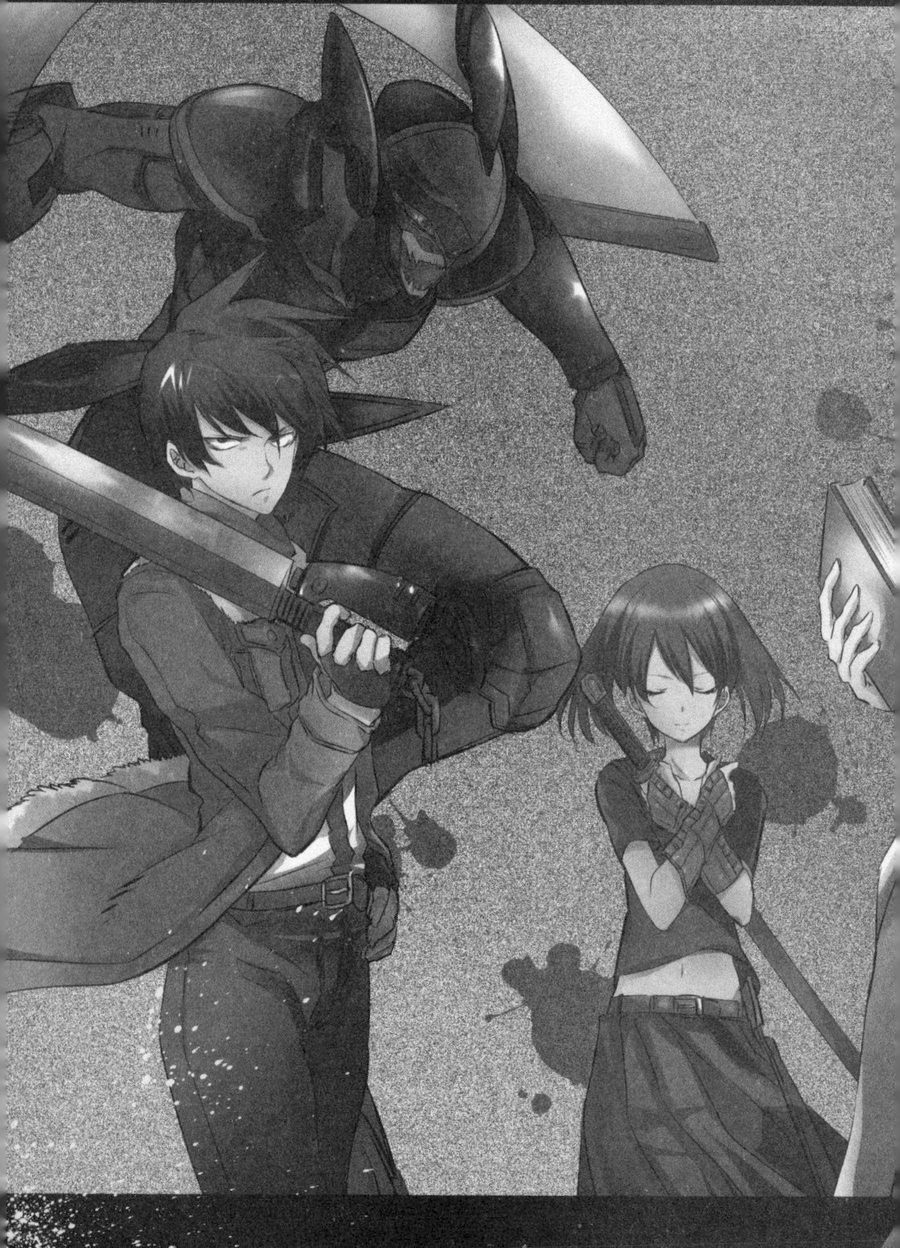

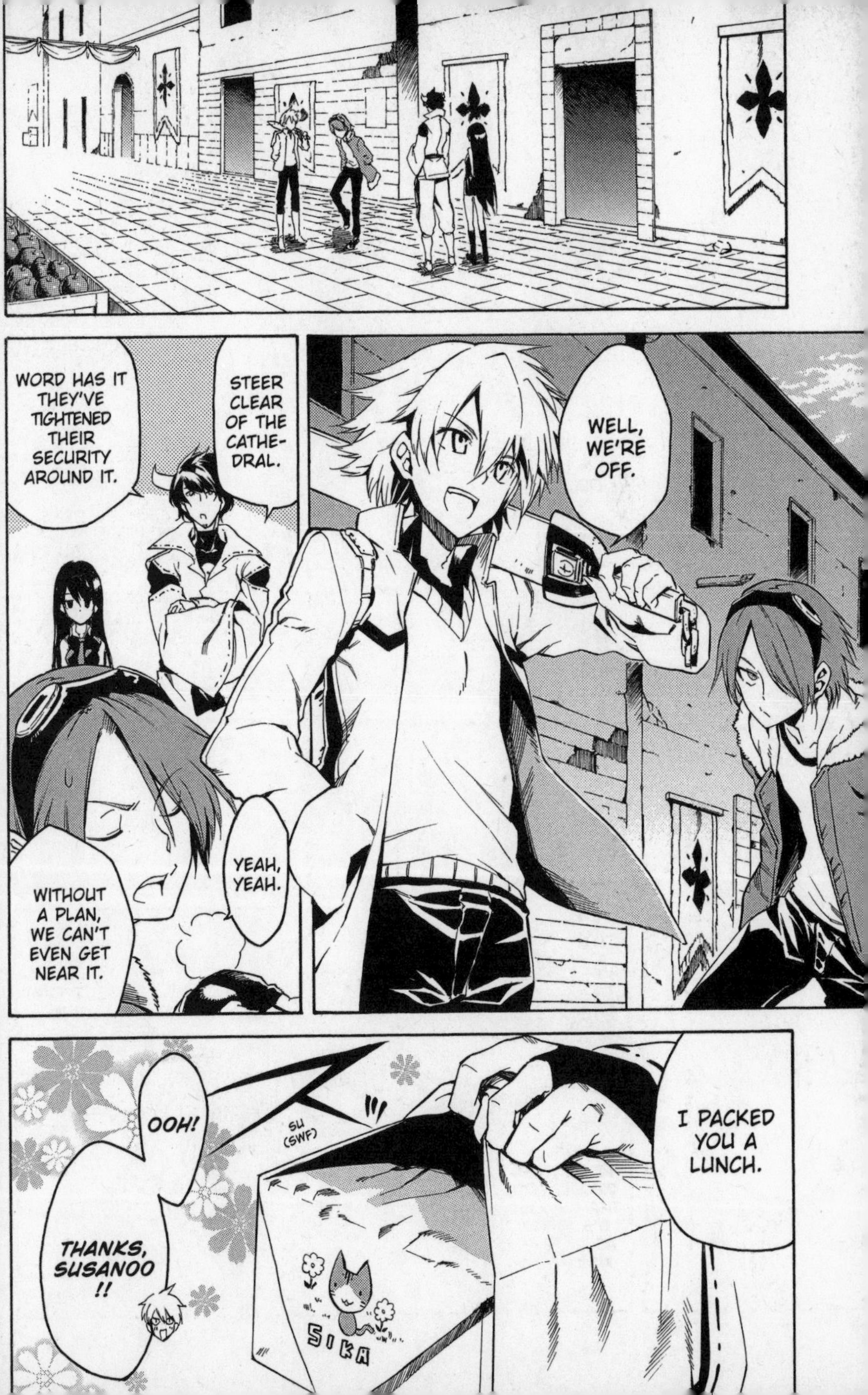
WELL, WE'RE OFF.
STEER CLEAR OF THE CATHEDRAL.
WORD HAS IT THEY'VE TIGHTENED THEIR SECURITY AROUND IT.
YEAH, YEAH.
WITHOUT A PLAN, WE CAN'T EVEN GET NEAR IT.
I PACKED YOU A LUNCH.
SU (SWF)
OOH!
THANKS, SUSANOO !!
SIKA

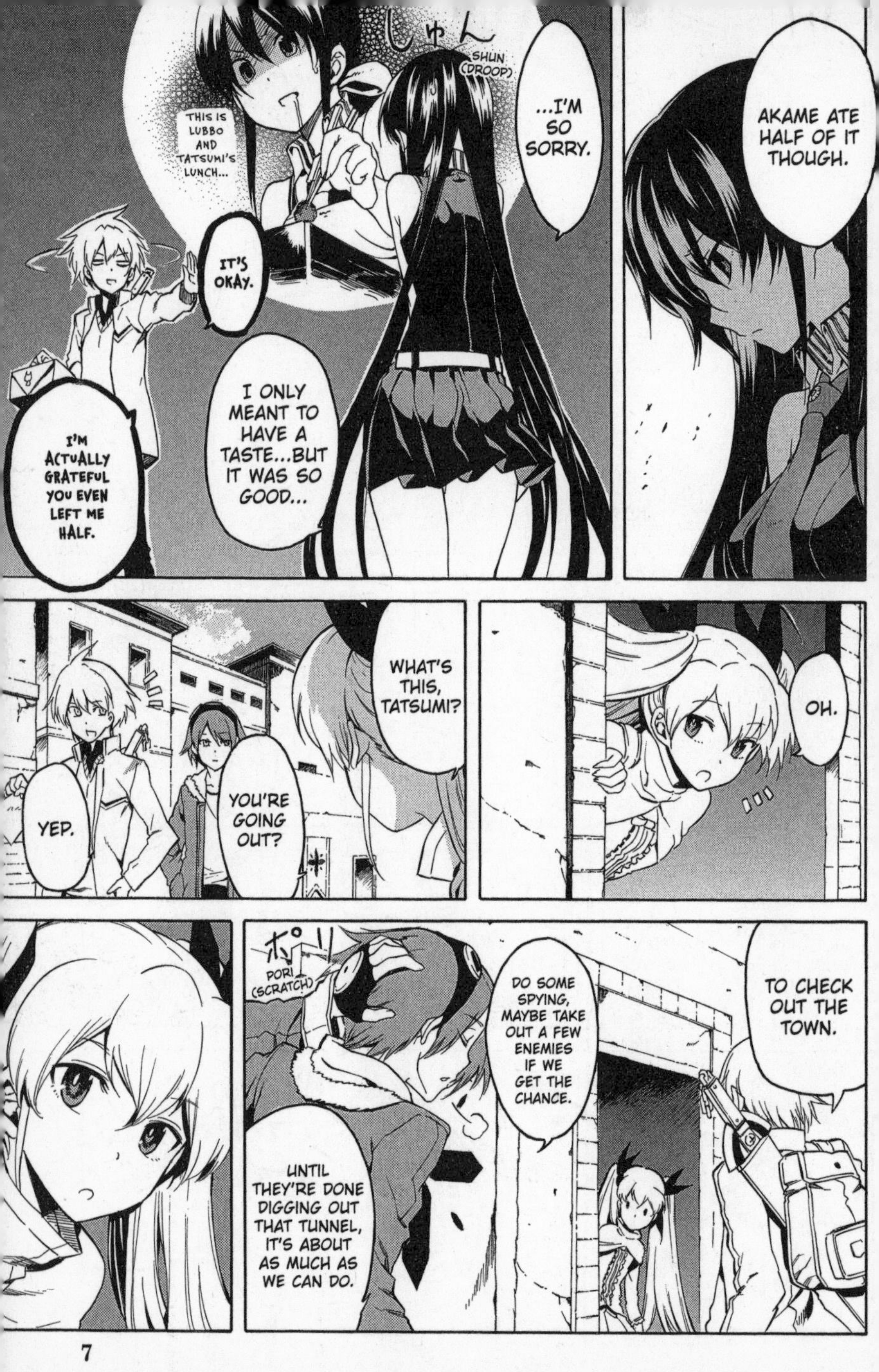
AKAME ATE HALF OF IT THOUGH.
しゅん
SHUN (DROOP)
...I'M SO SORRY.
THIS IS LUBBO AND TATSUMI'S LUNCH...
IT'S OKAY.
I ONLY MEANT TO HAVE A TASTE...BUT IT WAS SO GOOD...
I'M ACTUALLY GRATEFUL YOU EVEN LEFT ME HALF.
OH.
WHAT'S THIS, TATSUMI?
YOU'RE GOING OUT?
YEP.
TO CHECK OUT THE TOWN.
DO SOME SPYING, MAYBE TAKE OUT A FEW ENEMIES IF WE GET THE CHANCE.
ポリ
PORI (SCRATCH)
UNTIL THEY'RE DONE DIGGING OUT THAT TUNNEL, IT'S ABOUT AS MUCH AS WE CAN DO.

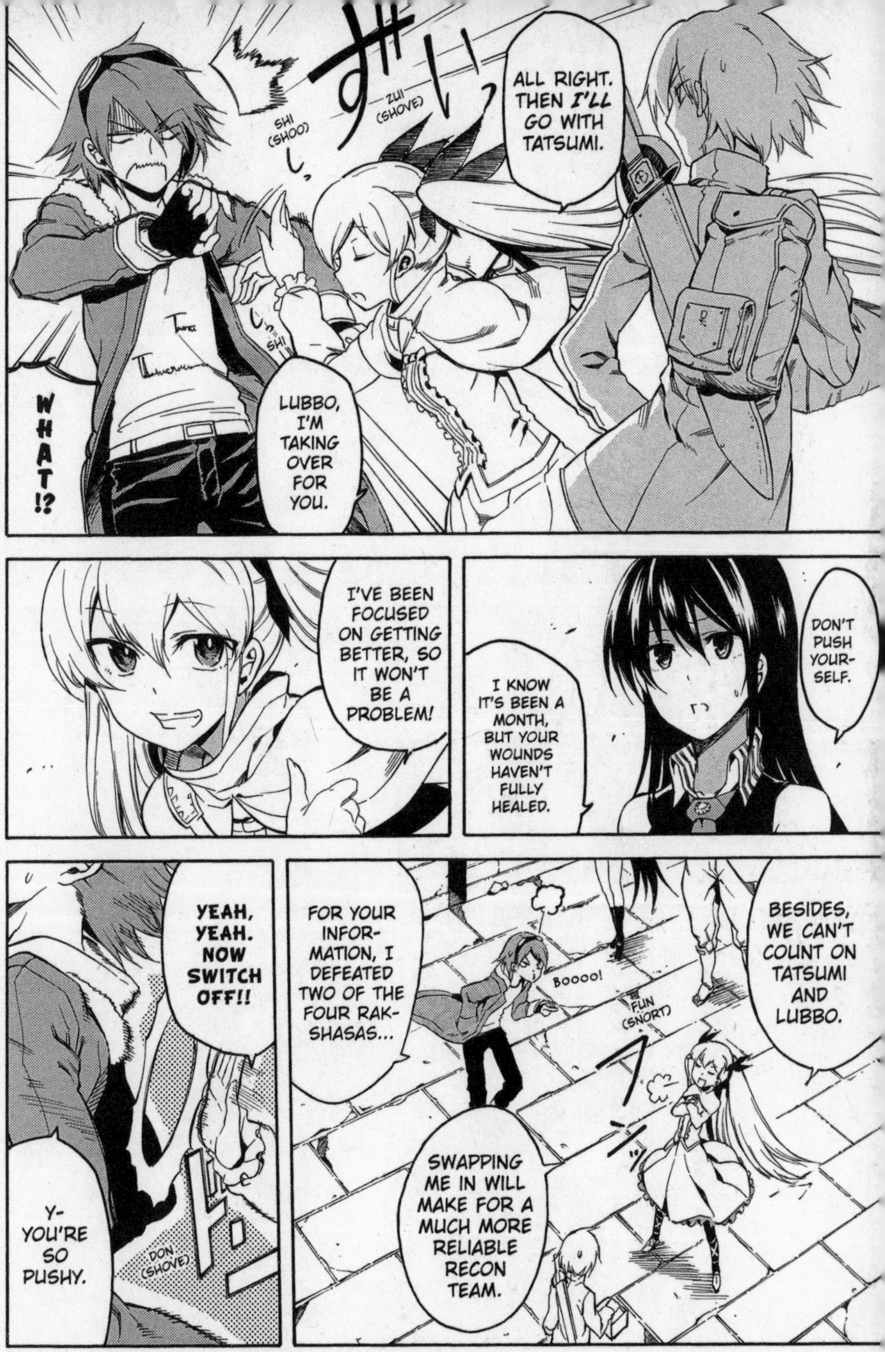
ALL RIGHT. THEN *I'LL* GO WITH TATSUMI.
ZUI (SHOVE)
SHI (SHOO)
SHI
LUBBO, I'M TAKING OVER FOR YOU.
WHAT!?
DON'T PUSH YOURSELF.
I KNOW IT'S BEEN A MONTH, BUT YOUR WOUNDS HAVEN'T FULLY HEALED.
I'VE BEEN FOCUSED ON GETTING BETTER, SO IT WON'T BE A PROBLEM!
BESIDES, WE CAN'T COUNT ON TATSUMI AND LUBBO.
FUN (SNORT)
BOOOO!
FOR YOUR INFORMATION, I DEFEATED TWO OF THE FOUR RAKSHASAS...
SWAPPING ME IN WILL MAKE FOR A MUCH MORE RELIABLE RECON TEAM.
YEAH, YEAH. NOW SWITCH OFF!!
DON (SHOVE)
Y-YOU'RE SO PUSHY.

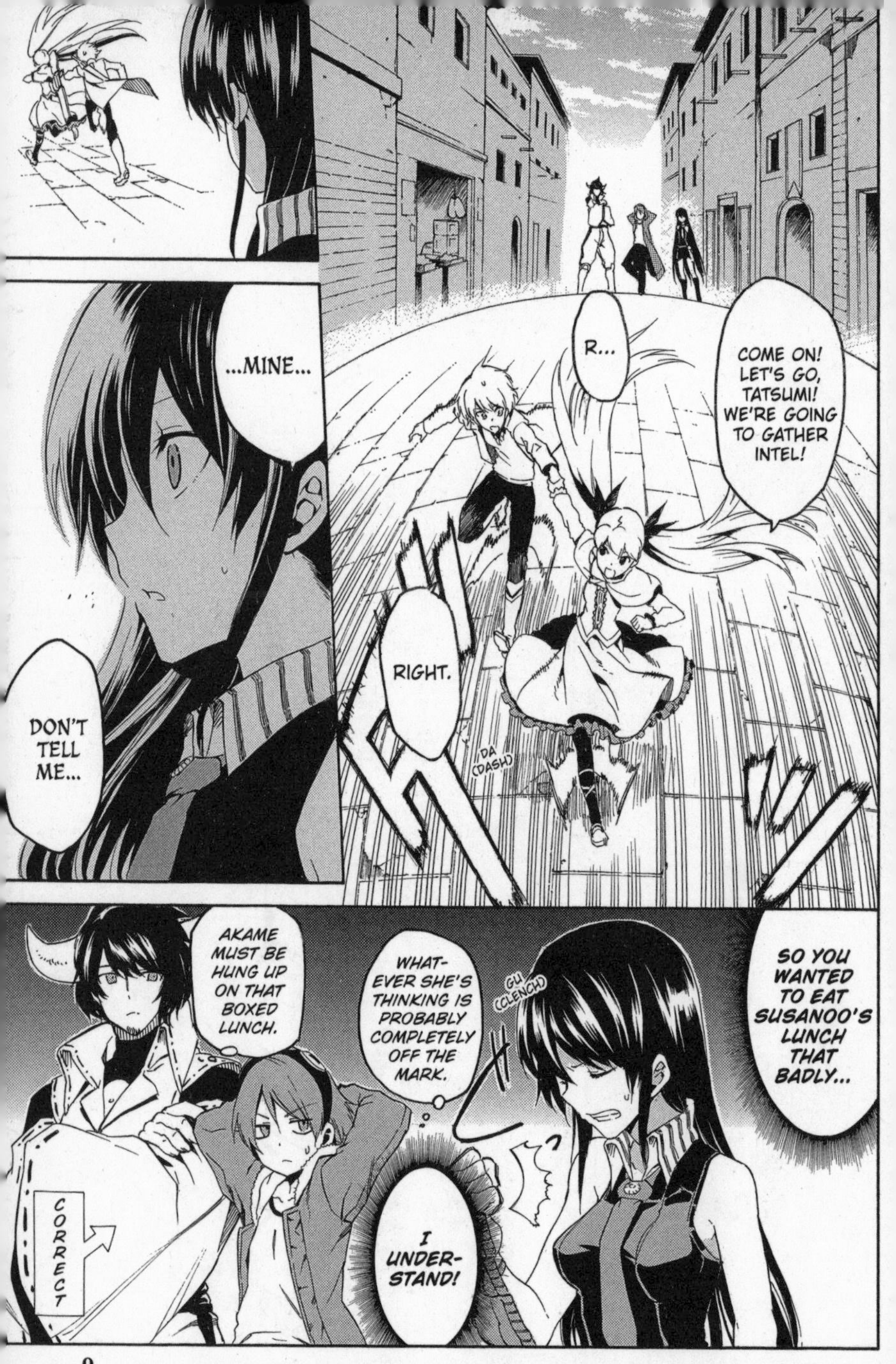
COME ON! LET'S GO, TATSUMI! WE'RE GOING TO GATHER INTEL!
R...
RIGHT.
DA (DASH)
...MINE...
DON'T TELL ME...
SO YOU WANTED TO EAT SUSANOO'S LUNCH THAT BADLY...
GU (CLENCH)
I UNDER-STAND!
WHAT-EVER SHE'S THINKING IS PROBABLY COMPLETELY OFF THE MARK.
AKAME MUST BE HUNG UP ON THAT BOXED LUNCH.
CORRECT

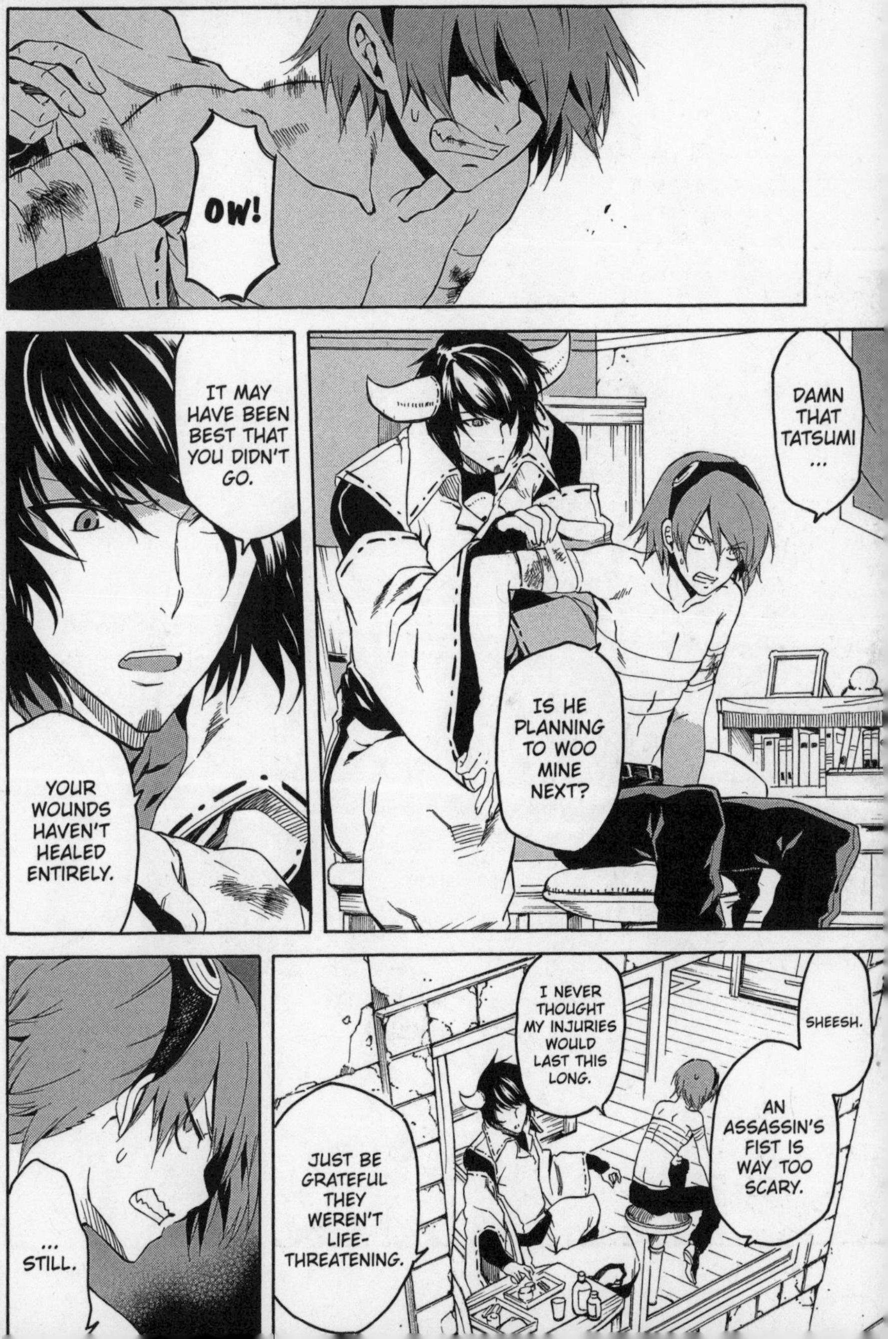
OW!
DAMN THAT TATSUMI ...
IS HE PLANNING TO WOO MINE NEXT?
IT MAY HAVE BEEN BEST THAT YOU DIDN'T GO.
YOUR WOUNDS HAVEN'T HEALED ENTIRELY.
SHEESH.
I NEVER THOUGHT MY INJURIES WOULD LAST THIS LONG.
AN ASSASSIN'S FIST IS WAY TOO SCARY.
JUST BE GRATEFUL THEY WEREN'T LIFE-THREATENING.
... STILL.

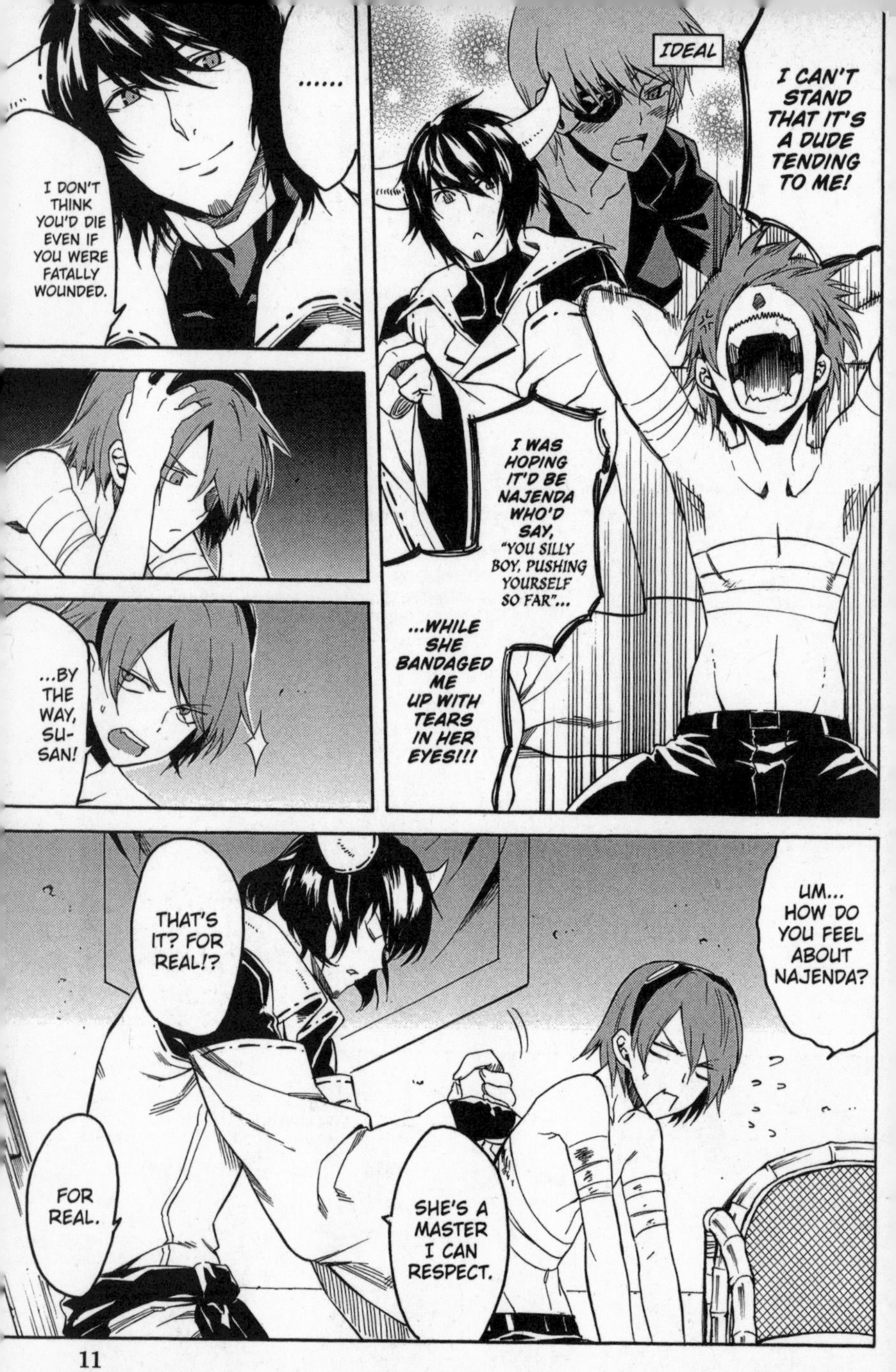
IDEAL
I CAN'T STAND THAT IT'S A DUDE TENDING TO ME!
I WAS HOPING IT'D BE NAJENDA WHO'D SAY, "YOU SILLY BOY, PUSHING YOURSELF SO FAR"...
...WHILE SHE BANDAGED ME UP WITH TEARS IN HER EYES!!!
......
I DON'T THINK YOU'D DIE EVEN IF YOU WERE FATALLY WOUNDED.
...BY THE WAY, SU-SAN!
UM... HOW DO YOU FEEL ABOUT NAJENDA?
SHE'S A MASTER I CAN RESPECT.
THAT'S IT? FOR REAL!?
FOR REAL.

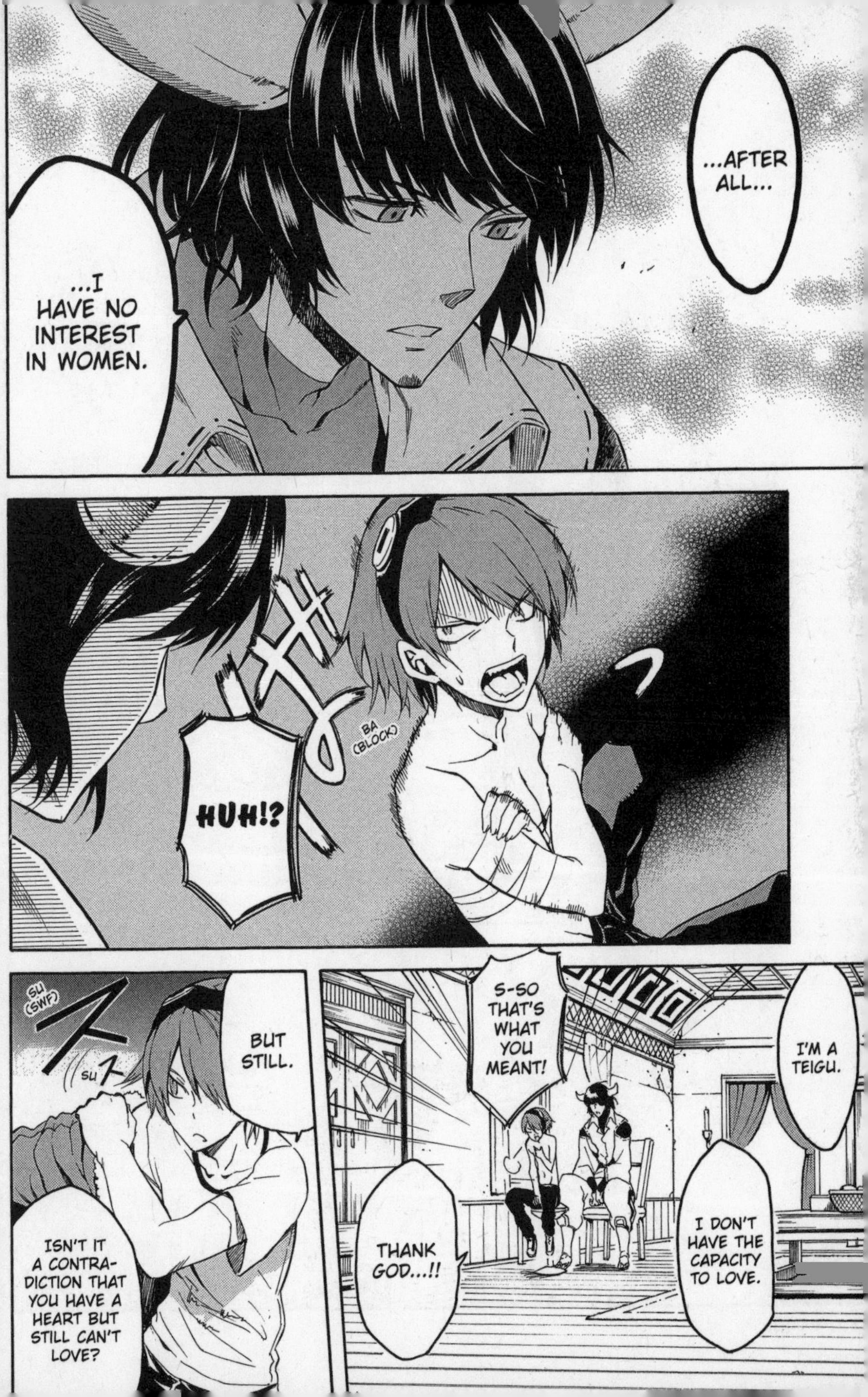
...AFTER ALL...
...I HAVE NO INTEREST IN WOMEN.
BA (BLOCK)
HUH!?
I'M A TEIGU.
I DON'T HAVE THE CAPACITY TO LOVE.
S-SO THAT'S WHAT YOU MEANT!
THANK GOD...!!
SU (SWF)
SU
BUT STILL.
ISN'T IT A CONTRA-DICTION THAT YOU HAVE A HEART BUT STILL CAN'T LOVE?

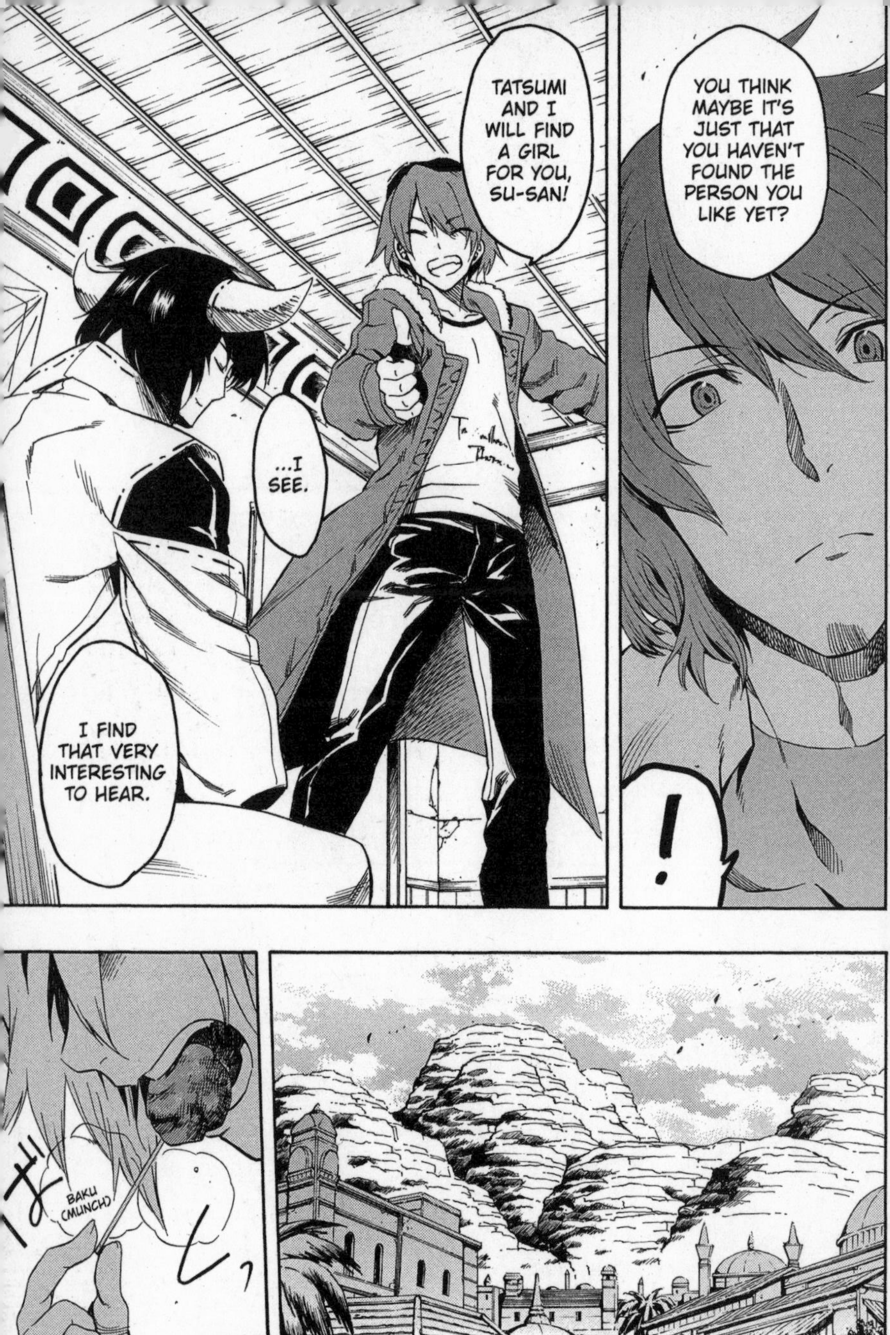
YOU THINK MAYBE IT'S JUST THAT YOU HAVEN'T FOUND THE PERSON YOU LIKE YET?
!
TATSUMI AND I WILL FIND A GIRL FOR YOU, SU-SAN!
...I SEE.
I FIND THAT VERY INTERESTING TO HEAR.
BAKU (MUNCH)

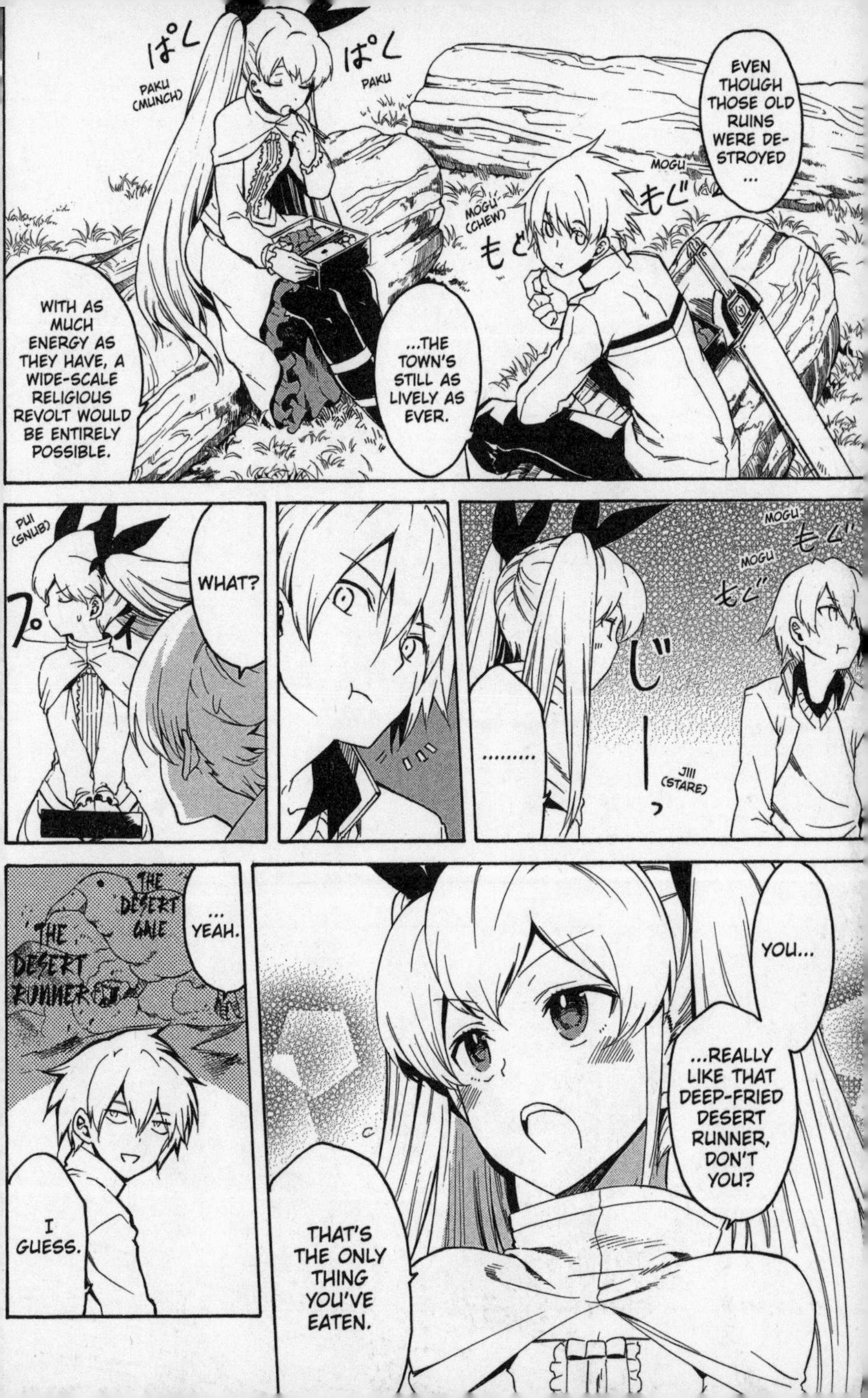
EVEN THOUGH THOSE OLD RUINS WERE DE-STROYED...
MOGU
もぐ
MOGU (CHEW)
もぐ
ぱく
PAKU
...THE TOWN'S STILL AS LIVELY AS EVER.
ぱく
PAKU (MUNCH)
WITH AS MUCH ENERGY AS THEY HAVE, A WIDE-SCALE RELIGIOUS REVOLT WOULD BE ENTIRELY POSSIBLE.
MOGU
もぐ
MOGU
もぐ
じーっ
JIII (STARE)
....
WHAT?
プイ
PUI (SNUB)
YOU...
...REALLY LIKE THAT DEEP-FRIED DESERT RUNNER, DON'T YOU?
THAT'S THE ONLY THING YOU'VE EATEN.
...YEAH.
THE DESERT GALE
THE DESERT RUNNER
I GUESS.

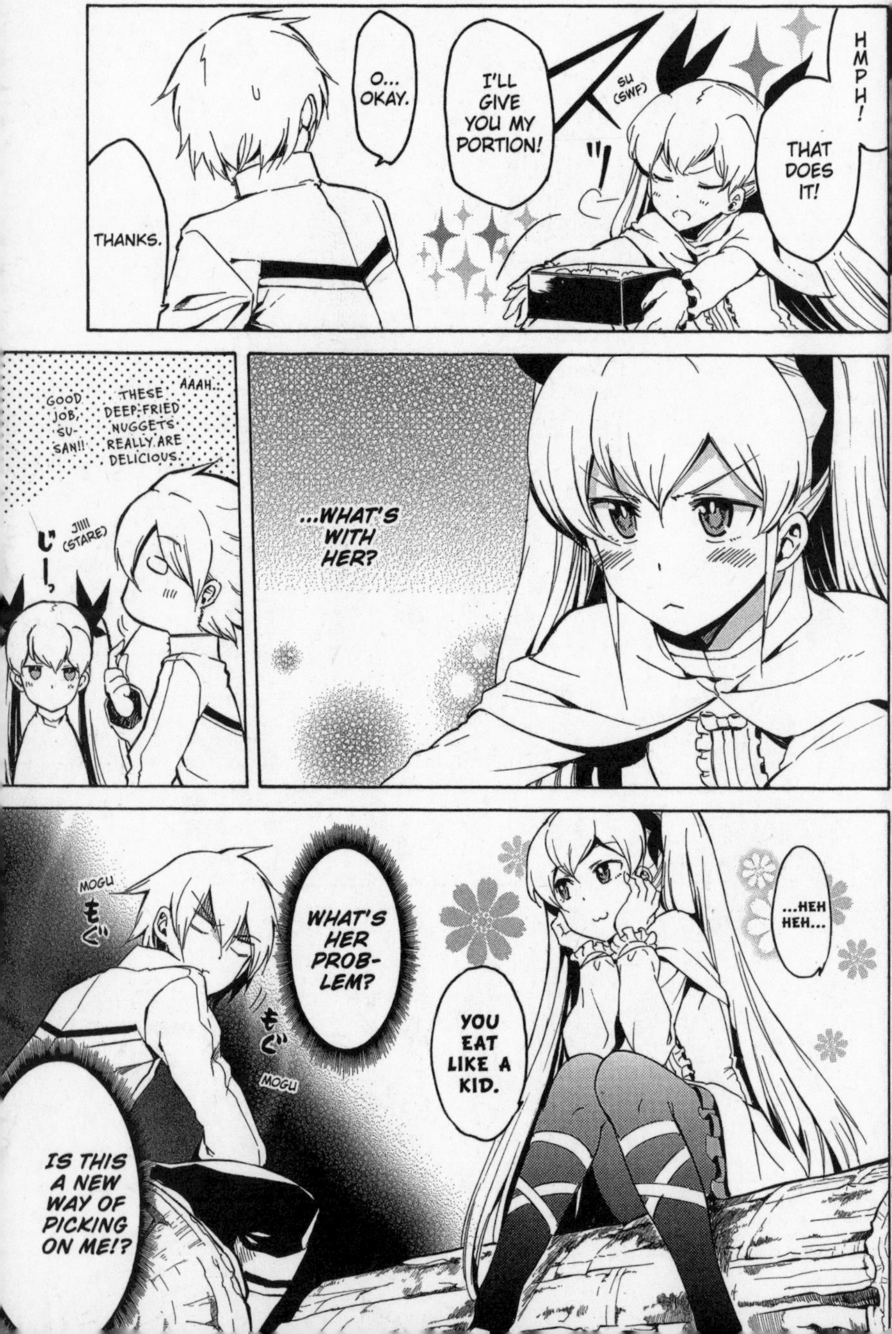
HMPH!
THAT DOES IT!
SU (SWF)
I'LL GIVE YOU MY PORTION!
O... OKAY.
THANKS.
...WHAT'S WITH HER?
AAAH... THESE DEEP-FRIED NUGGETS REALLY ARE DELICIOUS.
GOOD JOB, SU-SAN!!
じー
JIIII (STARE)
...HEH HEH...
YOU EAT LIKE A KID.
WHAT'S HER PROB-LEM?
もぐ
MOGU
もぐ
MOGU
IS THIS A NEW WAY OF PICKING ON ME!?

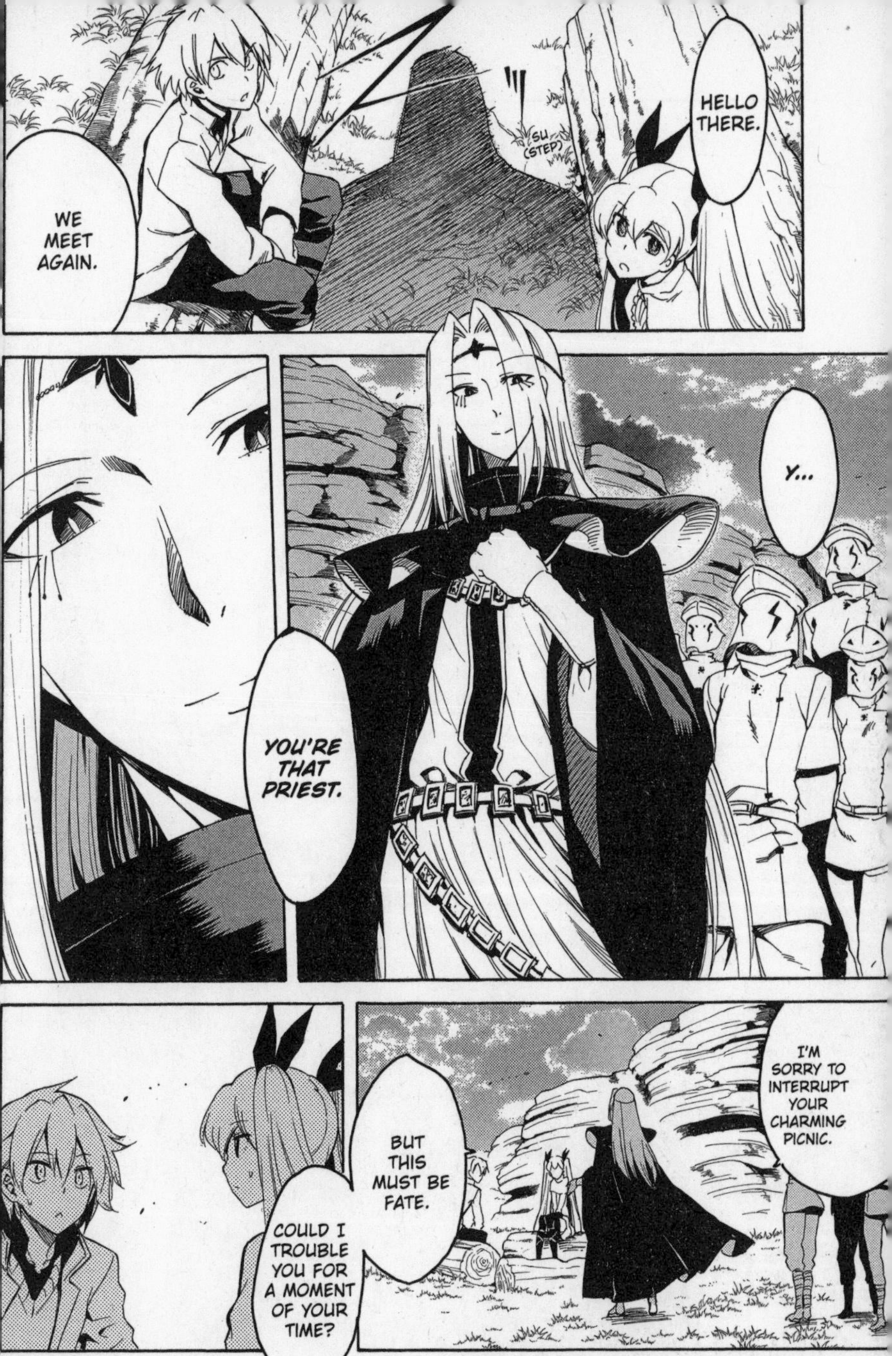
HELLO THERE.
SU (STEP)
WE MEET AGAIN.
Y...
YOU'RE THAT PRIEST.
I'M SORRY TO INTERRUPT YOUR CHARMING PICNIC.
BUT THIS MUST BE FATE.
COULD I TROUBLE YOU FOR A MOMENT OF YOUR TIME?

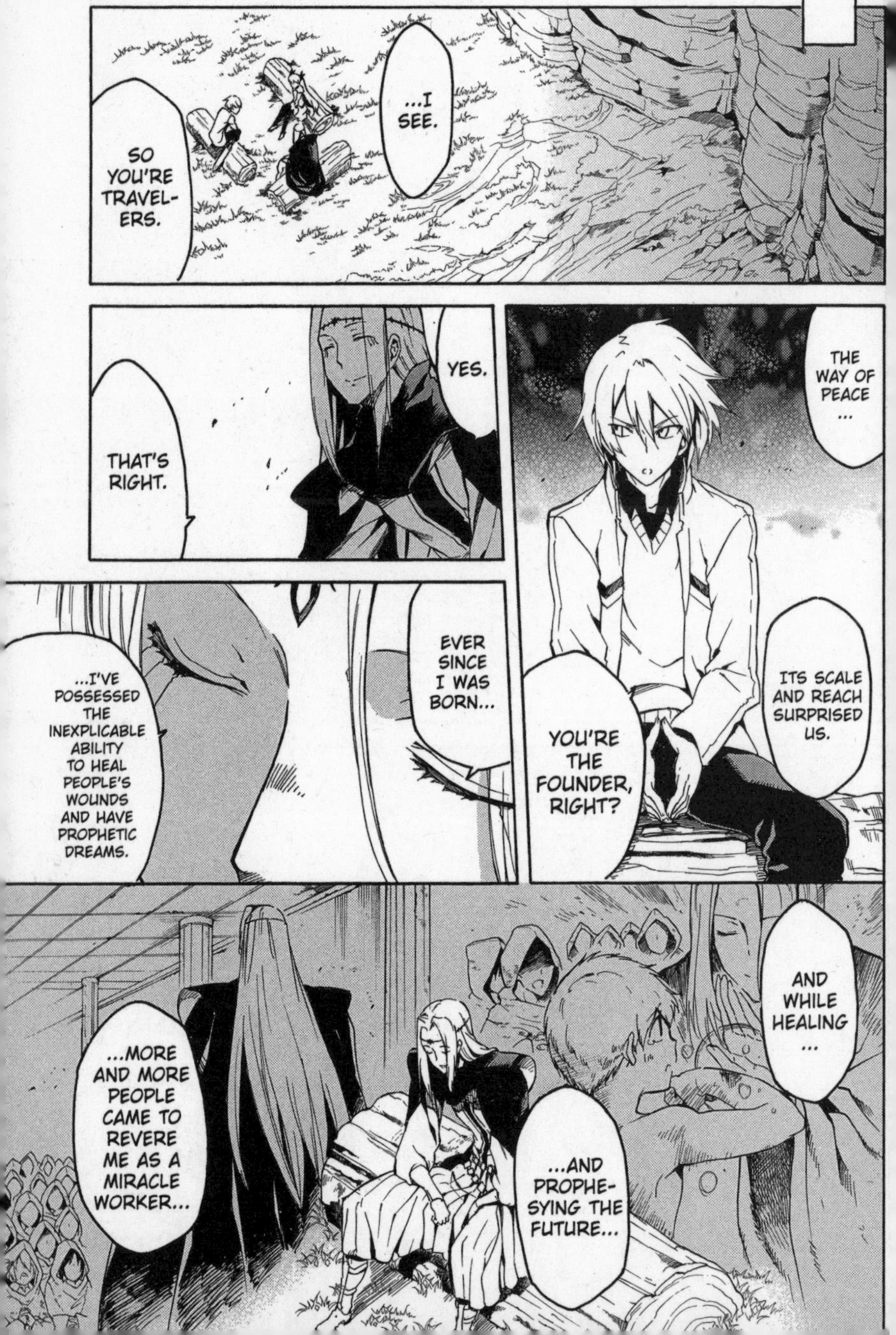
...I SEE.
SO YOU'RE TRAVEL-ERS.
THE WAY OF PEACE...
ITS SCALE AND REACH SURPRISED US.
YOU'RE THE FOUNDER, RIGHT?
YES.
THAT'S RIGHT.
EVER SINCE I WAS BORN...
...I'VE POSSESSED THE INEXPLICABLE ABILITY TO HEAL PEOPLE'S WOUNDS AND HAVE PROPHETIC DREAMS.
AND WHILE HEALING...
...AND PROPHE-SYING THE FUTURE...
...MORE AND MORE PEOPLE CAME TO REVERE ME AS A MIRACLE WORKER...

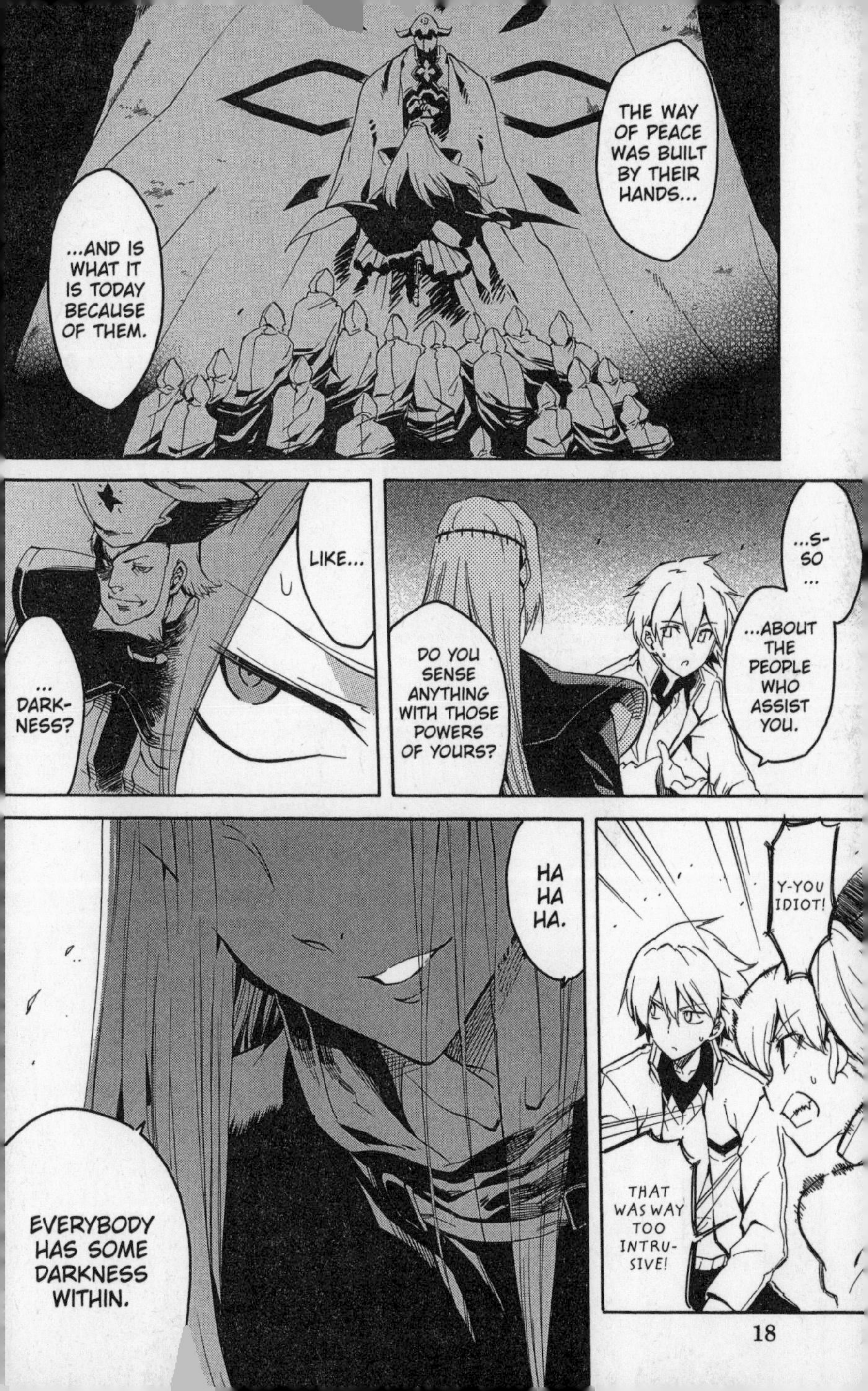
THE WAY OF PEACE WAS BUILT BY THEIR HANDS...
...AND IS WHAT IT IS TODAY BECAUSE OF THEM.
...S-SO...
...ABOUT THE PEOPLE WHO ASSIST YOU.
DO YOU SENSE ANYTHING WITH THOSE POWERS OF YOURS?
LIKE...
...DARKNESS?
Y-YOU IDIOT!
THAT WAS WAY TOO INTRUSIVE!
HA HA HA.
EVERYBODY HAS SOME DARKNESS WITHIN.

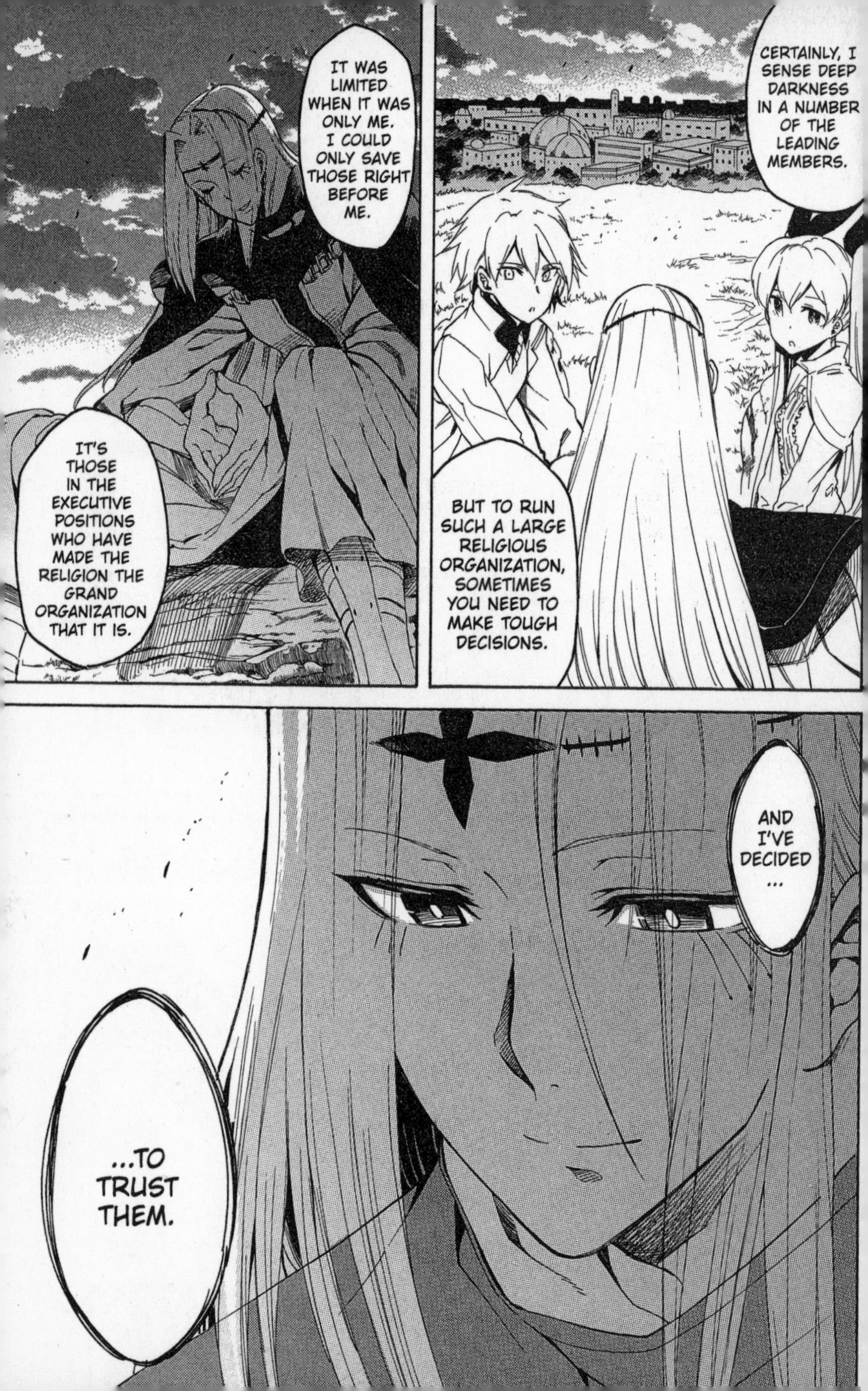
CERTAINLY, I SENSE DEEP DARKNESS IN A NUMBER OF THE LEADING MEMBERS.
BUT TO RUN SUCH A LARGE RELIGIOUS ORGANIZATION, SOMETIMES YOU NEED TO MAKE TOUGH DECISIONS.
IT WAS LIMITED WHEN IT WAS ONLY ME. I COULD ONLY SAVE THOSE RIGHT BEFORE ME.
IT'S THOSE IN THE EXECUTIVE POSITIONS WHO HAVE MADE THE RELIGION THE GRAND ORGANIZATION THAT IT IS.
AND I'VE DECIDED...
...TO TRUST THEM.

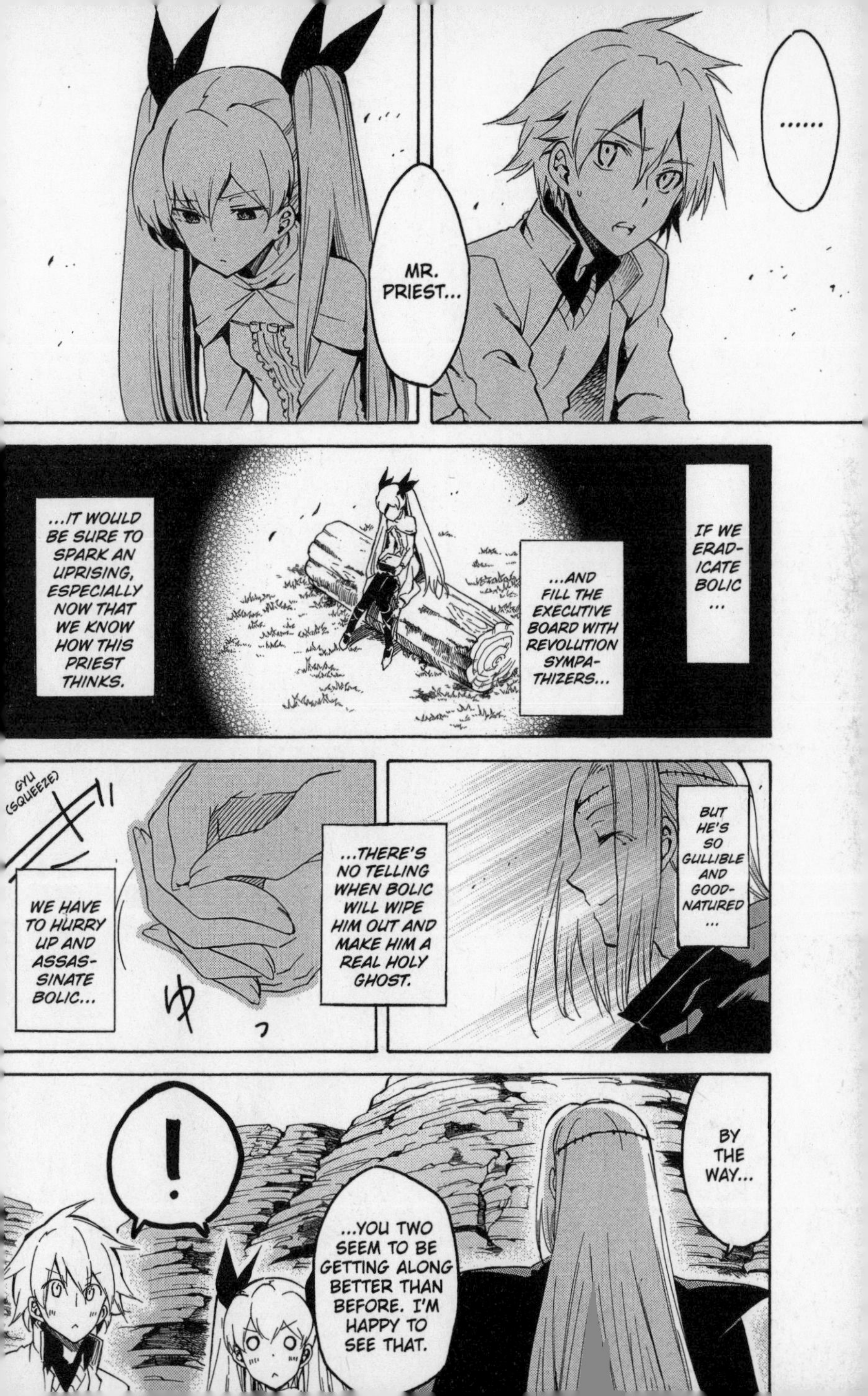
......
MR. PRIEST...
IF WE ERADICATE BOLIC...
...AND FILL THE EXECUTIVE BOARD WITH REVOLUTION SYMPATHIZERS...
...IT WOULD BE SURE TO SPARK AN UPRISING, ESPECIALLY NOW THAT WE KNOW HOW THIS PRIEST THINKS.
BUT HE'S SO GULLIBLE AND GOOD-NATURED...
...THERE'S NO TELLING WHEN BOLIC WILL WIPE HIM OUT AND MAKE HIM A REAL HOLY GHOST.
GYU (SQUEEZE)
WE HAVE TO HURRY UP AND ASSASSINATE BOLIC...
BY THE WAY...
...YOU TWO SEEM TO BE GETTING ALONG BETTER THAN BEFORE. I'M HAPPY TO SEE THAT.
!

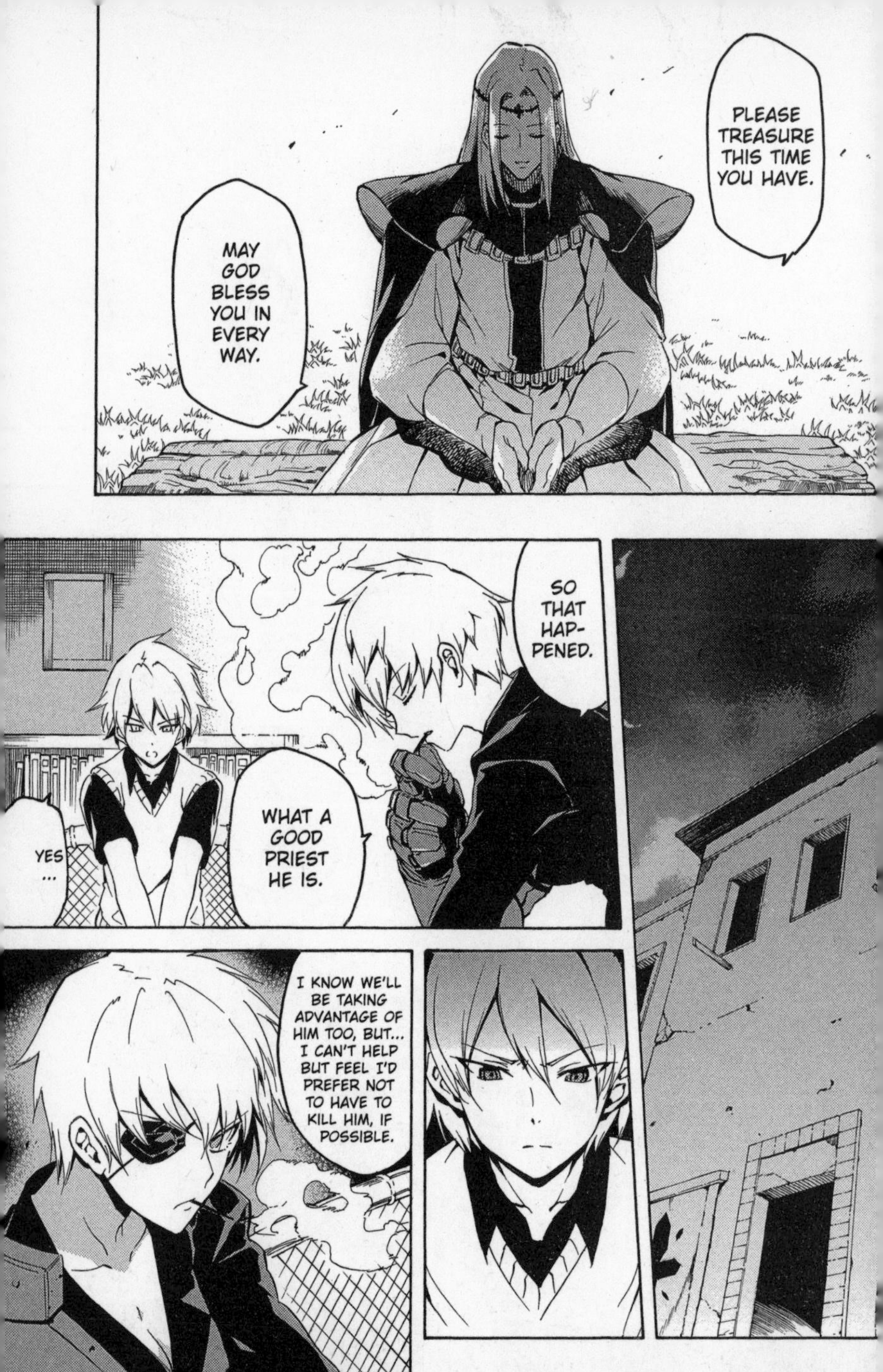
PLEASE TREASURE THIS TIME YOU HAVE.
MAY GOD BLESS YOU IN EVERY WAY.
SO THAT HAPPENED.
WHAT A GOOD PRIEST HE IS.
YES ...
I KNOW WE'LL BE TAKING ADVANTAGE OF HIM TOO, BUT... I CAN'T HELP BUT FEEL I'D PREFER NOT TO HAVE TO KILL HIM, IF POSSIBLE.

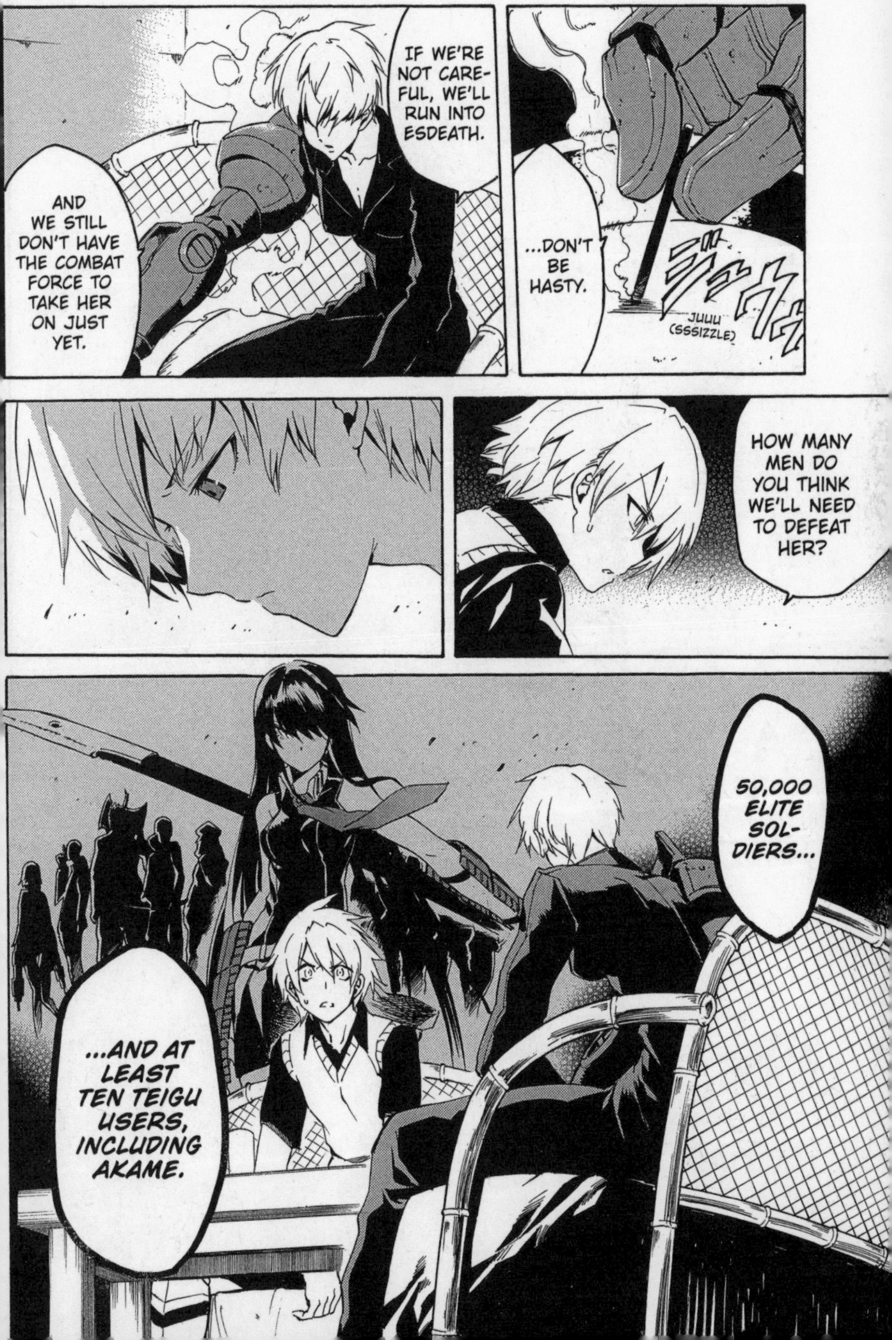
...DON'T BE HASTY.
JUUU (SSSIZZLE)
IF WE'RE NOT CAREFUL, WE'LL RUN INTO ESDEATH.
AND WE STILL DON'T HAVE THE COMBAT FORCE TO TAKE HER ON JUST YET.
HOW MANY MEN DO YOU THINK WE'LL NEED TO DEFEAT HER?
50,000 ELITE SOLDIERS...
...AND AT LEAST TEN TEIGU USERS, INCLUDING AKAME.

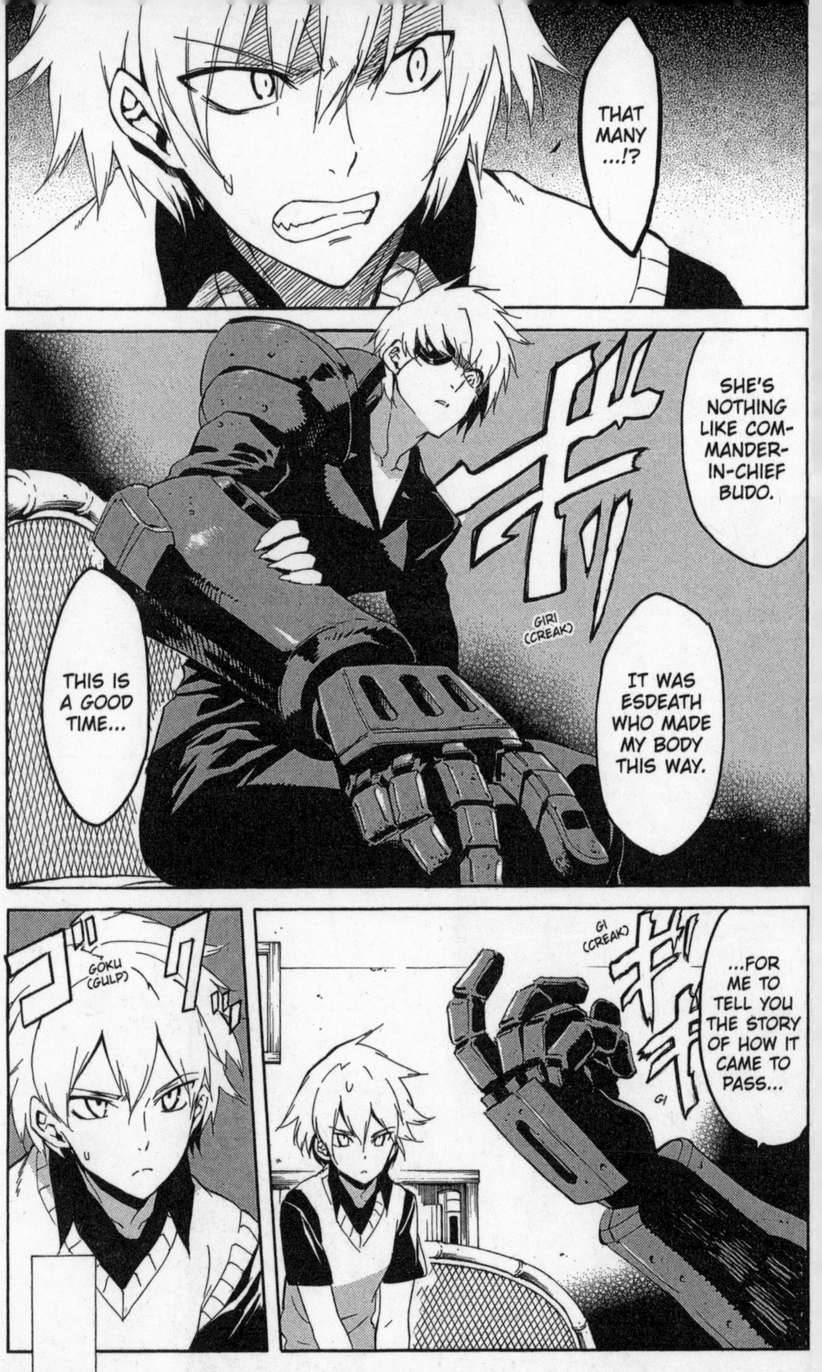
THAT MANY ...!?
SHE'S NOTHING LIKE COM-MANDER-IN-CHIEF BUDO.
GIRI (CREAK)
IT WAS ESDEATH WHO MADE MY BODY THIS WAY.
THIS IS A GOOD TIME...
GI (CREAK)
...FOR ME TO TELL YOU THE STORY OF HOW IT CAME TO PASS...
GI
GOKU (GULP)

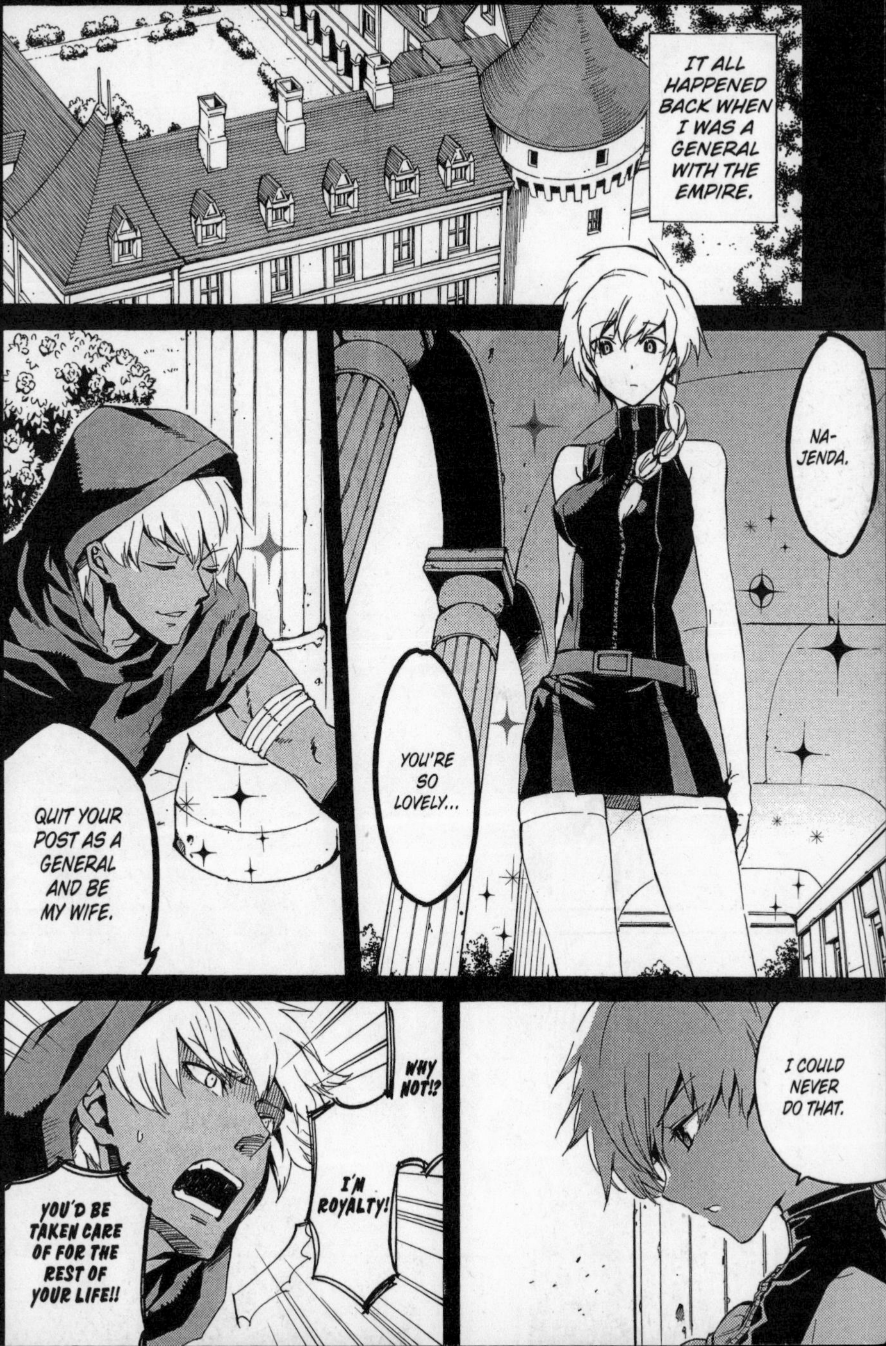
IT ALL HAPPENED BACK WHEN I WAS A GENERAL WITH THE EMPIRE.
NA-JENDA.
YOU'RE SO LOVELY...
QUIT YOUR POST AS A GENERAL AND BE MY WIFE.
I COULD NEVER DO THAT.
WHY NOT!?
I'M ROYALTY!
YOU'D BE TAKEN CARE OF FOR THE REST OF YOUR LIFE!!

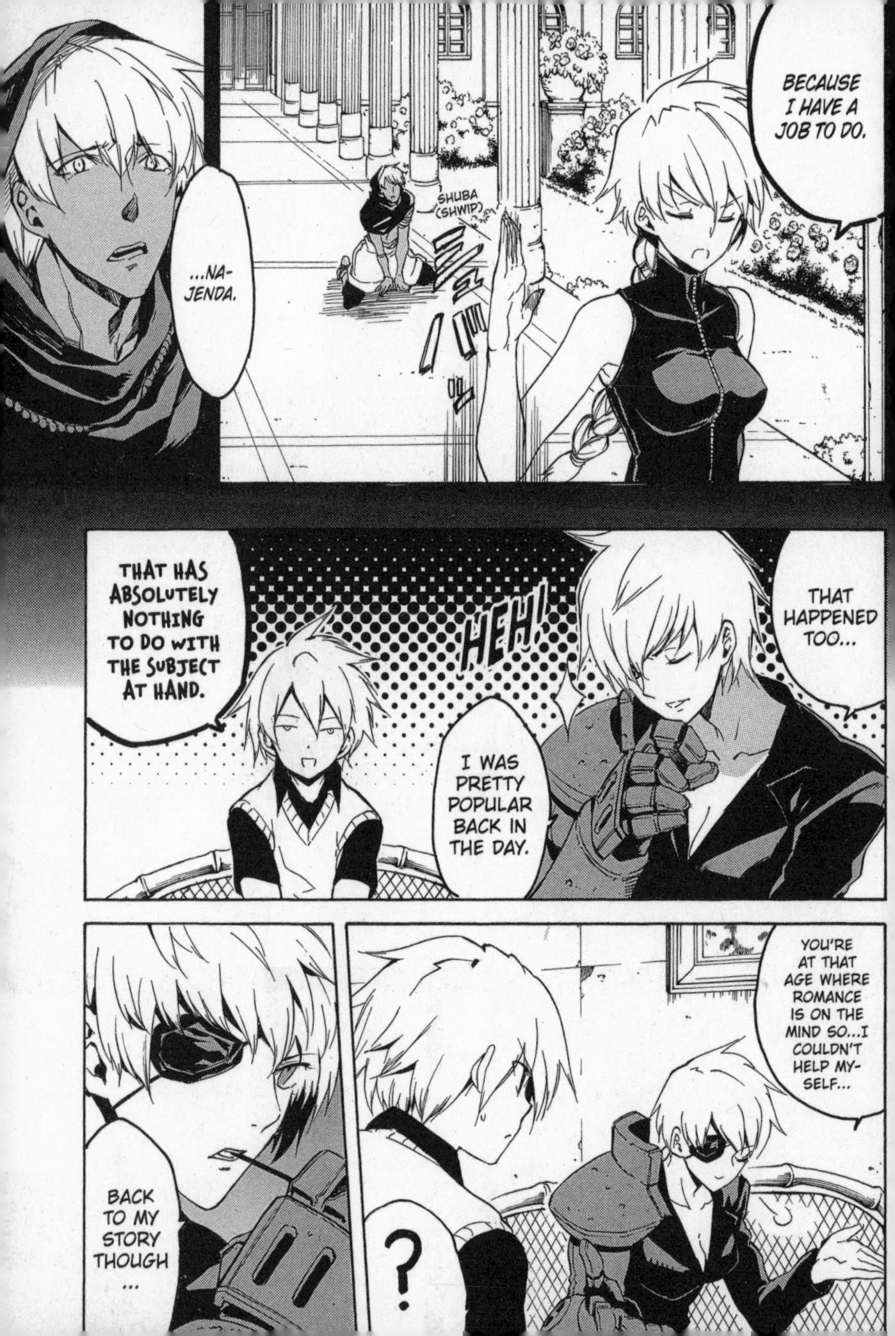
BECAUSE I HAVE A JOB TO DO.
SHUBA (SHWIP)
...NA-JENDA.
THAT HAPPENED TOO...
I WAS PRETTY POPULAR BACK IN THE DAY.
HEH!
THAT HAS ABSOLUTELY NOTHING TO DO WITH THE SUBJECT AT HAND.
YOU'RE AT THAT AGE WHERE ROMANCE IS ON THE MIND SO...I COULDN'T HELP MY-SELF...
?
BACK TO MY STORY THOUGH ...

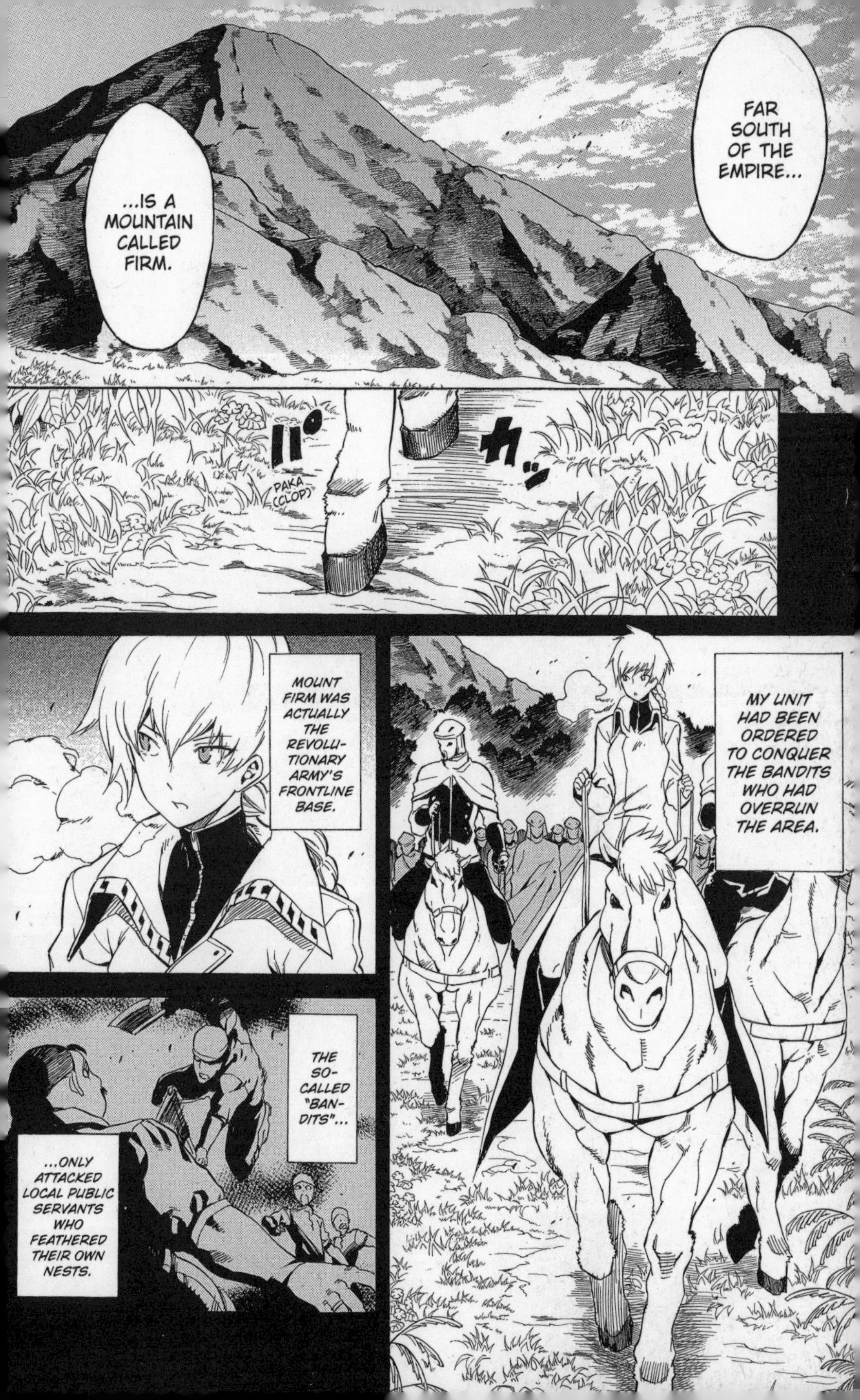
FAR SOUTH OF THE EMPIRE...
...IS A MOUNTAIN CALLED FIRM.
PAKA (CLOP)
MY UNIT HAD BEEN ORDERED TO CONQUER THE BANDITS WHO HAD OVERRUN THE AREA.
MOUNT FIRM WAS ACTUALLY THE REVOLUTIONARY ARMY'S FRONTLINE BASE.
THE SO-CALLED "BANDITS"...
...ONLY ATTACKED LOCAL PUBLIC SERVANTS WHO FEATHERED THEIR OWN NESTS.

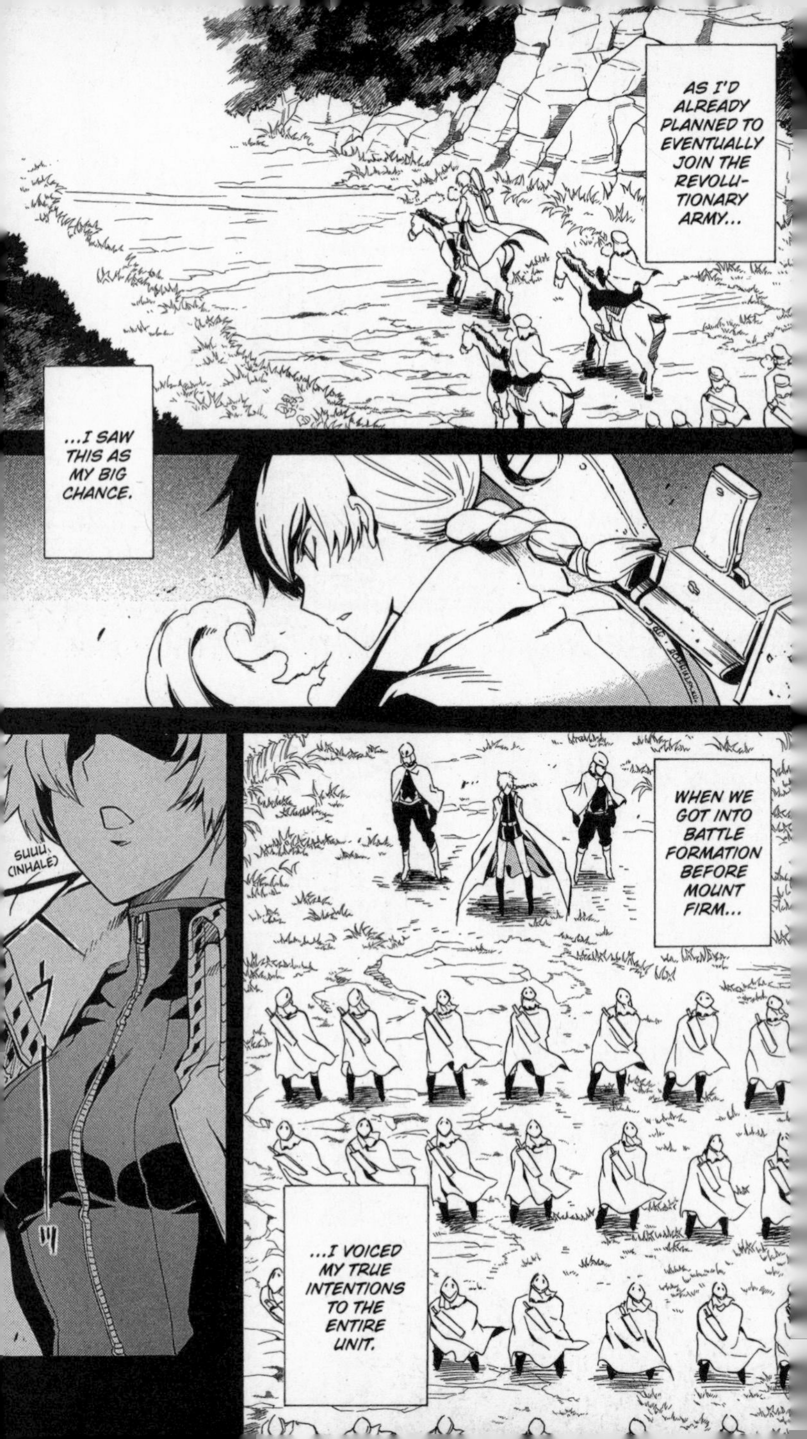
AS I'D ALREADY PLANNED TO EVENTUALLY JOIN THE REVOLUTIONARY ARMY...
...I SAW THIS AS MY BIG CHANCE.
WHEN WE GOT INTO BATTLE FORMATION BEFORE MOUNT FIRM...
...I VOICED MY TRUE INTENTIONS TO THE ENTIRE UNIT.
SUUU (INHALE)

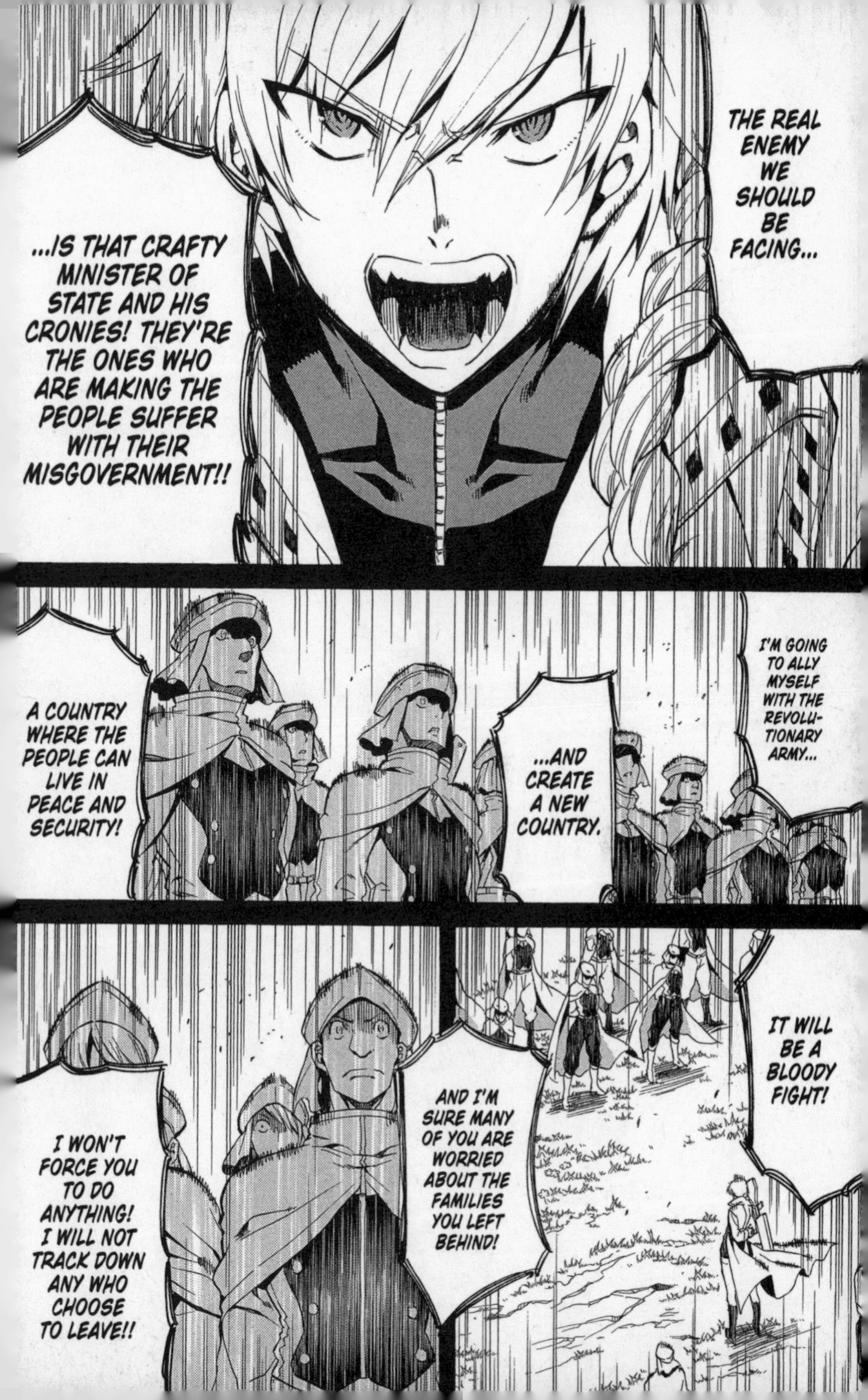
THE REAL ENEMY WE SHOULD BE FACING...
...IS THAT CRAFTY MINISTER OF STATE AND HIS CRONIES! THEY'RE THE ONES WHO ARE MAKING THE PEOPLE SUFFER WITH THEIR MISGOVERNMENT!!
I'M GOING TO ALLY MYSELF WITH THE REVOLU-TIONARY ARMY...
...AND CREATE A NEW COUNTRY.
A COUNTRY WHERE THE PEOPLE CAN LIVE IN PEACE AND SECURITY!
IT WILL BE A BLOODY FIGHT!
AND I'M SURE MANY OF YOU ARE WORRIED ABOUT THE FAMILIES YOU LEFT BEHIND!
I WON'T FORCE YOU TO DO ANYTHING! I WILL NOT TRACK DOWN ANY WHO CHOOSE TO LEAVE!!

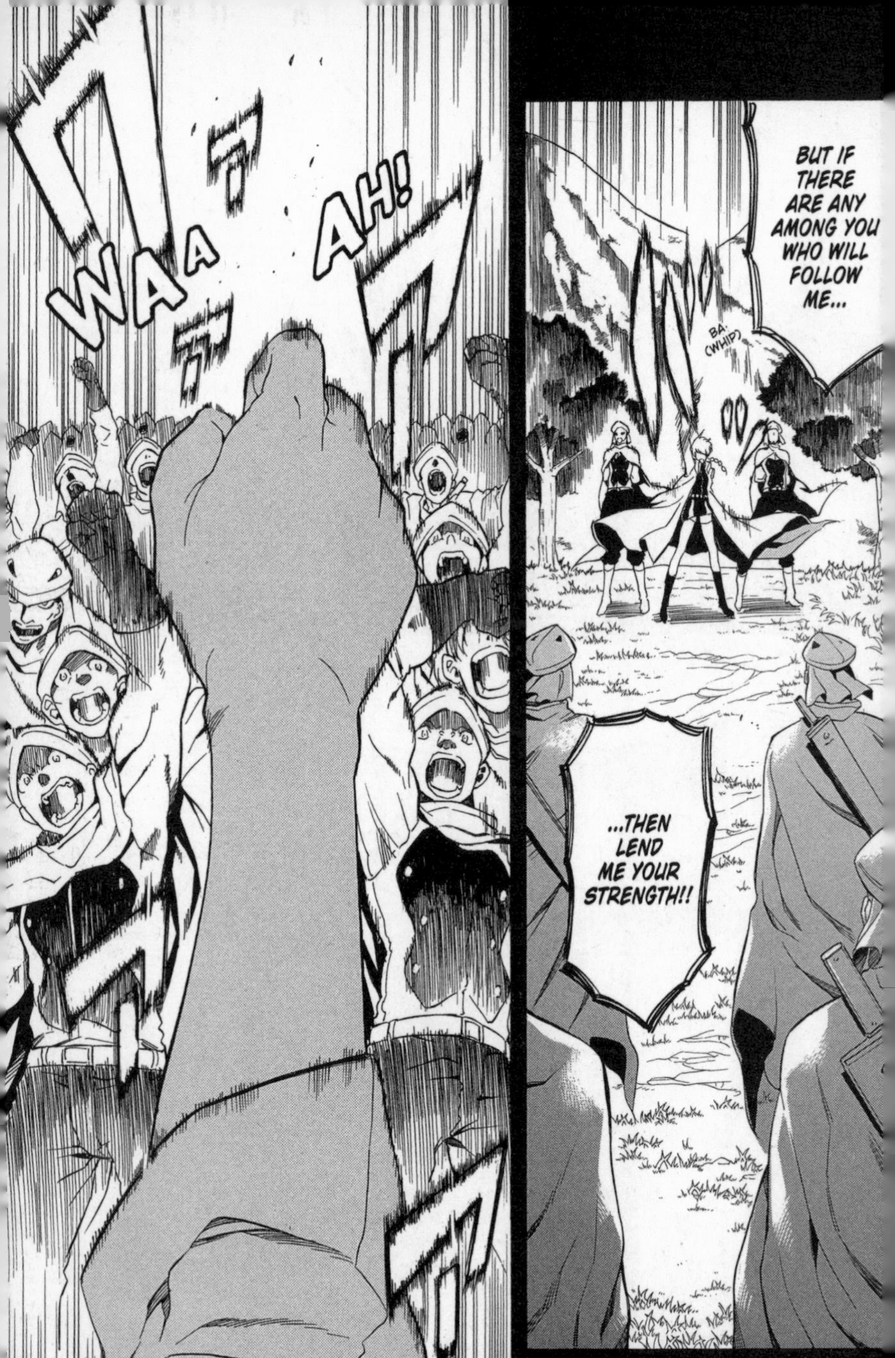
BUT IF THERE ARE ANY AMONG YOU WHO WILL FOLLOW ME...
BA (WHIP)
...THEN LEND ME YOUR STRENGTH!!
WA A AH!

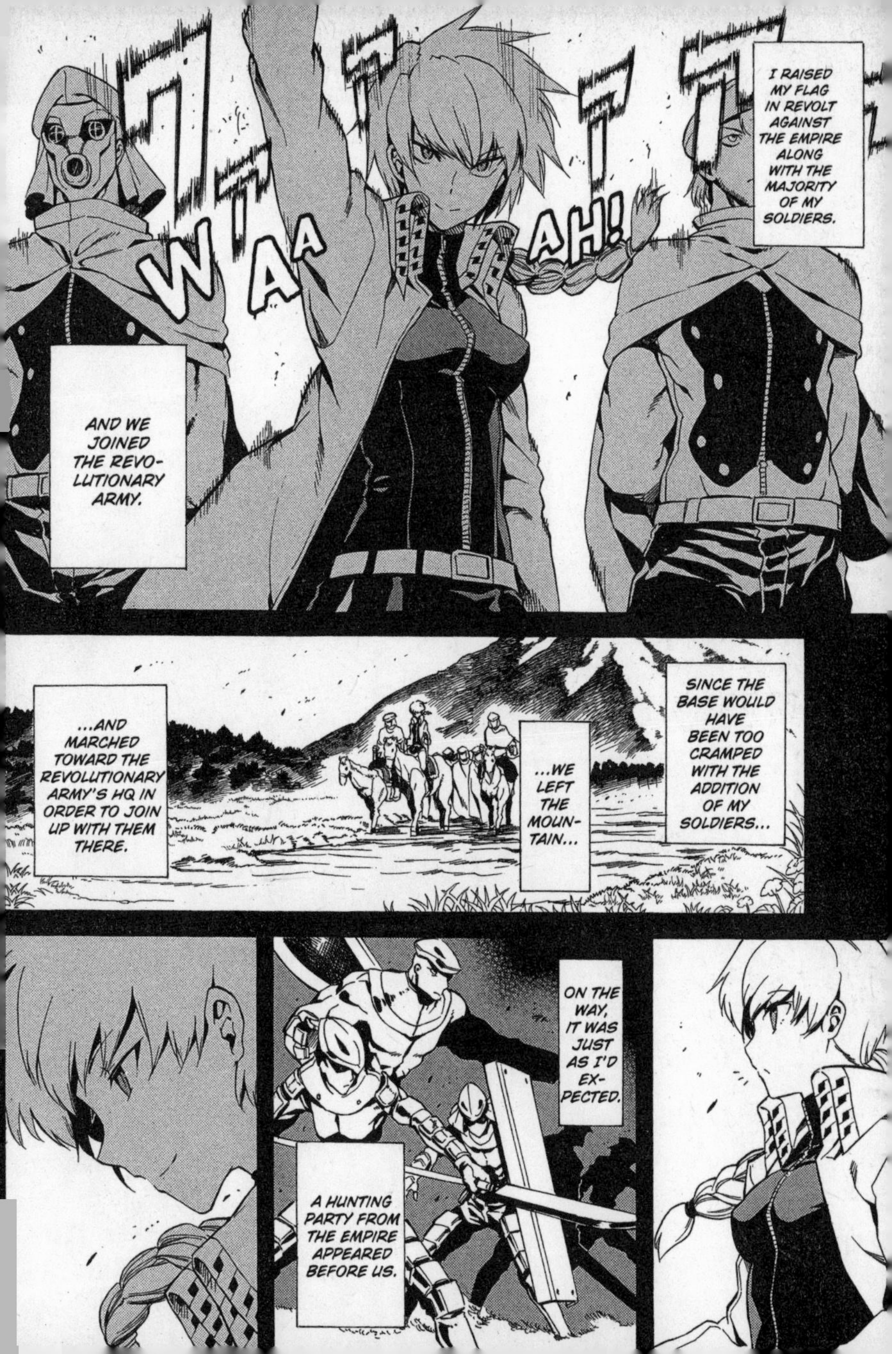
I RAISED MY FLAG IN REVOLT AGAINST THE EMPIRE ALONG WITH THE MAJORITY OF MY SOLDIERS.
WAAAH!
AND WE JOINED THE REVO-LUTIONARY ARMY.
SINCE THE BASE WOULD HAVE BEEN TOO CRAMPED WITH THE ADDITION OF MY SOLDIERS...
...WE LEFT THE MOUN-TAIN...
...AND MARCHED TOWARD THE REVOLUTIONARY ARMY'S HQ IN ORDER TO JOIN UP WITH THEM THERE.
ON THE WAY, IT WAS JUST AS I'D EX-PECTED.
A HUNTING PARTY FROM THE EMPIRE APPEARED BEFORE US.

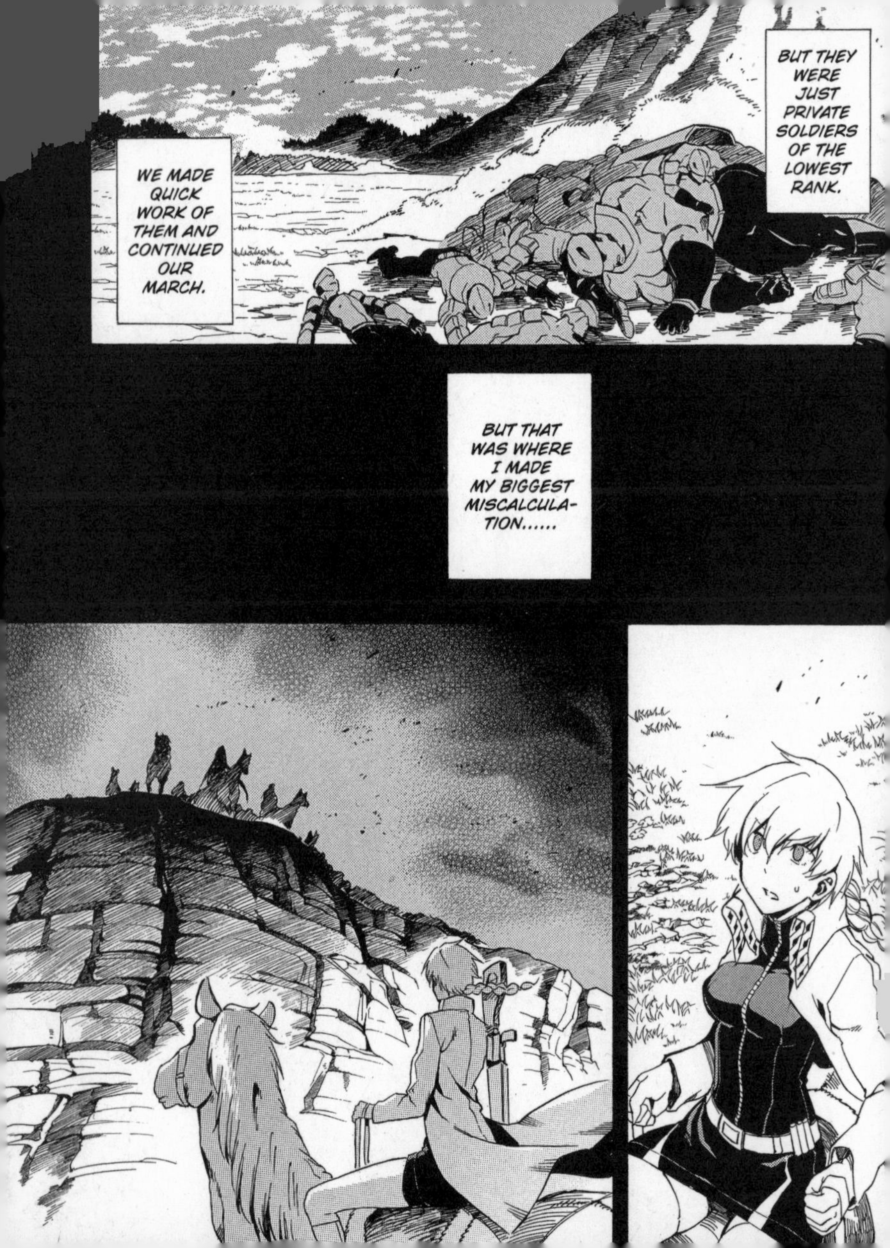
BUT THEY WERE JUST PRIVATE SOLDIERS OF THE LOWEST RANK.
WE MADE QUICK WORK OF THEM AND CONTINUED OUR MARCH.
BUT THAT WAS WHERE I MADE MY BIGGEST MISCALCULA-TION......

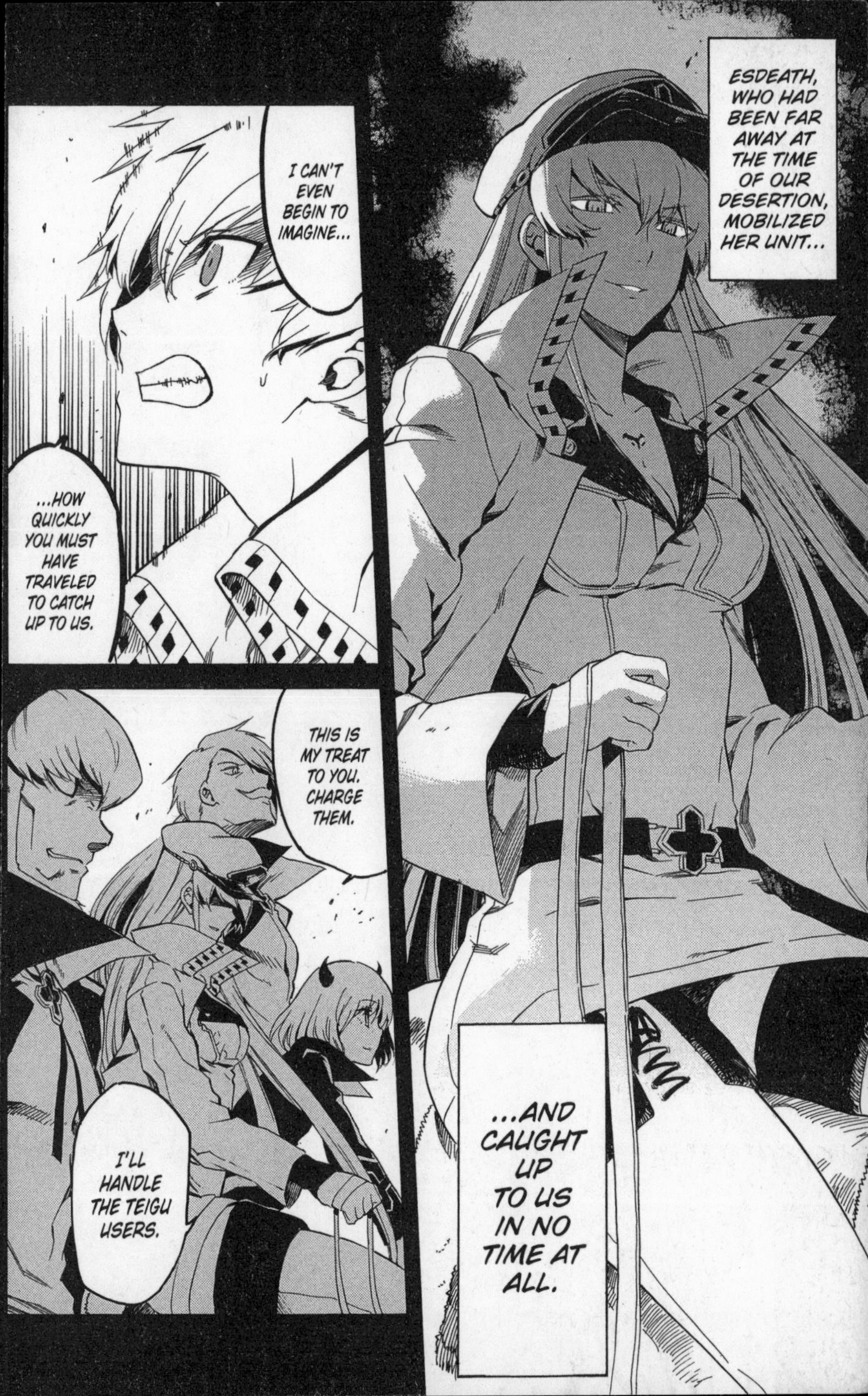
ESDEATH, WHO HAD BEEN FAR AWAY AT THE TIME OF OUR DESERTION, MOBILIZED HER UNIT...
...AND CAUGHT UP TO US IN NO TIME AT ALL.
I CAN'T EVEN BEGIN TO IMAGINE...
...HOW QUICKLY YOU MUST HAVE TRAVELED TO CATCH UP TO US.
THIS IS MY TREAT TO YOU. CHARGE THEM.
I'LL HANDLE THE TEIGU USERS.

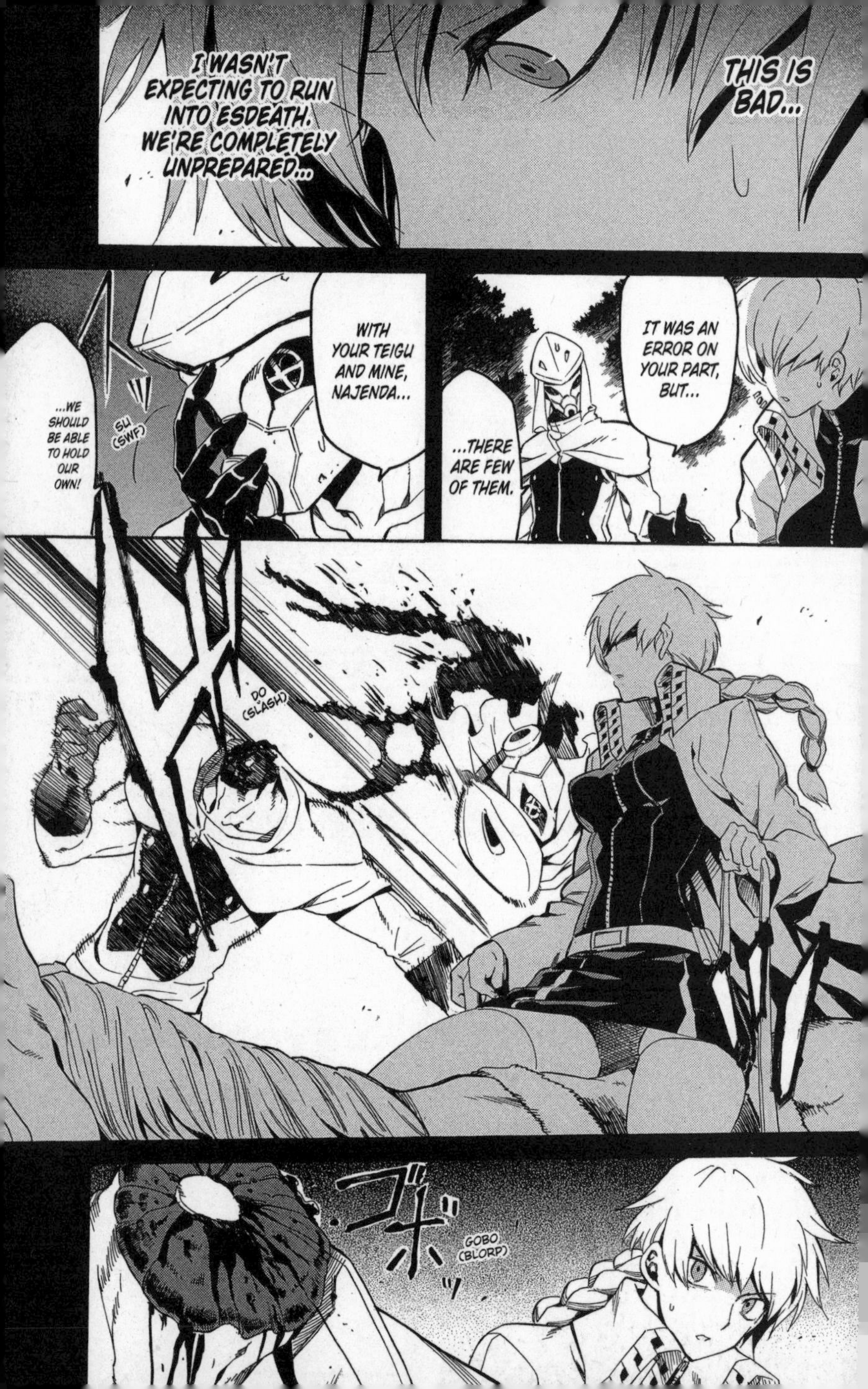
THIS IS BAD...
I WASN'T EXPECTING TO RUN INTO ESDEATH. WE'RE COMPLETELY UNPREPARED...
IT WAS AN ERROR ON YOUR PART, BUT...
...THERE ARE FEW OF THEM.
WITH YOUR TEIGU AND MINE, NAJENDA...
SU (SWF)
...WE SHOULD BE ABLE TO HOLD OUR OWN!
DO (SLASH)
ゴボッ
GOBO (BLORP)

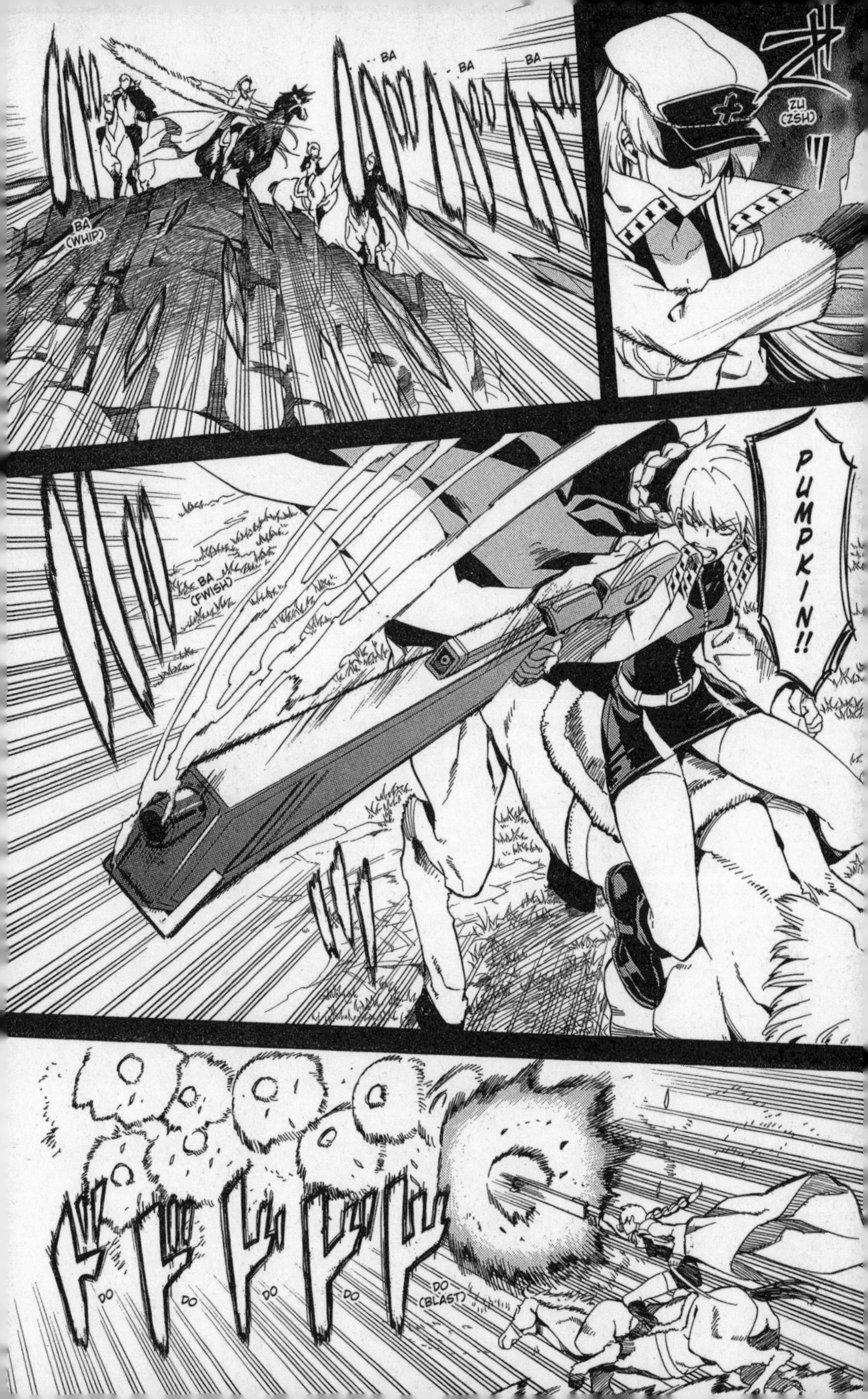
ZU (ZSH)
- - BA
- - BA
- - BA
BA (WHIP)
PUMPKIN!!
BA (FWISH)
DO (BLAST)
DO
DO
DO
DO

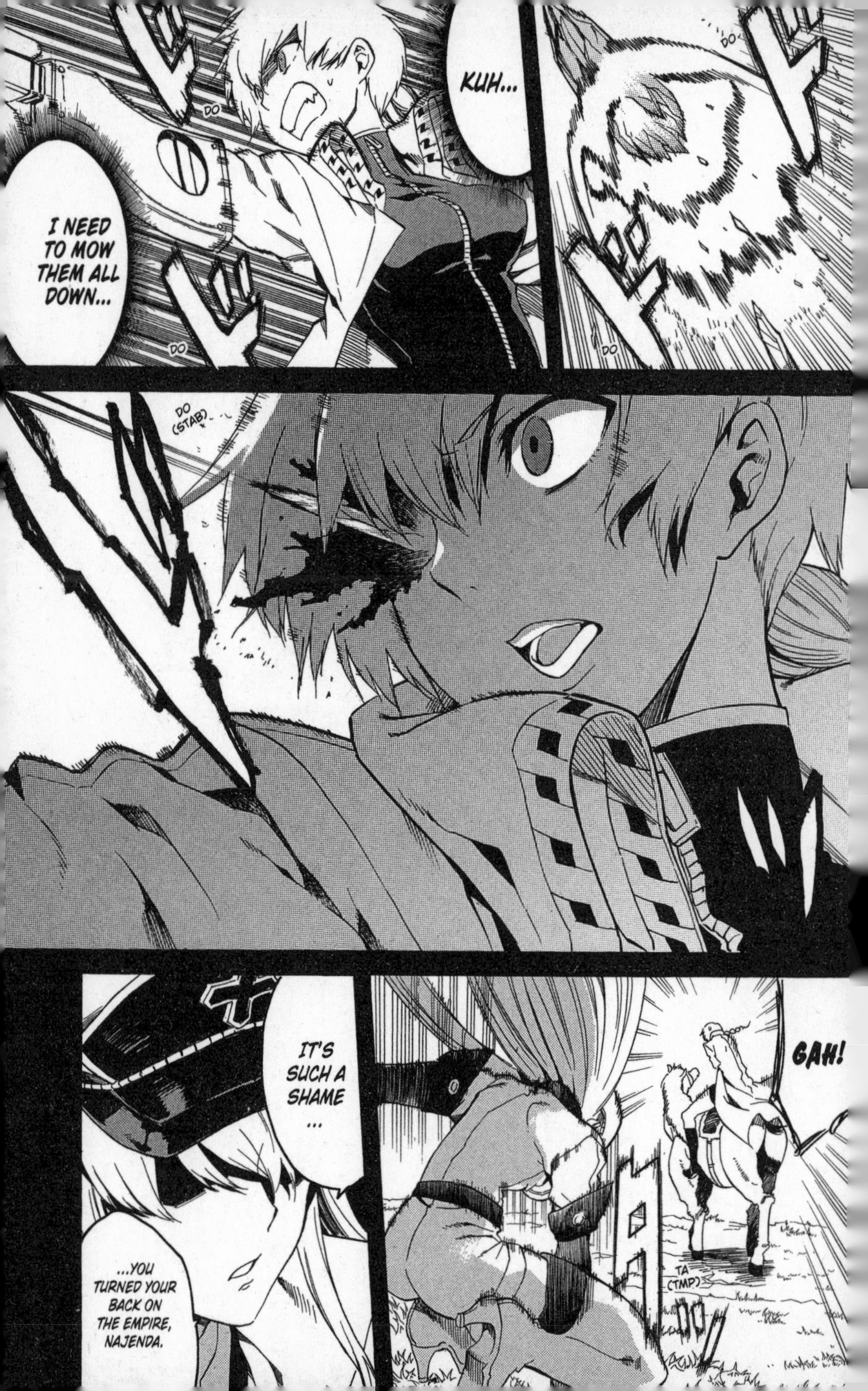
DO
DO
KUH...
I NEED TO MOW THEM ALL DOWN...
DO
DO
DO (STAB)
GAH!
TA (TMP)
IT'S SUCH A SHAME ...
...YOU TURNED YOUR BACK ON THE EMPIRE, NAJENDA.

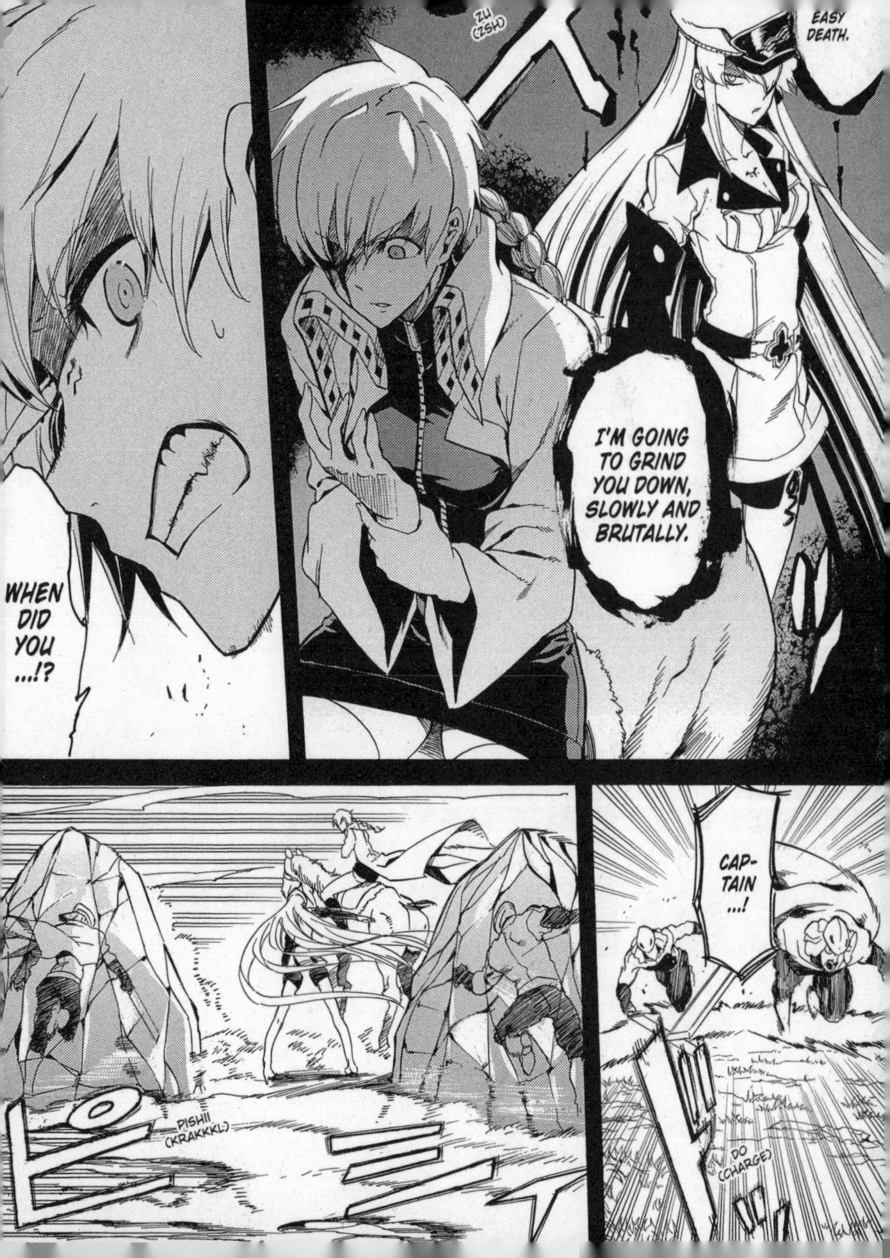
EASY DEATH.
ZU (ZSH)
I'M GOING TO GRIND YOU DOWN, SLOWLY AND BRUTALLY.
WHEN DID YOU ...!?
CAP-TAIN ...!
DO (CHARGE)
PISHII (KRAKKKL)

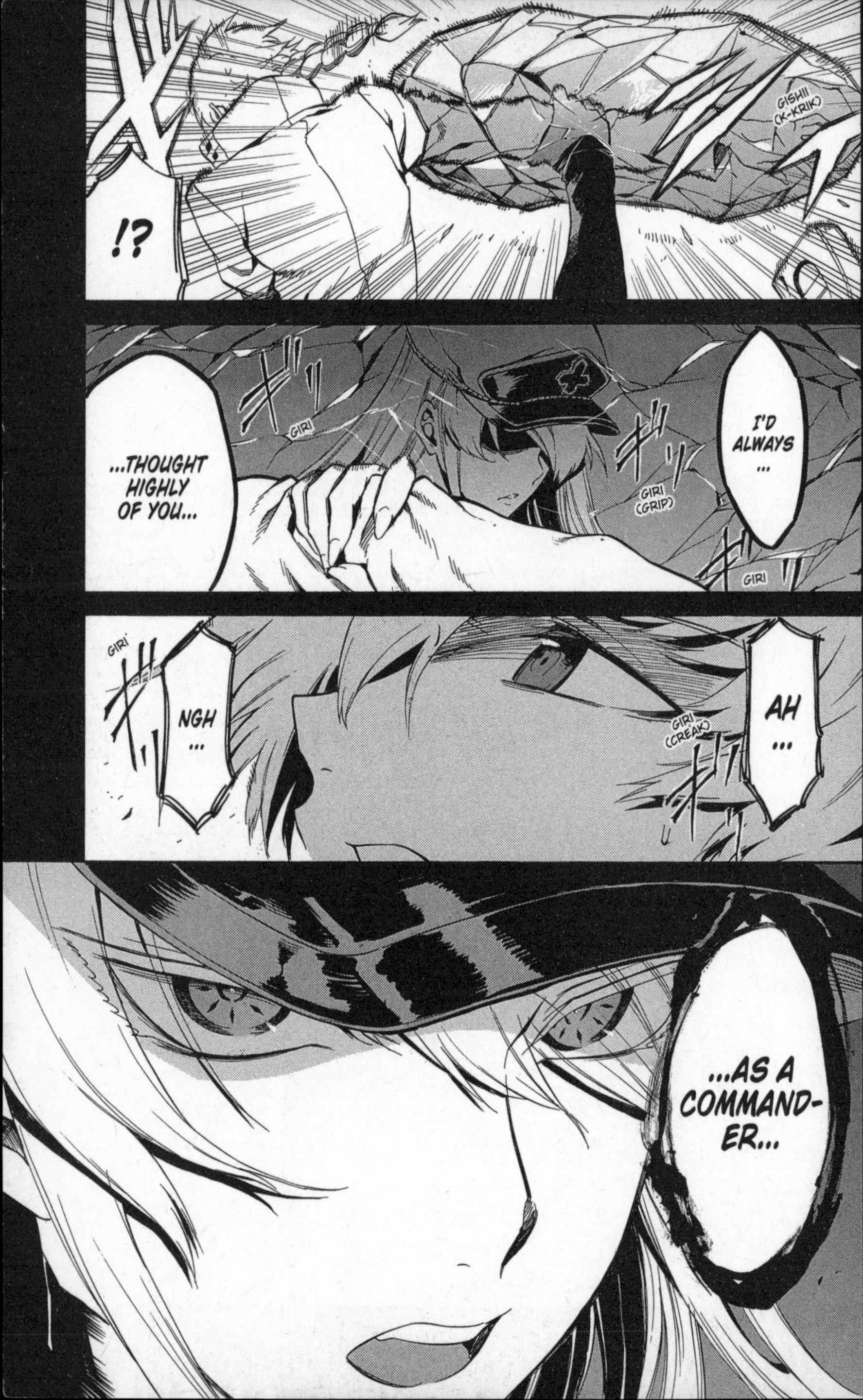
GISHI (K-KRIK)
!?
I'D ALWAYS ...
GIRI (GRIP)
GIRI
GIRI
...THOUGHT HIGHLY OF YOU...
AH ...
GIRI (CREAK)
NGH ...
GIRI
...AS A COMMAND-ER...

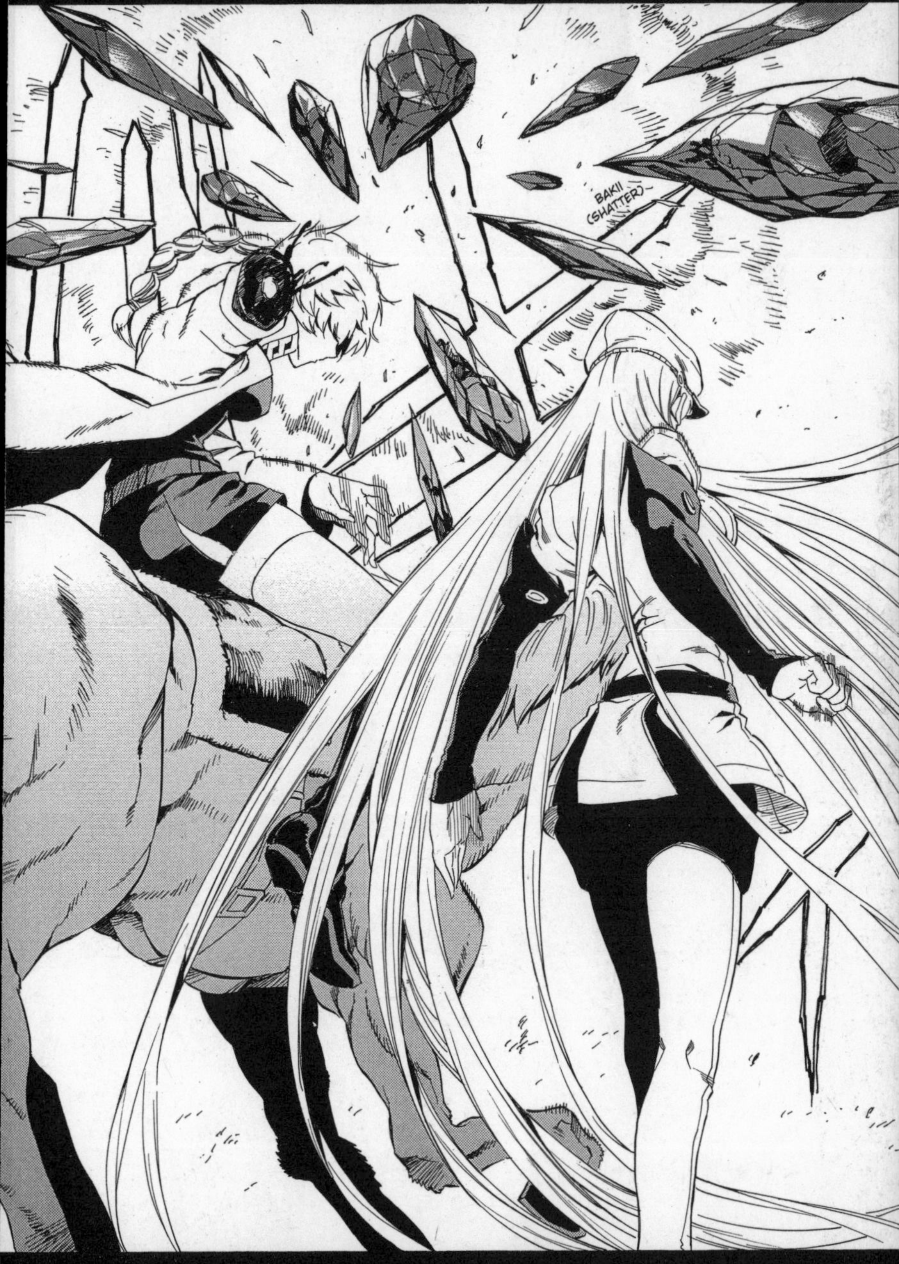
BAKII (SHATTER)

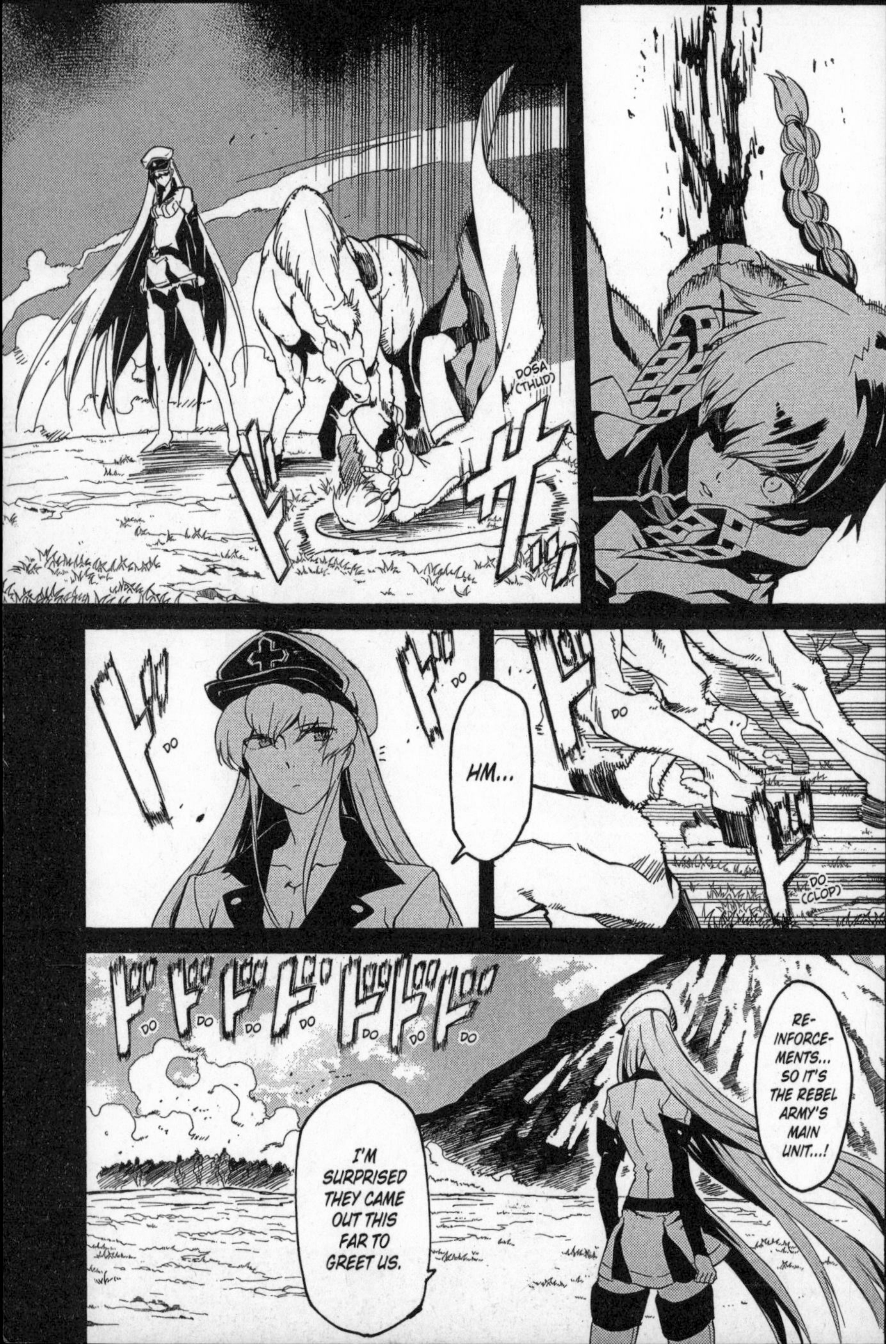
DOSA (THUD)
DO
DO
HM...
DO
DO (CLOP)
DO DO DO DO DO DO DO
RE-INFORCE-MENTS... SO IT'S THE REBEL ARMY'S MAIN UNIT...!
I'M SURPRISED THEY CAME OUT THIS FAR TO GREET US.

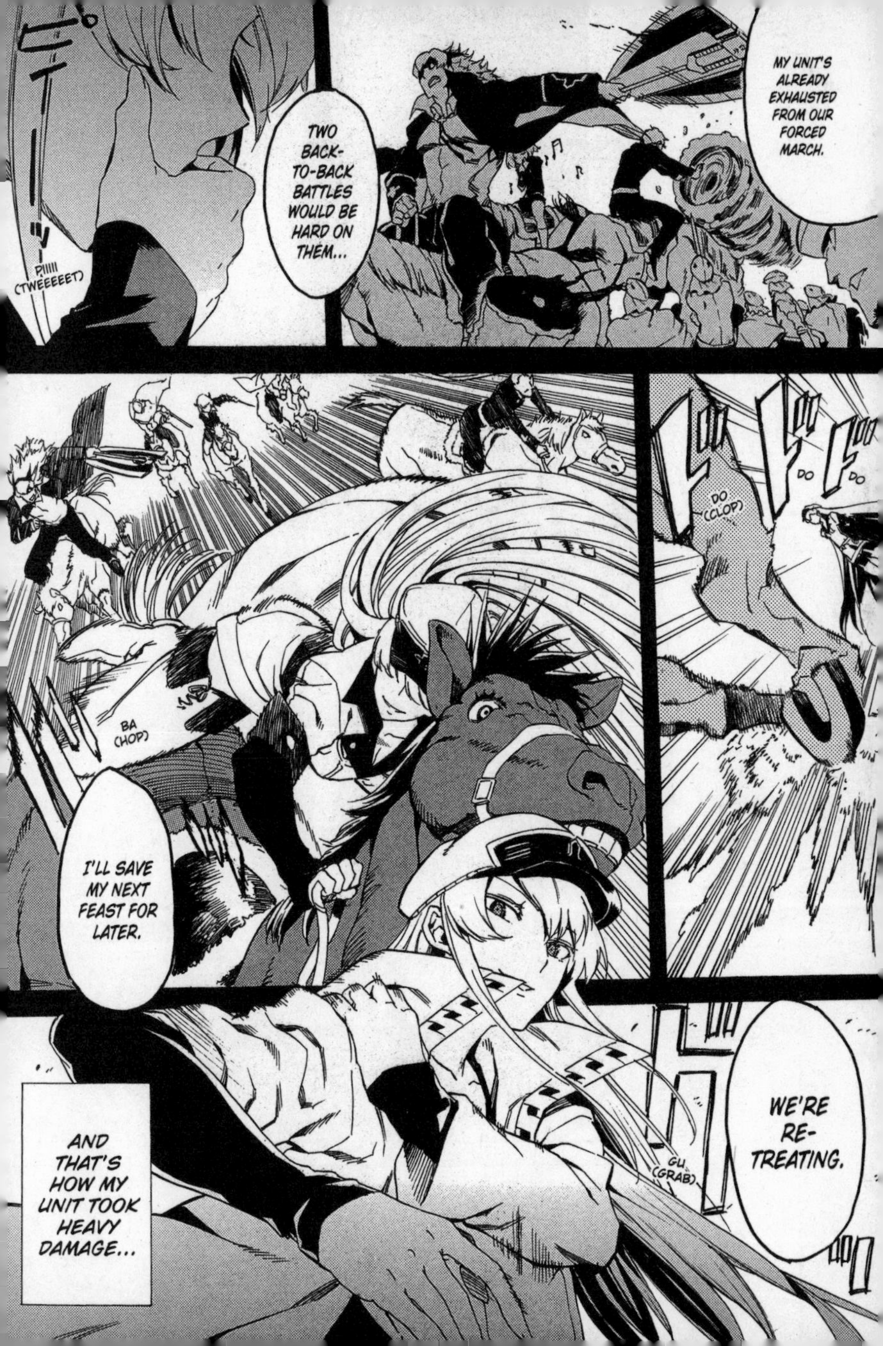
MY UNIT'S ALREADY EXHAUSTED FROM OUR FORCED MARCH.
TWO BACK-TO-BACK BATTLES WOULD BE HARD ON THEM...
PIIIII (TWEEEEET)
DO DO
DO (CLOP)
BA (HOP)
I'LL SAVE MY NEXT FEAST FOR LATER.
WE'RE RE-TREATING.
GU (GRAB)
AND THAT'S HOW MY UNIT TOOK HEAVY DAMAGE...

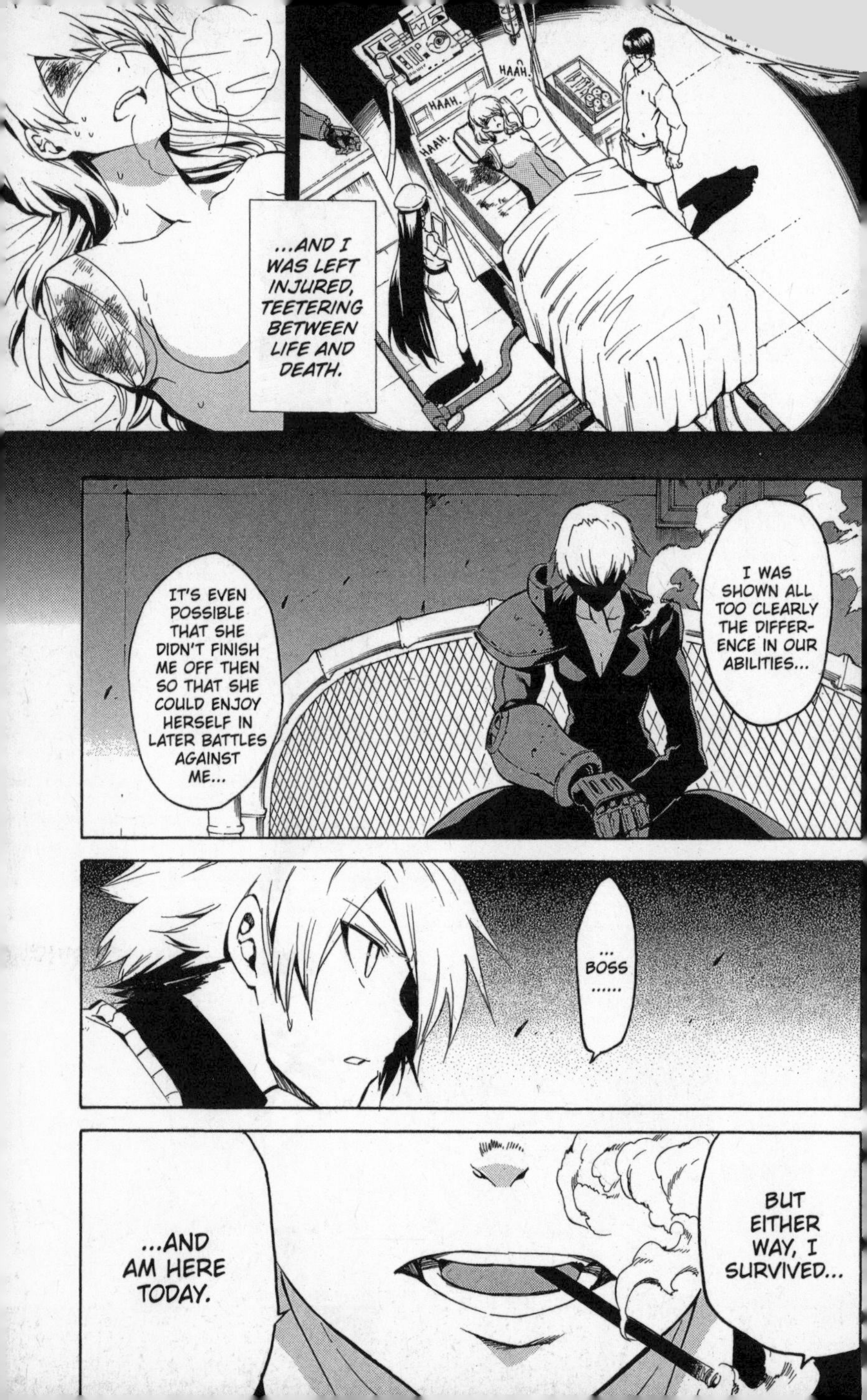
HAAH.
HAAH.
HAAH.
...AND I WAS LEFT INJURED, TEETERING BETWEEN LIFE AND DEATH.
I WAS SHOWN ALL TOO CLEARLY THE DIFFERENCE IN OUR ABILITIES...
IT'S EVEN POSSIBLE THAT SHE DIDN'T FINISH ME OFF THEN SO THAT SHE COULD ENJOY HERSELF IN LATER BATTLES AGAINST ME...
... BOSS ......
BUT EITHER WAY, I SURVIVED...
...AND AM HERE TODAY.

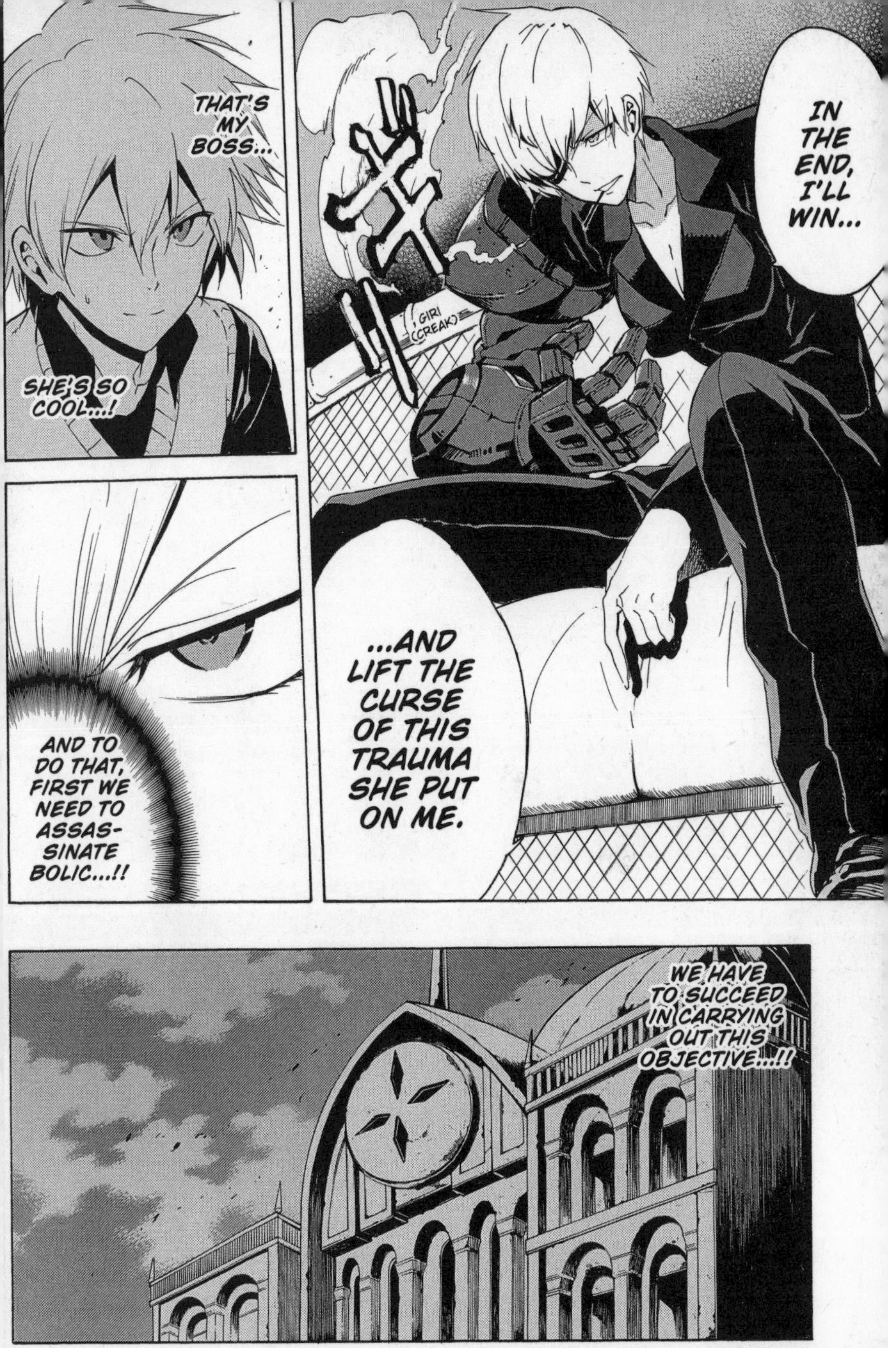
IN THE END, I'LL WIN...
GIRI (CREAK)
...AND LIFT THE CURSE OF THIS TRAUMA SHE PUT ON ME.
THAT'S MY BOSS...
SHE'S SO COOL...!
AND TO DO THAT, FIRST WE NEED TO ASSAS- SINATE BOLIC...!!
WE HAVE TO SUCCEED IN CARRYING OUT THIS OBJECTIVE...!!

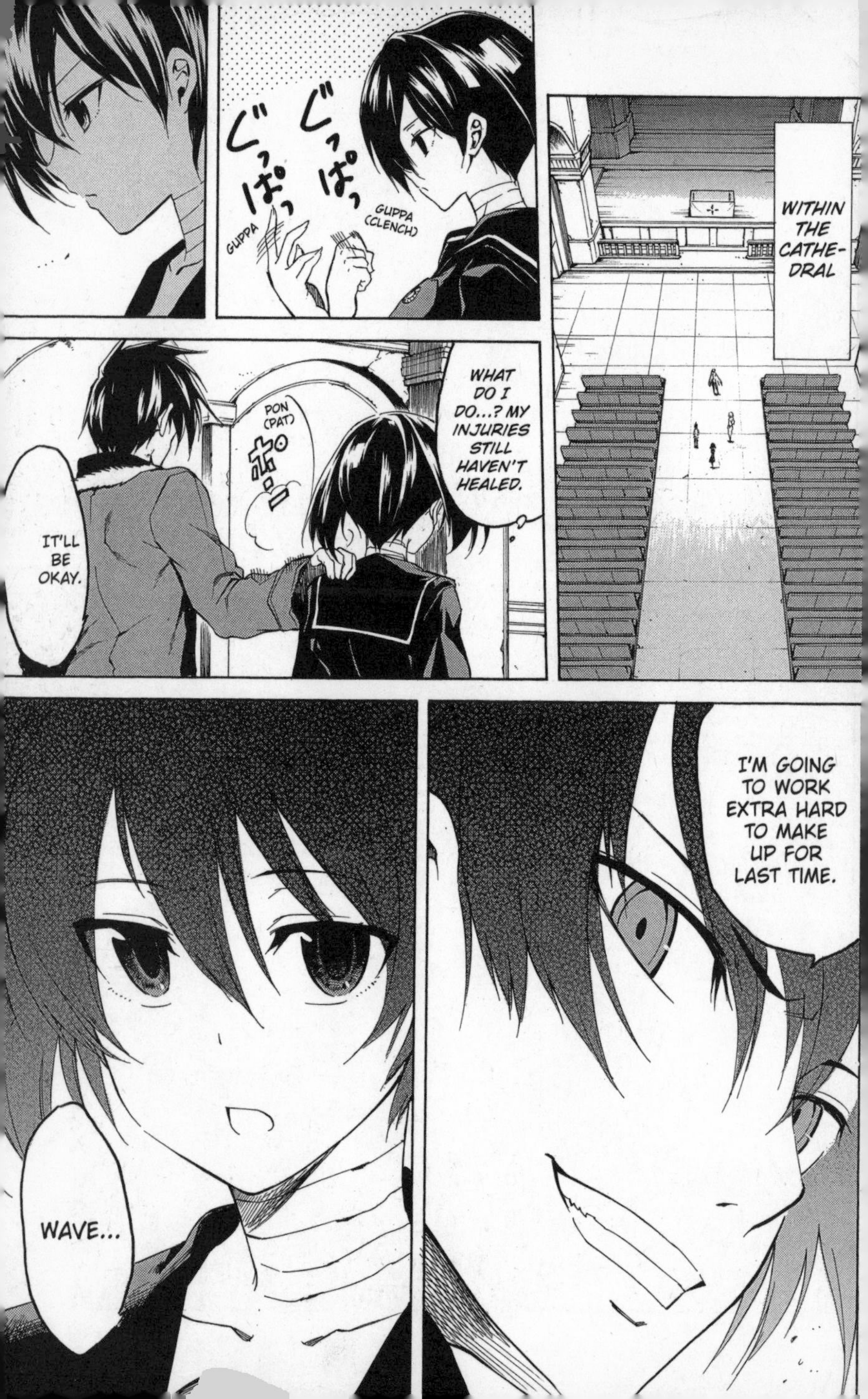
WITHIN THE CATHE-DRAL
ぐっぱっ
GUPPA (CLENCH)
ぐっぱっ
GUPPA
...
WHAT DO I DO...? MY INJURIES STILL HAVEN'T HEALED.
PON (PAT)
IT'LL BE OKAY.
I'M GOING TO WORK EXTRA HARD TO MAKE UP FOR LAST TIME.
WAVE...

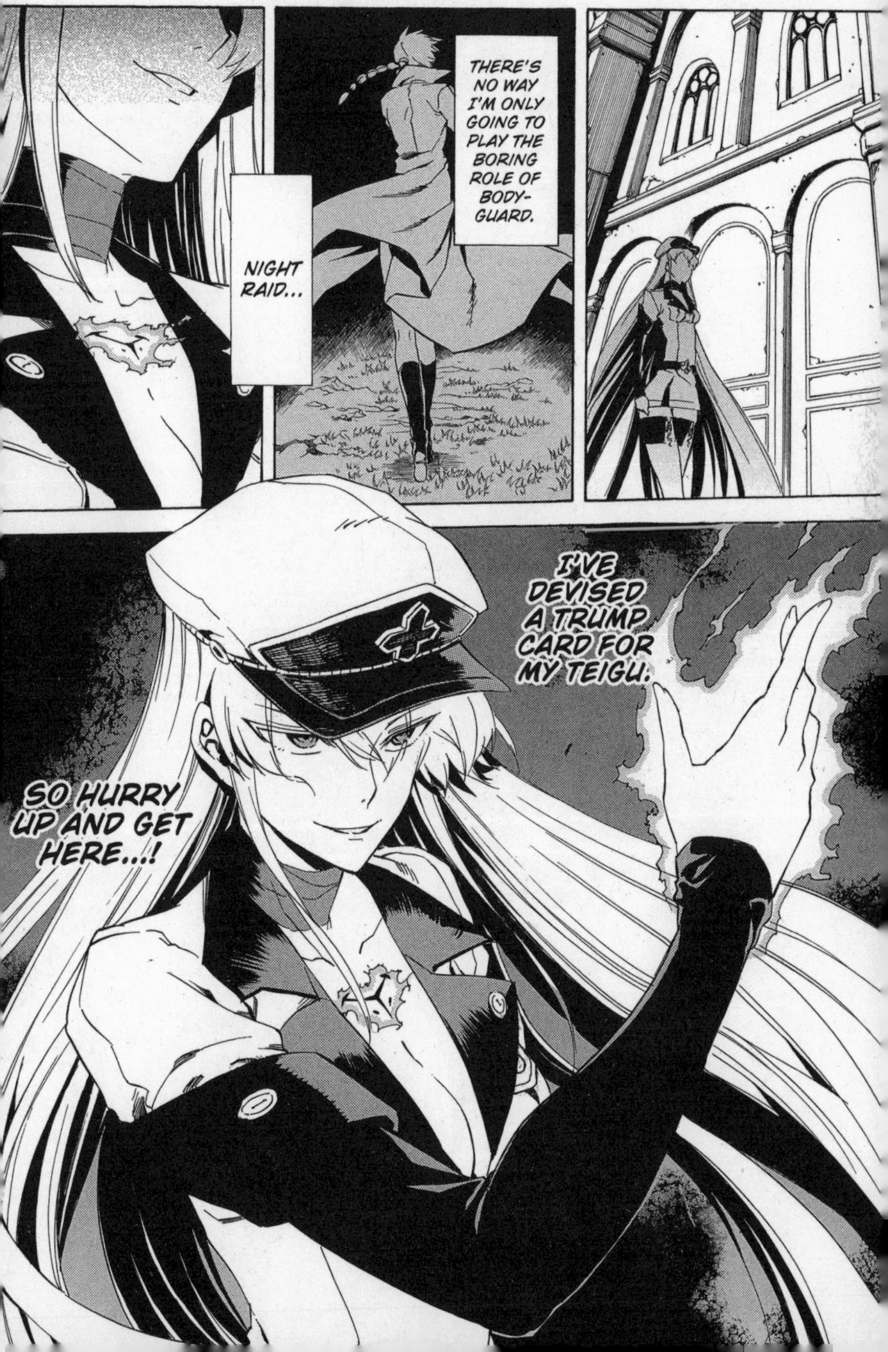
THERE'S NO WAY I'M ONLY GOING TO PLAY THE BORING ROLE OF BODY-GUARD.
NIGHT RAID...
I'VE DEVISED A TRUMP CARD FOR MY TEIGU.
SO HURRY UP AND GET HERE...!

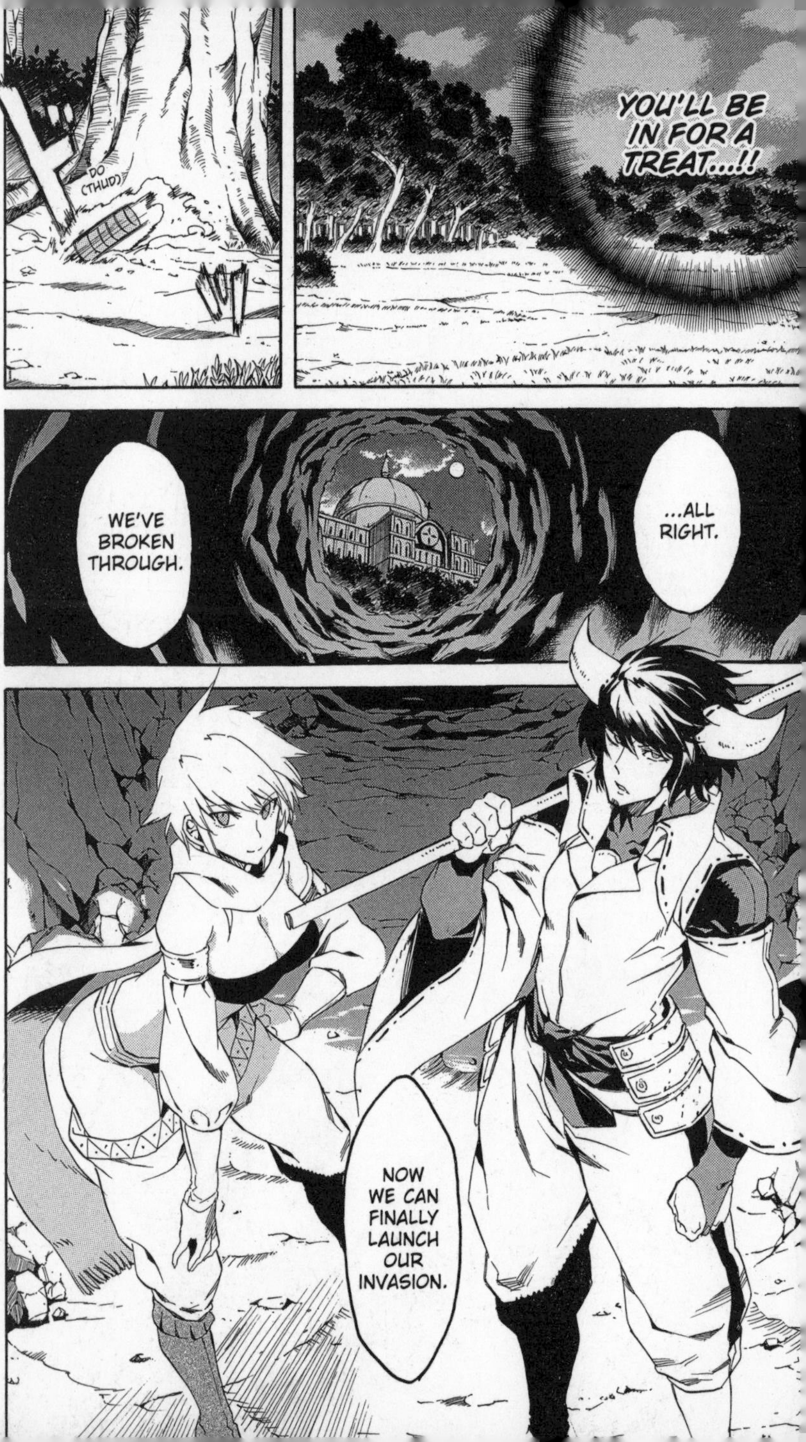
YOU'LL BE IN FOR A TREAT...!!
DO (THUD)
...ALL RIGHT.
WE'VE BROKEN THROUGH.
NOW WE CAN FINALLY LAUNCH OUR INVASION.

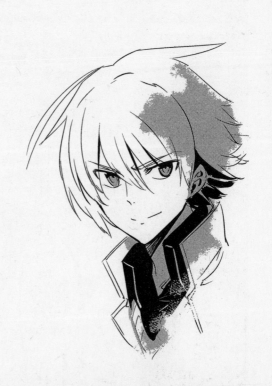

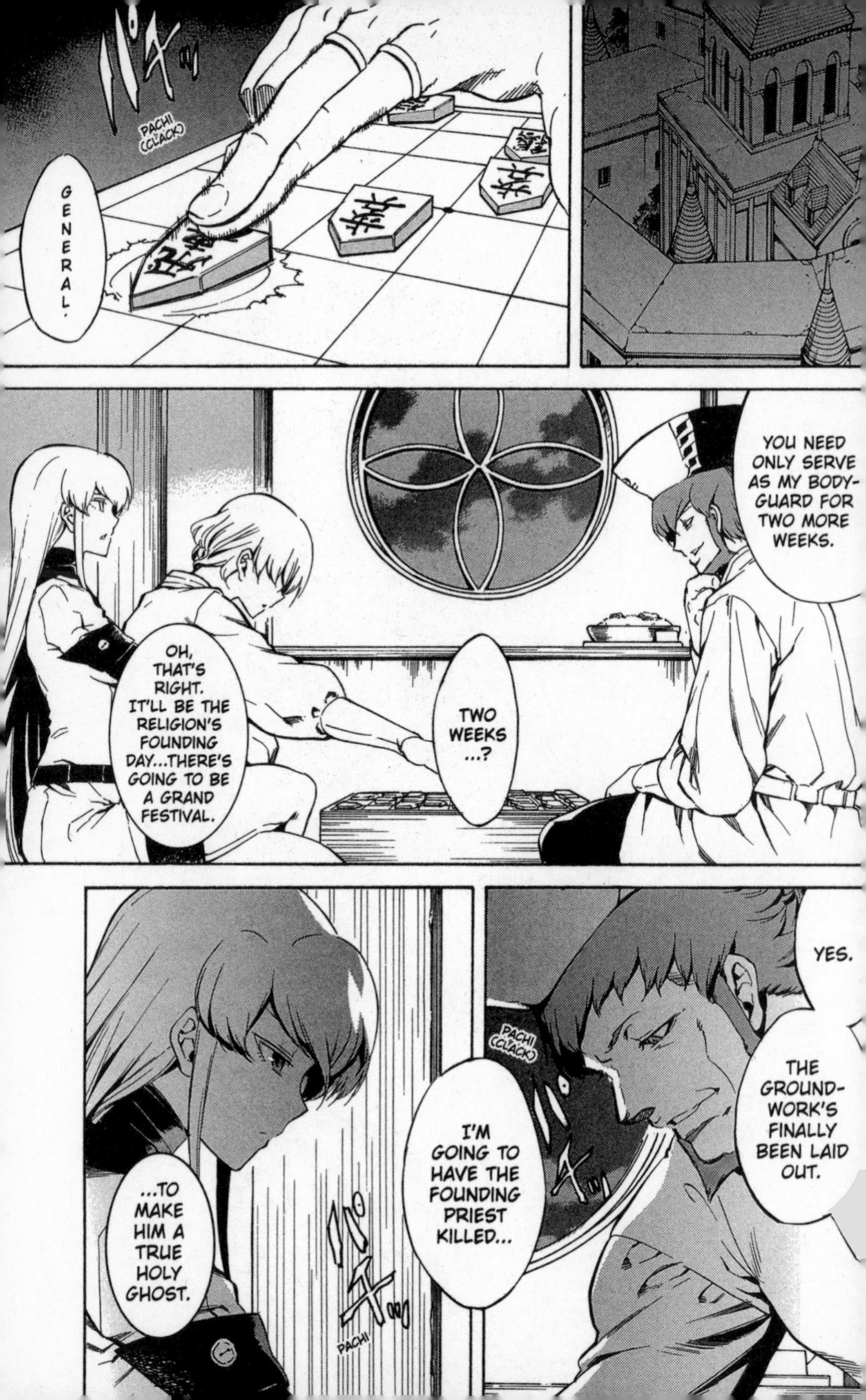
PACHI (CLACK)
GENERAL.
YOU NEED ONLY SERVE AS MY BODYGUARD FOR TWO MORE WEEKS.
TWO WEEKS ...?
OH, THAT'S RIGHT. IT'LL BE THE RELIGION'S FOUNDING DAY...THERE'S GOING TO BE A GRAND FESTIVAL.
YES.
THE GROUNDWORK'S FINALLY BEEN LAID OUT.
PACHI (CLACK)
I'M GOING TO HAVE THE FOUNDING PRIEST KILLED...
PACHI
...TO MAKE HIM A TRUE HOLY GHOST.

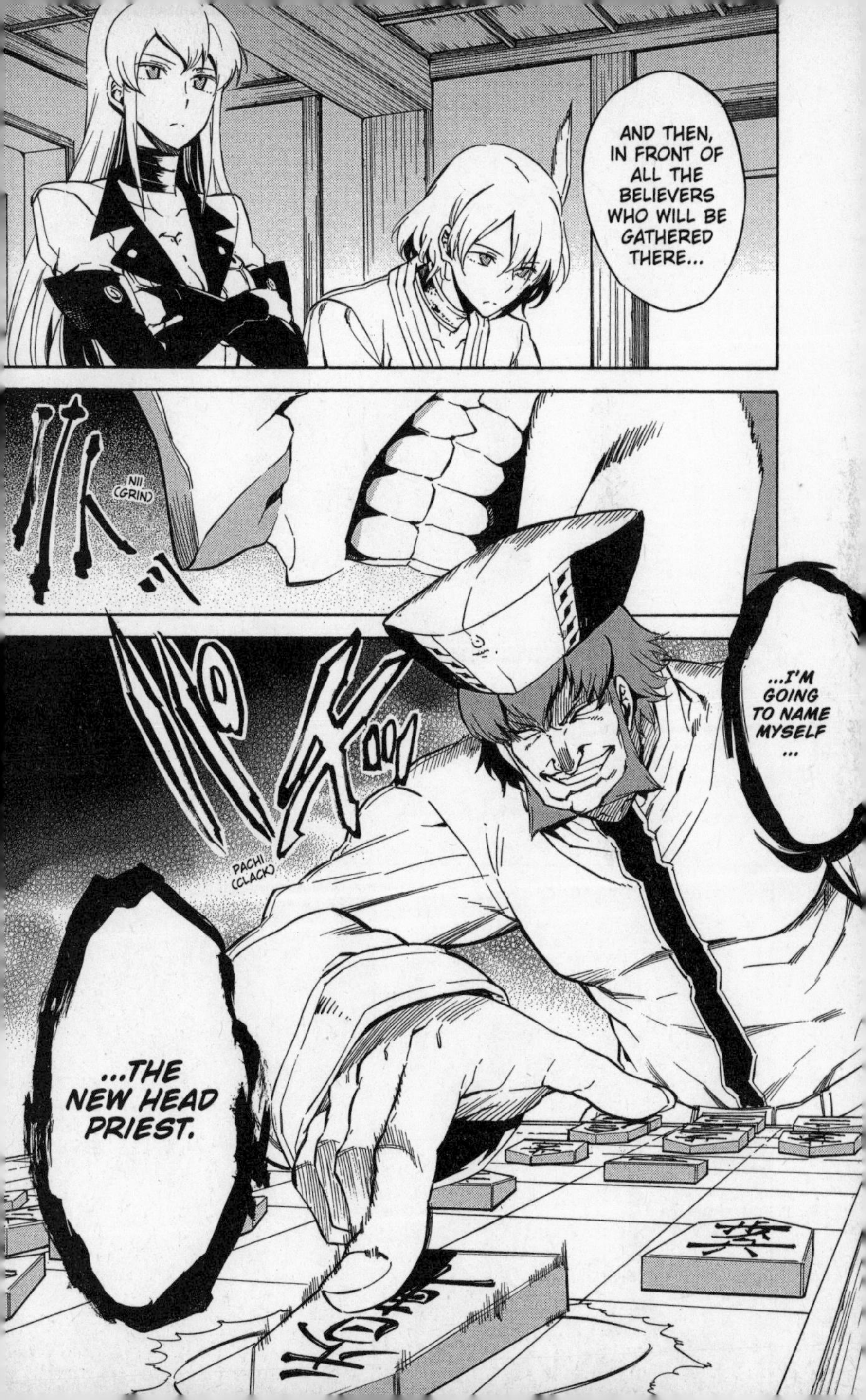
AND THEN, IN FRONT OF ALL THE BELIEVERS WHO WILL BE GATHERED THERE...
NII (GRIN)
...I'M GOING TO NAME MYSELF ...
PACHI (CLACK)
...THE NEW HEAD PRIEST.

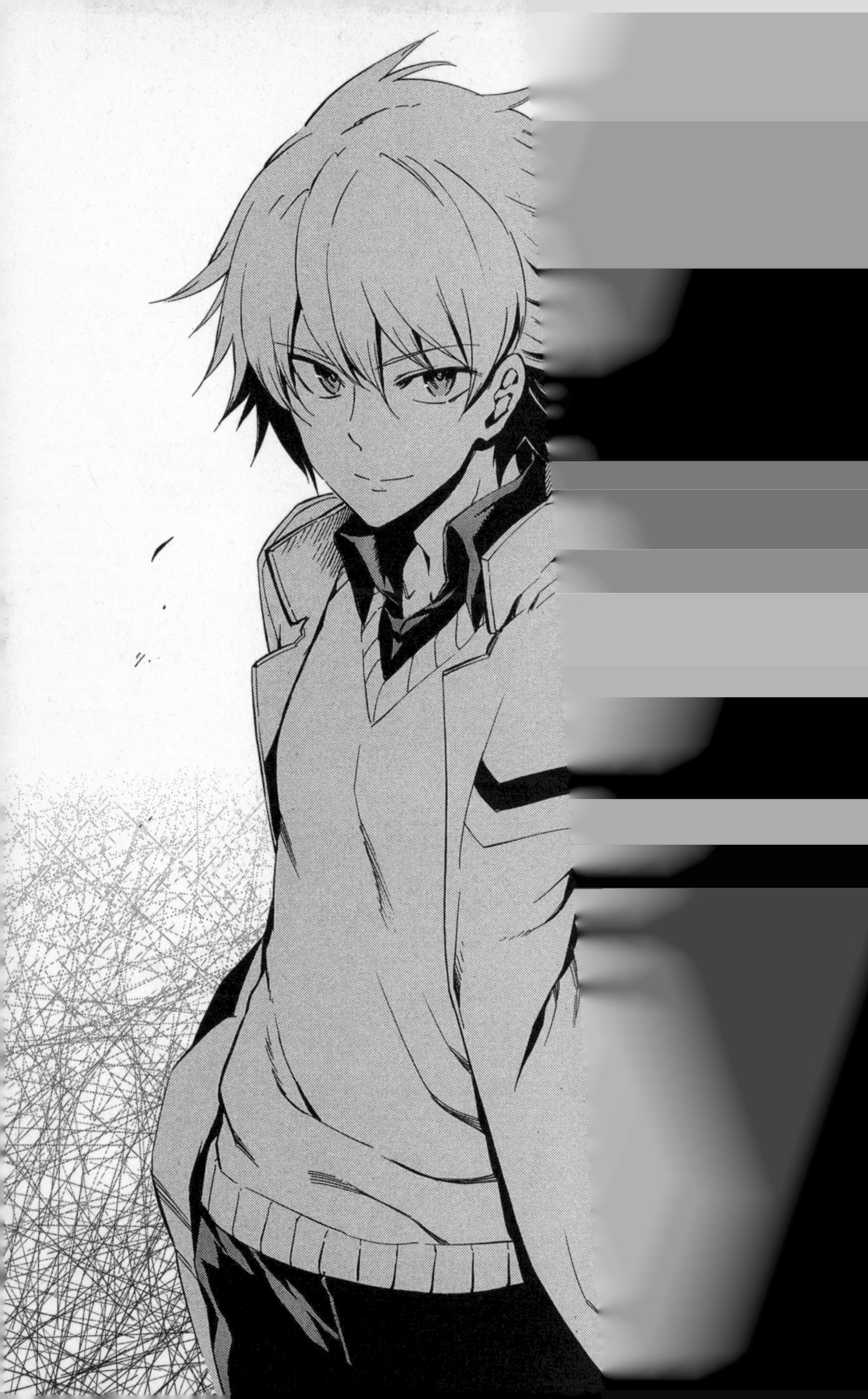

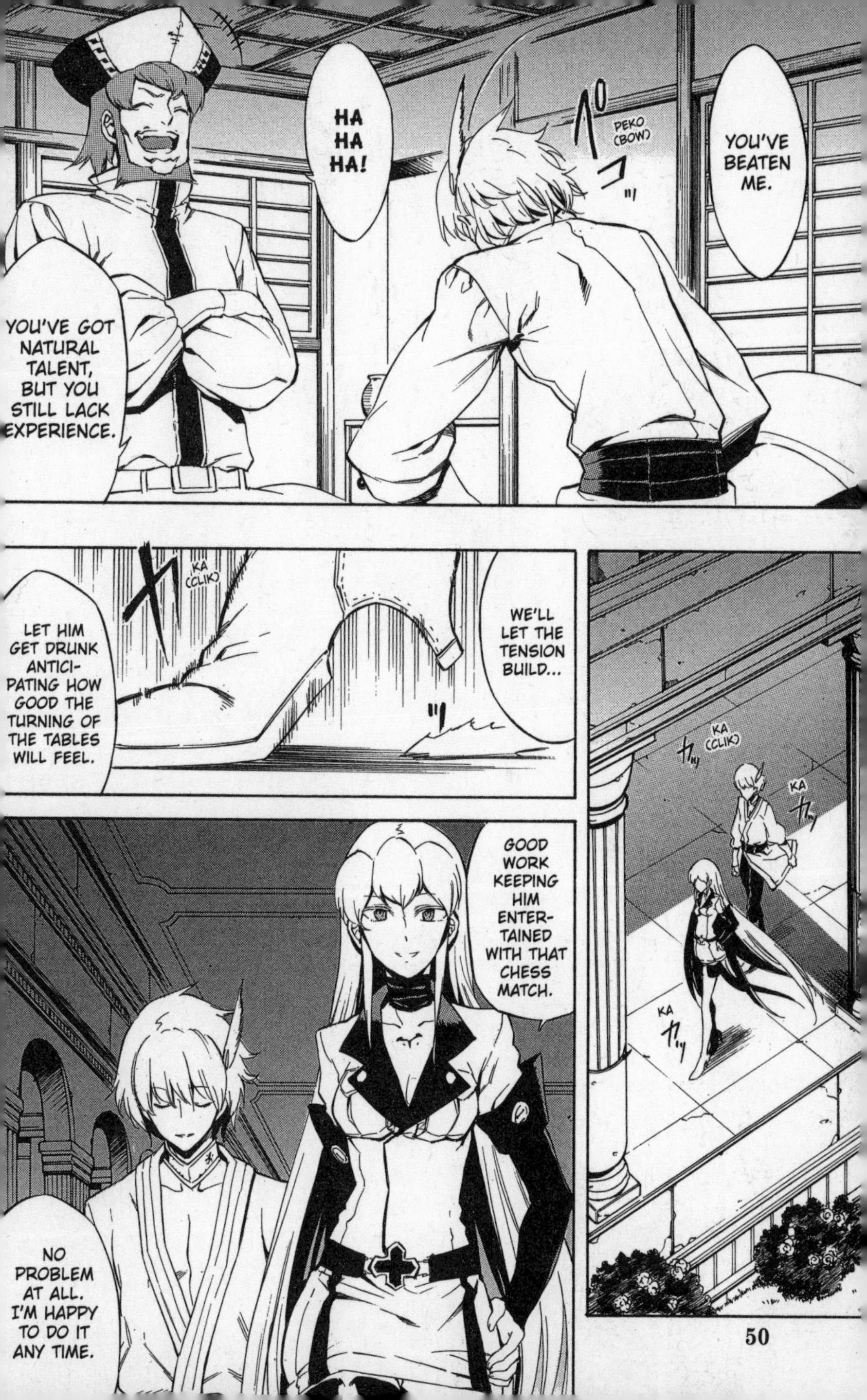
YOU'VE BEATEN ME.
PEKO (BOW)
HA HA HA!
YOU'VE GOT NATURAL TALENT, BUT YOU STILL LACK EXPERIENCE.
KA (CLIK)
KA
KA
WE'LL LET THE TENSION BUILD...
KA (CLIK)
LET HIM GET DRUNK ANTICI- PATING HOW GOOD THE TURNING OF THE TABLES WILL FEEL.
GOOD WORK KEEPING HIM ENTER- TAINED WITH THAT CHESS MATCH.
NO PROBLEM AT ALL. I'M HAPPY TO DO IT ANY TIME.

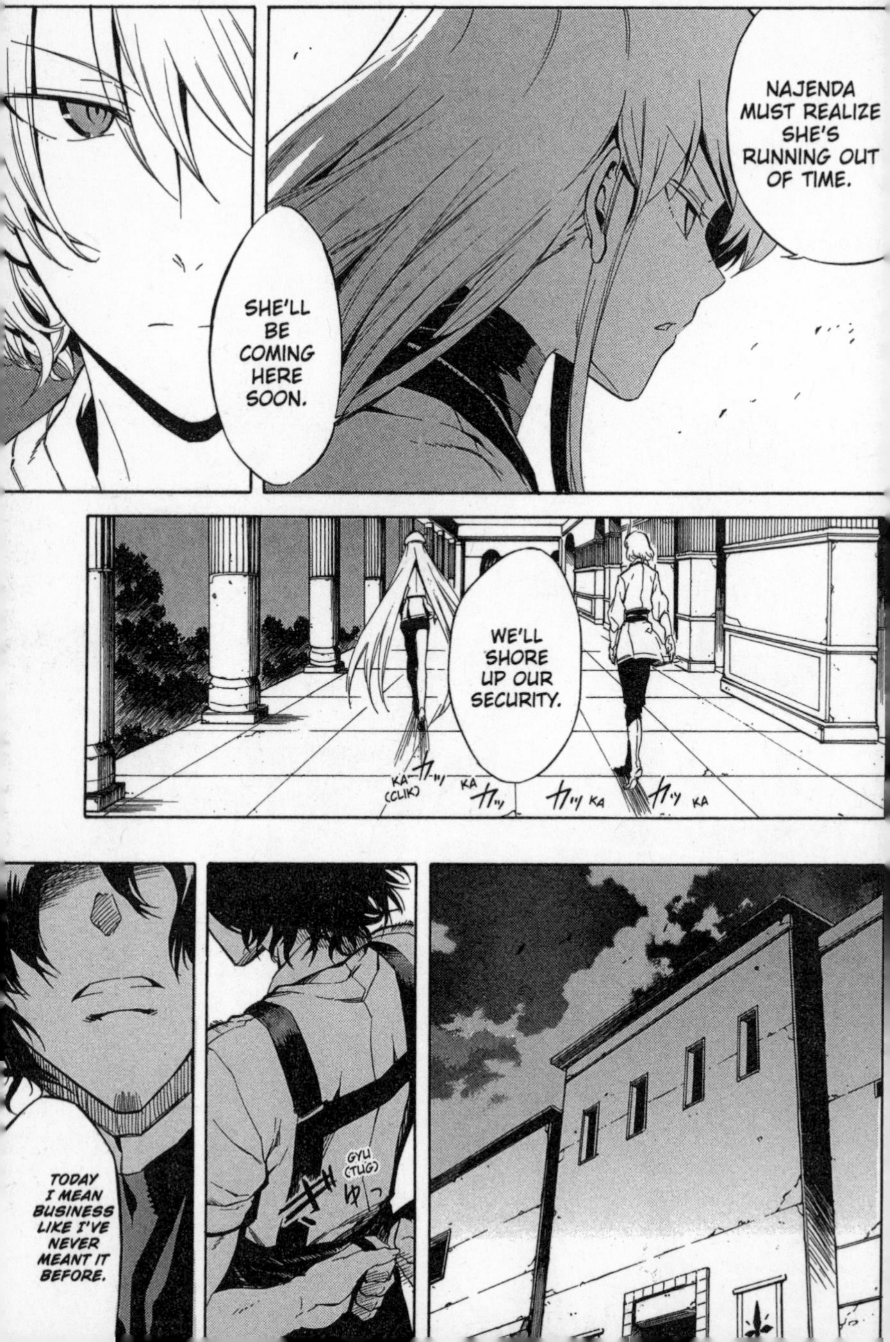
NAJENDA MUST REALIZE SHE'S RUNNING OUT OF TIME.
SHE'LL BE COMING HERE SOON.
WE'LL SHORE UP OUR SECURITY.
KA KA KA KA (CLIK)
GYU (TUG)
TODAY I MEAN BUSINESS LIKE I'VE NEVER MEANT IT BEFORE.

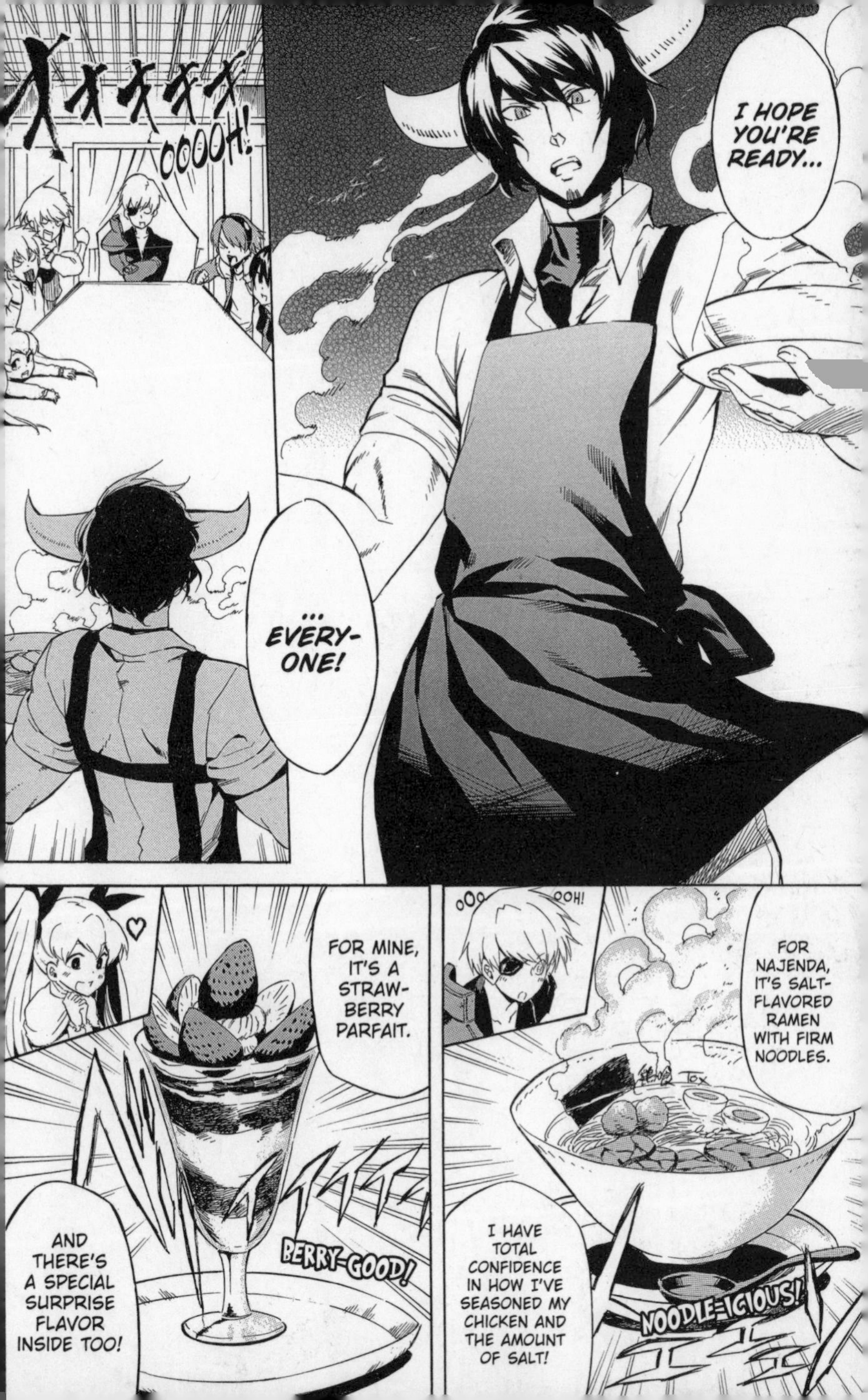
I HOPE YOU'RE READY...
... EVERY-ONE!
OOOOH!
OOO OOH!
FOR NAJENDA, IT'S SALT-FLAVORED RAMEN WITH FIRM NOODLES.
I HAVE TOTAL CONFIDENCE IN HOW I'VE SEASONED MY CHICKEN AND THE AMOUNT OF SALT!
NOODLE-ICIOUS!
FOR MINE, IT'S A STRAW-BERRY PARFAIT.
AND THERE'S A SPECIAL SURPRISE FLAVOR INSIDE TOO!
BERRY-GOOD!

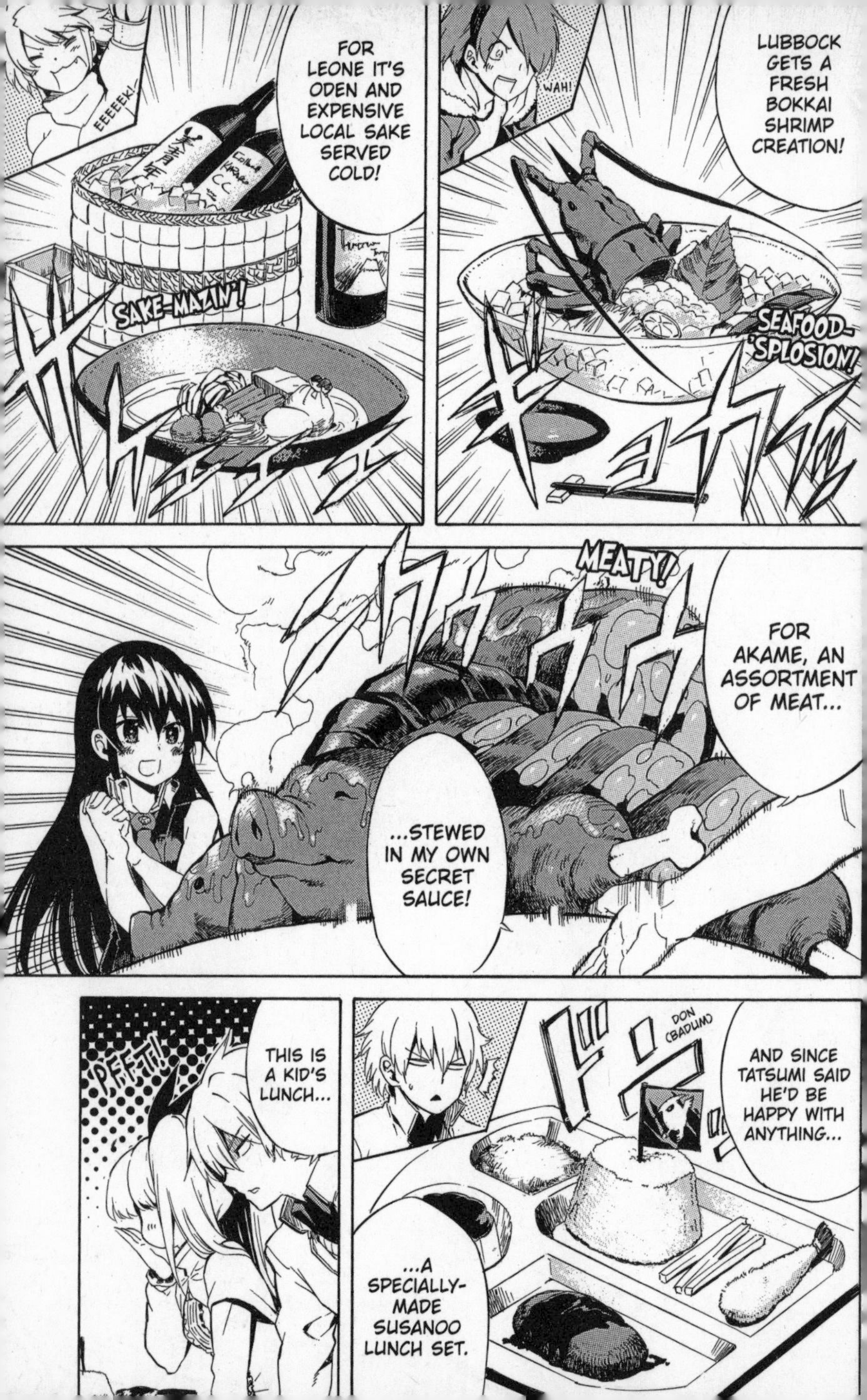
LUBBOCK GETS A FRESH BOKKAI SHRIMP CREATION!
WAH!
SEAFOOD-'SPLOSION!
FOR LEONE IT'S ODEN AND EXPENSIVE LOCAL SAKE SERVED COLD!
EEEEEK!
SAKE-MAZIN'!
MEATY!
FOR AKAME, AN ASSORTMENT OF MEAT...
...STEWED IN MY OWN SECRET SAUCE!
AND SINCE TATSUMI SAID HE'D BE HAPPY WITH ANYTHING...
DON (BADUM)
...A SPECIALLY-MADE SUSANOO LUNCH SET.
THIS IS A KID'S LUNCH...
PFFFT!

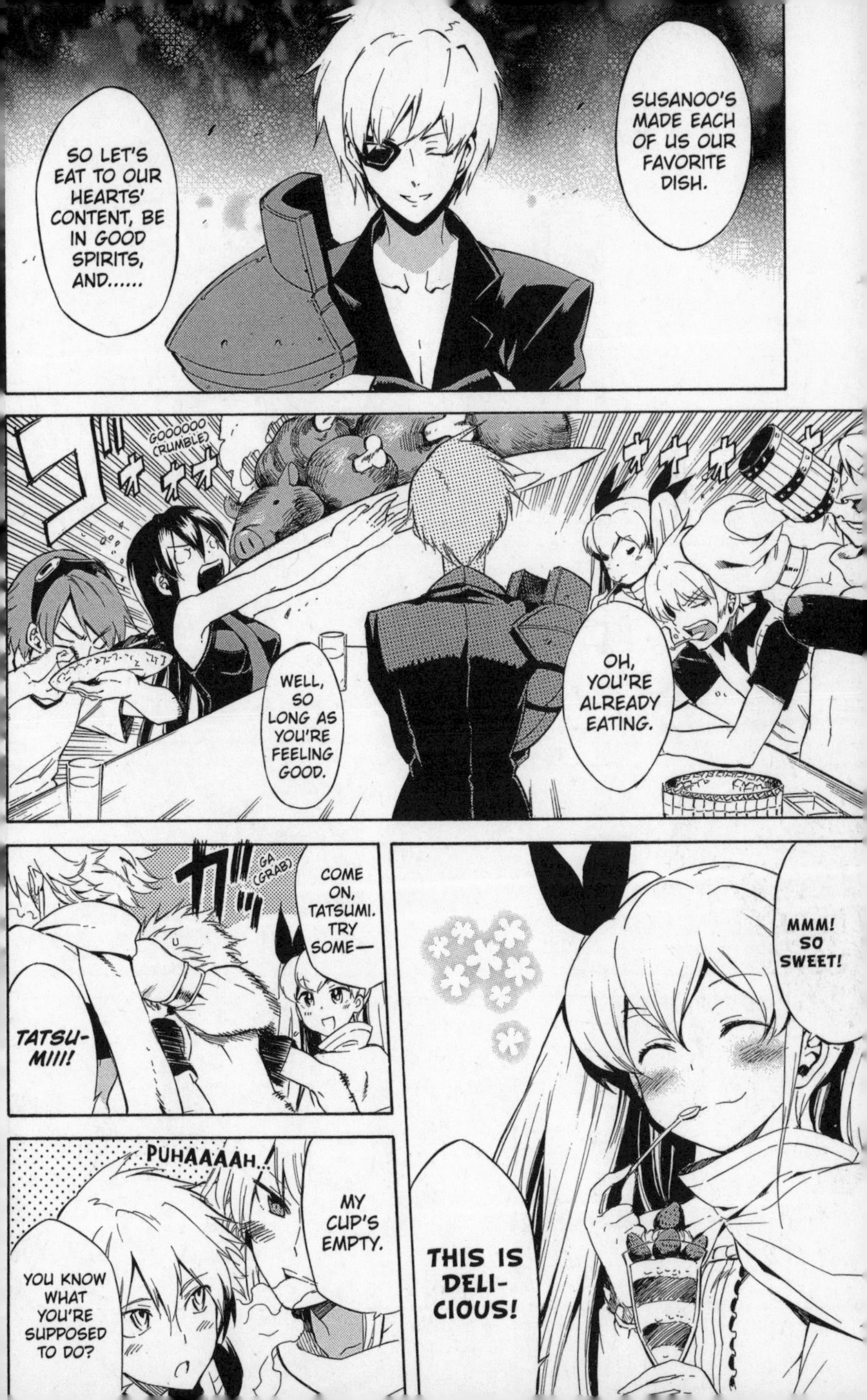
SUSANOO'S MADE EACH OF US OUR FAVORITE DISH.
SO LET'S EAT TO OUR HEARTS' CONTENT, BE IN GOOD SPIRITS, AND......
GOOOOOO (RUMBLE)
OH, YOU'RE ALREADY EATING.
WELL, SO LONG AS YOU'RE FEELING GOOD.
MMM! SO SWEET!
THIS IS DELI-CIOUS!
GA (GRAB)
COME ON, TATSUMI. TRY SOME—
TATSU-MIII!
PUHAAAAH..!
MY CUP'S EMPTY.
YOU KNOW WHAT YOU'RE SUPPOSED TO DO?

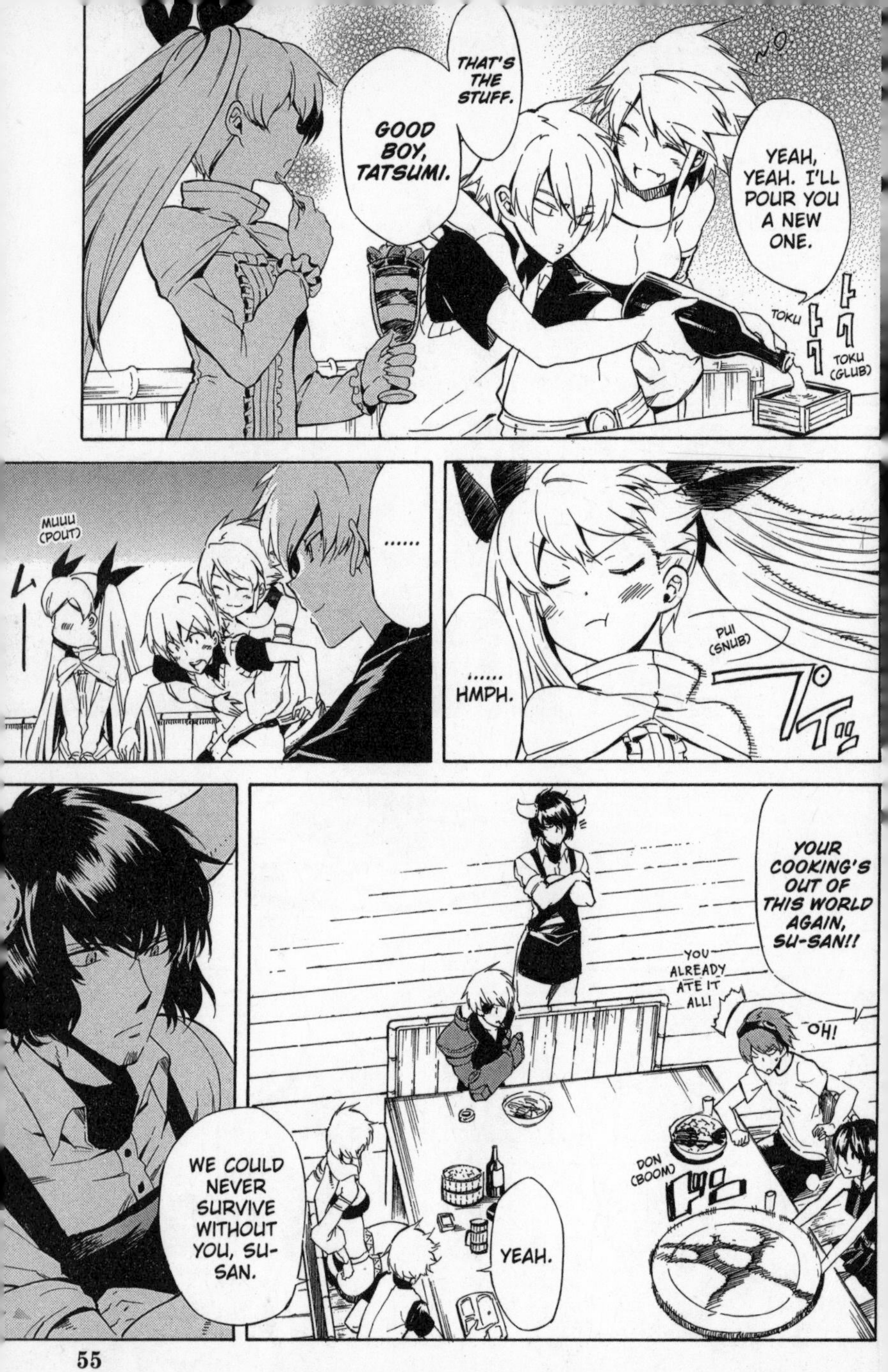

YEAH, YEAH. I'LL POUR YOU A NEW ONE.
TOKU
TOKU (GLUB)
THAT'S THE STUFF.
GOOD BOY, TATSUMI.
PUI (SNUB)
...... HMPH.
......
MUUU (POUT)
YOUR COOKING'S OUT OF THIS WORLD AGAIN, SU-SAN!!
OH!
YOU ALREADY ATE IT ALL!
DON (BOOM)
YEAH.
WE COULD NEVER SURVIVE WITHOUT YOU, SU-SAN.

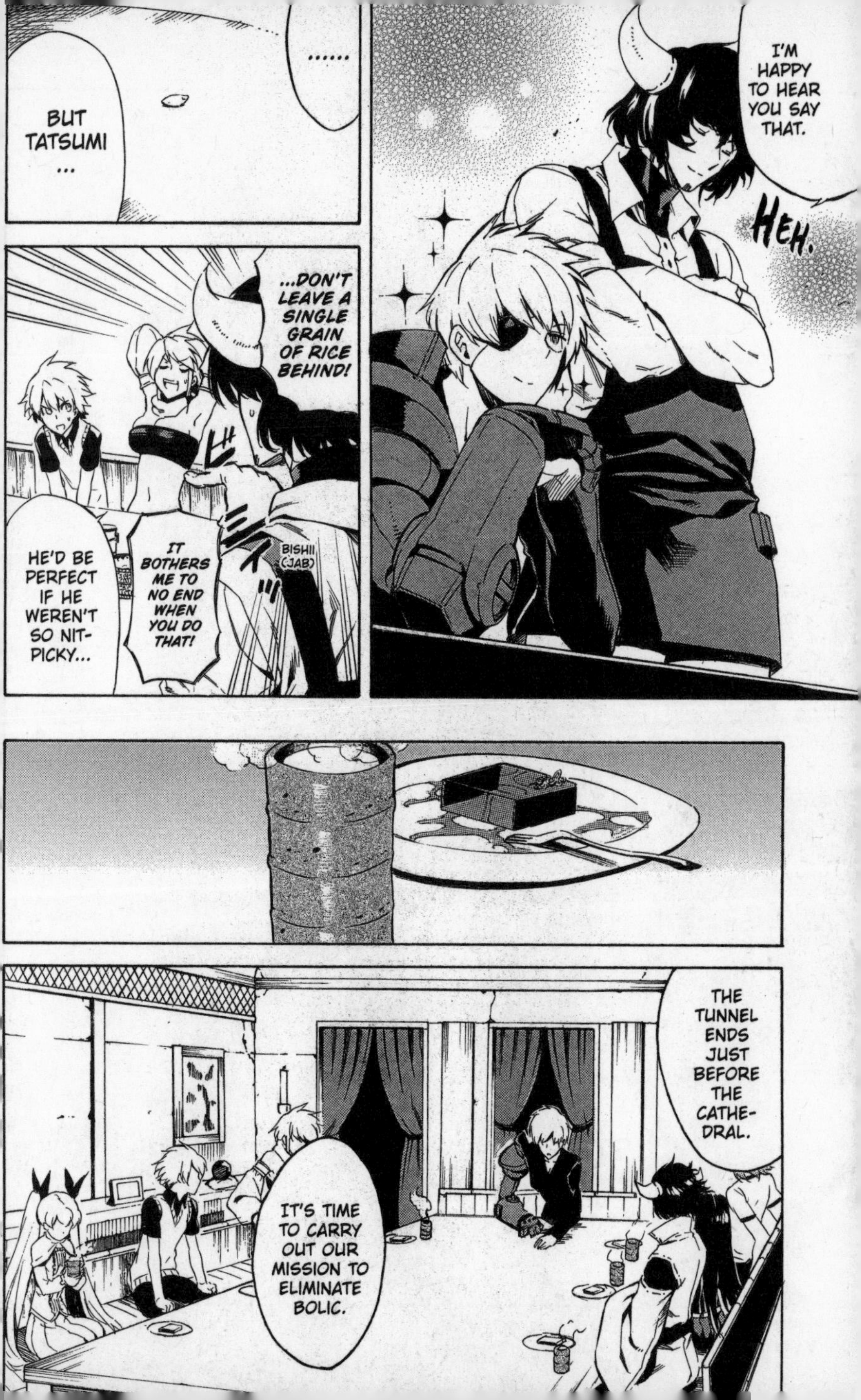
I'M HAPPY TO HEAR YOU SAY THAT.
HEH.
......
BUT TATSUMI ...
...DON'T LEAVE A SINGLE GRAIN OF RICE BEHIND!
BISHII (JAB)
IT BOTHERS ME TO NO END WHEN YOU DO THAT!
HE'D BE PERFECT IF HE WEREN'T SO NIT-PICKY...
THE TUNNEL ENDS JUST BEFORE THE CATHE-DRAL.
IT'S TIME TO CARRY OUT OUR MISSION TO ELIMINATE BOLIC.

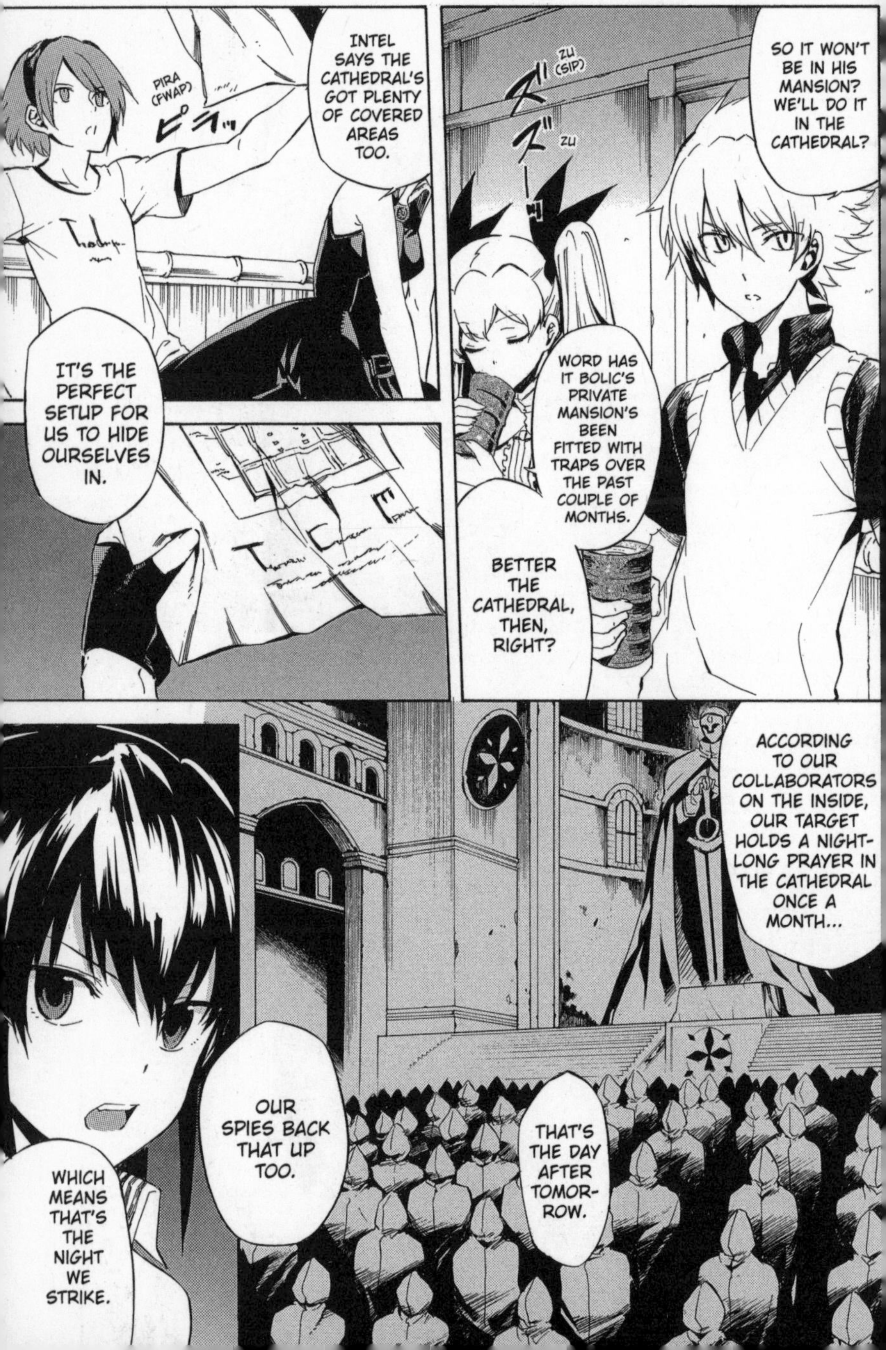
SO IT WON'T BE IN HIS MANSION? WE'LL DO IT IN THE CATHEDRAL?
ZU (SIP)
ZU
WORD HAS IT BOLIC'S PRIVATE MANSION'S BEEN FITTED WITH TRAPS OVER THE PAST COUPLE OF MONTHS.
BETTER THE CATHEDRAL, THEN, RIGHT?
INTEL SAYS THE CATHEDRAL'S GOT PLENTY OF COVERED AREAS TOO.
PIRA (FWAP)
IT'S THE PERFECT SETUP FOR US TO HIDE OURSELVES IN.
ACCORDING TO OUR COLLABORATORS ON THE INSIDE, OUR TARGET HOLDS A NIGHT-LONG PRAYER IN THE CATHEDRAL ONCE A MONTH...
THAT'S THE DAY AFTER TOMOR-ROW.
OUR SPIES BACK THAT UP TOO.
WHICH MEANS THAT'S THE NIGHT WE STRIKE.

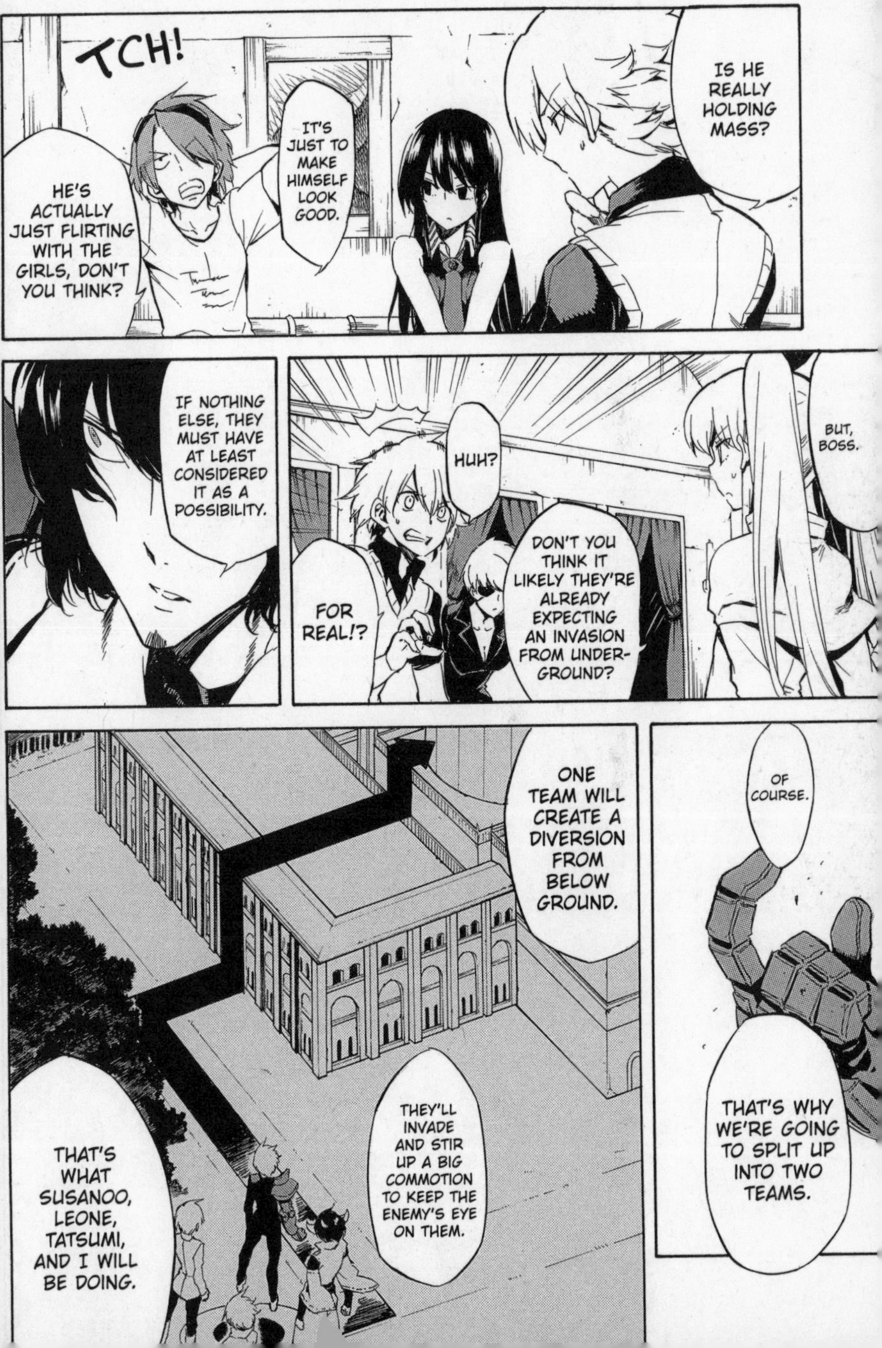
IS HE REALLY HOLDING MASS?
TCH!
IT'S JUST TO MAKE HIMSELF LOOK GOOD.
HE'S ACTUALLY JUST FLIRTING WITH THE GIRLS, DON'T YOU THINK?
BUT, BOSS.
DON'T YOU THINK IT LIKELY THEY'RE ALREADY EXPECTING AN INVASION FROM UNDER-GROUND?
HUH?
FOR REAL!?
IF NOTHING ELSE, THEY MUST HAVE AT LEAST CONSIDERED IT AS A POSSIBILITY.
OF COURSE.
THAT'S WHY WE'RE GOING TO SPLIT UP INTO TWO TEAMS.
ONE TEAM WILL CREATE A DIVERSION FROM BELOW GROUND.
THEY'LL INVADE AND STIR UP A BIG COMMOTION TO KEEP THE ENEMY'S EYE ON THEM.
THAT'S WHAT SUSANOO, LEONE, TATSUMI, AND I WILL BE DOING.

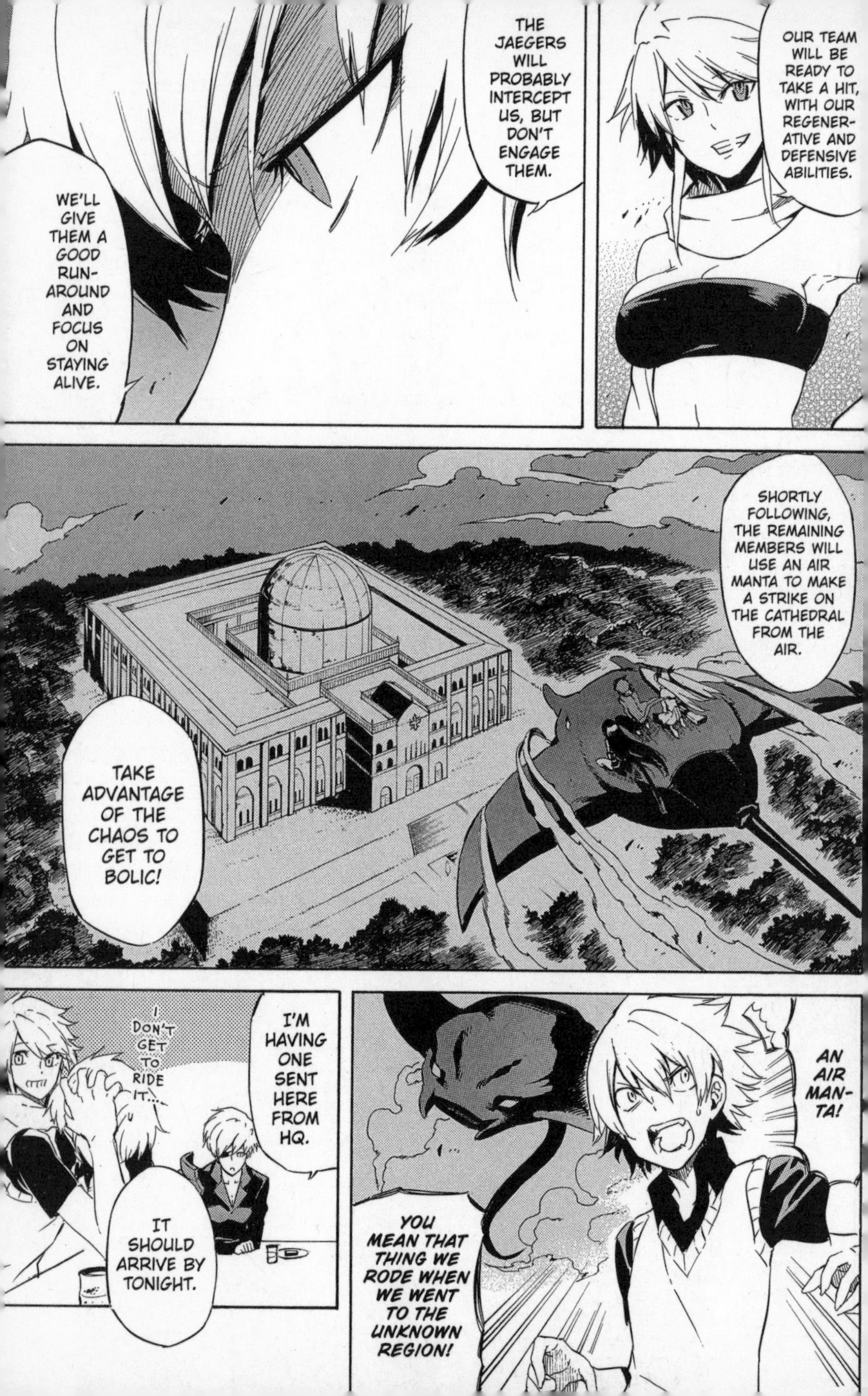
OUR TEAM WILL BE READY TO TAKE A HIT, WITH OUR REGENERATIVE AND DEFENSIVE ABILITIES.
THE JAEGERS WILL PROBABLY INTERCEPT US, BUT DON'T ENGAGE THEM.
WE'LL GIVE THEM A GOOD RUN-AROUND AND FOCUS ON STAYING ALIVE.
SHORTLY FOLLOWING, THE REMAINING MEMBERS WILL USE AN AIR MANTA TO MAKE A STRIKE ON THE CATHEDRAL FROM THE AIR.
TAKE ADVANTAGE OF THE CHAOS TO GET TO BOLIC!
AN AIR MANTA!
YOU MEAN THAT THING WE RODE WHEN WE WENT TO THE UNKNOWN REGION!
I'M HAVING ONE SENT HERE FROM HQ.
I DON'T GET TO RIDE IT...
IT SHOULD ARRIVE BY TONIGHT.

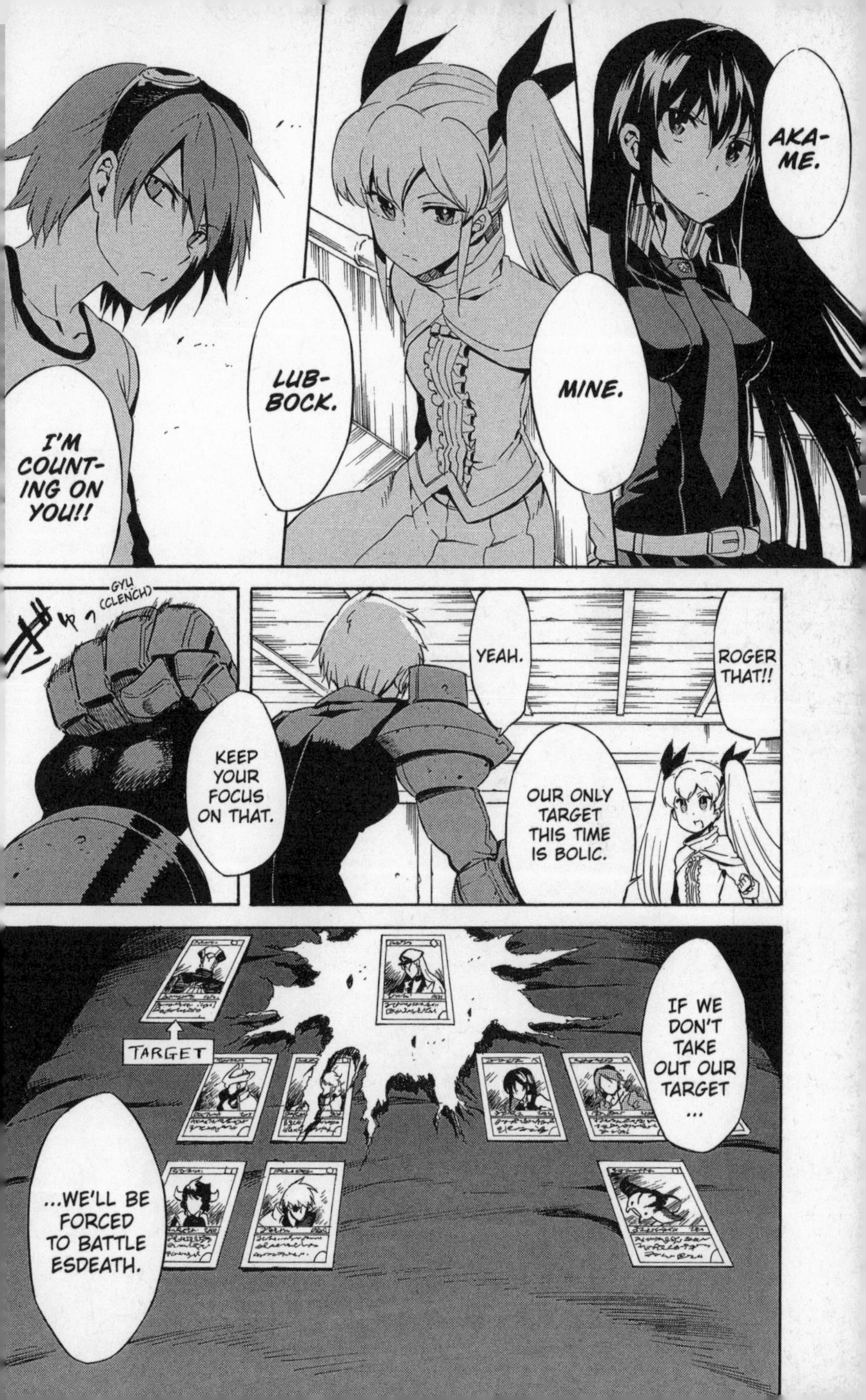
AKA-ME.
MINE.
LUB-BOCK.
I'M COUNTING ON YOU!!
ROGER THAT!!
YEAH.
OUR ONLY TARGET THIS TIME IS BOLIC.
KEEP YOUR FOCUS ON THAT.
GYU (CLENCH)
IF WE DON'T TAKE OUT OUR TARGET ...
TARGET
...WE'LL BE FORCED TO BATTLE ESDEATH.

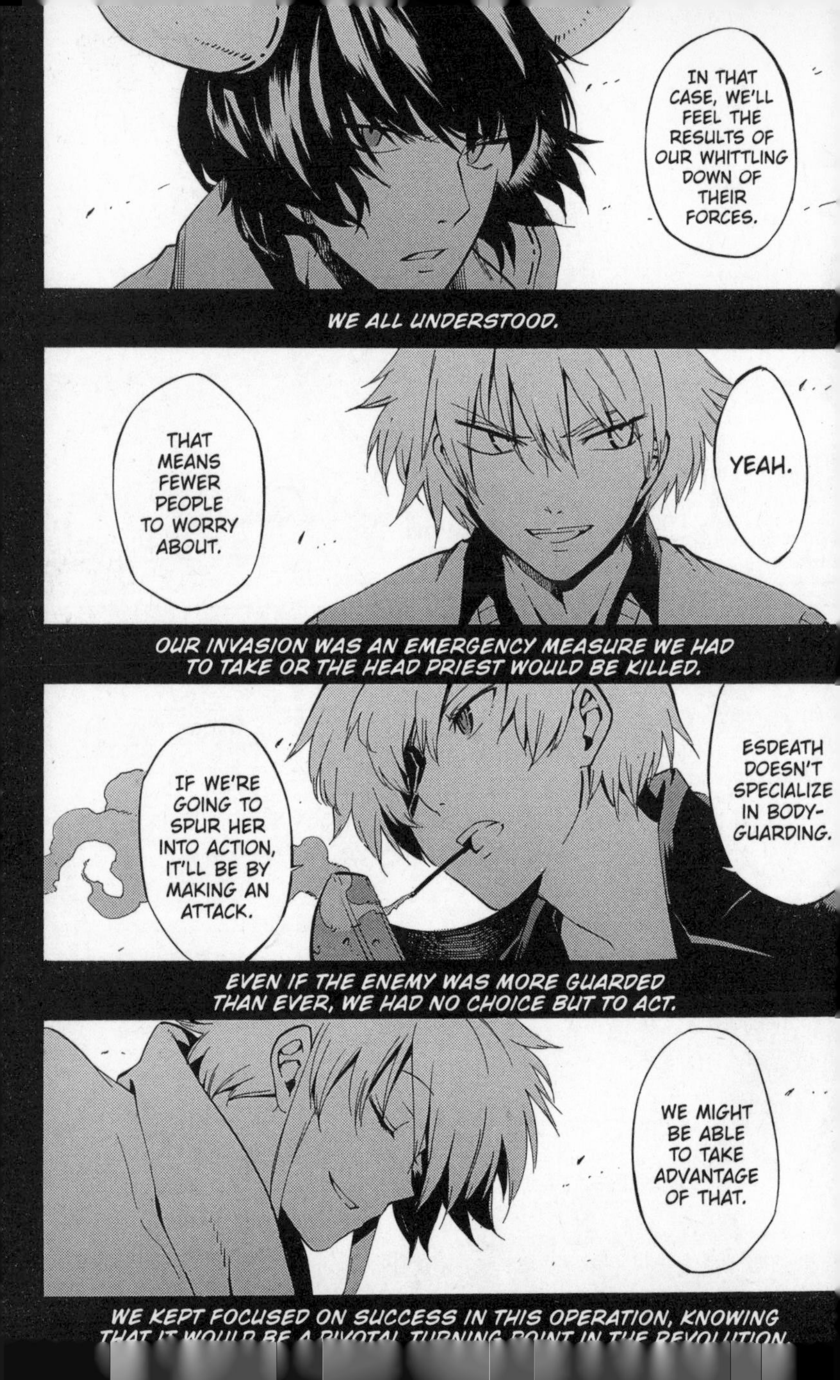
IN THAT CASE, WE'LL FEEL THE RESULTS OF OUR WHITTLING DOWN OF THEIR FORCES.
WE ALL UNDERSTOOD.
YEAH.
THAT MEANS FEWER PEOPLE TO WORRY ABOUT.
OUR INVASION WAS AN EMERGENCY MEASURE WE HAD TO TAKE OR THE HEAD PRIEST WOULD BE KILLED.
ESDEATH DOESN'T SPECIALIZE IN BODY-GUARDING.
IF WE'RE GOING TO SPUR HER INTO ACTION, IT'LL BE BY MAKING AN ATTACK.
EVEN IF THE ENEMY WAS MORE GUARDED THAN EVER, WE HAD NO CHOICE BUT TO ACT.
WE MIGHT BE ABLE TO TAKE ADVANTAGE OF THAT.
WE KEPT FOCUSED ON SUCCESS IN THIS OPERATION, KNOWING THAT IT WOULD BE A PIVOTAL TURNING POINT IN THE REVOLUTION.

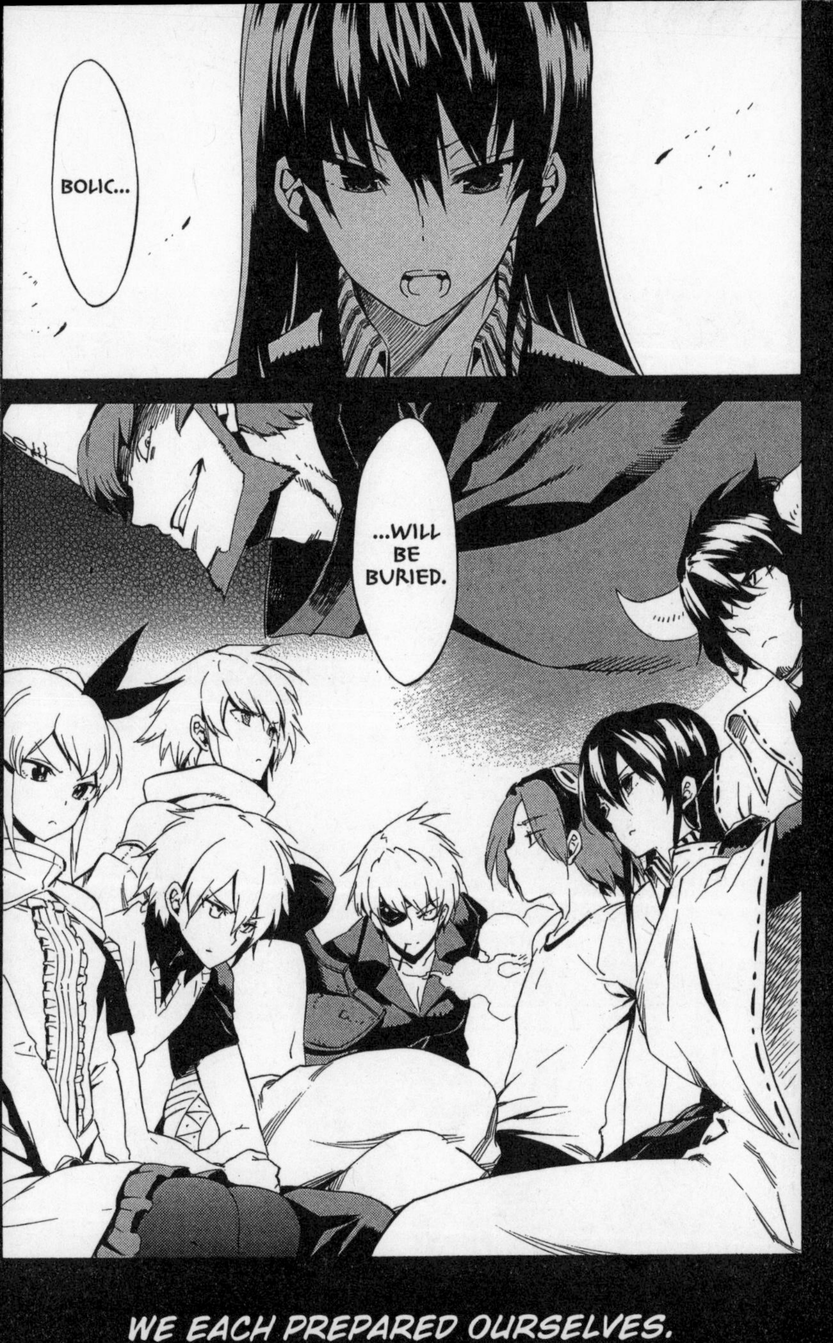
BOLIC...
...WILL BE BURIED.
WE EACH PREPARED OURSELVES.

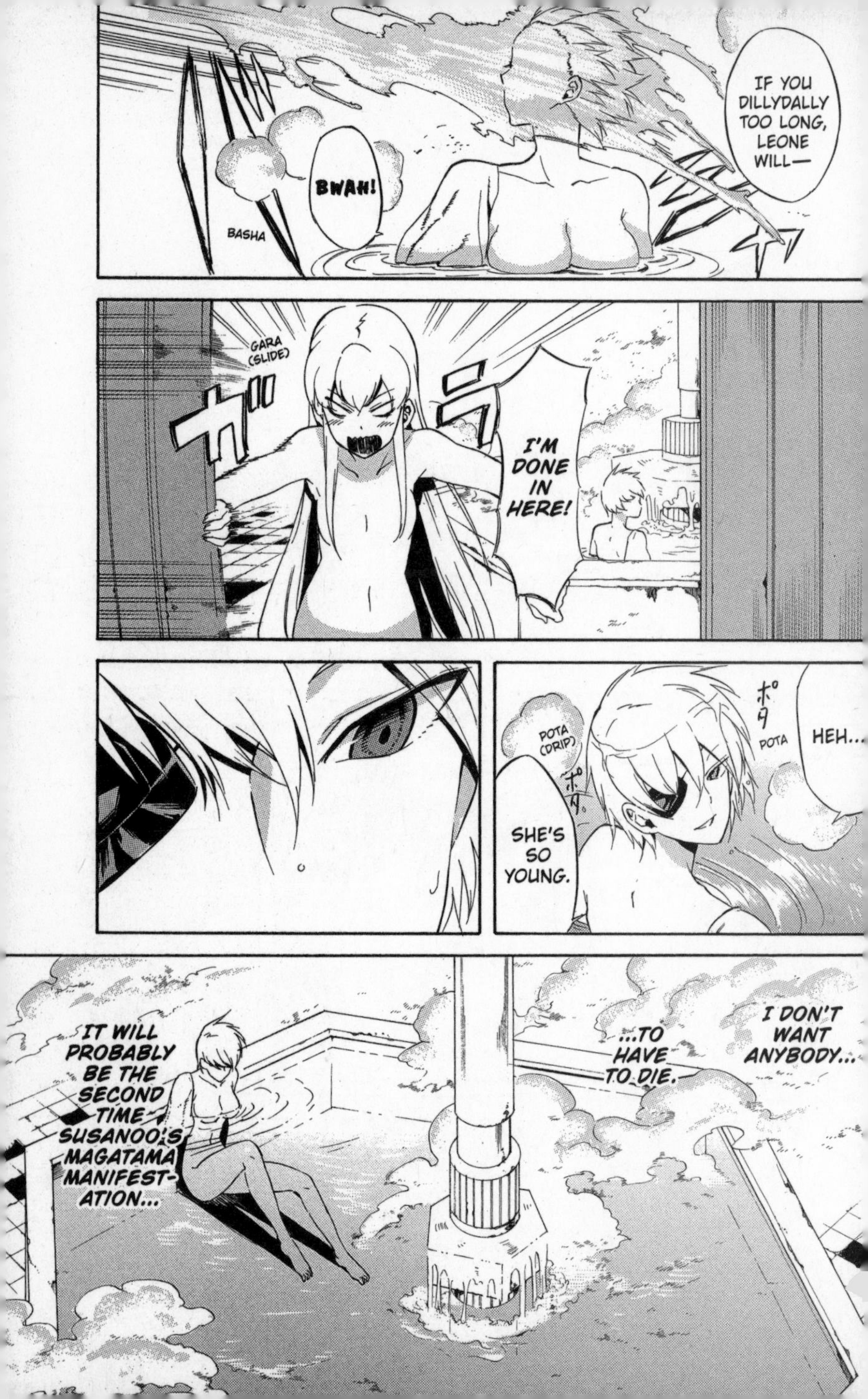
IF YOU DILLYDALLY TOO LONG, LEONE WILL—
BWAH!
BASHA
GARA (SLIDE)
I'M DONE IN HERE!
HEH...
POTA
POTA (DRIP)
SHE'S SO YOUNG.
I DON'T WANT ANYBODY...
...TO HAVE TO DIE.
IT WILL PROBABLY BE THE SECOND TIME SUSANOO'S MAGATAMA MANIFEST-ATION...

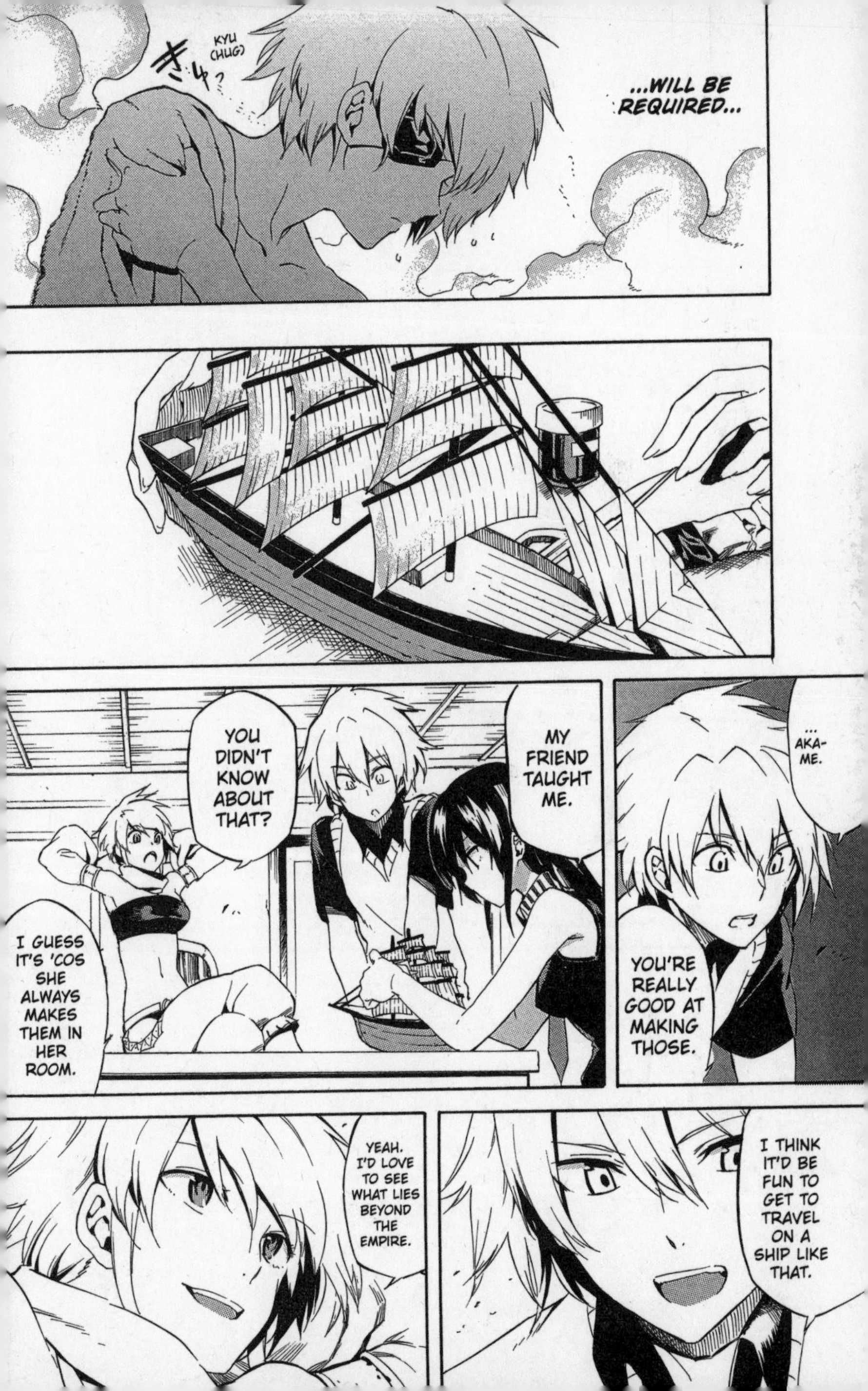

...WILL BE REQUIRED...
KYU (HUG)
...AKA-ME.
YOU'RE REALLY GOOD AT MAKING THOSE.
MY FRIEND TAUGHT ME.
YOU DIDN'T KNOW ABOUT THAT?
I GUESS IT'S 'COS SHE ALWAYS MAKES THEM IN HER ROOM.
I THINK IT'D BE FUN TO GET TO TRAVEL ON A SHIP LIKE THAT.
YEAH. I'D LOVE TO SEE WHAT LIES BEYOND THE EMPIRE.

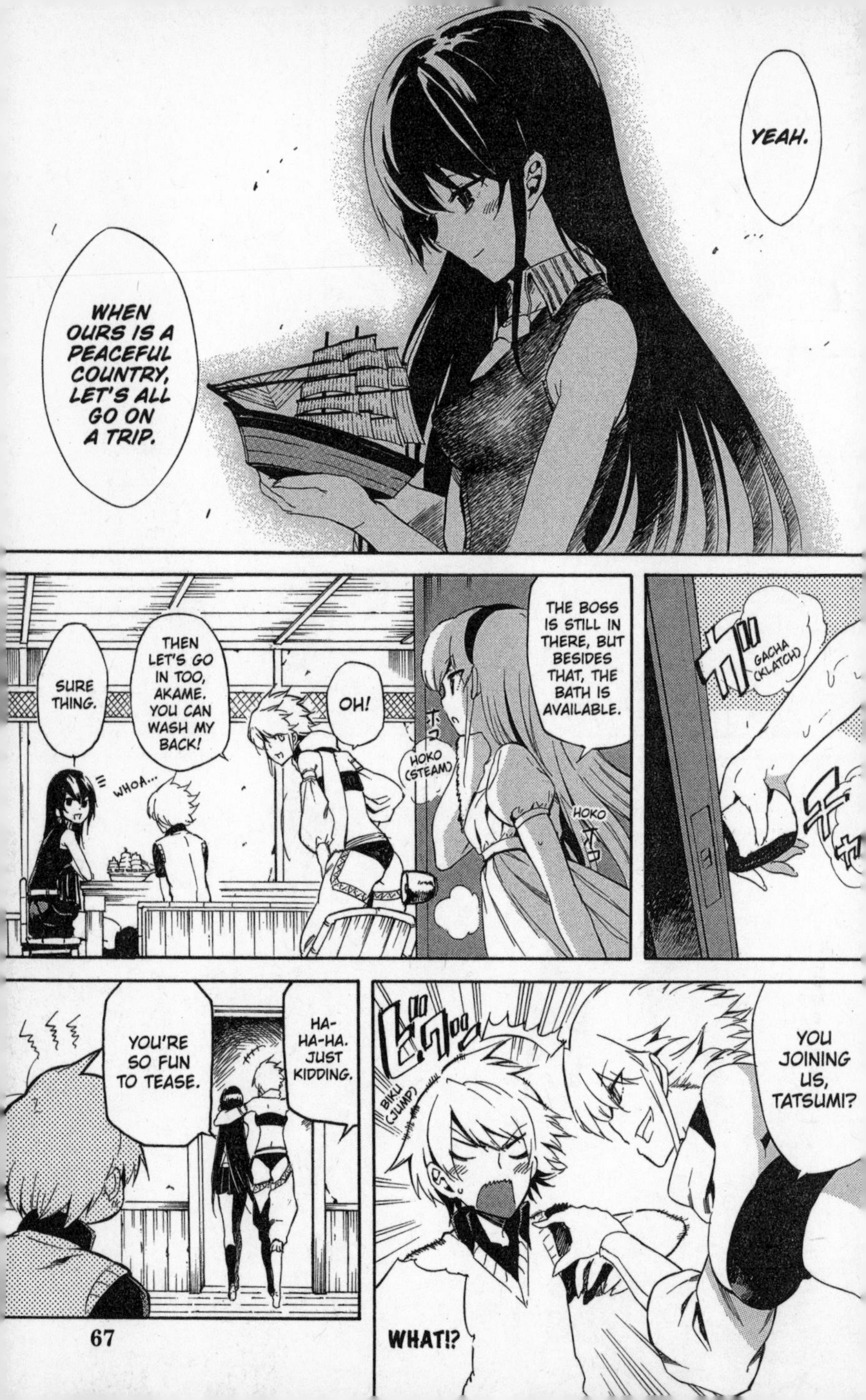
YEAH.
WHEN OURS IS A PEACEFUL COUNTRY, LET'S ALL GO ON A TRIP.
GACHA (KLATCH)
THE BOSS IS STILL IN THERE, BUT BESIDES THAT, THE BATH IS AVAILABLE.
HOKO (STEAM)
HOKO
OH!
THEN LET'S GO IN TOO, AKAME. YOU CAN WASH MY BACK!
SURE THING.
WHOA...
YOU JOINING US, TATSUMI?
BIKU (JUMP)
WHAT!?
HA-HA-HA. JUST KIDDING.
YOU'RE SO FUN TO TEASE.

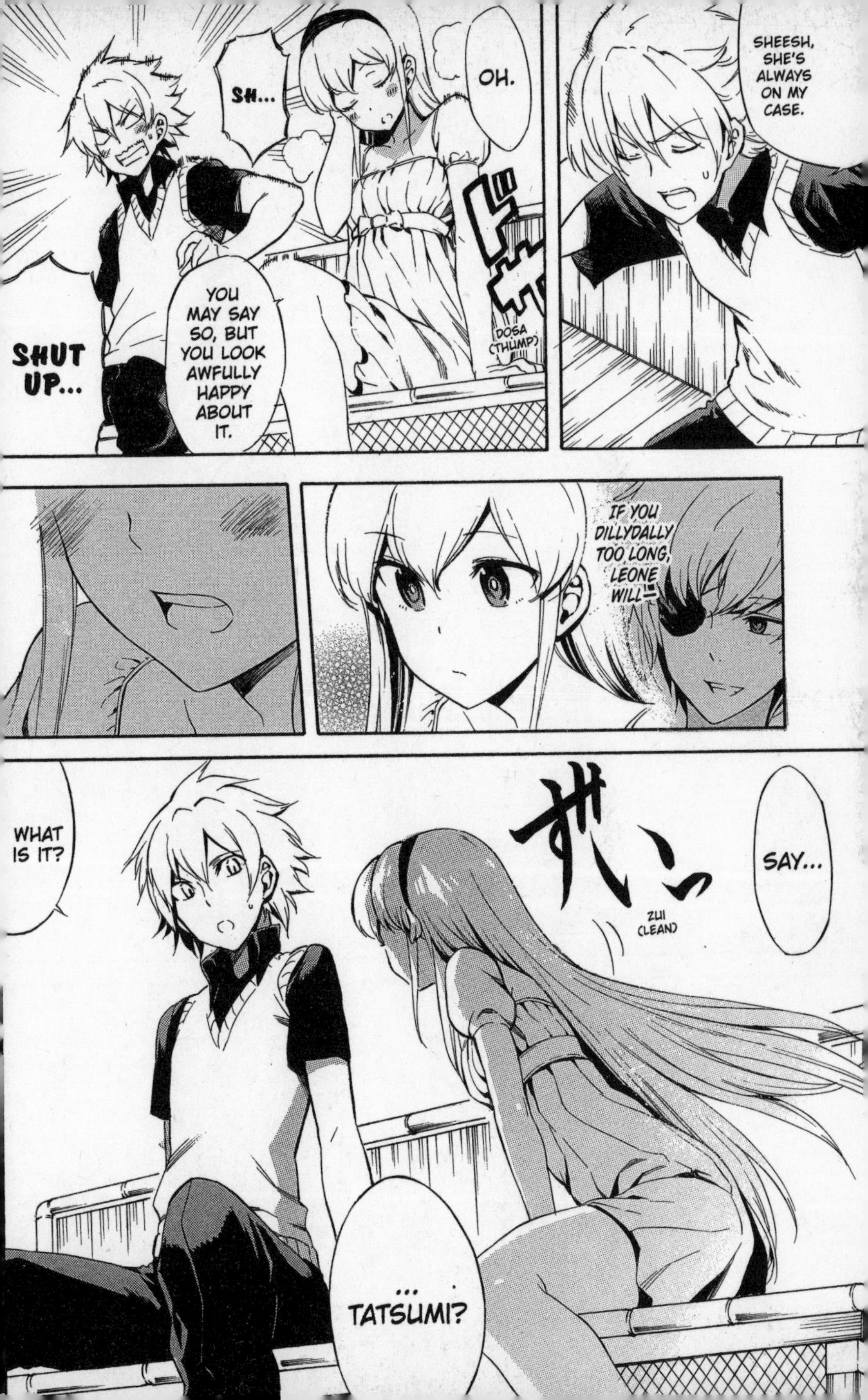
SHEESH, SHE'S ALWAYS ON MY CASE.
OH.
DOSA (THUMP)
SH...
YOU MAY SAY SO, BUT YOU LOOK AWFULLY HAPPY ABOUT IT.
SHUT UP...
IF YOU DILLYDALLY TOO LONG, LEONE WILL—
SAY...
ZUI (LEAN)
WHAT IS IT?
... TATSUMI?

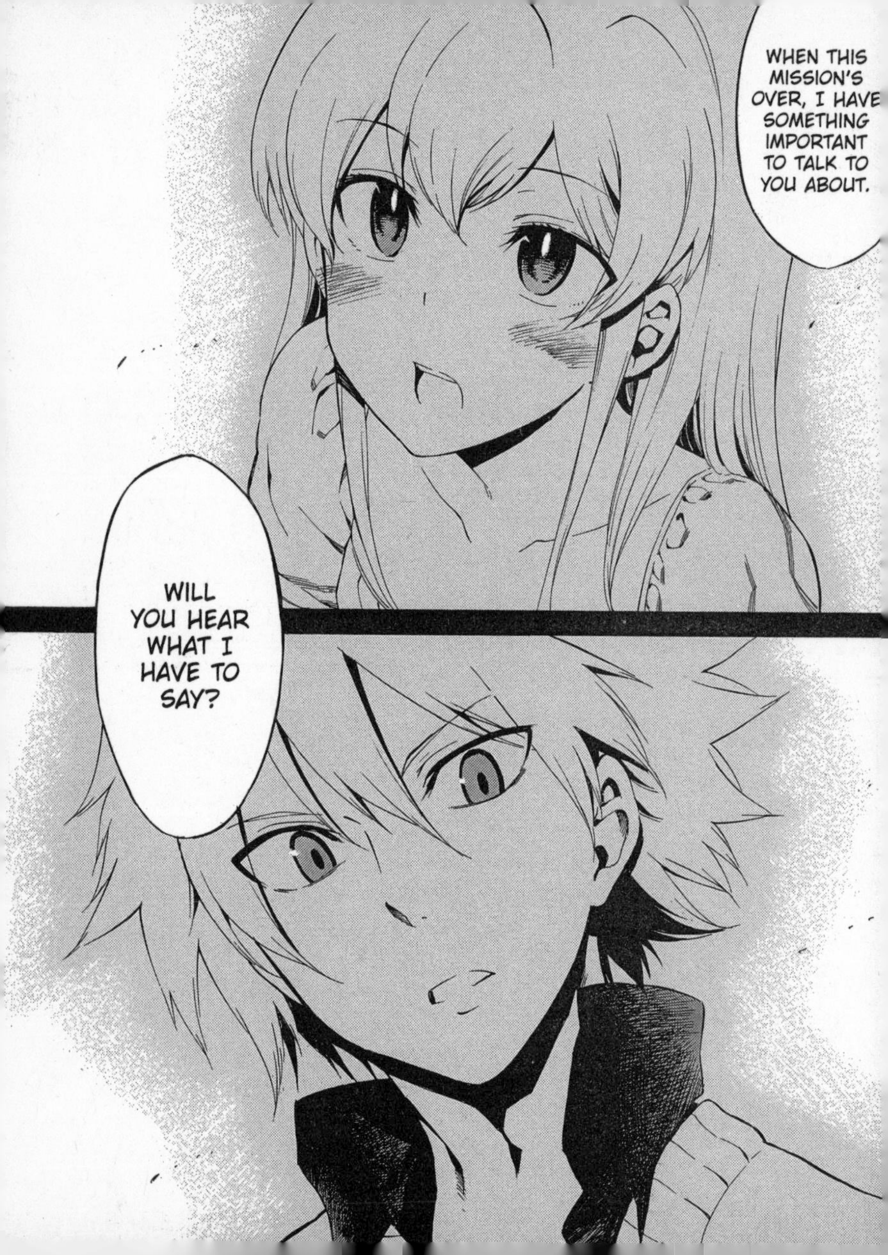
WHEN THIS MISSION'S OVER, I HAVE SOMETHING IMPORTANT TO TALK TO YOU ABOUT.
WILL YOU HEAR WHAT I HAVE TO SAY?

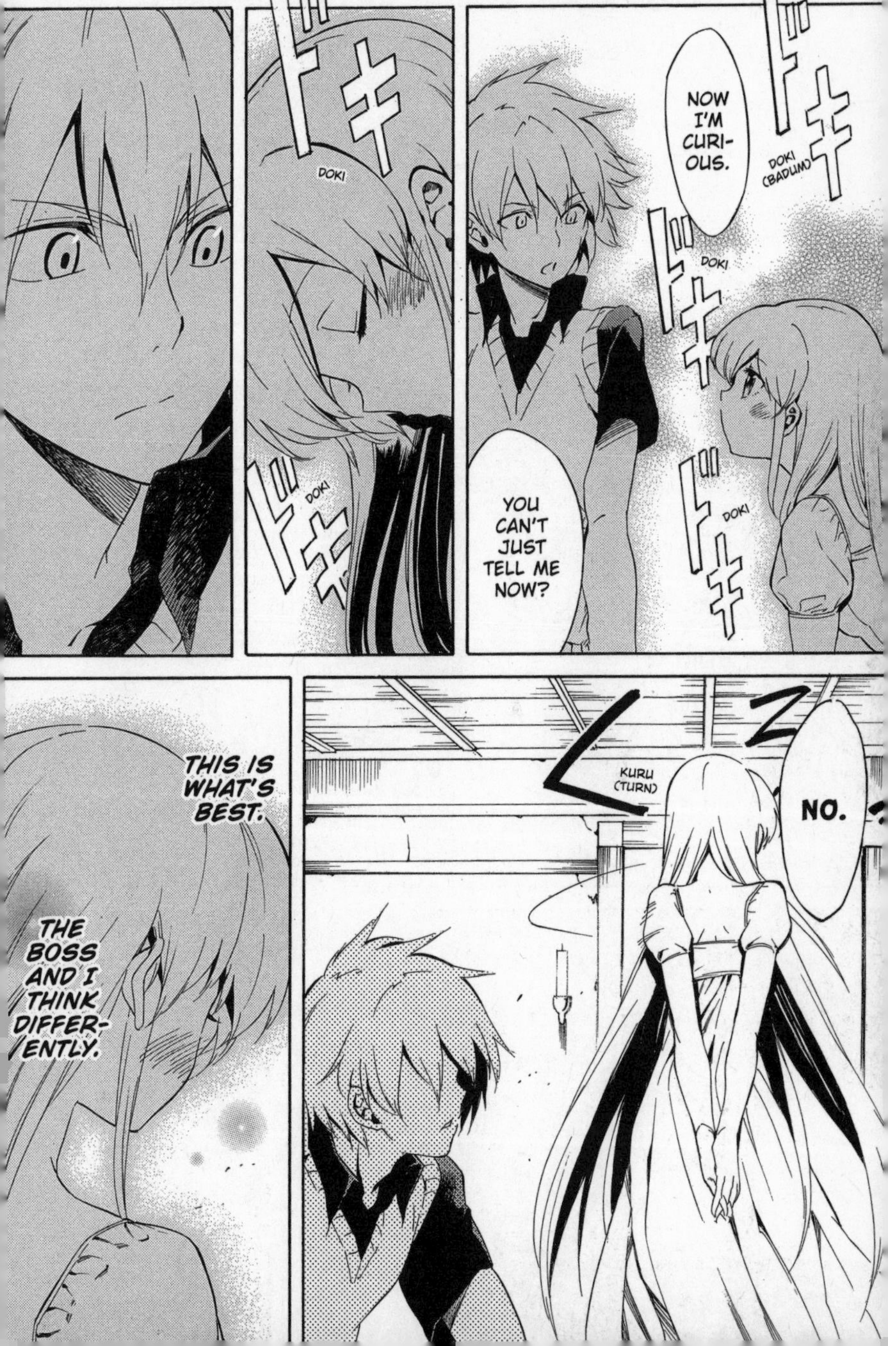
ドキ
DOKI (BADUM)
NOW I'M CURI-OUS.
ドキ
DOKI
YOU CAN'T JUST TELL ME NOW?
ドキ
DOKI
ドキ
DOKI
ドキ
DOKI
NO.
KURU (TURN)
THIS IS WHAT'S BEST.
THE BOSS AND I THINK DIFFER-ENTLY.

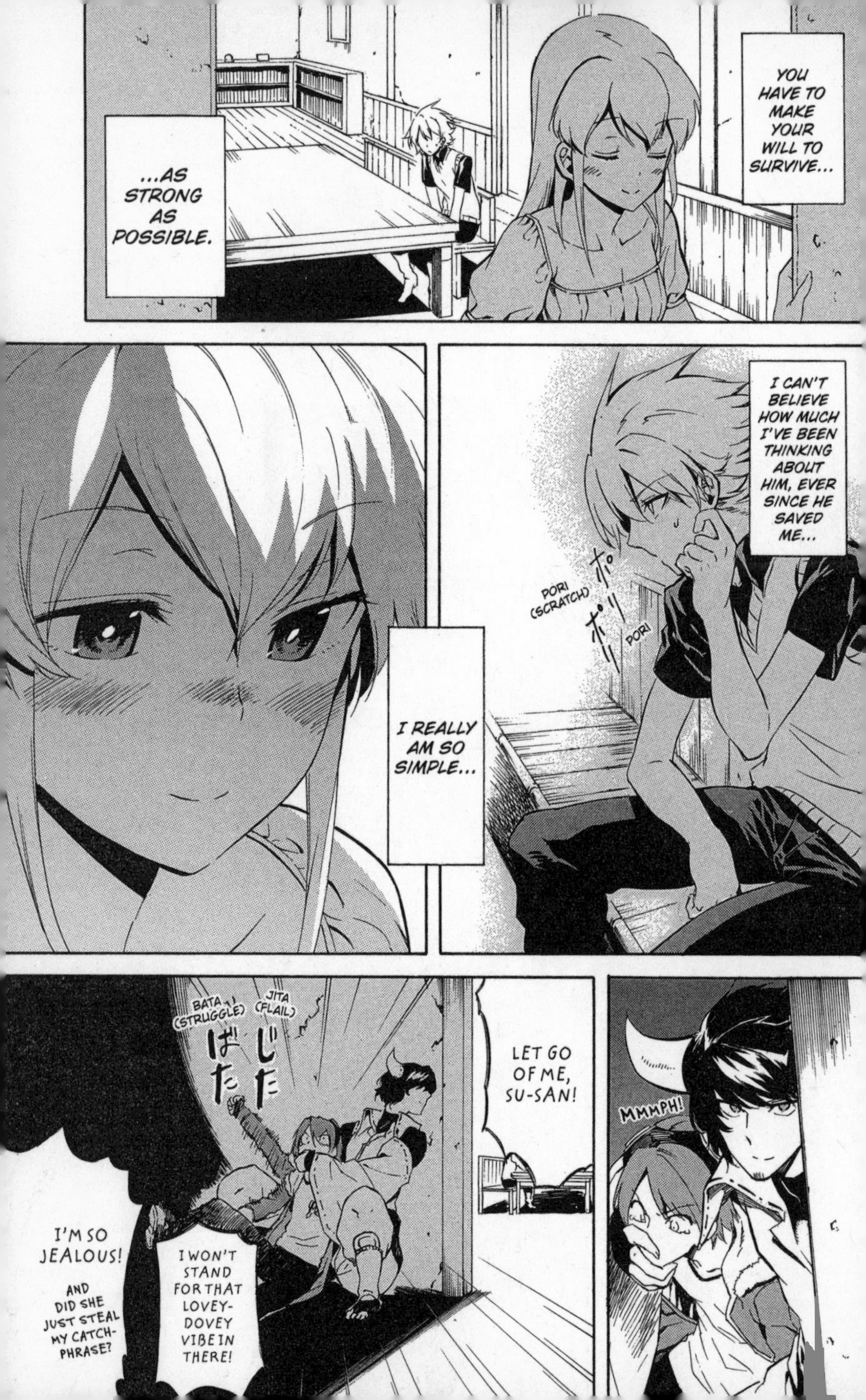
YOU HAVE TO MAKE YOUR WILL TO SURVIVE...
...AS STRONG AS POSSIBLE.
I CAN'T BELIEVE HOW MUCH I'VE BEEN THINKING ABOUT HIM, EVER SINCE HE SAVED ME...
ポリポリ
PORI (SCRATCH)
PORI
I REALLY AM SO SIMPLE...
MMMPH!
LET GO OF ME, SU-SAN!
ばたじた
BATA (STRUGGLE)
JITA (FLAIL)
I WON'T STAND FOR THAT LOVEY-DOVEY VIBE IN THERE!
I'M SO JEALOUS!
AND DID SHE JUST STEAL MY CATCH-PHRASE?

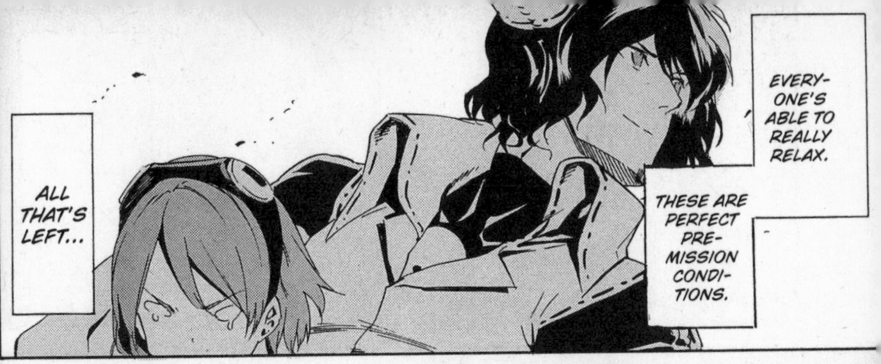
EVERYONE'S ABLE TO REALLY RELAX.
THESE ARE PERFECT PRE-MISSION CONDITIONS.
ALL THAT'S LEFT...

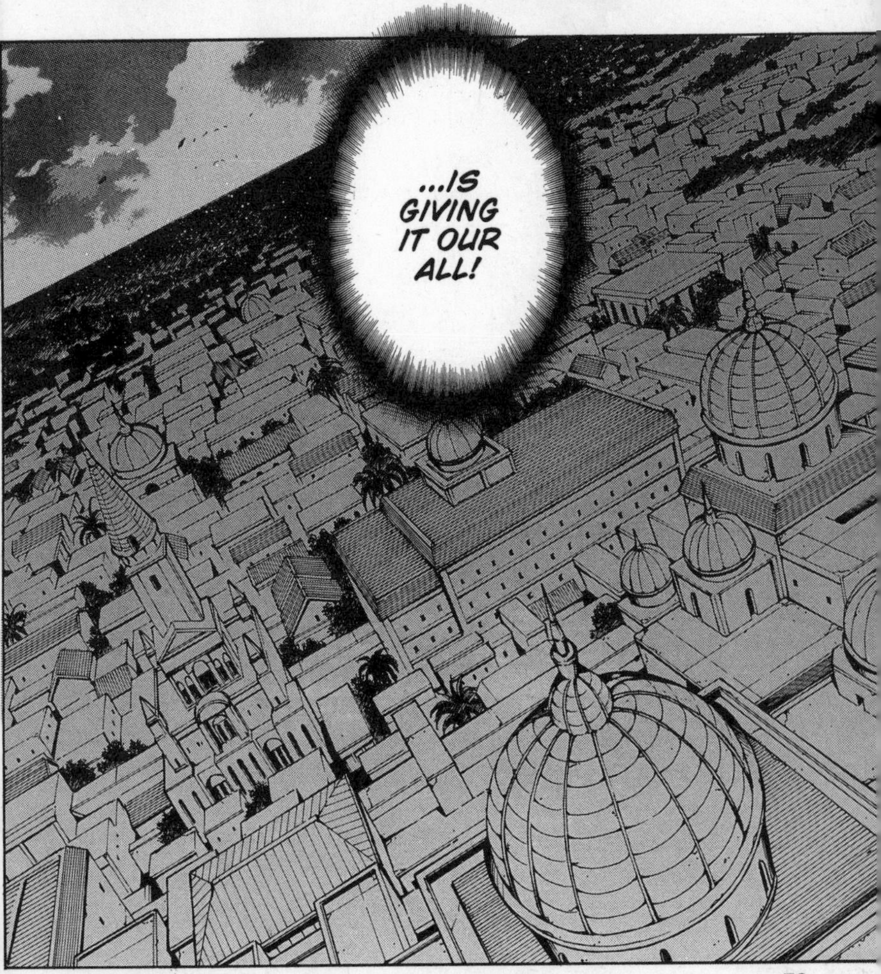
...IS GIVING IT OUR ALL!

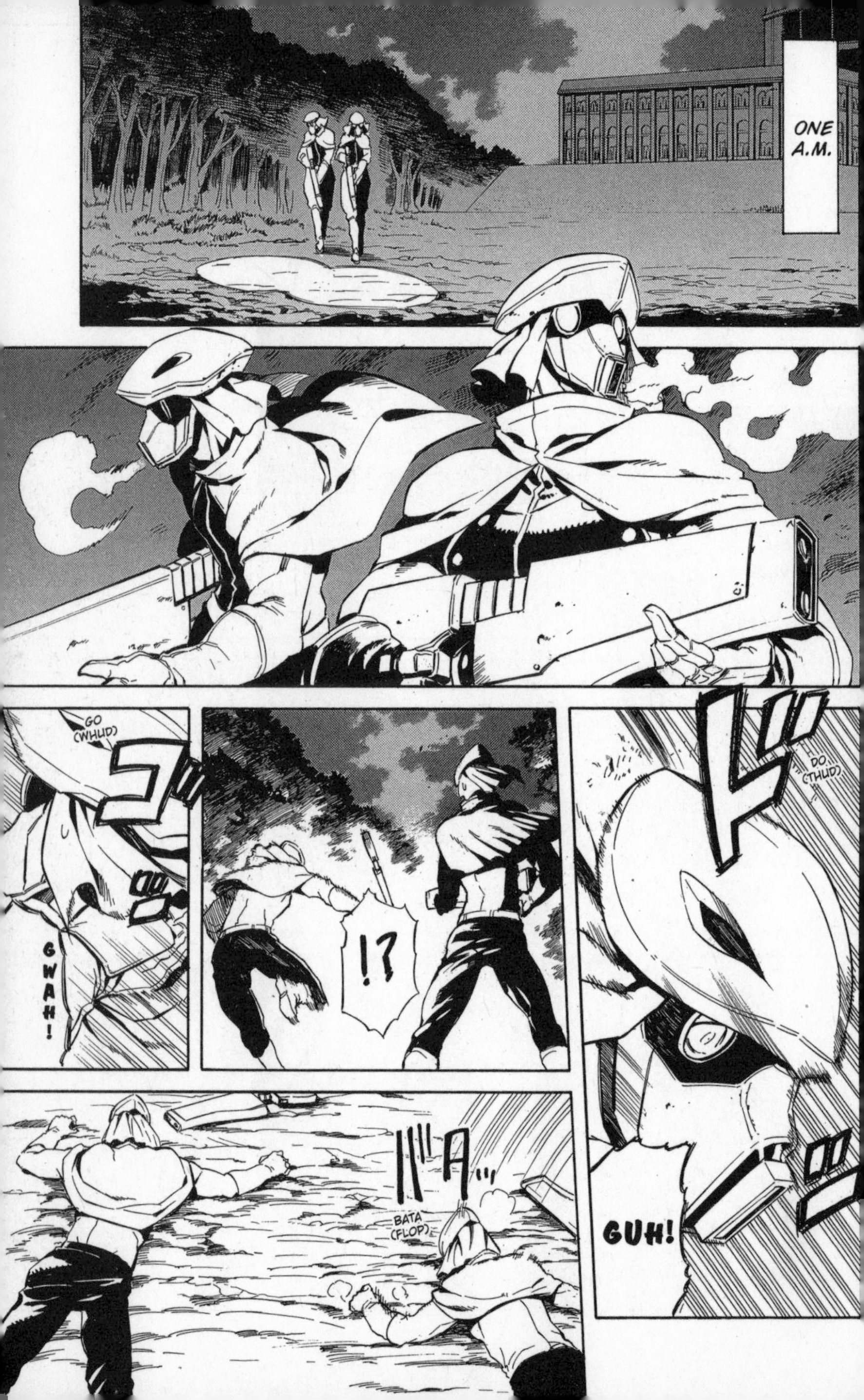
ONE A.M.
DO (THUD)
GUH!
!?
GO (WHUD)
GWAH!
BATA (FLOP)

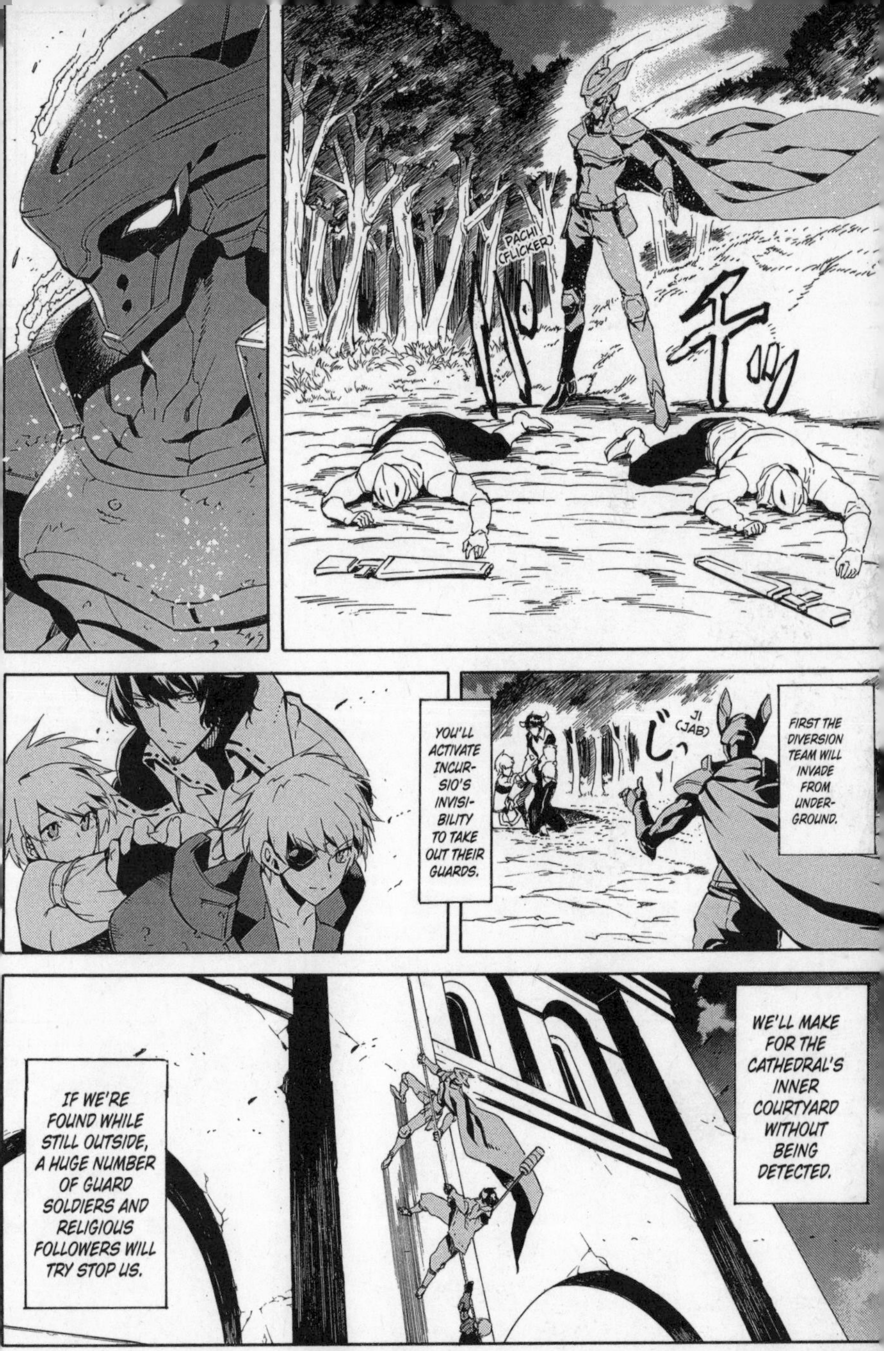
PACHI (FLICKER)
FIRST THE DIVERSION TEAM WILL INVADE FROM UNDER-GROUND.
JI (JAB)
YOU'LL ACTIVATE INCUR-SIO'S INVISI-BILITY TO TAKE OUT THEIR GUARDS.
WE'LL MAKE FOR THE CATHEDRAL'S INNER COURTYARD WITHOUT BEING DETECTED.
IF WE'RE FOUND WHILE STILL OUTSIDE, A HUGE NUMBER OF GUARD SOLDIERS AND RELIGIOUS FOLLOWERS WILL TRY STOP US.

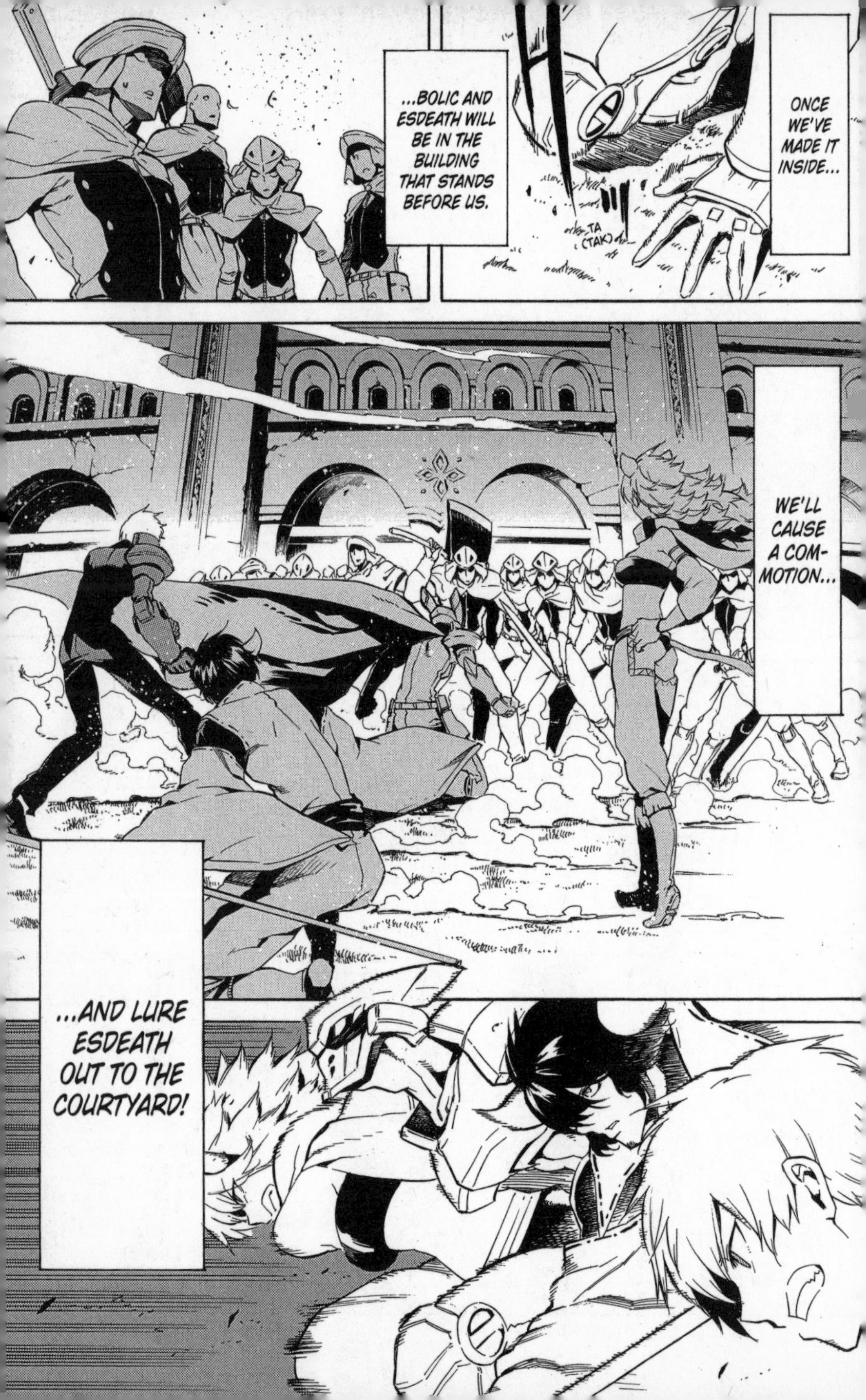
ONCE WE'VE MADE IT INSIDE...
TA (TAK)
...BOLIC AND ESDEATH WILL BE IN THE BUILDING THAT STANDS BEFORE US.
WE'LL CAUSE A COM-MOTION...
...AND LURE ESDEATH OUT TO THE COURTYARD!

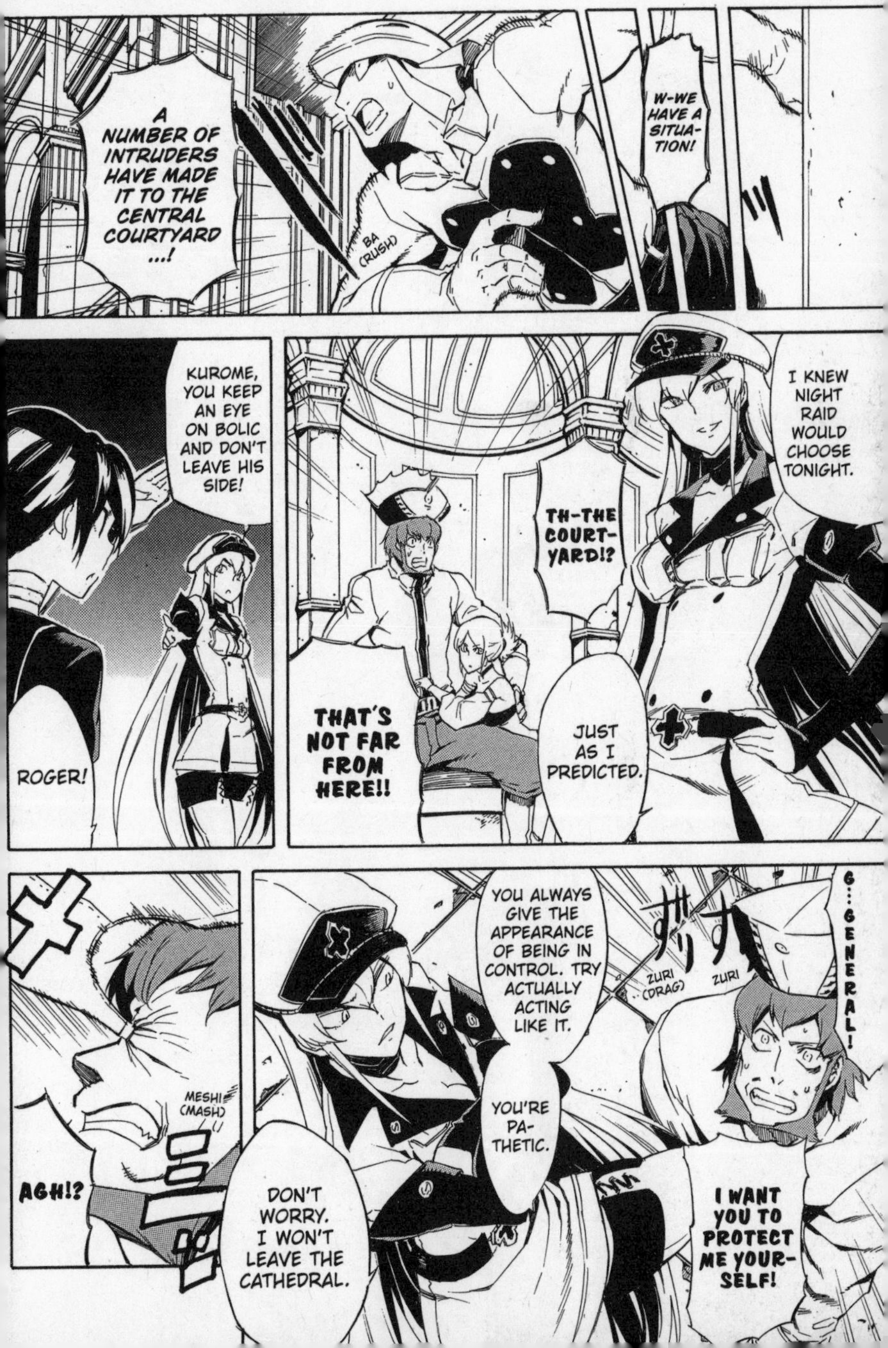
W-WE HAVE A SITUATION!
A NUMBER OF INTRUDERS HAVE MADE IT TO THE CENTRAL COURTYARD ...!
BA (RUSH)
I KNEW NIGHT RAID WOULD CHOOSE TONIGHT.
TH-THE COURTYARD!?
JUST AS I PREDICTED.
THAT'S NOT FAR FROM HERE!!
KUROME, YOU KEEP AN EYE ON BOLIC AND DON'T LEAVE HIS SIDE!
ROGER!
G...GENERAL!
ZURI (DRAG)
ZURI
YOU ALWAYS GIVE THE APPEARANCE OF BEING IN CONTROL. TRY ACTUALLY ACTING LIKE IT.
YOU'RE PATHETIC.
I WANT YOU TO PROTECT ME YOURSELF!
DON'T WORRY. I WON'T LEAVE THE CATHEDRAL.
MESHI (MASH)
AGH!?

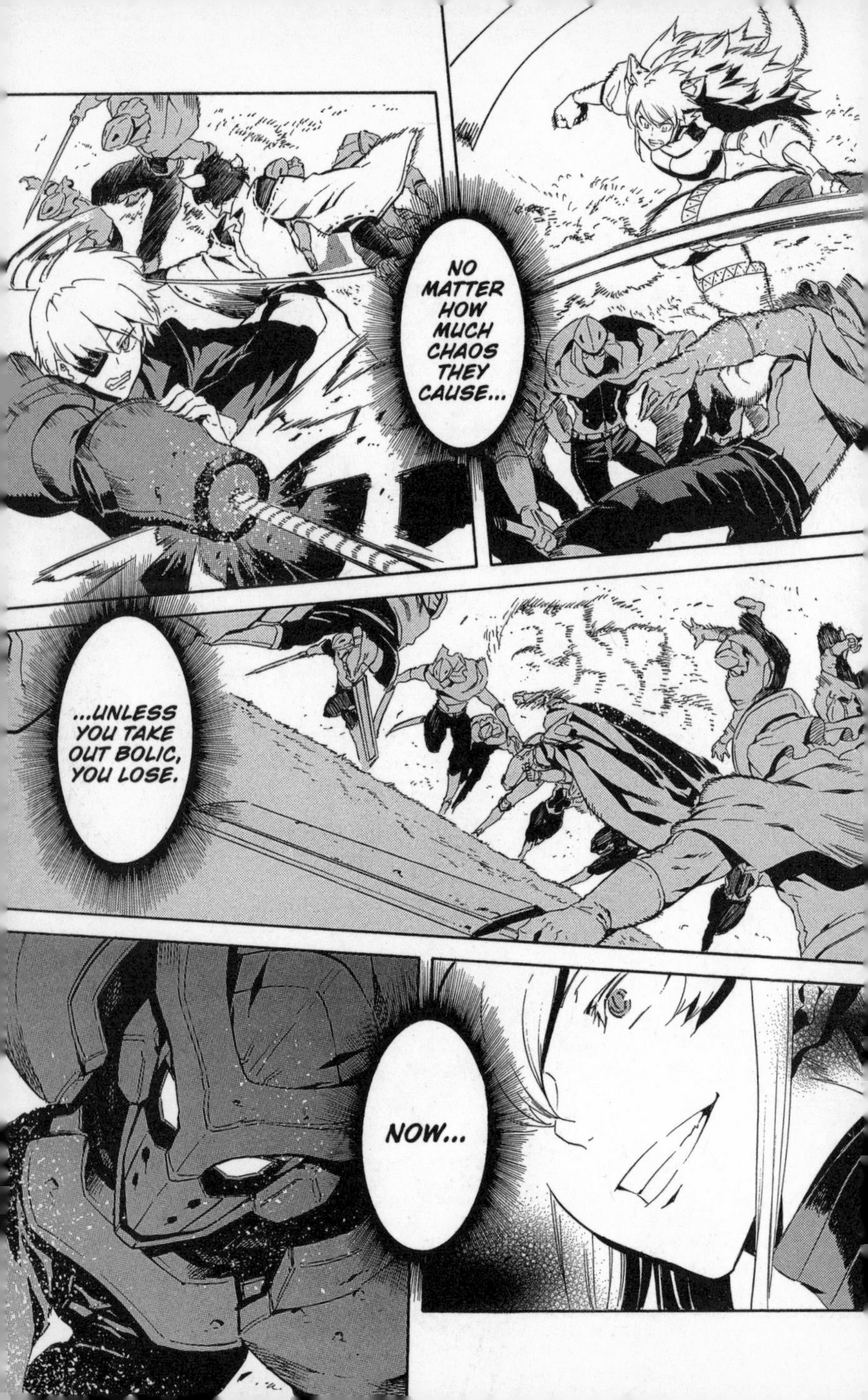
NO MATTER HOW MUCH CHAOS THEY CAUSE...
...UNLESS YOU TAKE OUT BOLIC, YOU LOSE.
NOW...

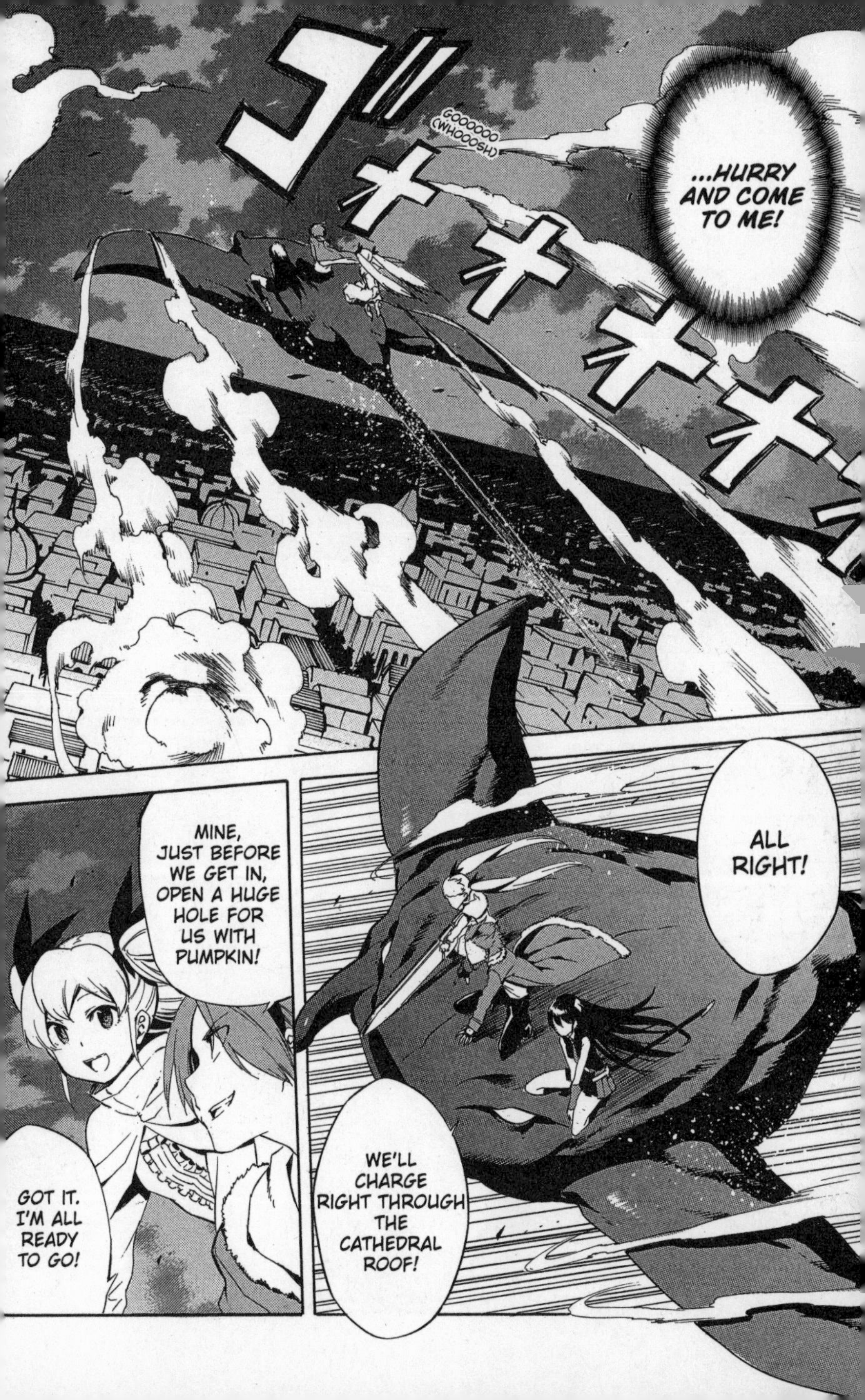
...HURRY AND COME TO ME!
GOOOOOO (WHOOOSH)
ALL RIGHT!
WE'LL CHARGE RIGHT THROUGH THE CATHEDRAL ROOF!
MINE, JUST BEFORE WE GET IN, OPEN A HUGE HOLE FOR US WITH PUMPKIN!
GOT IT. I'M ALL READY TO GO!

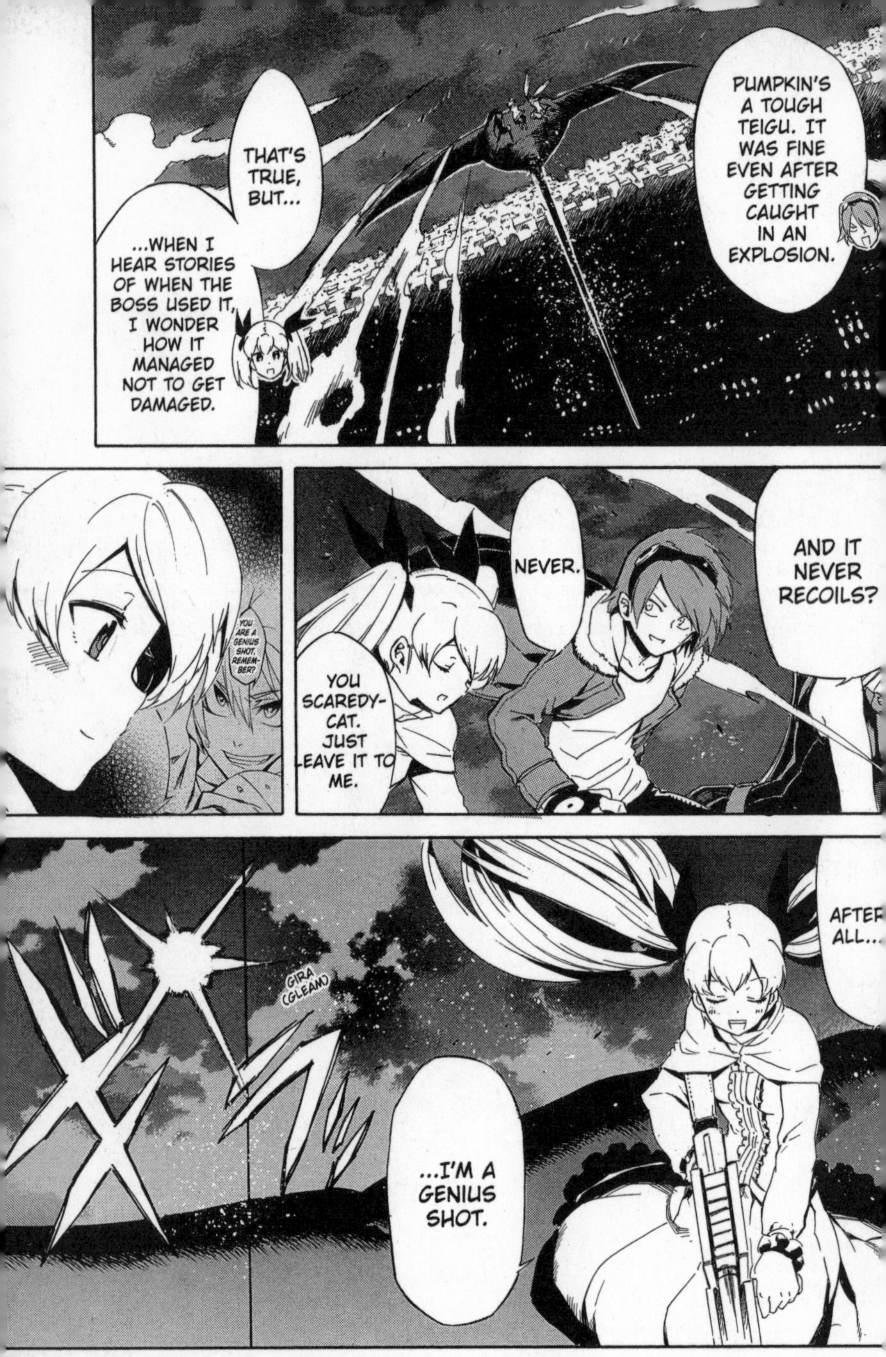
PUMPKIN'S A TOUGH TEIGU. IT WAS FINE EVEN AFTER GETTING CAUGHT IN AN EXPLOSION.
THAT'S TRUE, BUT...
...WHEN I HEAR STORIES OF WHEN THE BOSS USED IT, I WONDER HOW IT MANAGED NOT TO GET DAMAGED.
AND IT NEVER RECOILS?
NEVER.
YOU SCAREDY-CAT. JUST LEAVE IT TO ME.
YOU ARE A GENIUS SHOT, REMEMBER?
AFTER ALL...
GIRA (GLEAM)
...I'M A GENIUS SHOT.

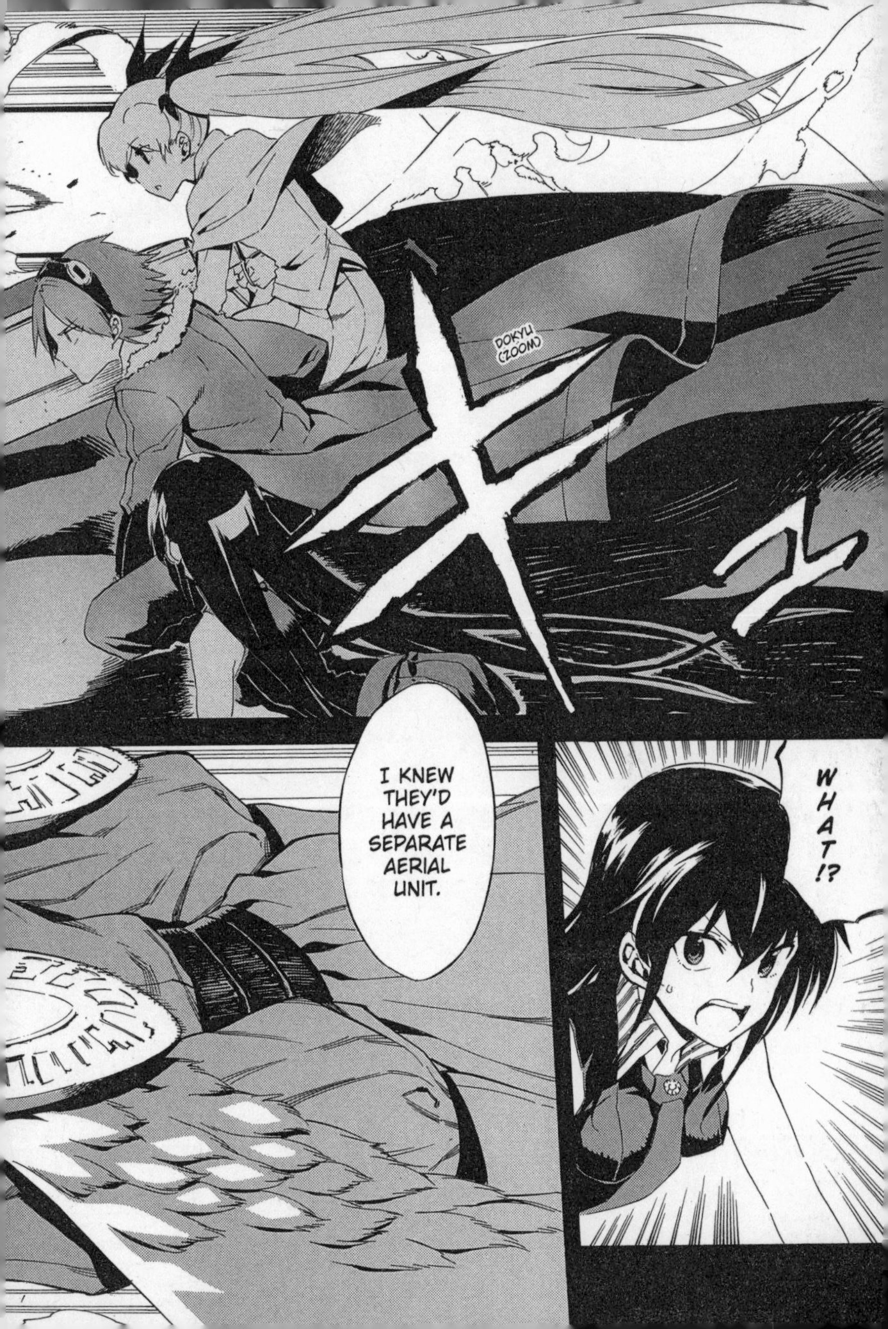
DOKYU (ZOOM)
WHAT!?
I KNEW THEY'D HAVE A SEPARATE AERIAL UNIT.

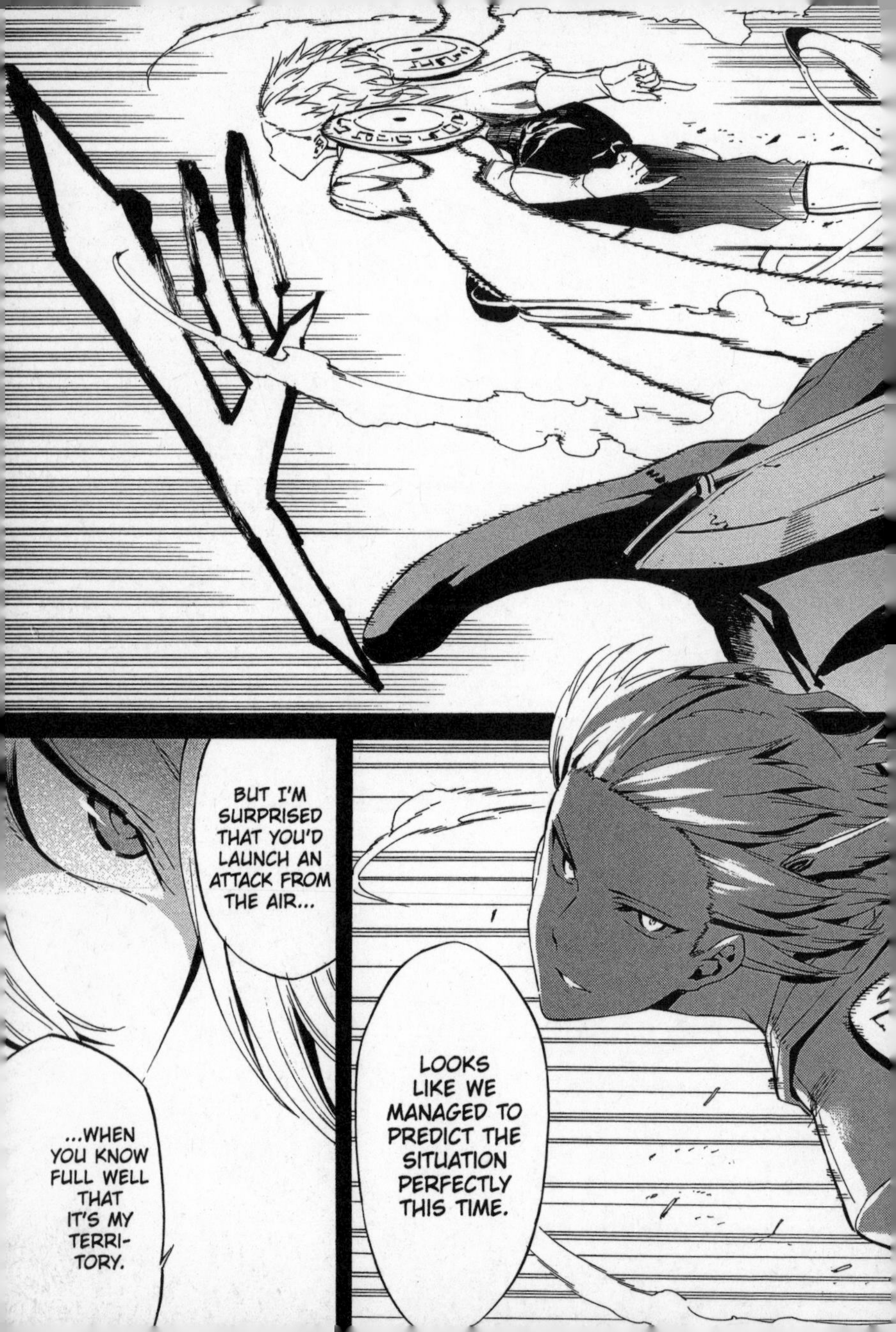
LOOKS LIKE WE MANAGED TO PREDICT THE SITUATION PERFECTLY THIS TIME.
BUT I'M SURPRISED THAT YOU'D LAUNCH AN ATTACK FROM THE AIR...
...WHEN YOU KNOW FULL WELL THAT IT'S MY TERRITORY.

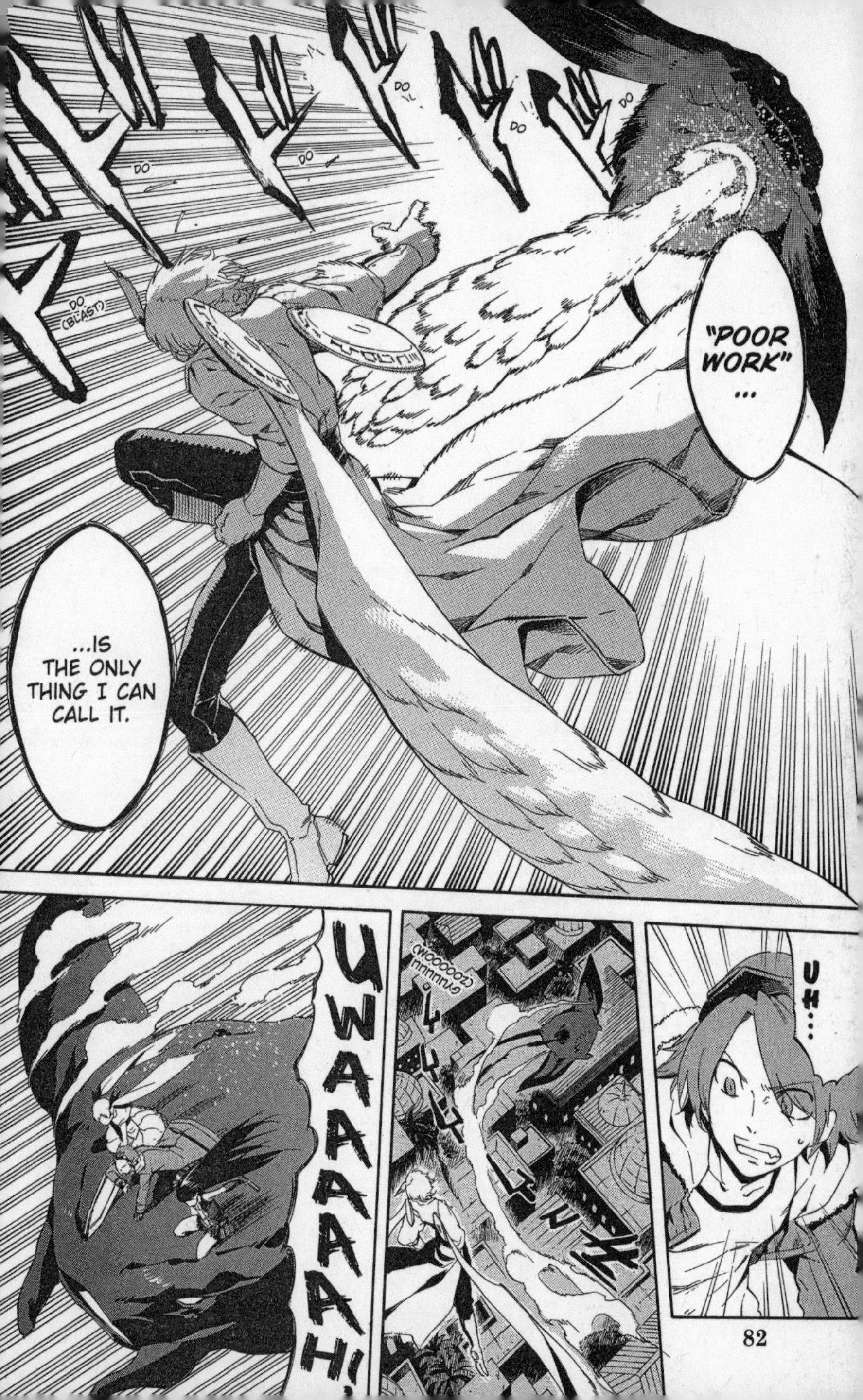
DO
DO
DO
DO
DO
DO
DO (BLAST)
"POOR WORK" ...
...IS THE ONLY THING I CAN CALL IT.
UH...
GYUUUUN (ZOOOOOM)
UWAAAAAH!

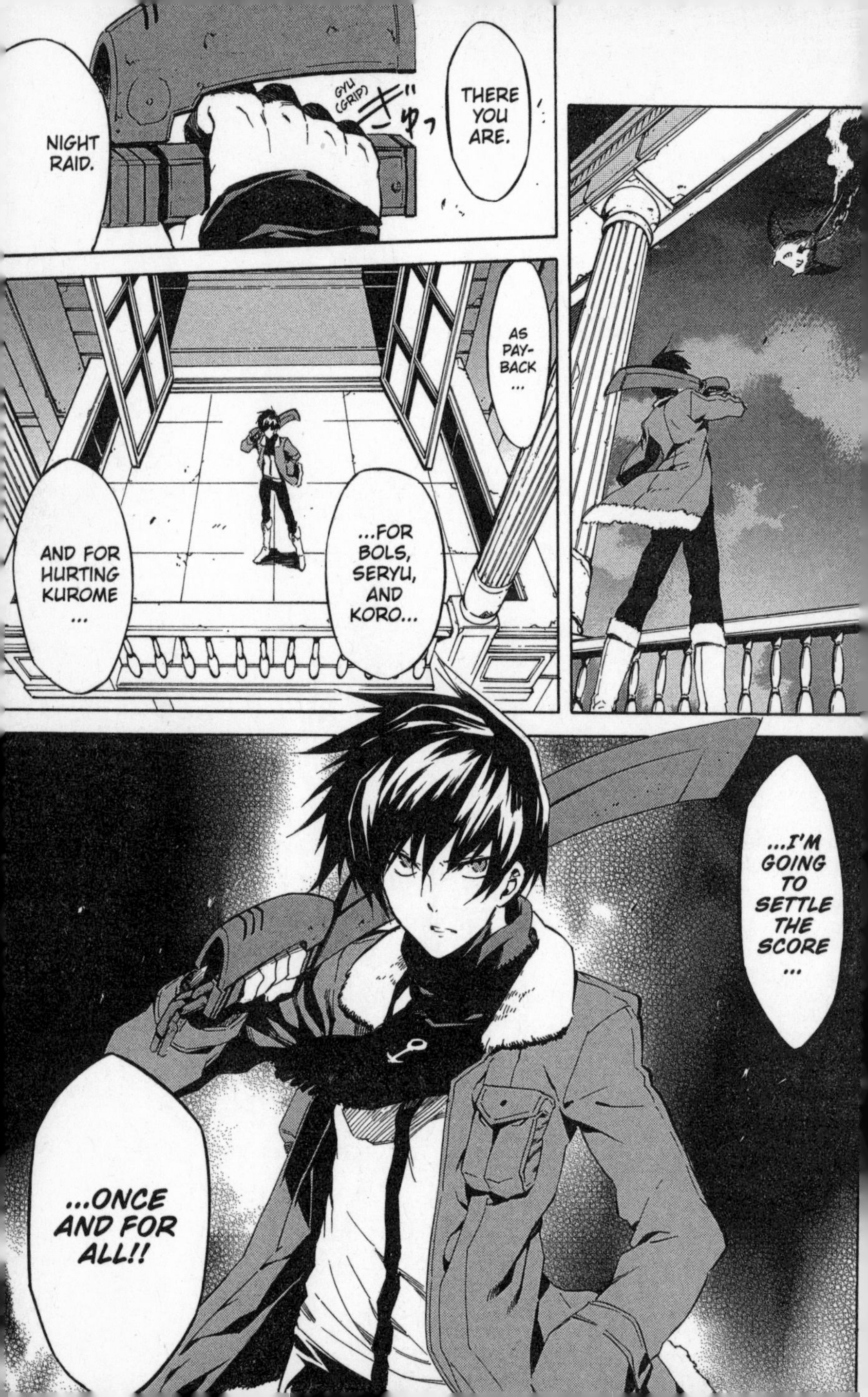
THERE YOU ARE.
GYU (GRIP)
NIGHT RAID.
AS PAY-BACK...
...FOR BOLS, SERYU, AND KORO...
AND FOR HURTING KUROME...
...I'M GOING TO SETTLE THE SCORE...
...ONCE AND FOR ALL!!

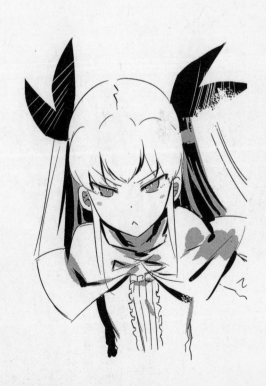

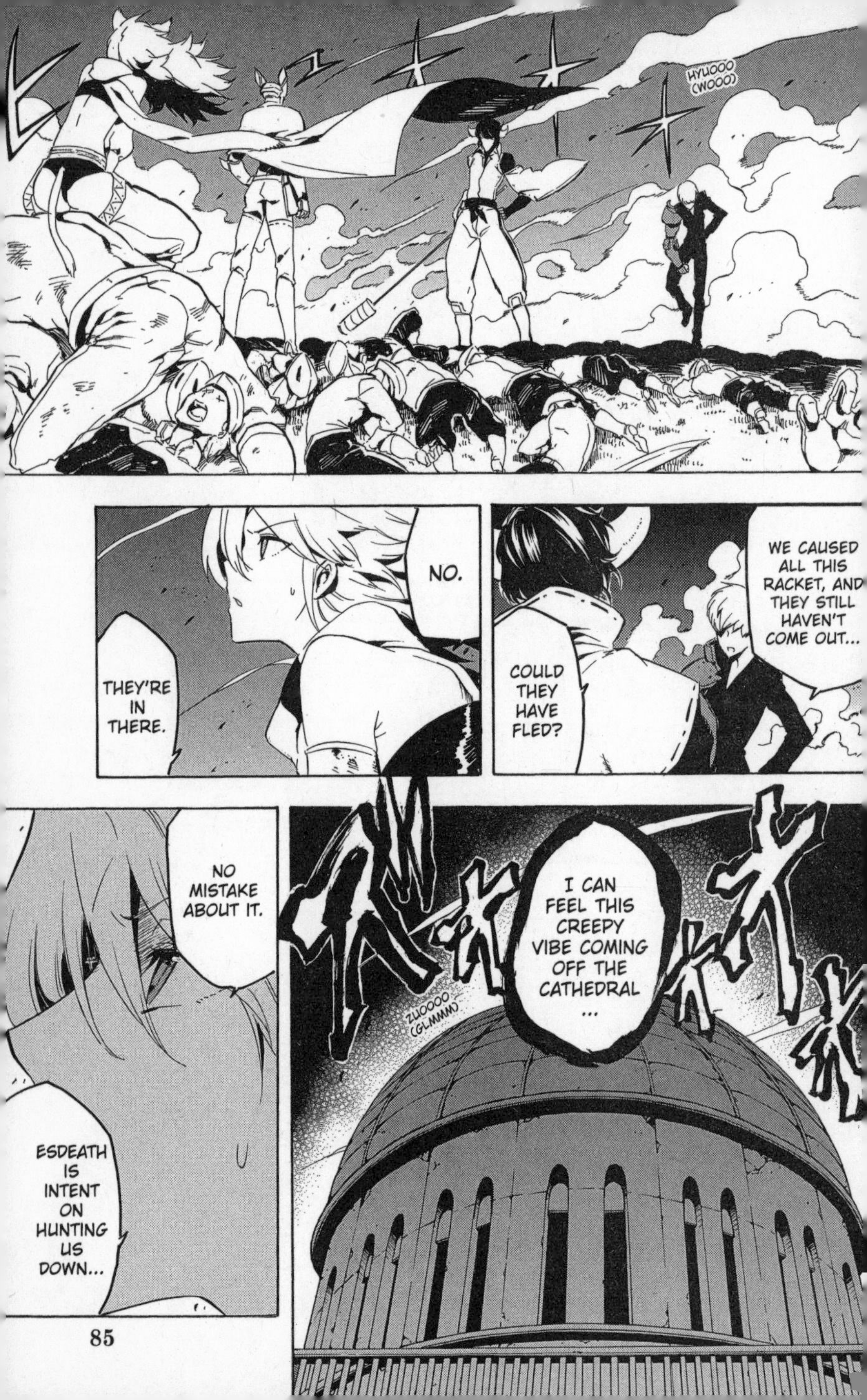
HYUOOO (WOOO)
WE CAUSED ALL THIS RACKET, AND THEY STILL HAVEN'T COME OUT...
COULD THEY HAVE FLED?
NO.
THEY'RE IN THERE.
I CAN FEEL THIS CREEPY VIBE COMING OFF THE CATHEDRAL ...
ZUOOOO (GLMMM)
NO MISTAKE ABOUT IT.
ESDEATH IS INTENT ON HUNTING US DOWN...

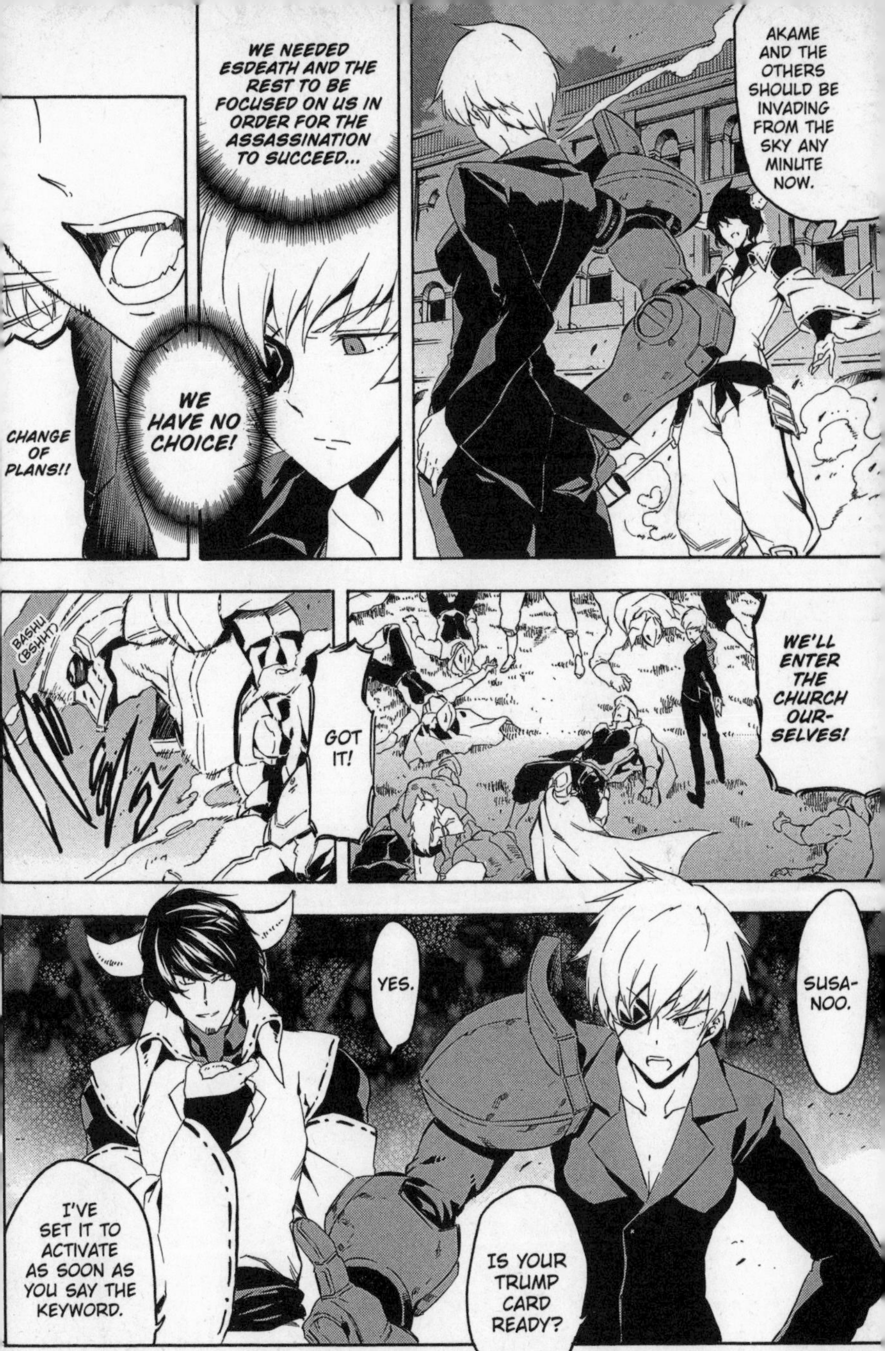
AKAME AND THE OTHERS SHOULD BE INVADING FROM THE SKY ANY MINUTE NOW.
WE NEEDED ESDEATH AND THE REST TO BE FOCUSED ON US IN ORDER FOR THE ASSASSINATION TO SUCCEED...
WE HAVE NO CHOICE!
CHANGE OF PLANS!!
WE'LL ENTER THE CHURCH OUR-SELVES!
GOT IT!
BASHU (BSHHT)
SUSA-NOO.
YES.
IS YOUR TRUMP CARD READY?
I'VE SET IT TO ACTIVATE AS SOON AS YOU SAY THE KEYWORD.

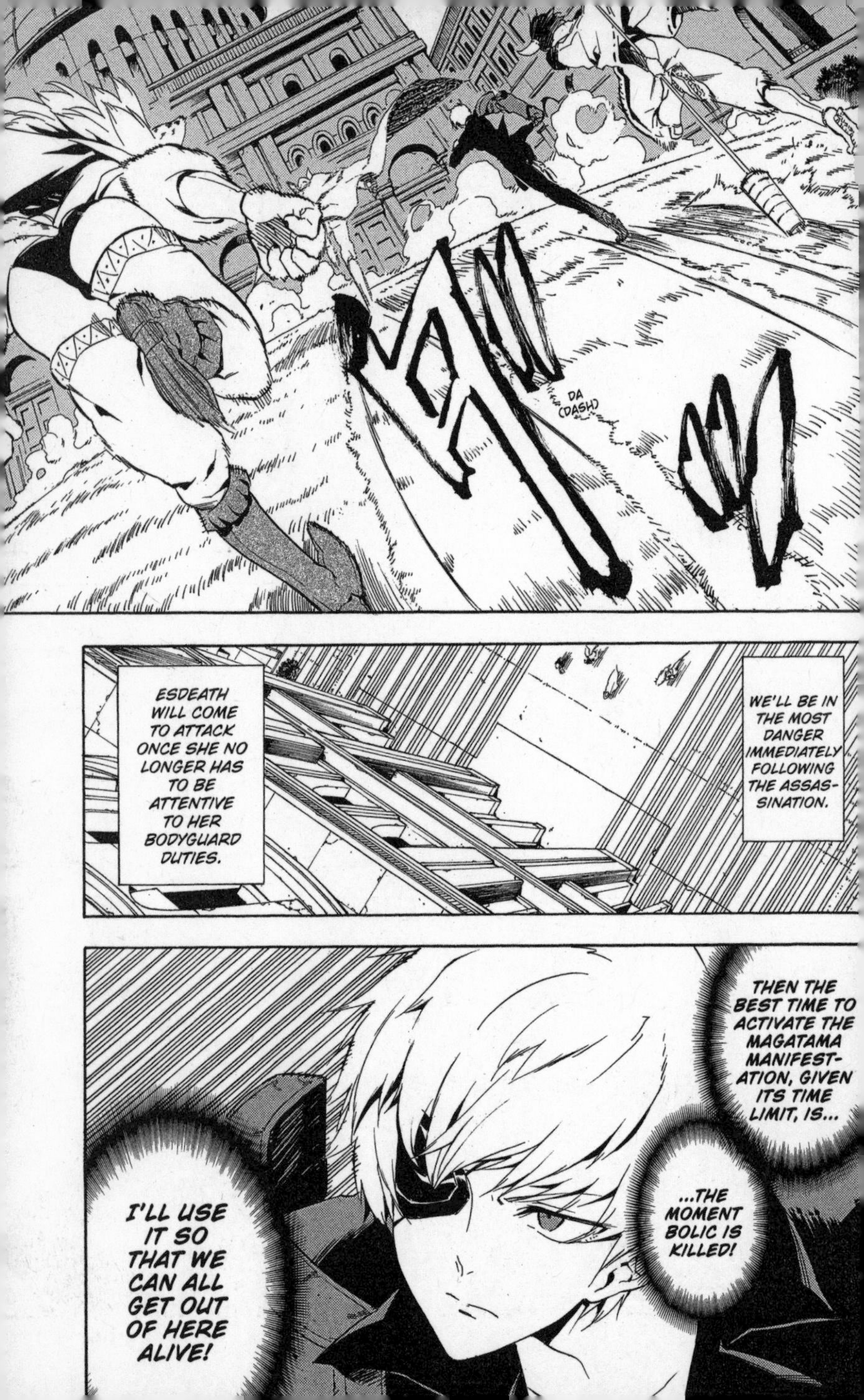
DA (DASH)
WE'LL BE IN THE MOST DANGER IMMEDIATELY FOLLOWING THE ASSAS-SINATION.
ESDEATH WILL COME TO ATTACK ONCE SHE NO LONGER HAS TO BE ATTENTIVE TO HER BODYGUARD DUTIES.
THEN THE BEST TIME TO ACTIVATE THE MAGATAMA MANIFEST-ATION, GIVEN ITS TIME LIMIT, IS...
...THE MOMENT BOLIC IS KILLED!
I'LL USE IT SO THAT WE CAN ALL GET OUT OF HERE ALIVE!

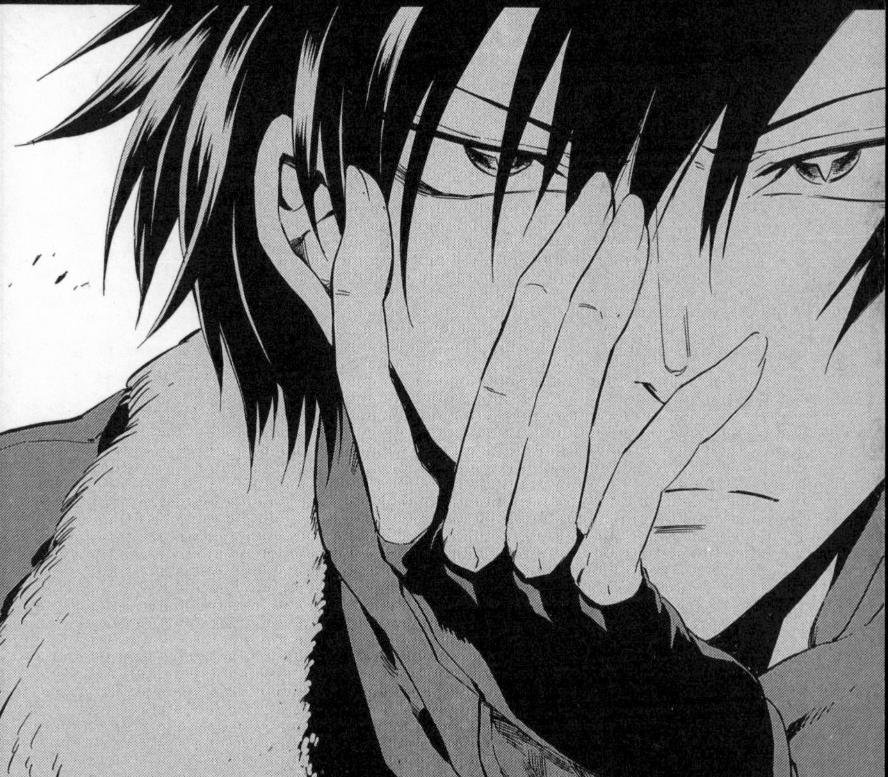

Chapter 41 - Kill the Wicked

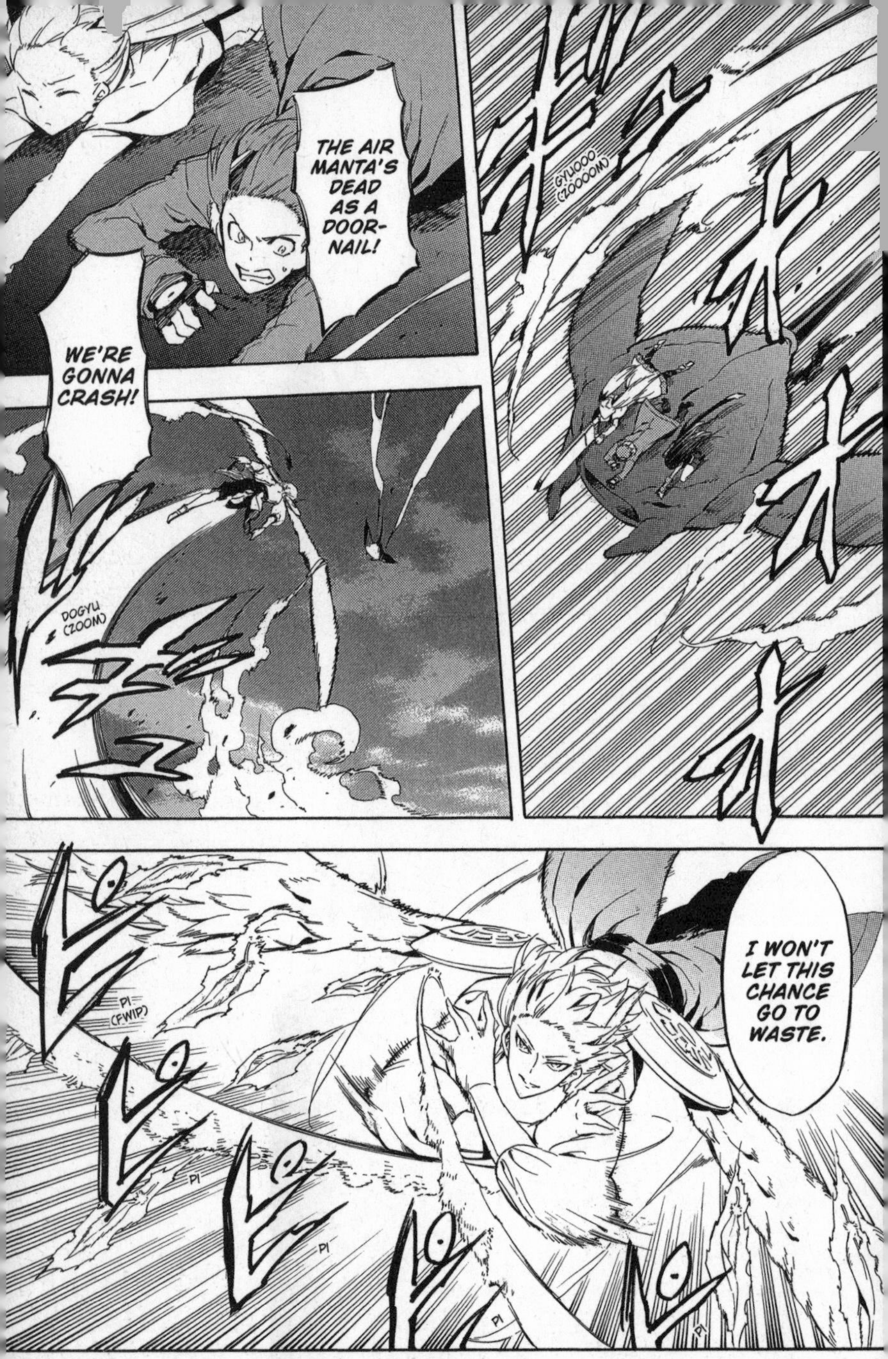
GYUOOO (ZOOOOM)
THE AIR MANTA'S DEAD AS A DOOR-NAIL!
WE'RE GONNA CRASH!
DOGYU (ZOOM)
I WON'T LET THIS CHANCE GO TO WASTE.
PI (FWIP)
PI
PI
PI
PI

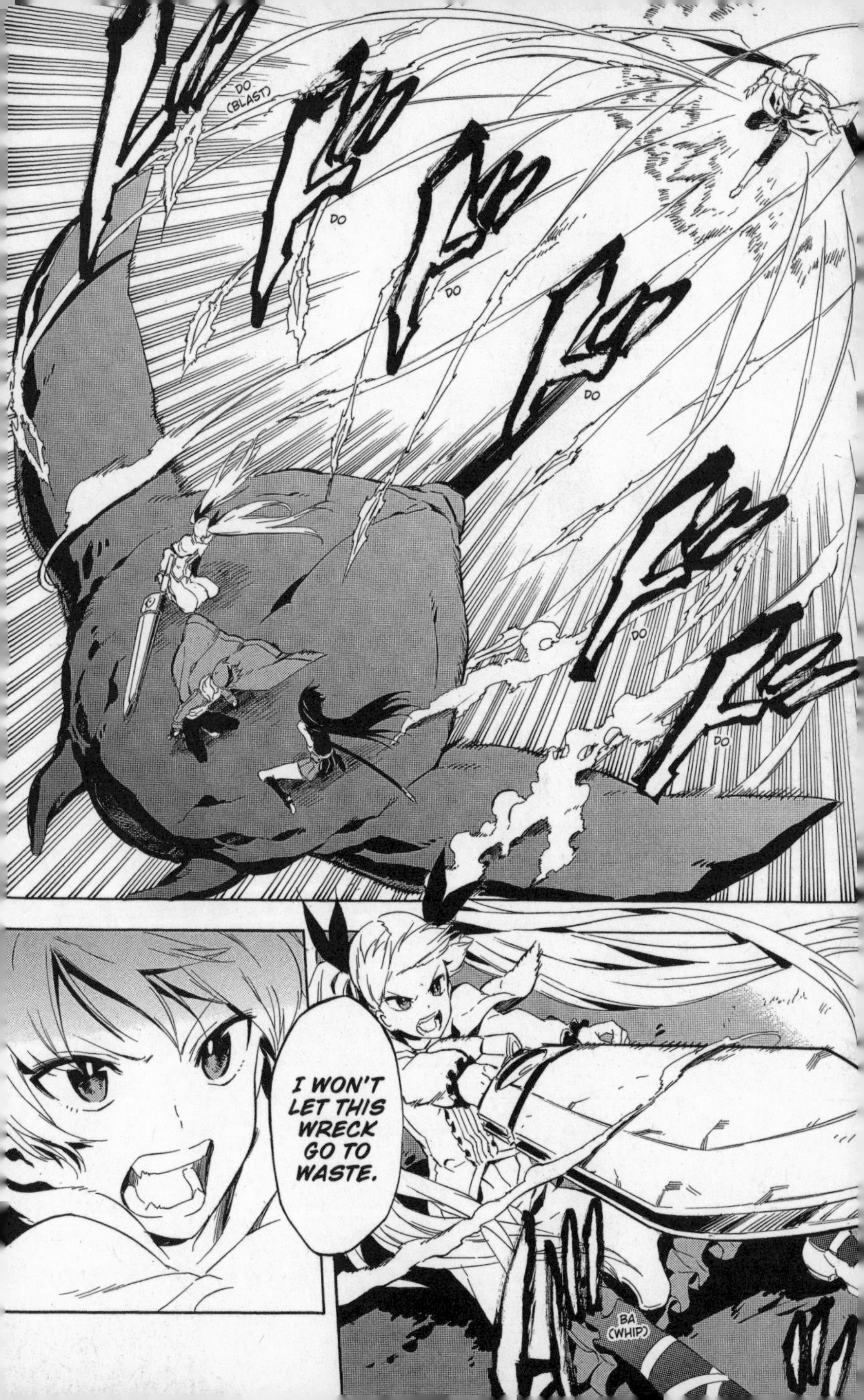
DO (BLAST)
DO
DO
DO
DO
DO
I WON'T LET THIS WRECK GO TO WASTE.
BA (WHIP)

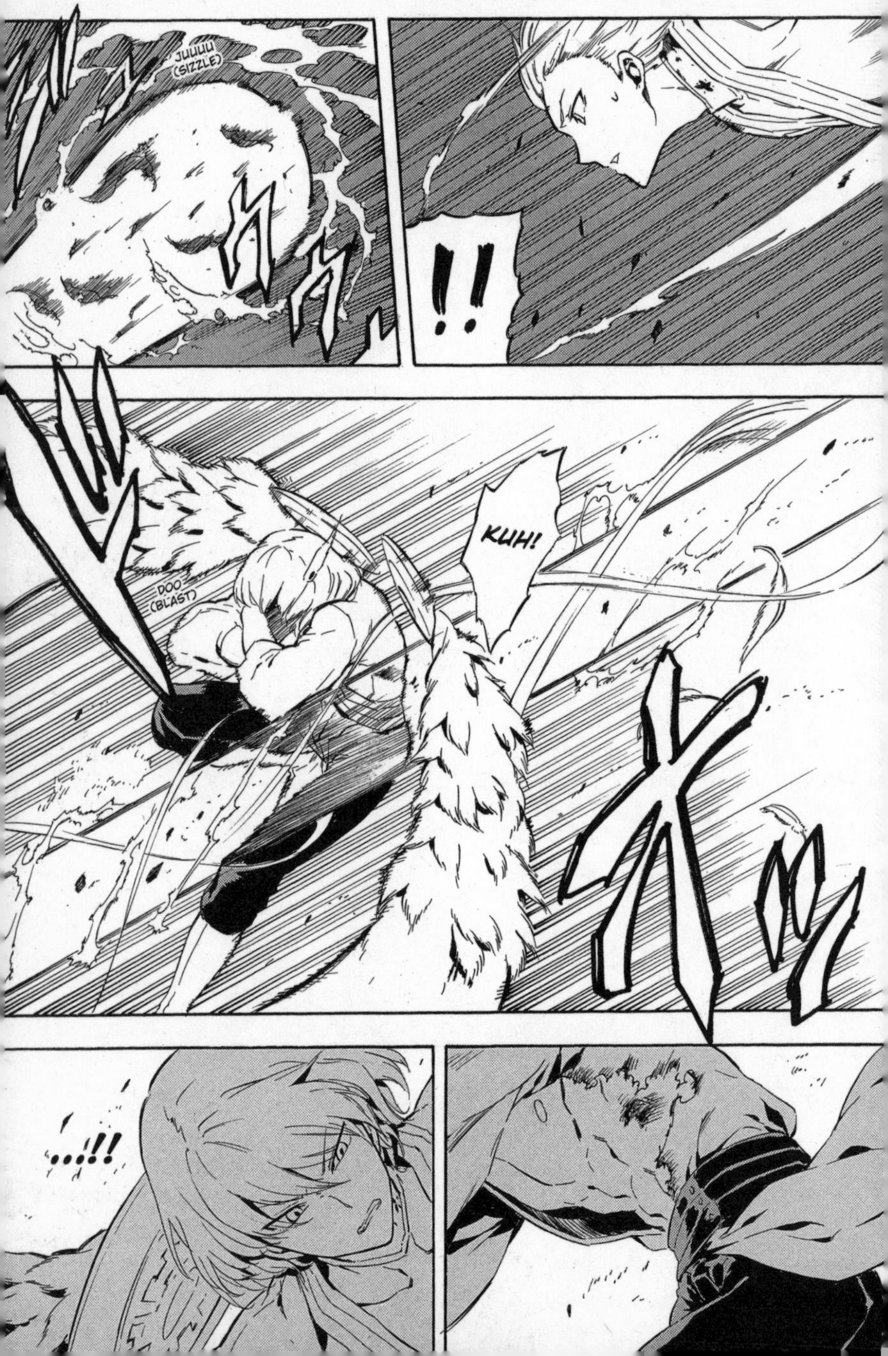
!!
JUUUU (SIZZLE)
KUH!
DOO (BLAST)
...!!

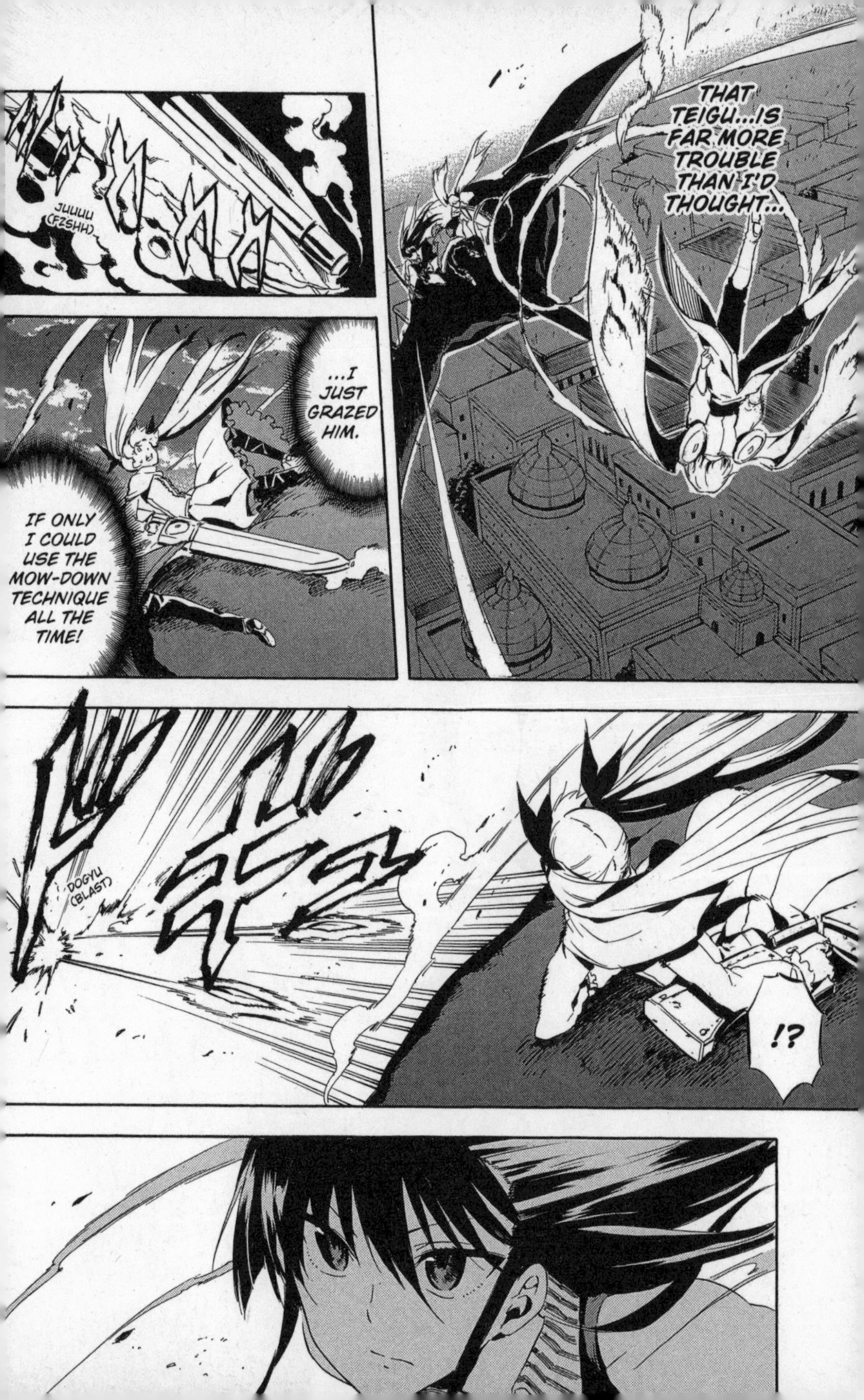
THAT TEIGU...IS FAR MORE TROUBLE THAN I'D THOUGHT...
JUUUU (FZSHH)
...I JUST GRAZED HIM.
IF ONLY I COULD USE THE MOW-DOWN TECHNIQUE ALL THE TIME!
!?
DOGYU (BLAST)

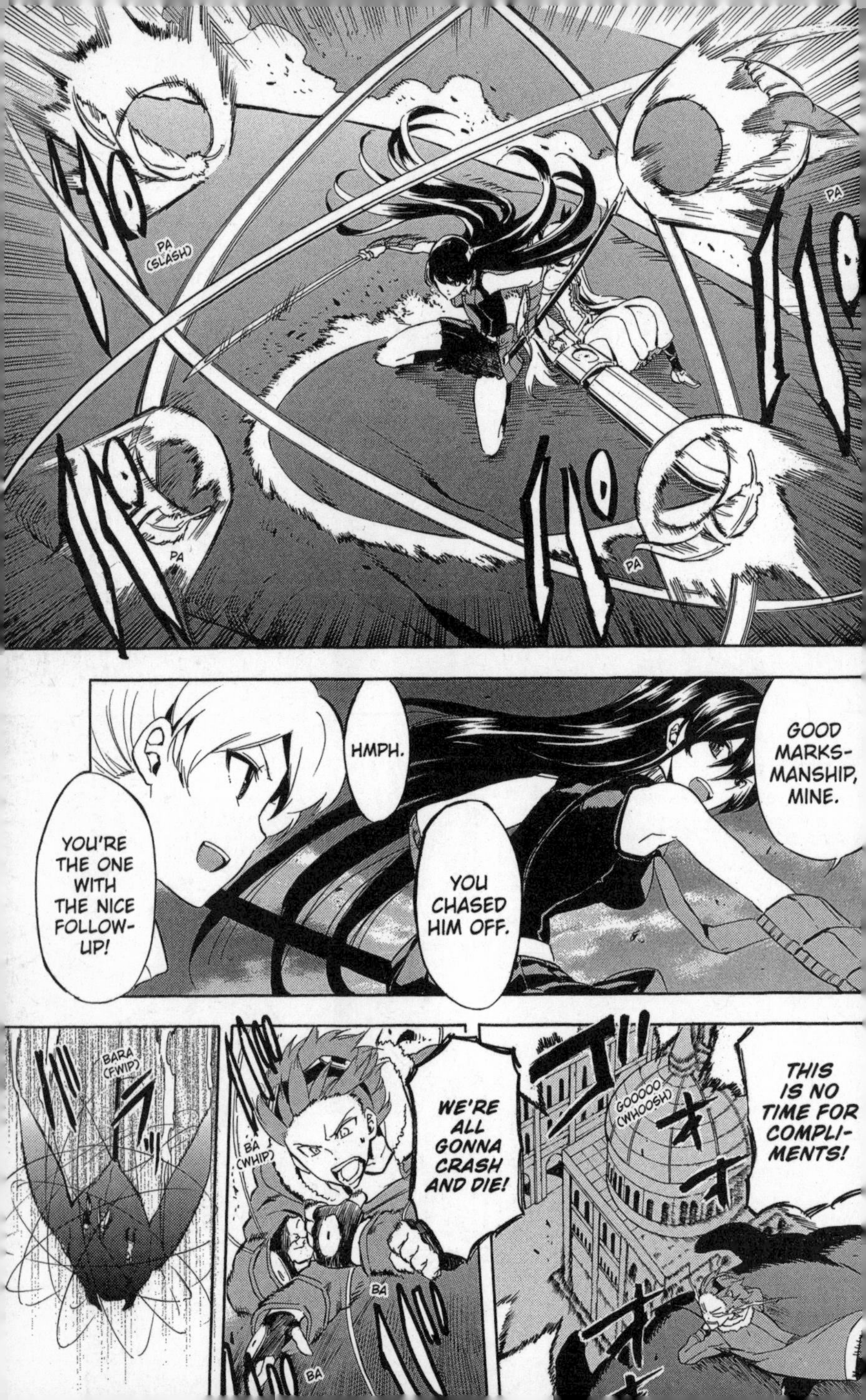
PA
PA
(SLASH)
PA
PA
GOOD MARKS-MANSHIP, MINE.
HMPH.
YOU CHASED HIM OFF.
YOU'RE THE ONE WITH THE NICE FOLLOW-UP!
THIS IS NO TIME FOR COMPLI-MENTS!
GOOOOO
(WHOOSH)
WE'RE ALL GONNA CRASH AND DIE!
BA
(WHIP)
BA
BA
BARA
(FWIP)

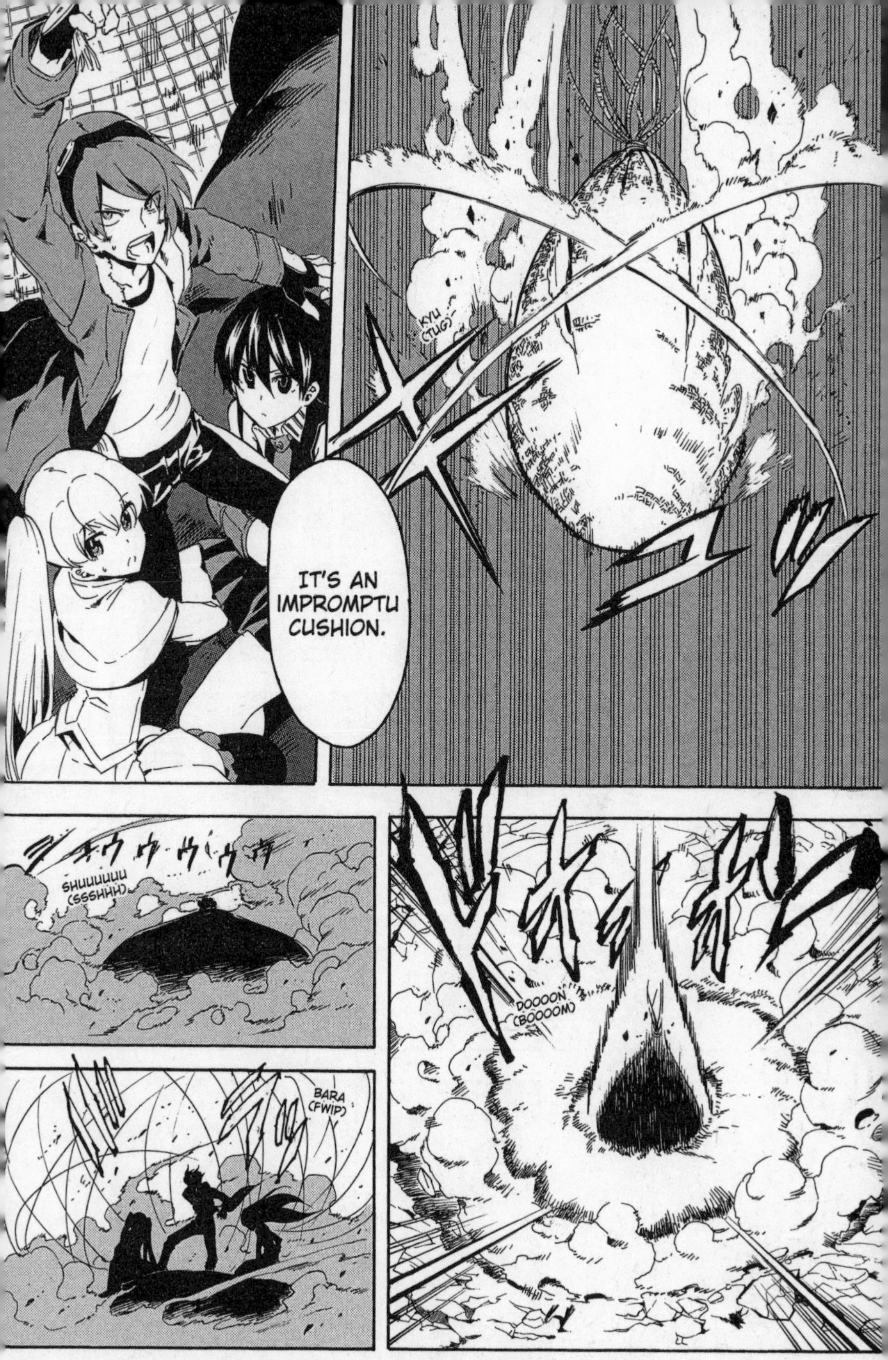
KYU (TUG)
IT'S AN IMPROMPTU CUSHION.
DOOOON (BOOOOM)
SHUUUUUU (SSSHHH)
BARA (FWIP)

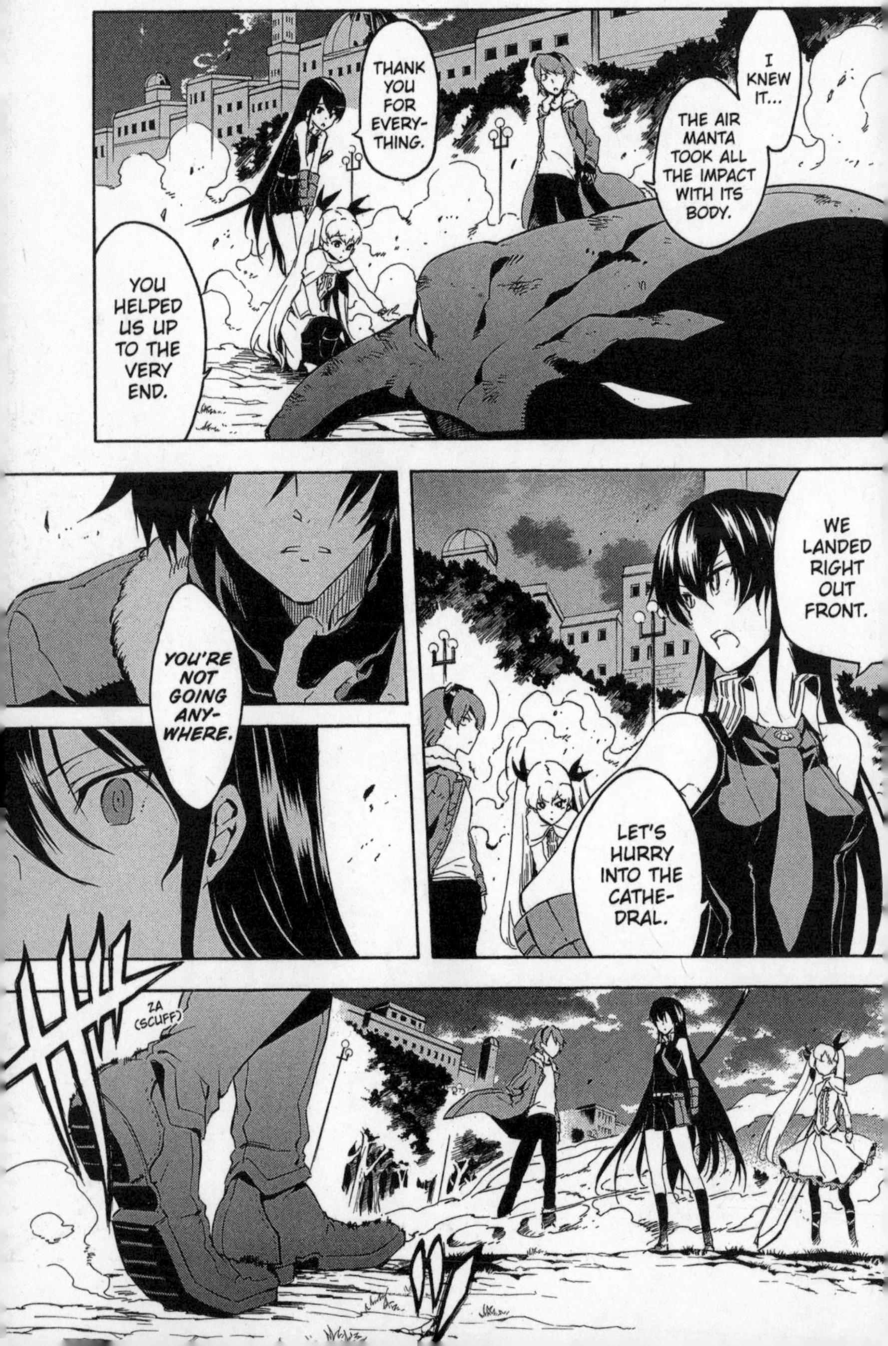
I KNEW IT...
THE AIR MANTA TOOK ALL THE IMPACT WITH ITS BODY.
THANK YOU FOR EVERY-THING.
YOU HELPED US UP TO THE VERY END.
WE LANDED RIGHT OUT FRONT.
LET'S HURRY INTO THE CATHE-DRAL.
...
YOU'RE NOT GOING ANY-WHERE.
...
ZA (SCUFF)

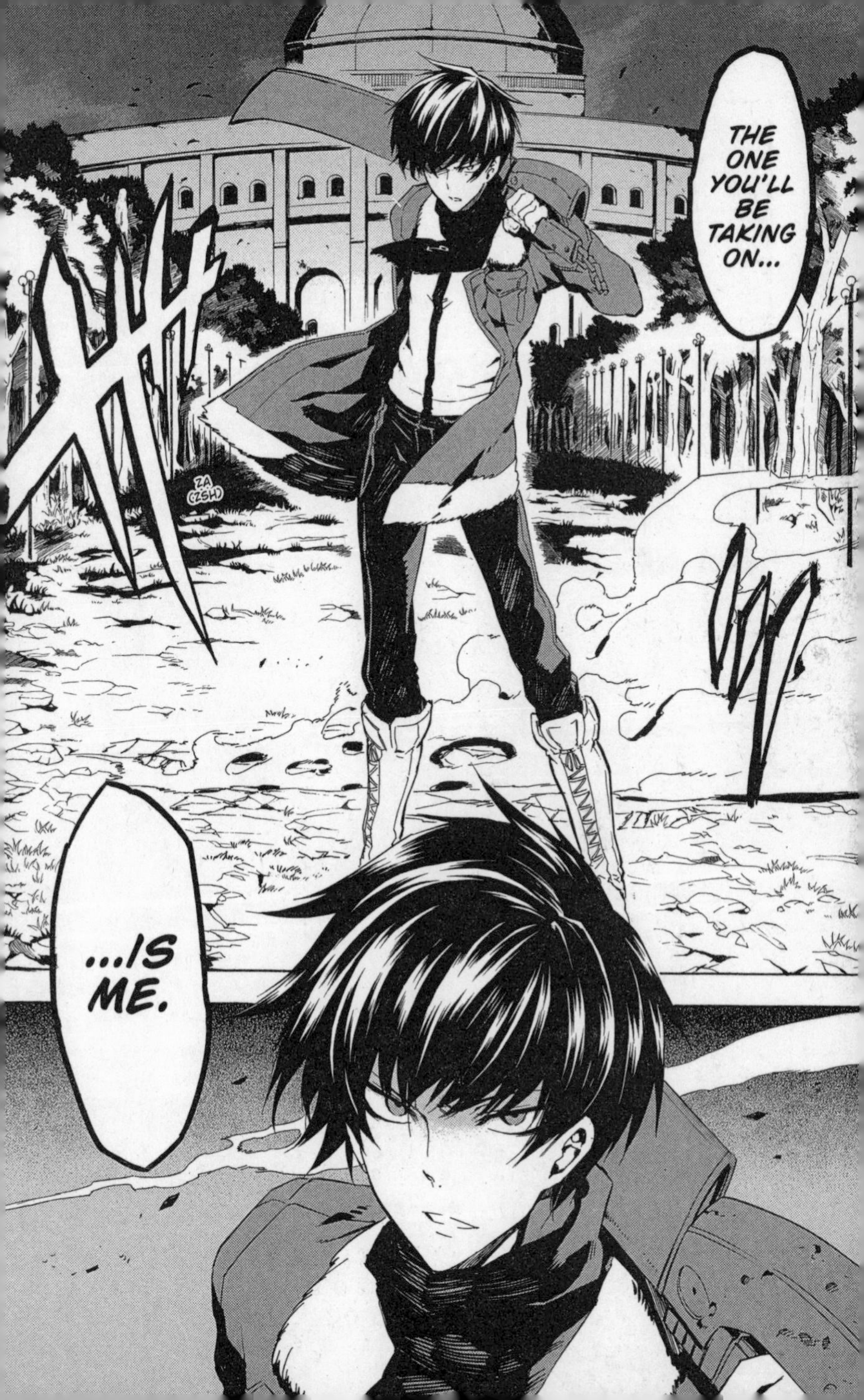
THE ONE YOU'LL BE TAKING ON...
ZA (ZSH)
...IS ME.

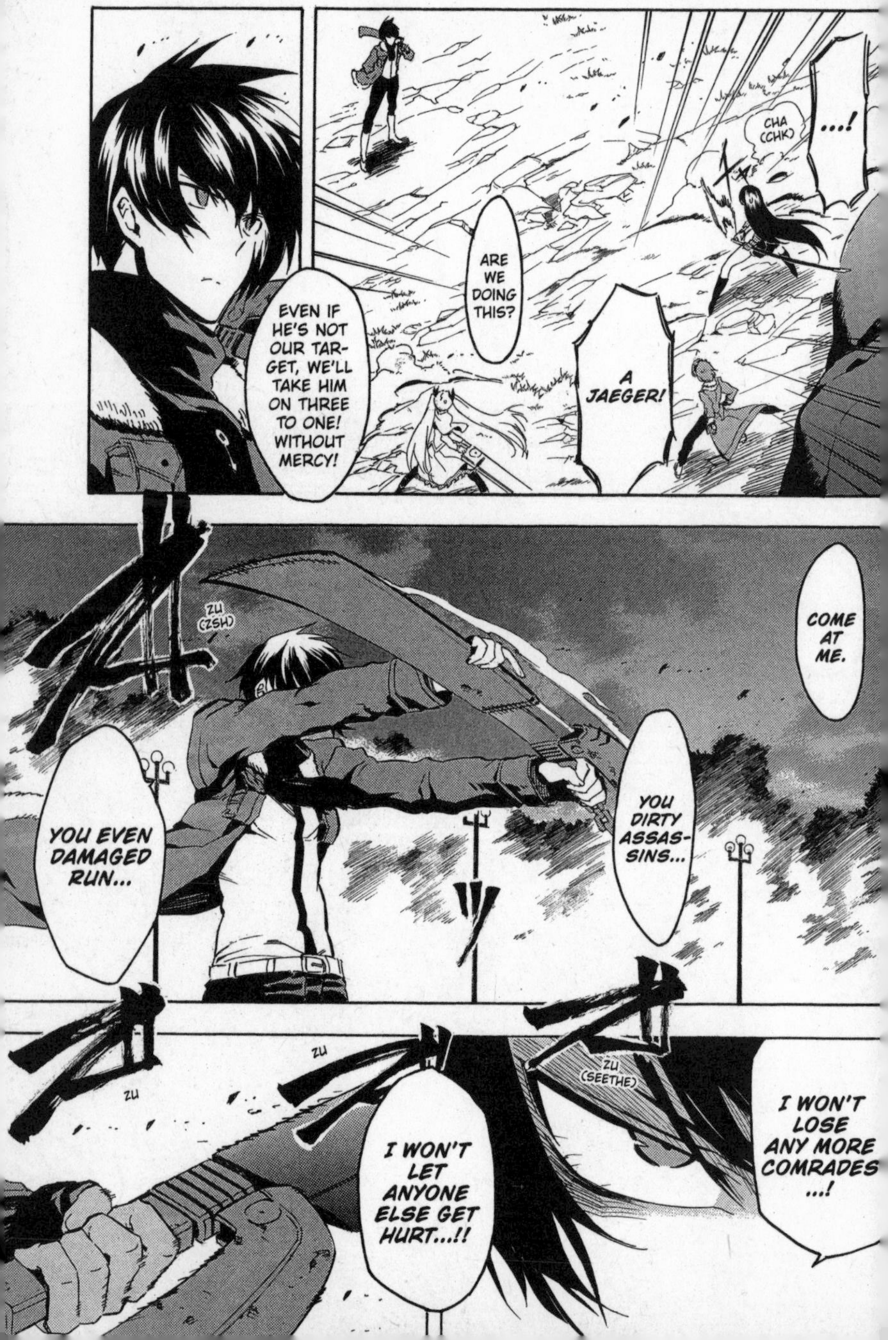
...!
CHA (CHK)
A JAEGER!
ARE WE DOING THIS?
...
EVEN IF HE'S NOT OUR TARGET, WE'LL TAKE HIM ON THREE TO ONE! WITHOUT MERCY!
COME AT ME.
ZU (ZSH)
YOU DIRTY ASSASSINS...
YOU EVEN DAMAGED RUN...
I WON'T LOSE ANY MORE COMRADES...!
ZU (SEETHE)
ZU
I WON'T LET ANYONE ELSE GET HURT...!!
ZU

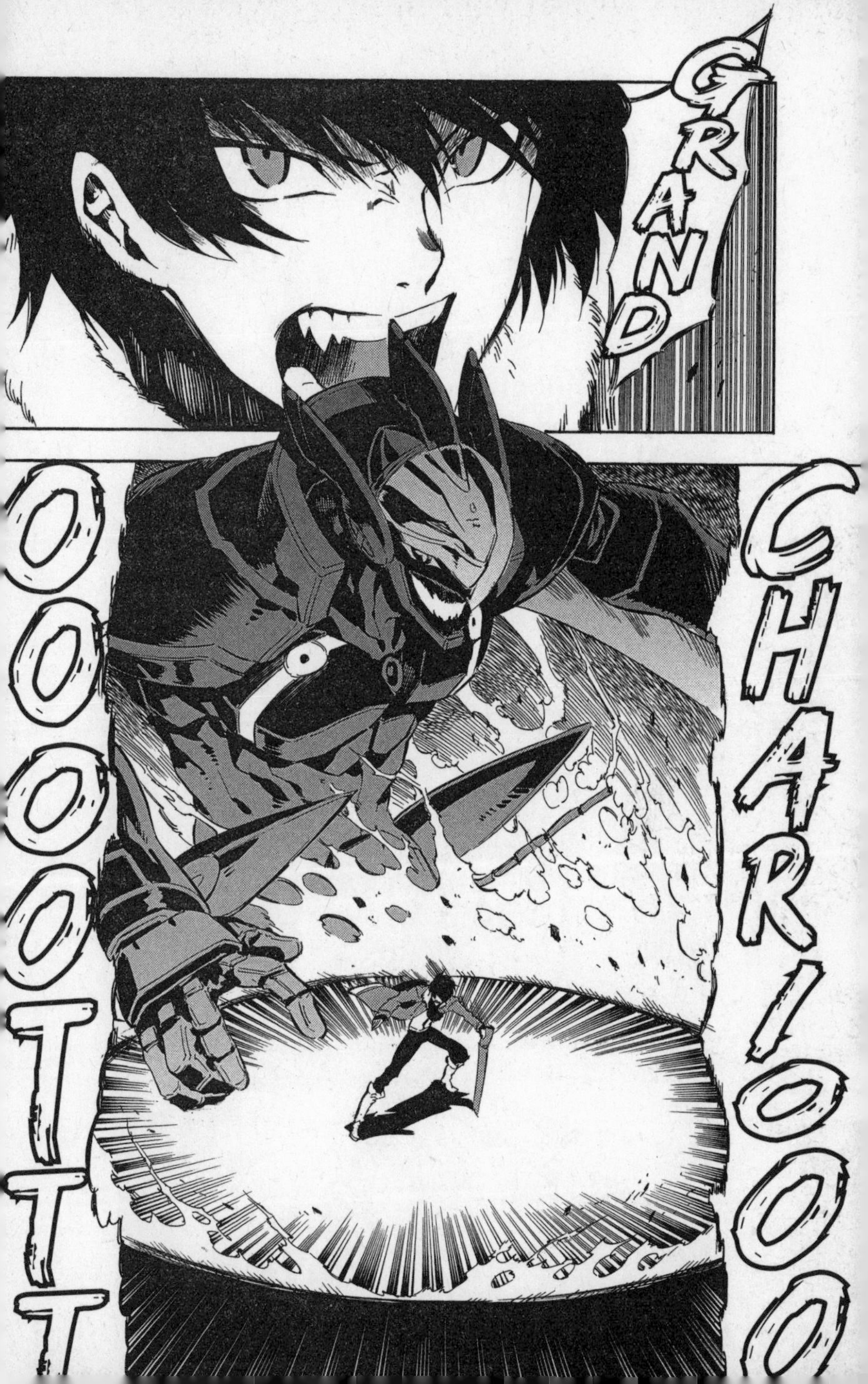
GRAND
CHARIOOO
OOOOOTTT

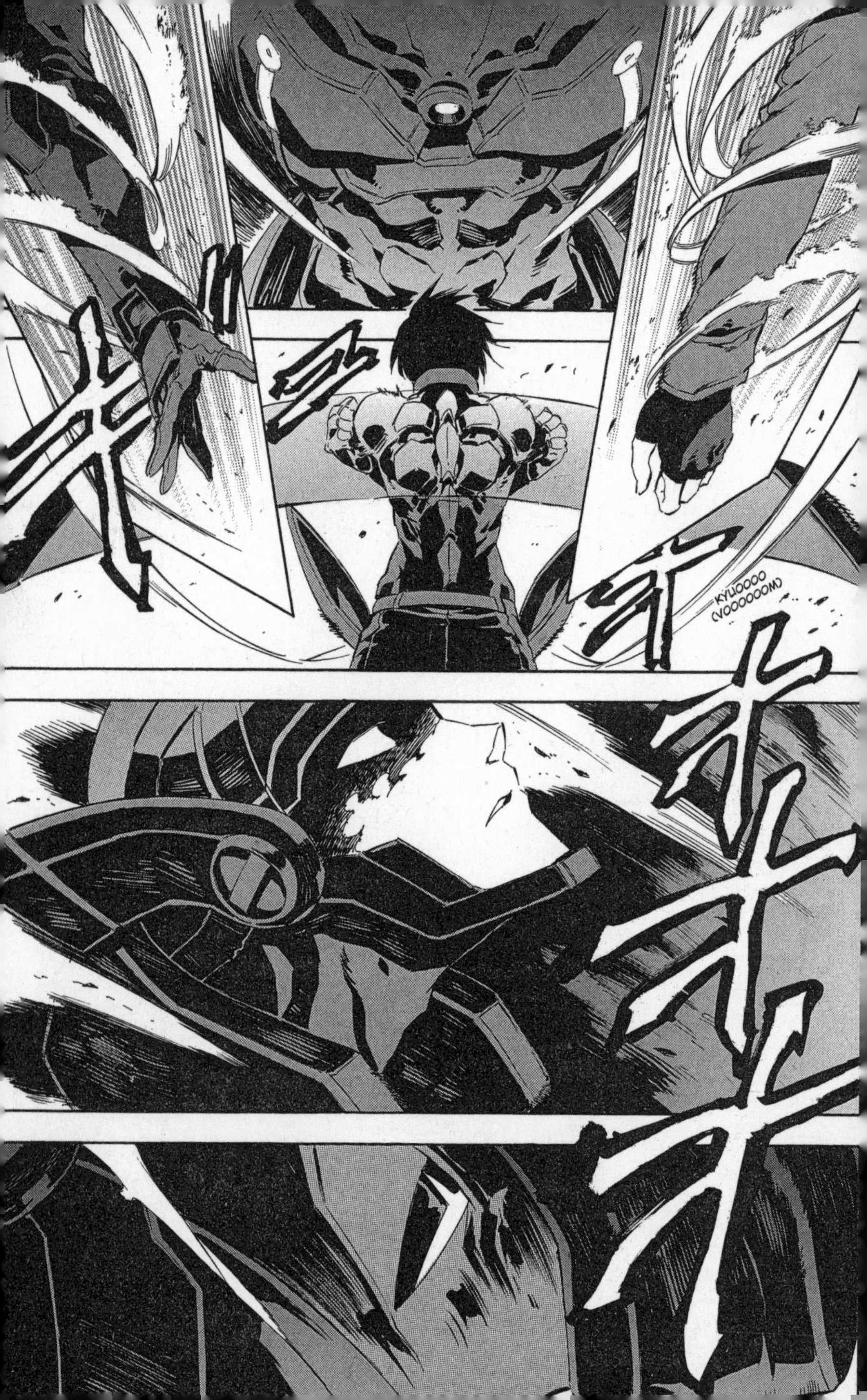
KYUOOOO
(VOOOOOOM)

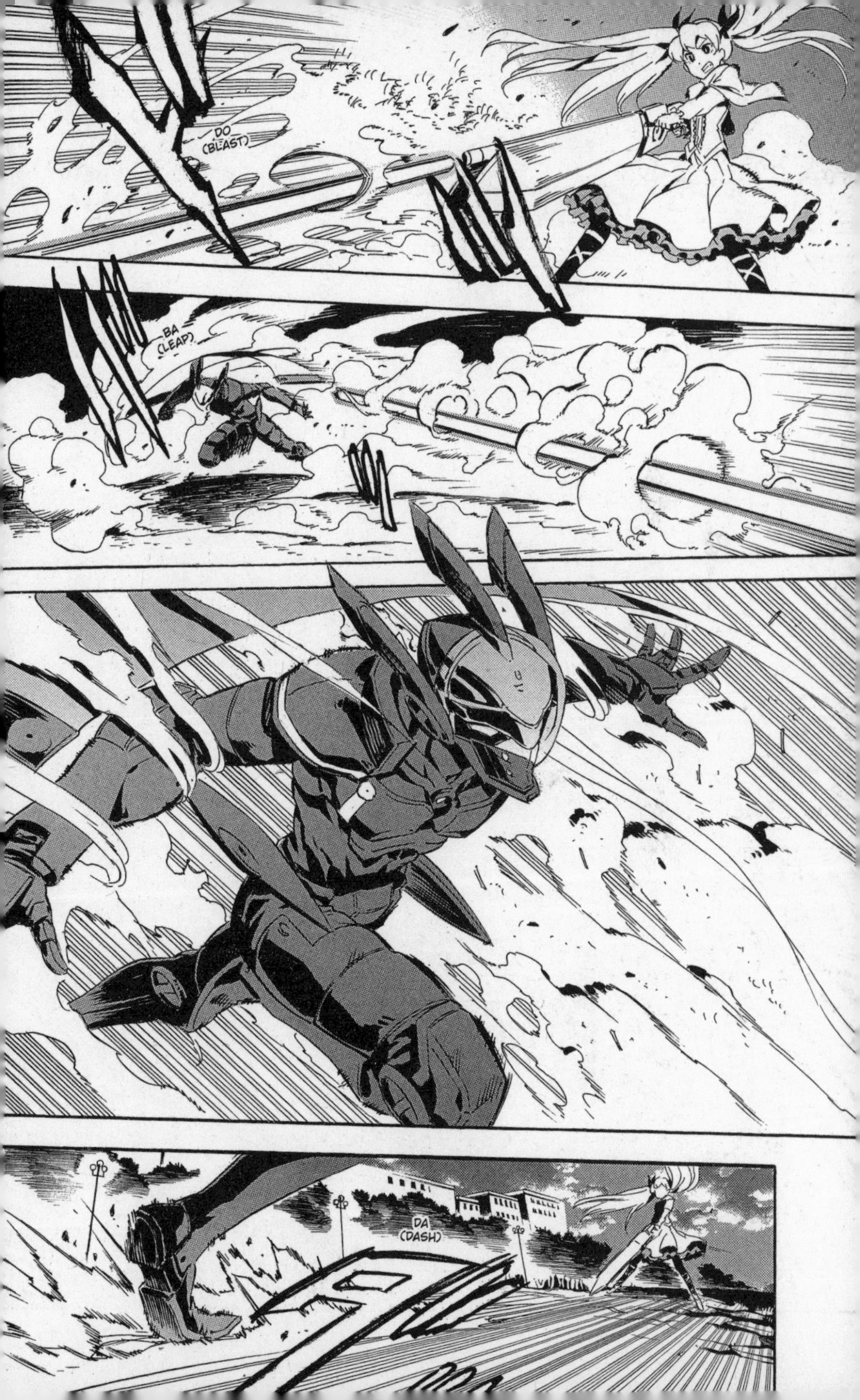
DO (BLAST)
BA (LEAP)
DA (DASH)

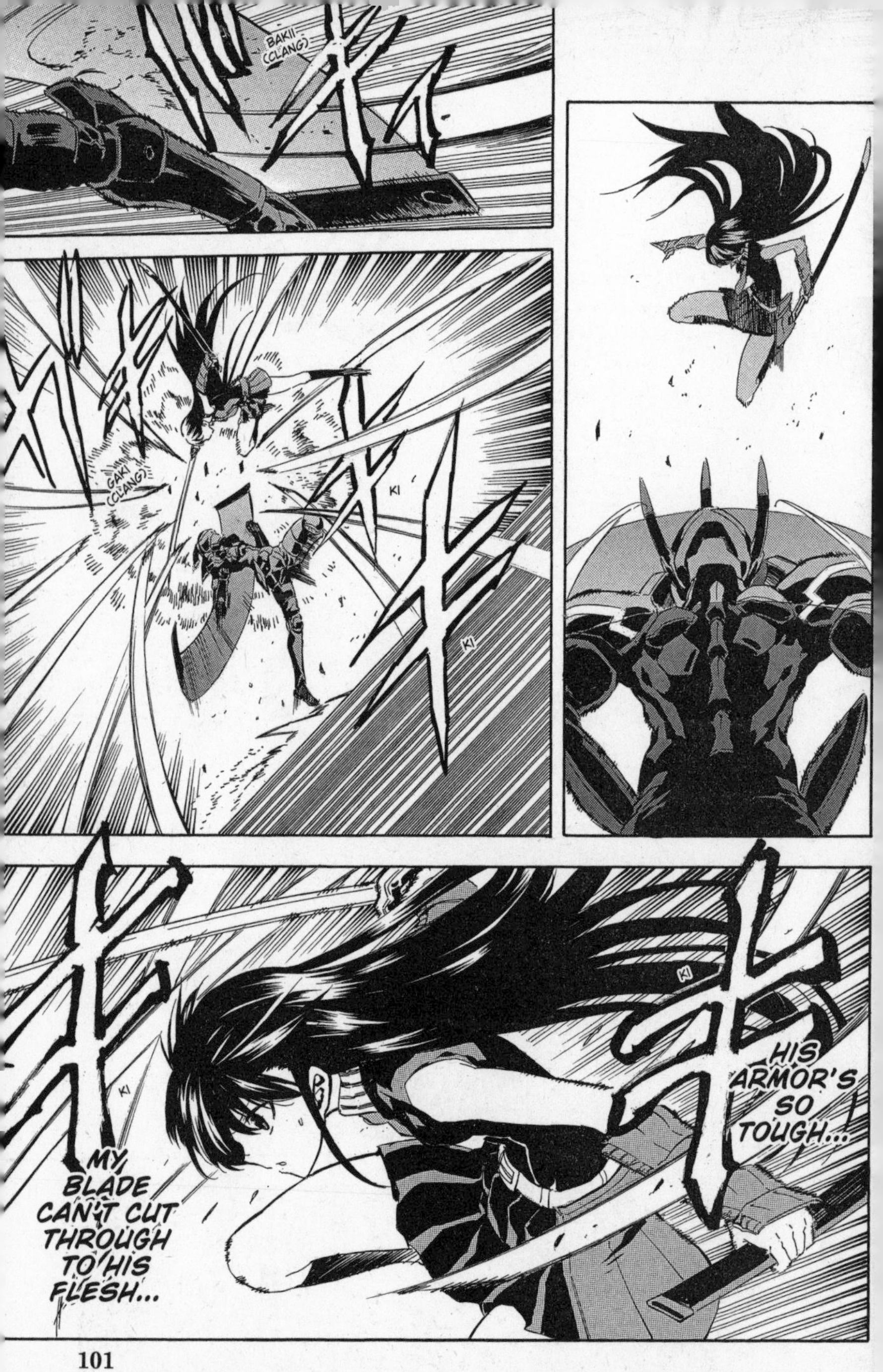
BAKII (CLANG)
GAKI (CLANG)
KI
KI
KI
HIS ARMOR'S SO TOUGH...!
KI
MY BLADE CAN'T CUT THROUGH TO HIS FLESH...

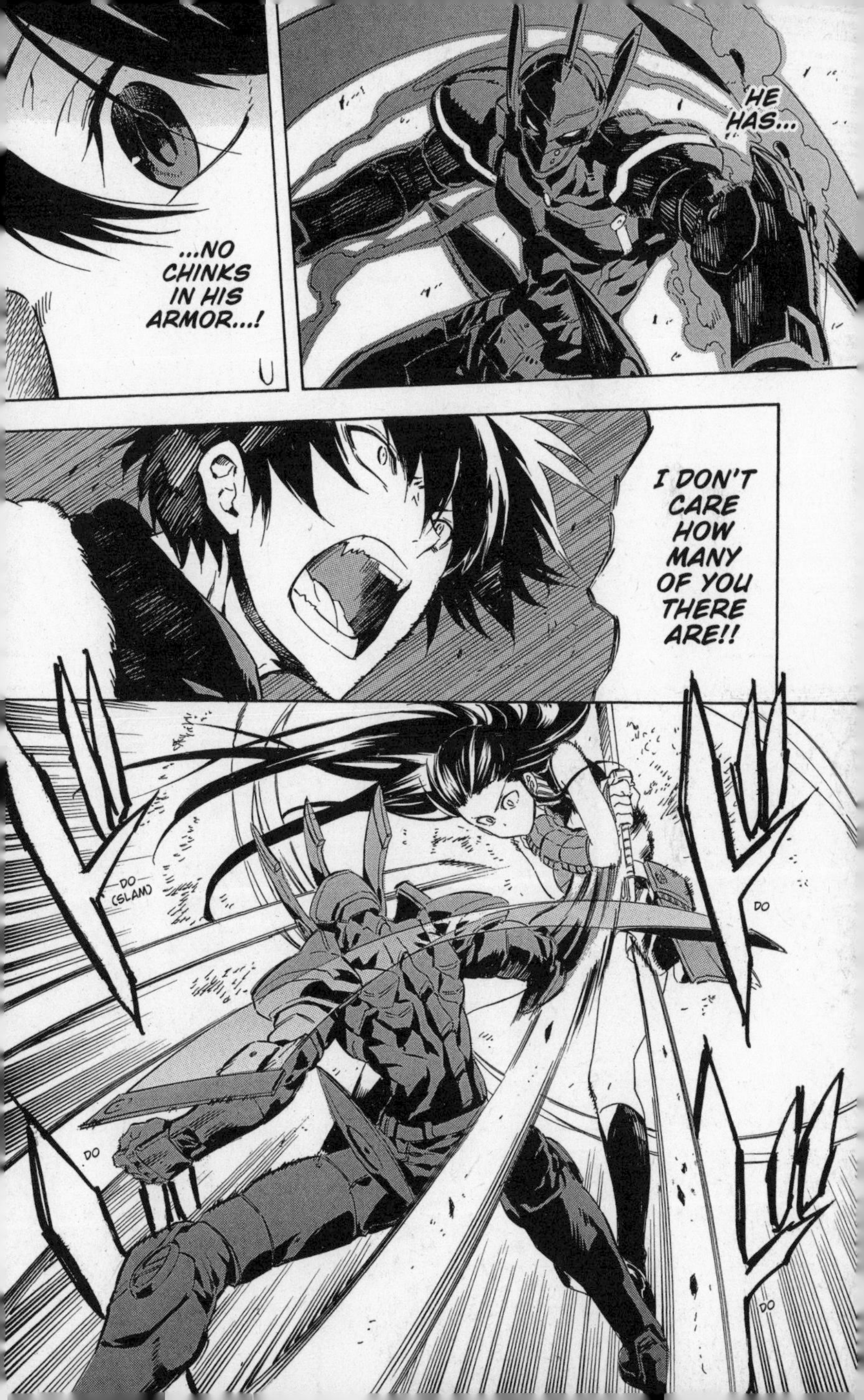
HE HAS...
...NO CHINKS IN HIS ARMOR...!
I DON'T CARE HOW MANY OF YOU THERE ARE!!
DO
DO (SLAM)
DO
DO

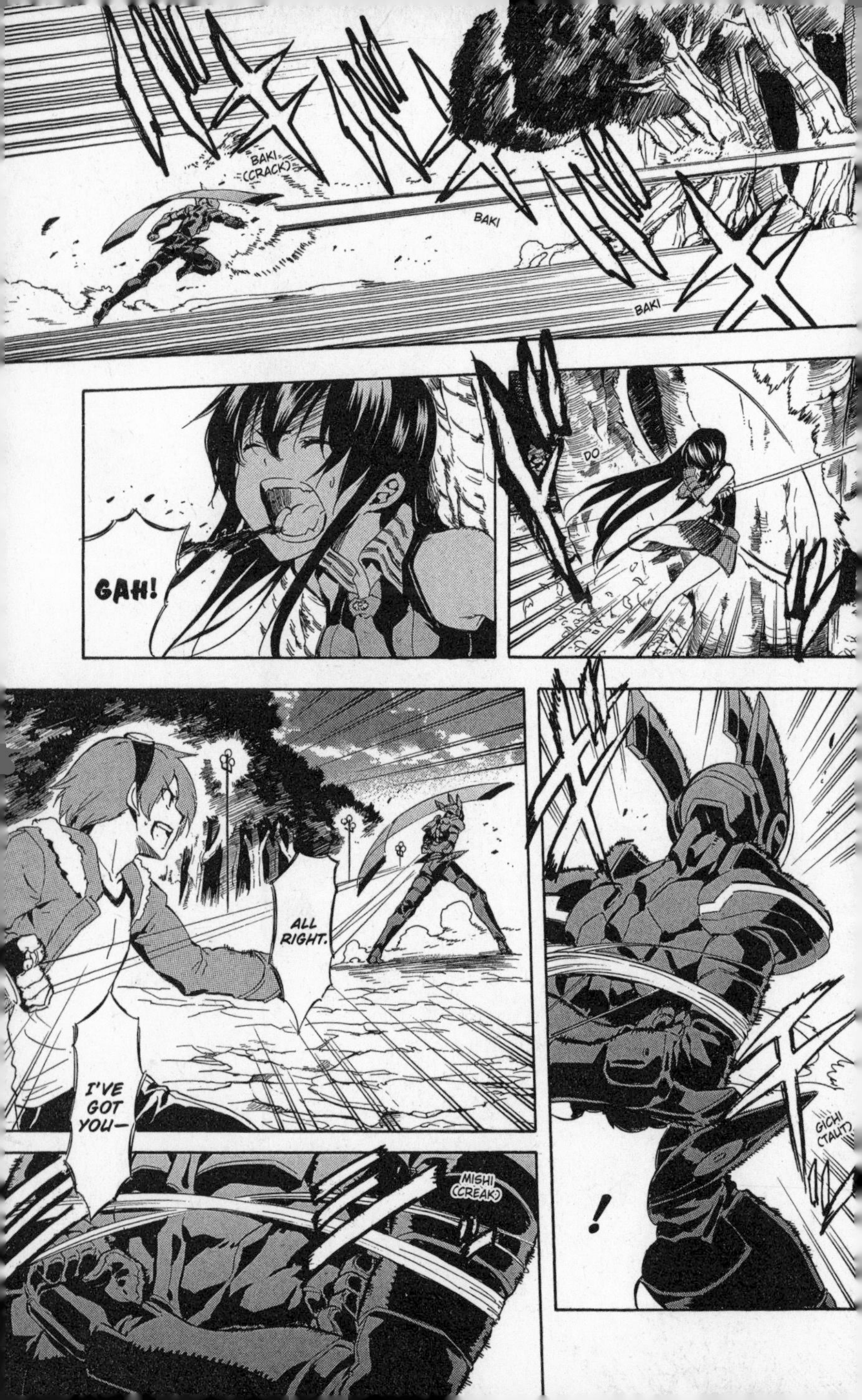
BAKI (CRACK)
BAKI
BAKI
DO
GAH!
GICHI (TAUT)
!
ALL RIGHT.
I'VE GOT YOU—
MISHI (CREAK)

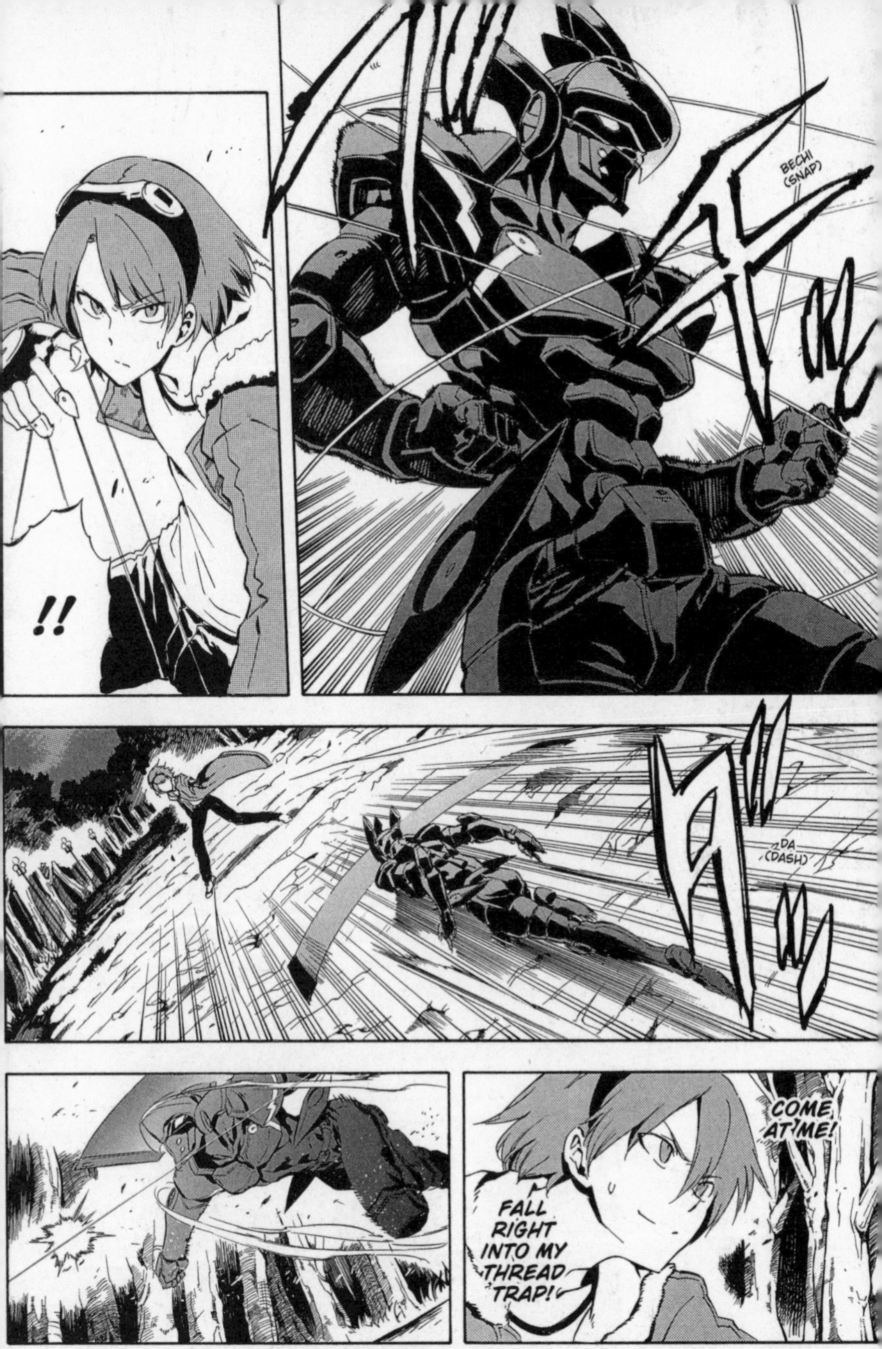
BECHI (SNAP)
!!
DA (DASH)
COME AT ME!
FALL RIGHT INTO MY THREAD TRAP!

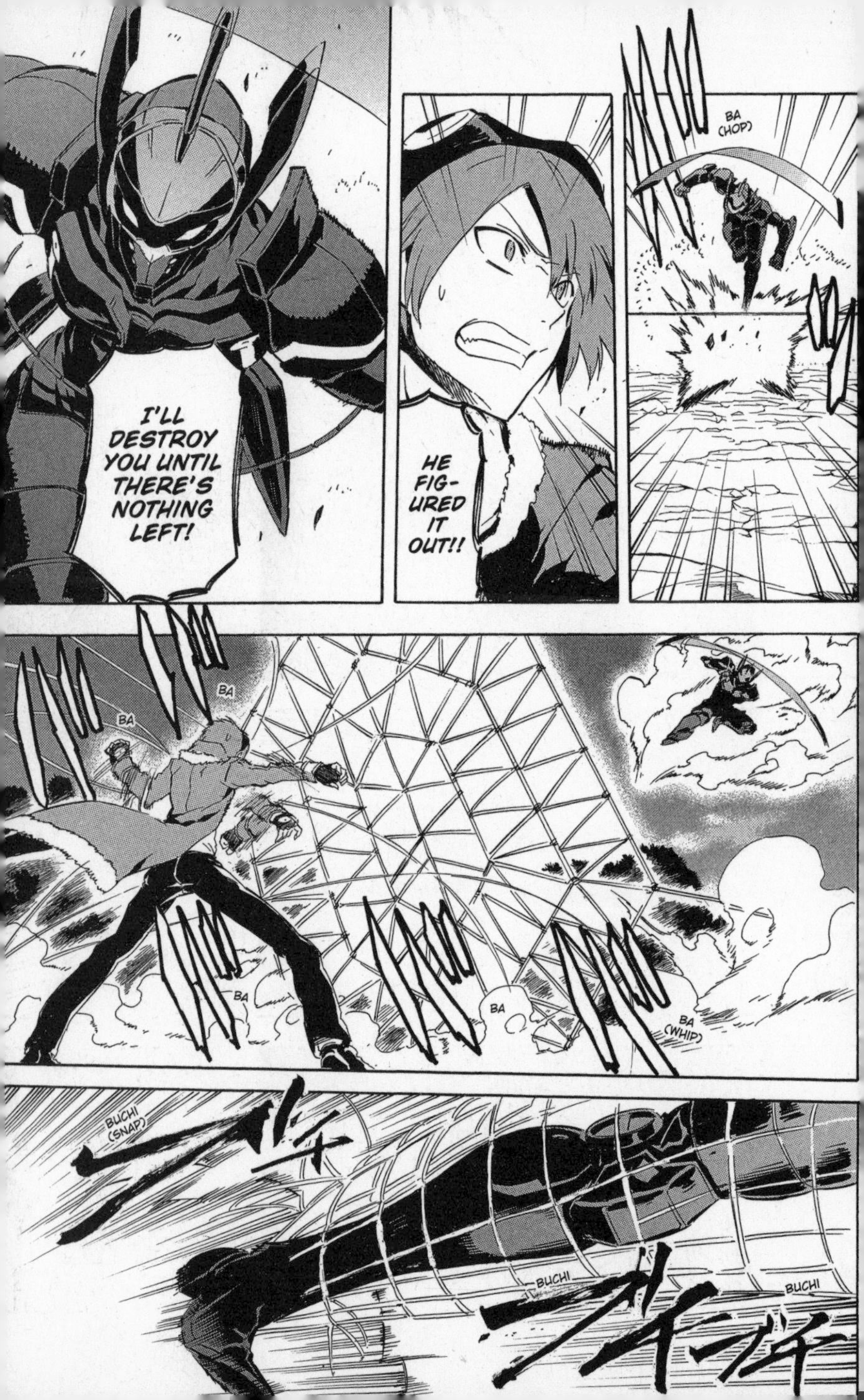
BA
(HOP)
HE FIG-URED IT OUT!!
I'LL DESTROY YOU UNTIL THERE'S NOTHING LEFT!
BA
BA
BA
(WHIP)
BA
BA
BUCHI
(SNAP)
BUCHI
BUCHI

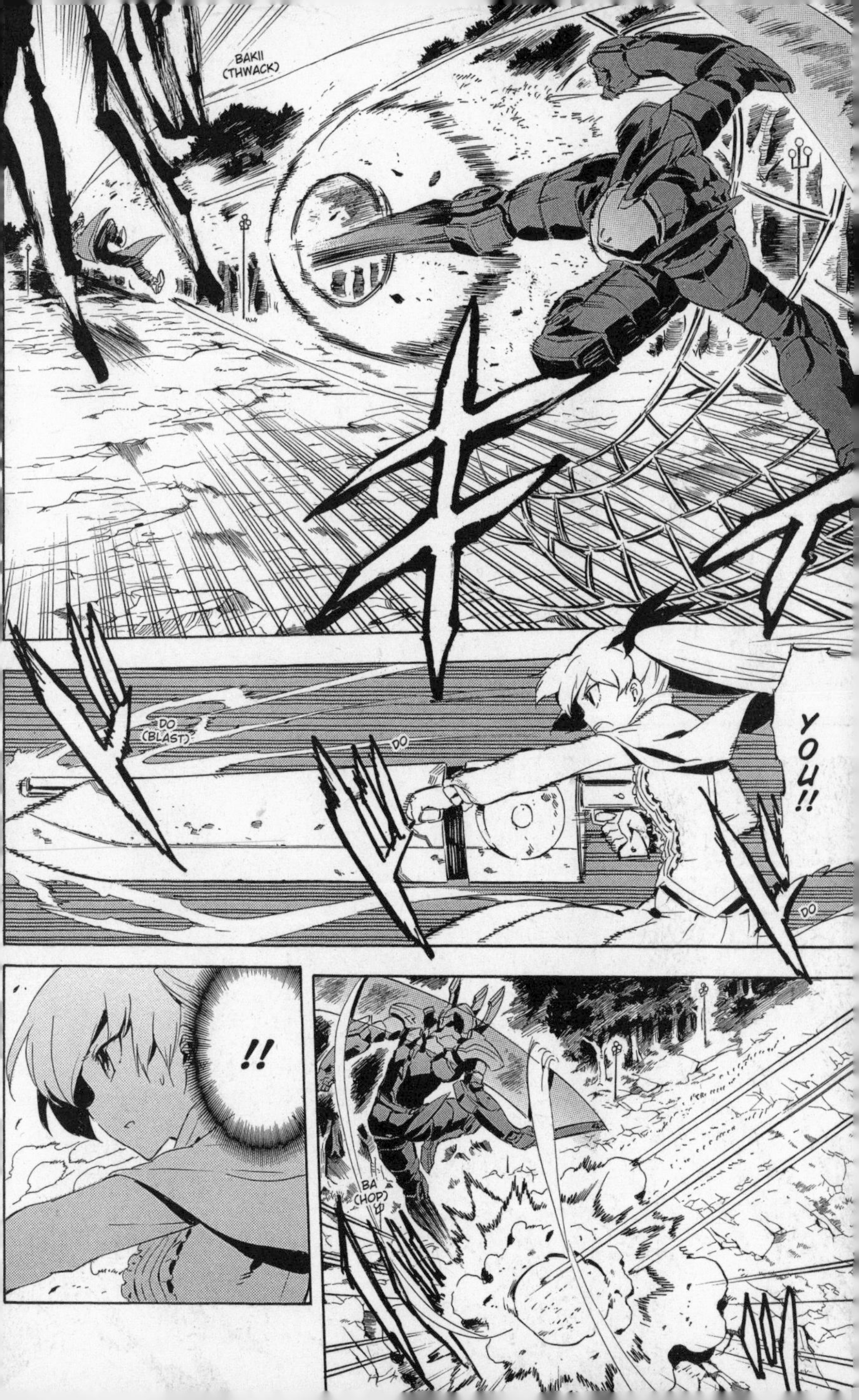
BAKII
(THWACK)
YOU!!
DO
DO
DO
(BLAST)
BA
(HOP)
!!

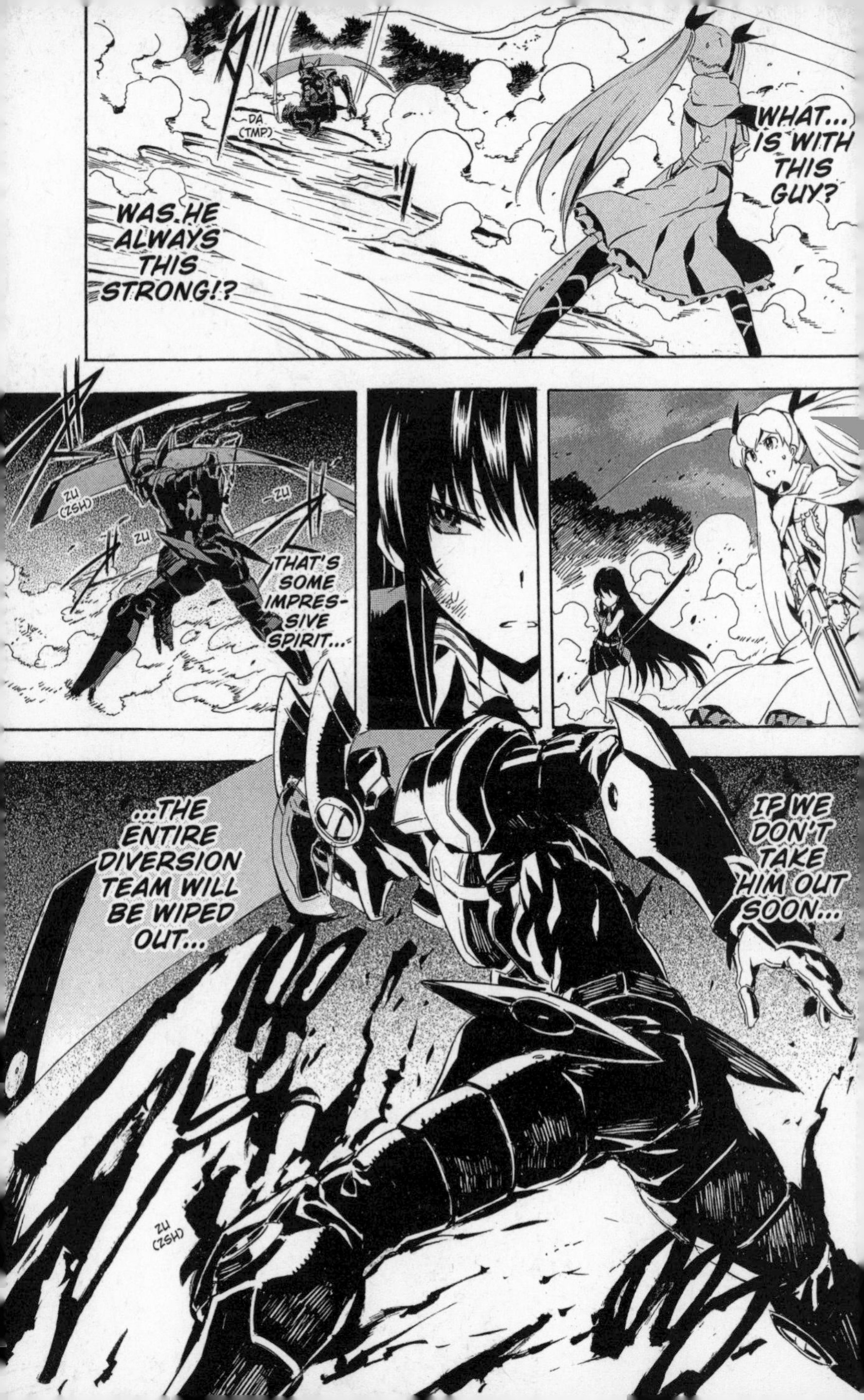
WHAT... IS WITH THIS GUY?
DA (TMP)
WAS HE ALWAYS THIS STRONG!?
THAT'S SOME IMPRESSIVE SPIRIT...
ZU
ZU (ZSH)
ZU
IF WE DON'T TAKE HIM OUT SOON...
...THE ENTIRE DIVERSION TEAM WILL BE WIPED OUT...
ZU (ZSH)

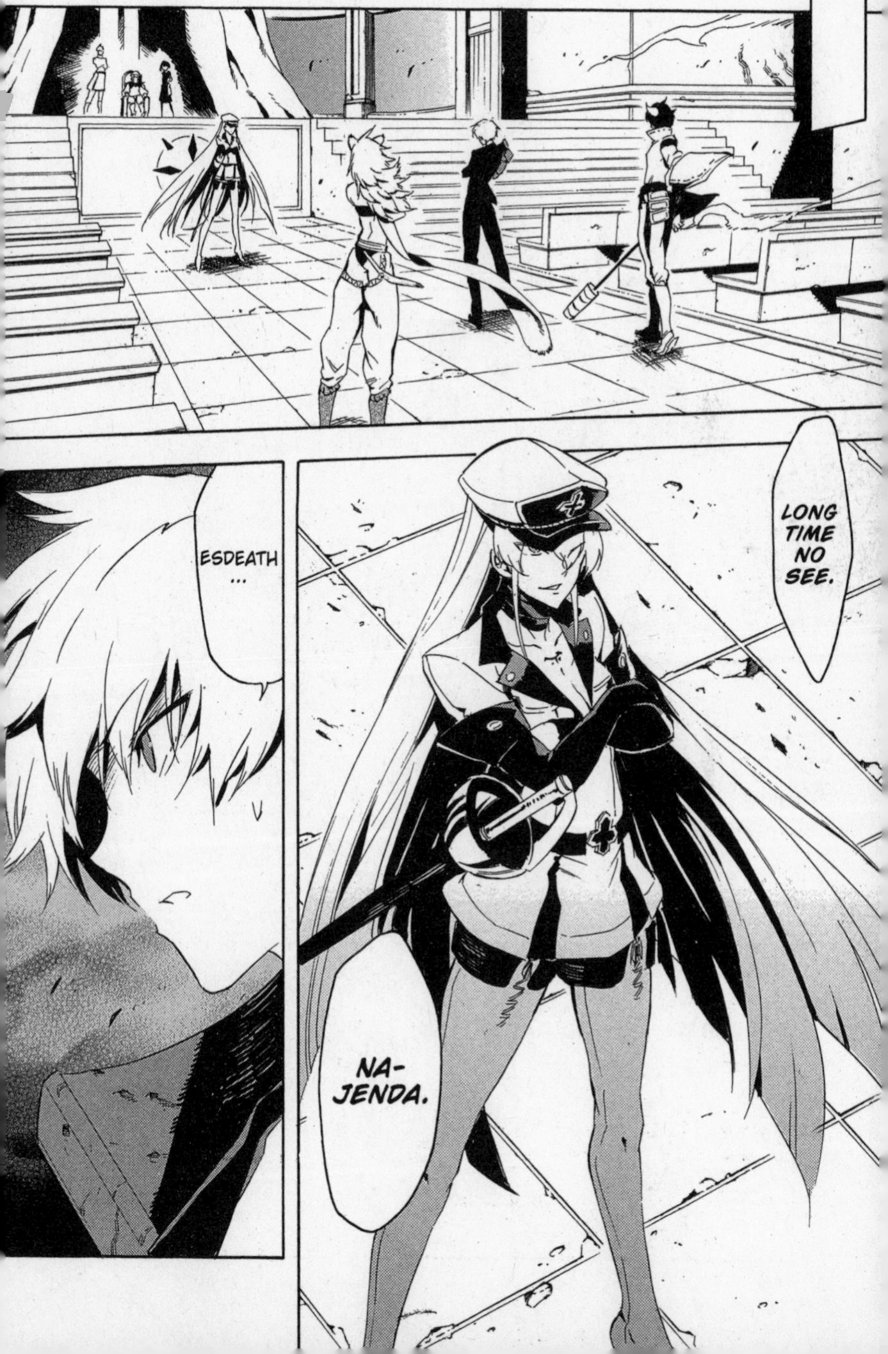
LONG TIME NO SEE.
NA-JENDA.
ESDEATH ...

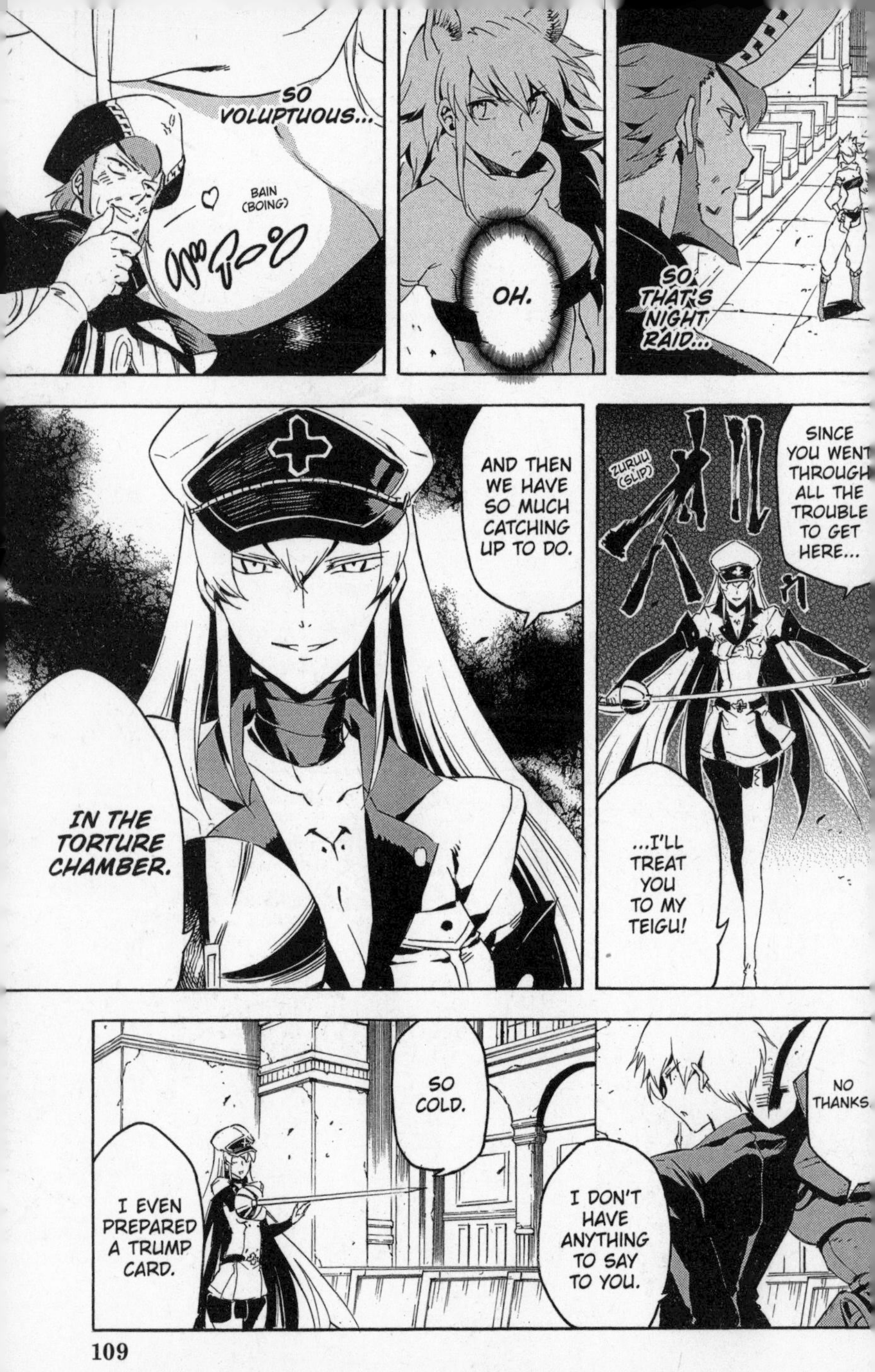
SO THAT'S NIGHT RAID...
OH.
SO VOLUPTUOUS...
BAIN (BOING)
SINCE YOU WENT THROUGH ALL THE TROUBLE TO GET HERE...
ZURUU (SLIP)
...I'LL TREAT YOU TO MY TEIGU!
AND THEN WE HAVE SO MUCH CATCHING UP TO DO.
IN THE TORTURE CHAMBER.
NO THANKS.
I DON'T HAVE ANYTHING TO SAY TO YOU.
SO COLD.
I EVEN PREPARED A TRUMP CARD.

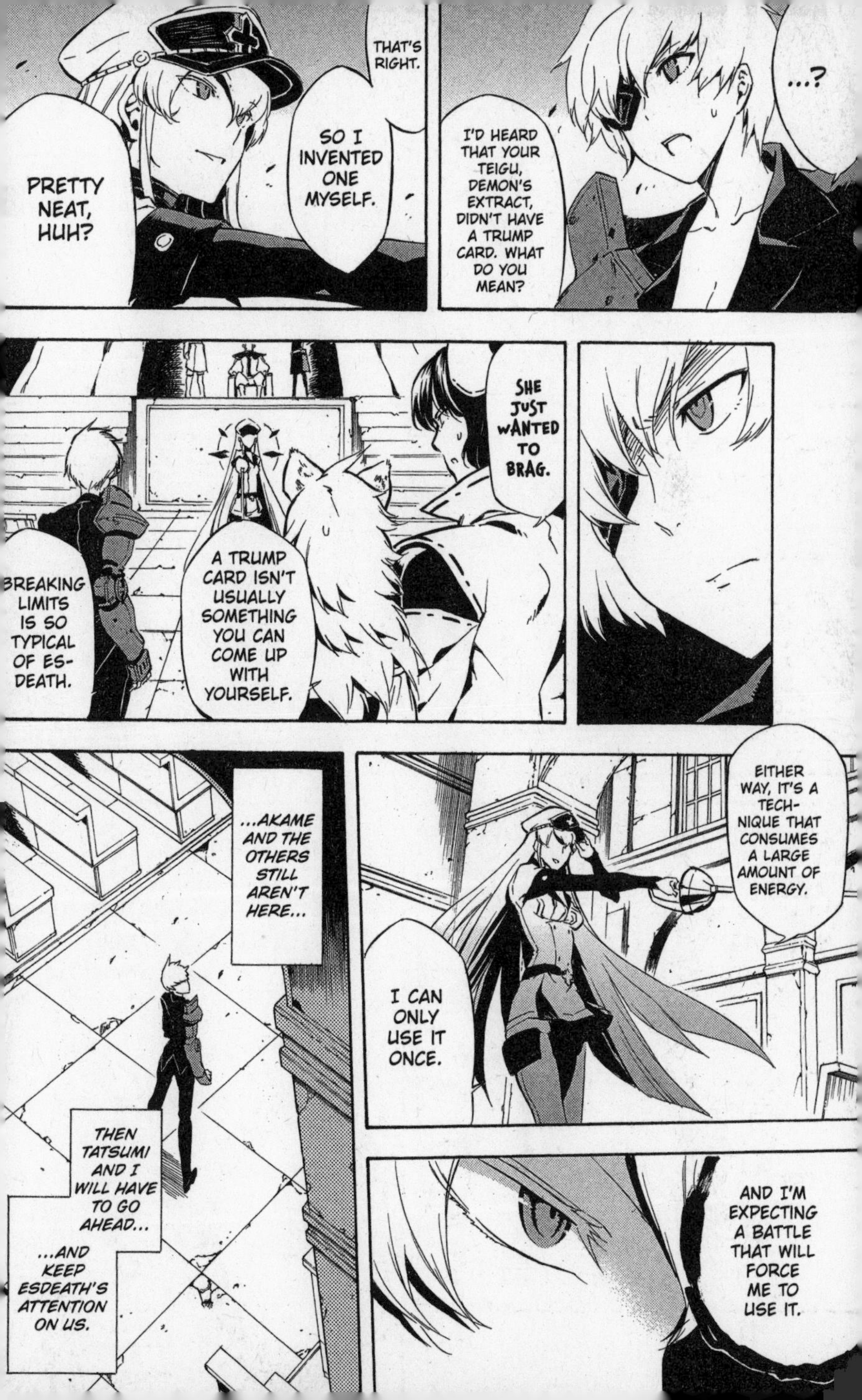
...?
I'D HEARD THAT YOUR TEIGU, DEMON'S EXTRACT, DIDN'T HAVE A TRUMP CARD. WHAT DO YOU MEAN?
THAT'S RIGHT.
SO I INVENTED ONE MYSELF.
PRETTY NEAT, HUH?
SHE JUST WANTED TO BRAG.
A TRUMP CARD ISN'T USUALLY SOMETHING YOU CAN COME UP WITH YOURSELF.
BREAKING LIMITS IS SO TYPICAL OF ES-DEATH.
EITHER WAY, IT'S A TECH-NIQUE THAT CONSUMES A LARGE AMOUNT OF ENERGY.
I CAN ONLY USE IT ONCE.
AND I'M EXPECTING A BATTLE THAT WILL FORCE ME TO USE IT.
...AKAME AND THE OTHERS STILL AREN'T HERE...
THEN TATSUMI AND I WILL HAVE TO GO AHEAD...
...AND KEEP ESDEATH'S ATTENTION ON US.

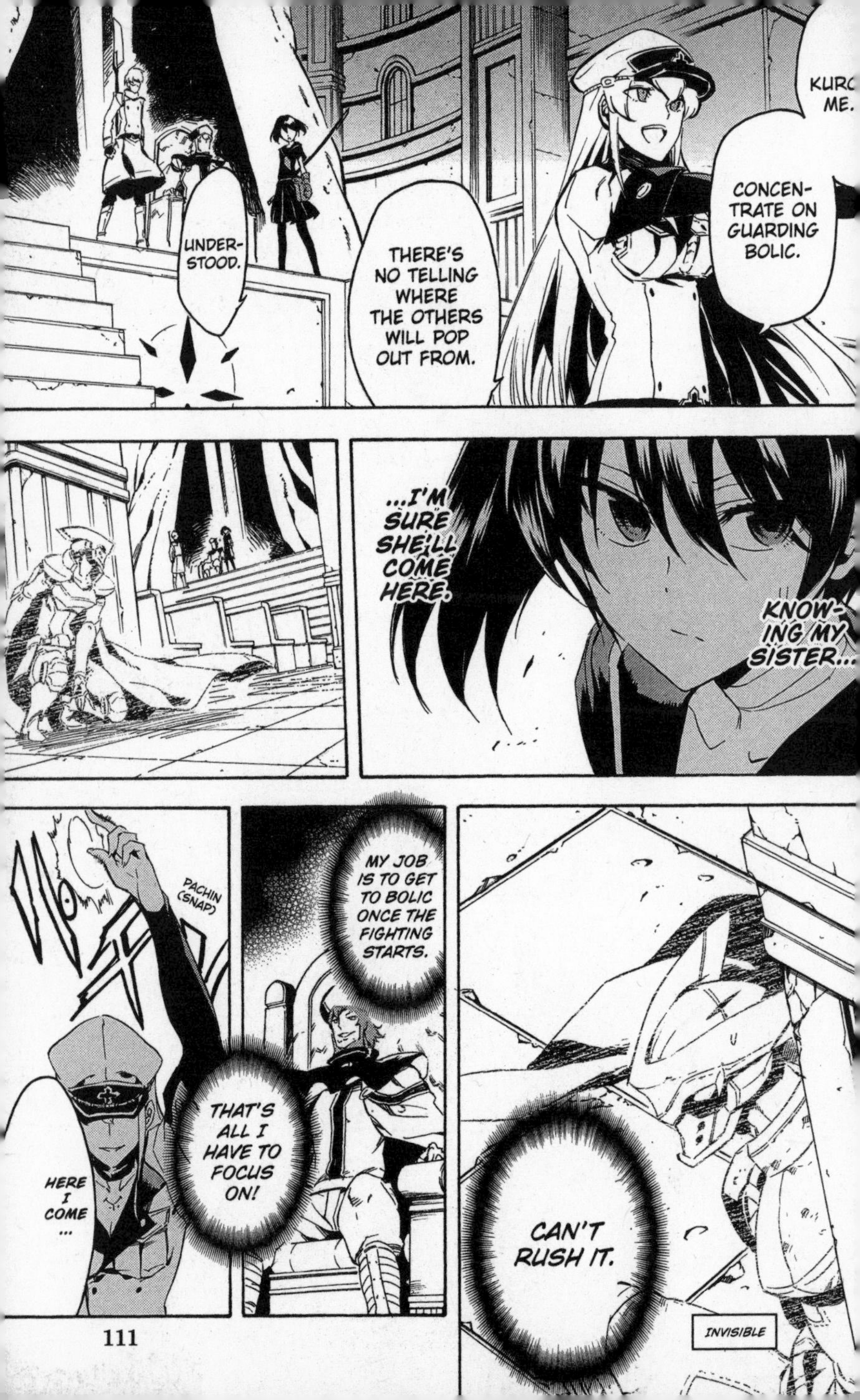
KURO ME.
CONCEN-TRATE ON GUARDING BOLIC.
THERE'S NO TELLING WHERE THE OTHERS WILL POP OUT FROM.
UNDER-STOOD.
KNOW-ING MY SISTER...
...I'M SURE SHE'LL COME HERE.
CAN'T RUSH IT.
INVISIBLE
MY JOB IS TO GET TO BOLIC ONCE THE FIGHTING STARTS.
THAT'S ALL I HAVE TO FOCUS ON!
PACHIN (SNAP)
HERE I COME ...

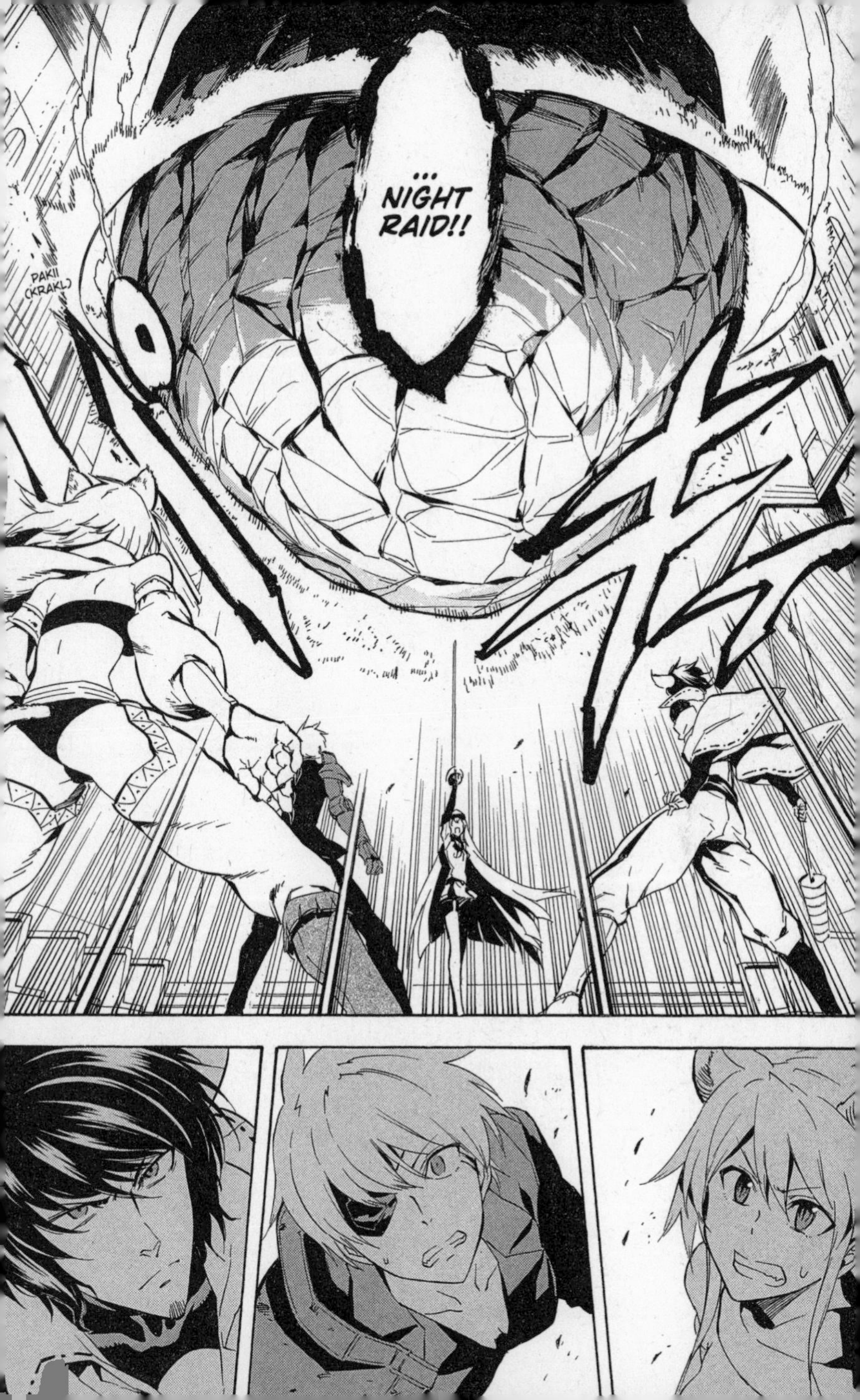
... NIGHT RAID!!
PAKII (KRAKL)

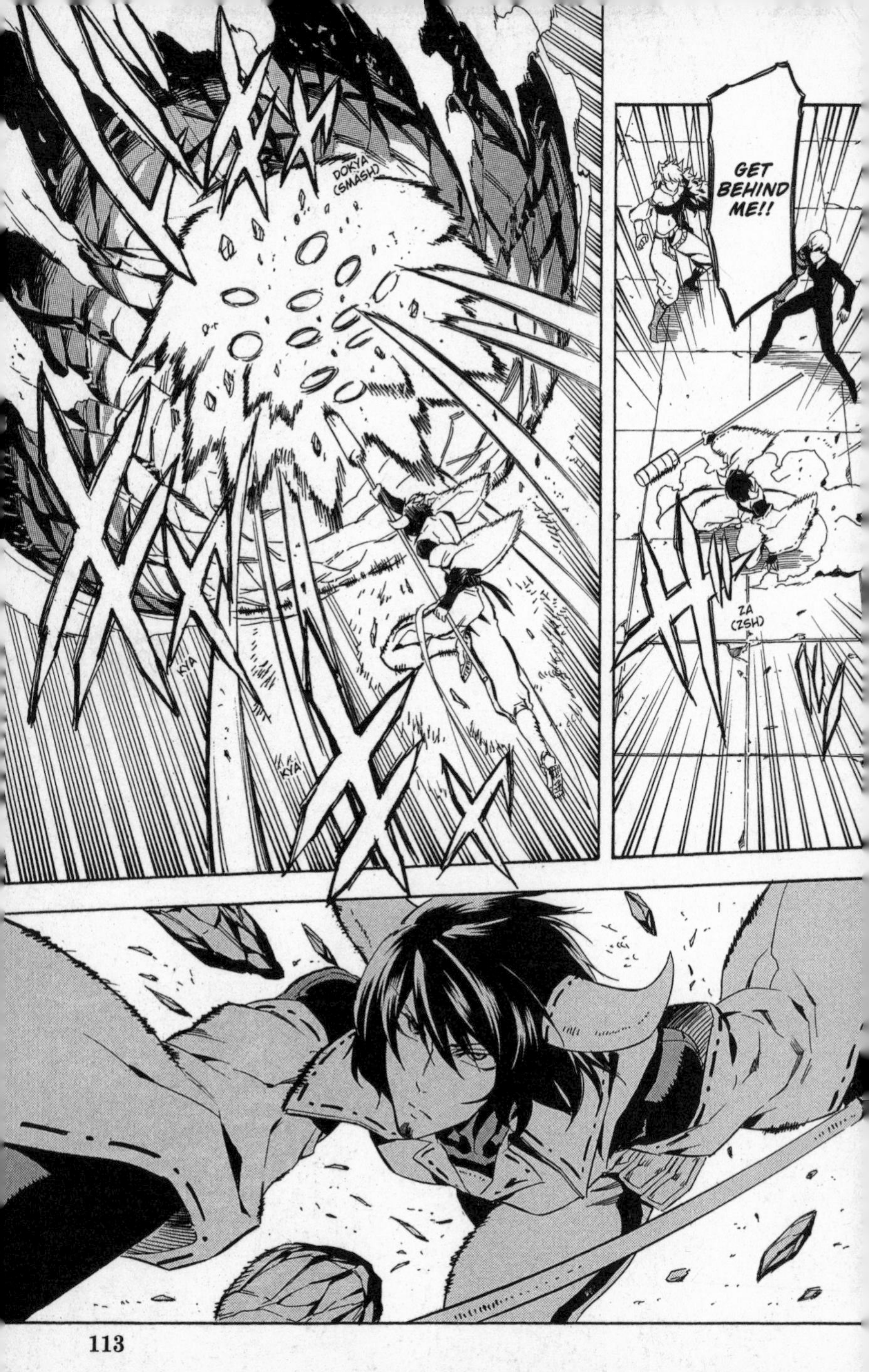
GET BEHIND ME!!
ZA (ZSH)
DOKYA (SMASH)
KYA
K-K-KYA

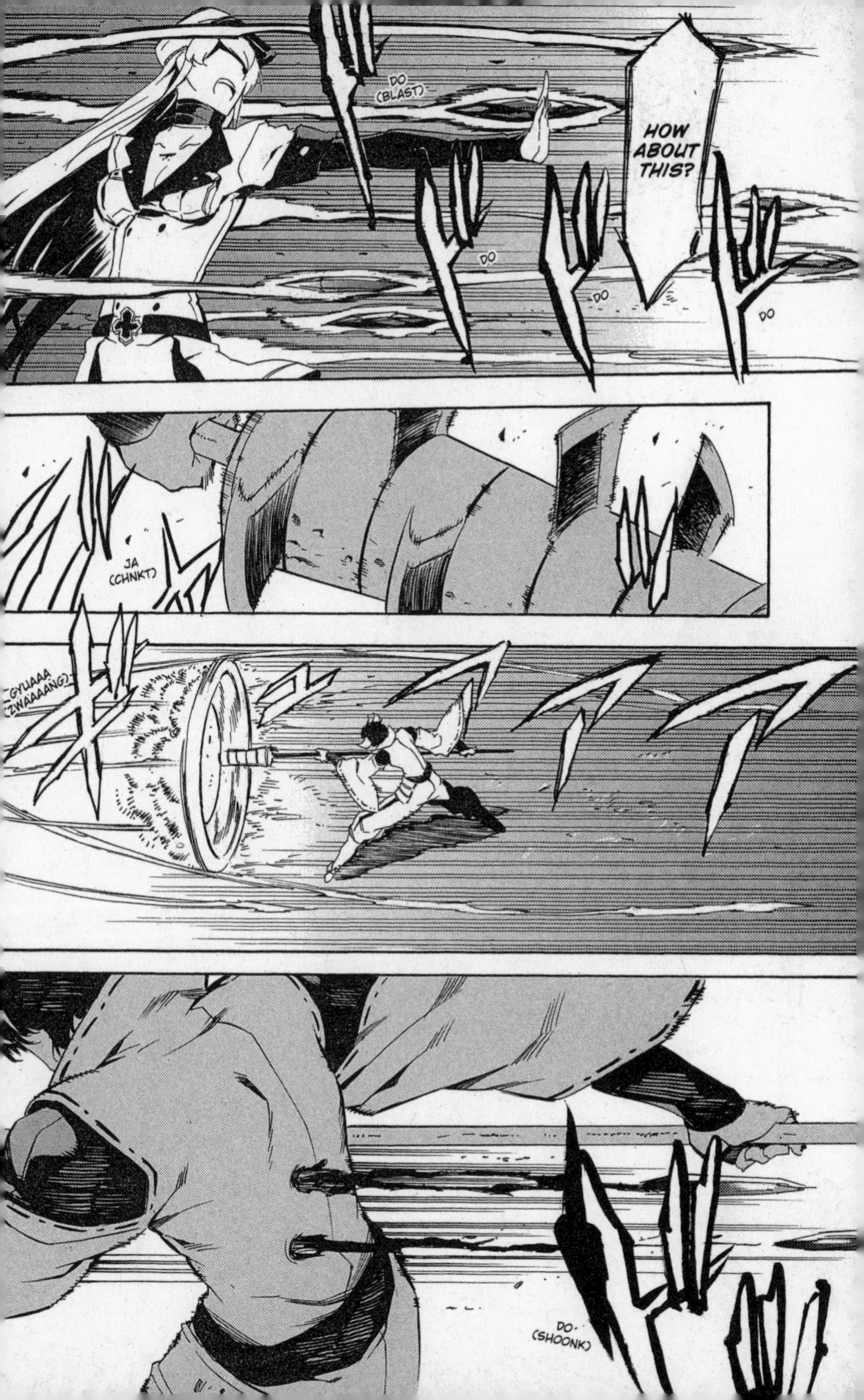
HOW ABOUT THIS?
DO (BLAST)
DO
DO
DO
JA (CHNKT)
GYUAAA (ZWAAAANG)
DO (SHOONK)

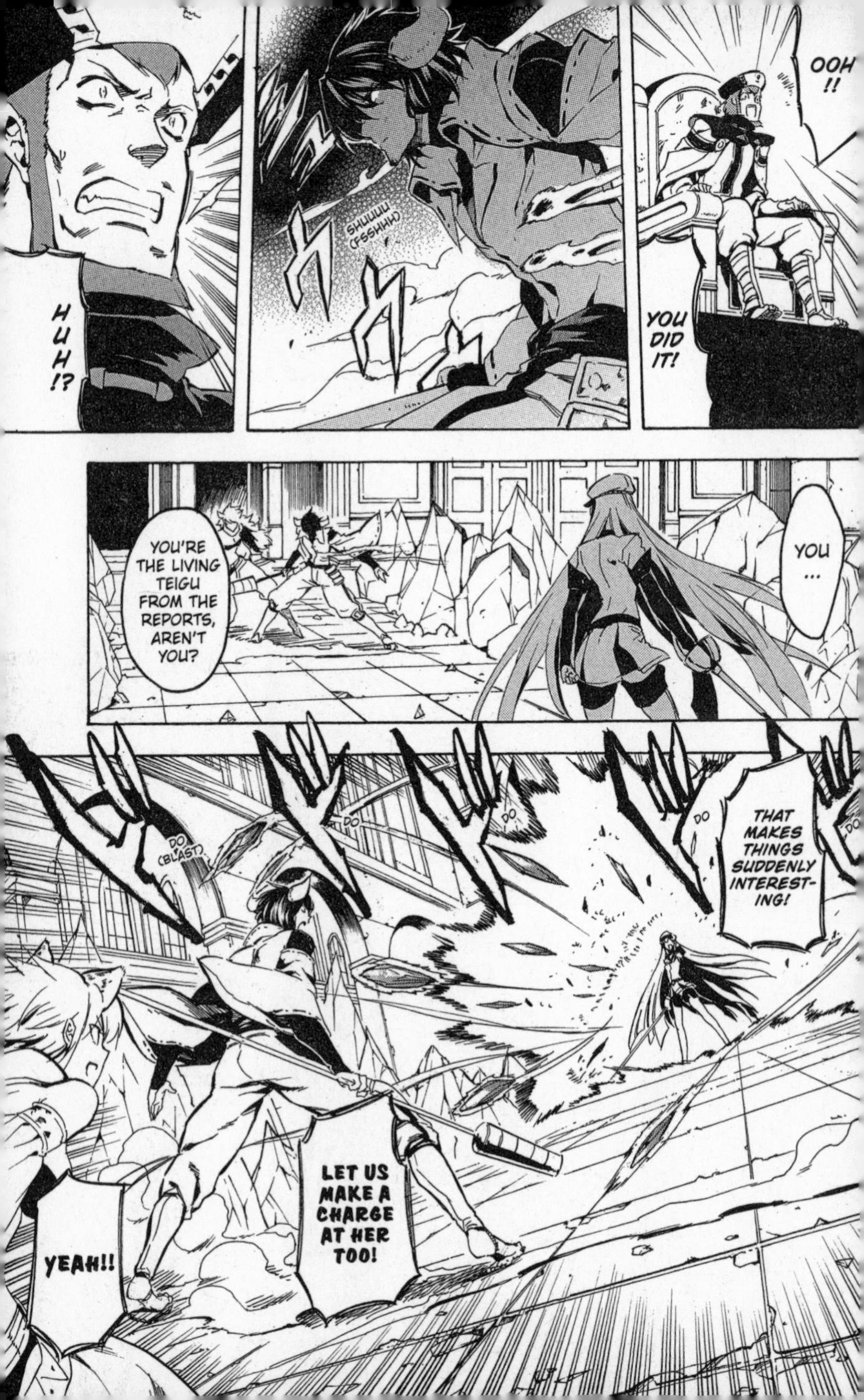
OOH!!
YOU DID IT!
SHUUUUN (FSSHHH)
HUH!?
YOU...
YOU'RE THE LIVING TEIGU FROM THE REPORTS, AREN'T YOU?
THAT MAKES THINGS SUDDENLY INTEREST-ING!
DO
DO
DO
DO (BLAST)
LET US MAKE A CHARGE AT HER TOO!
YEAH!!

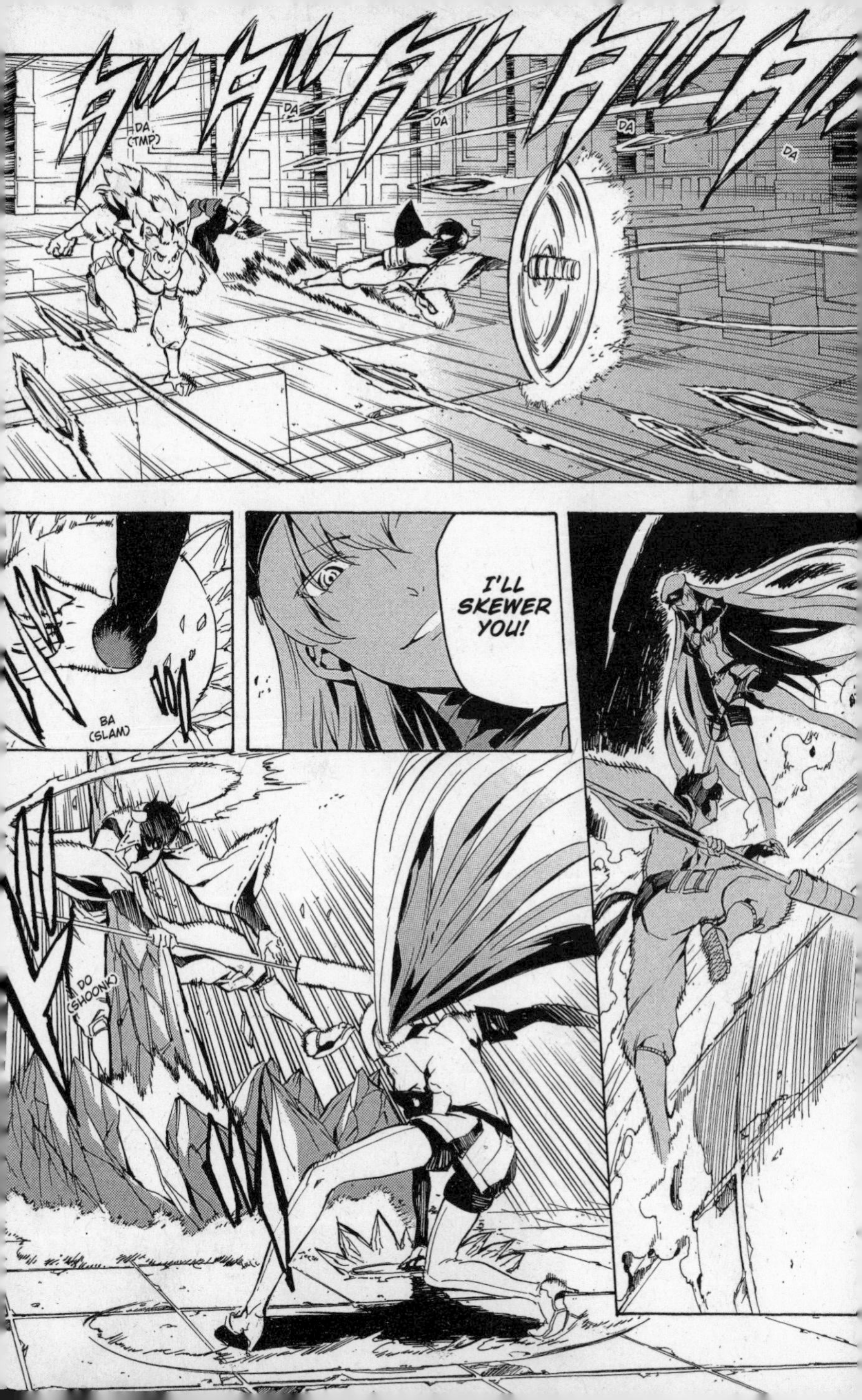

DA
DA
DA
DA
DA (TMP)
I'LL SKEWER YOU!
BA (SLAM)
DO (SHOONK)

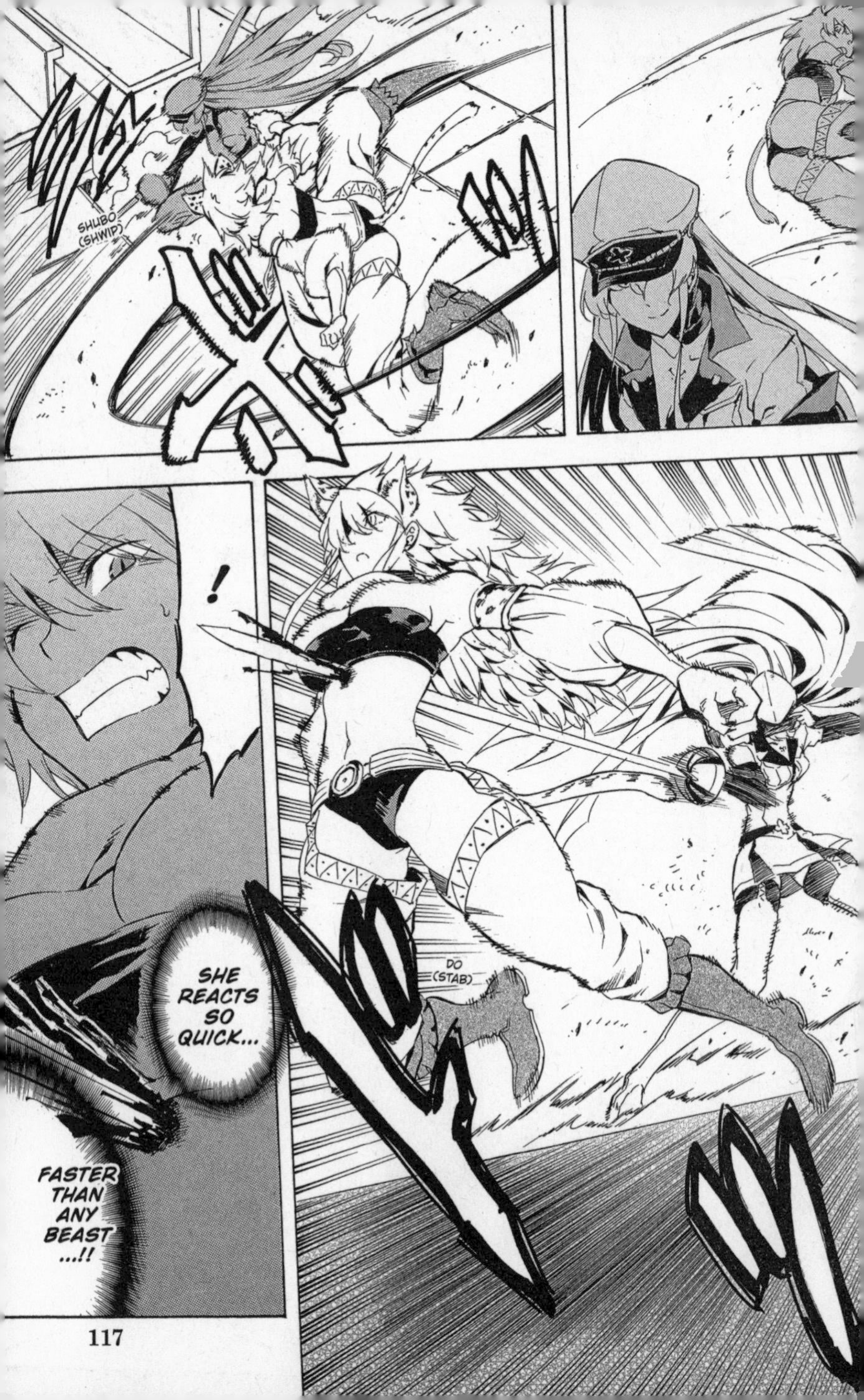
SHUBO (SHWIP)
DO (STAB)
!
SHE REACTS SO QUICK...
FASTER THAN ANY BEAST ...!!

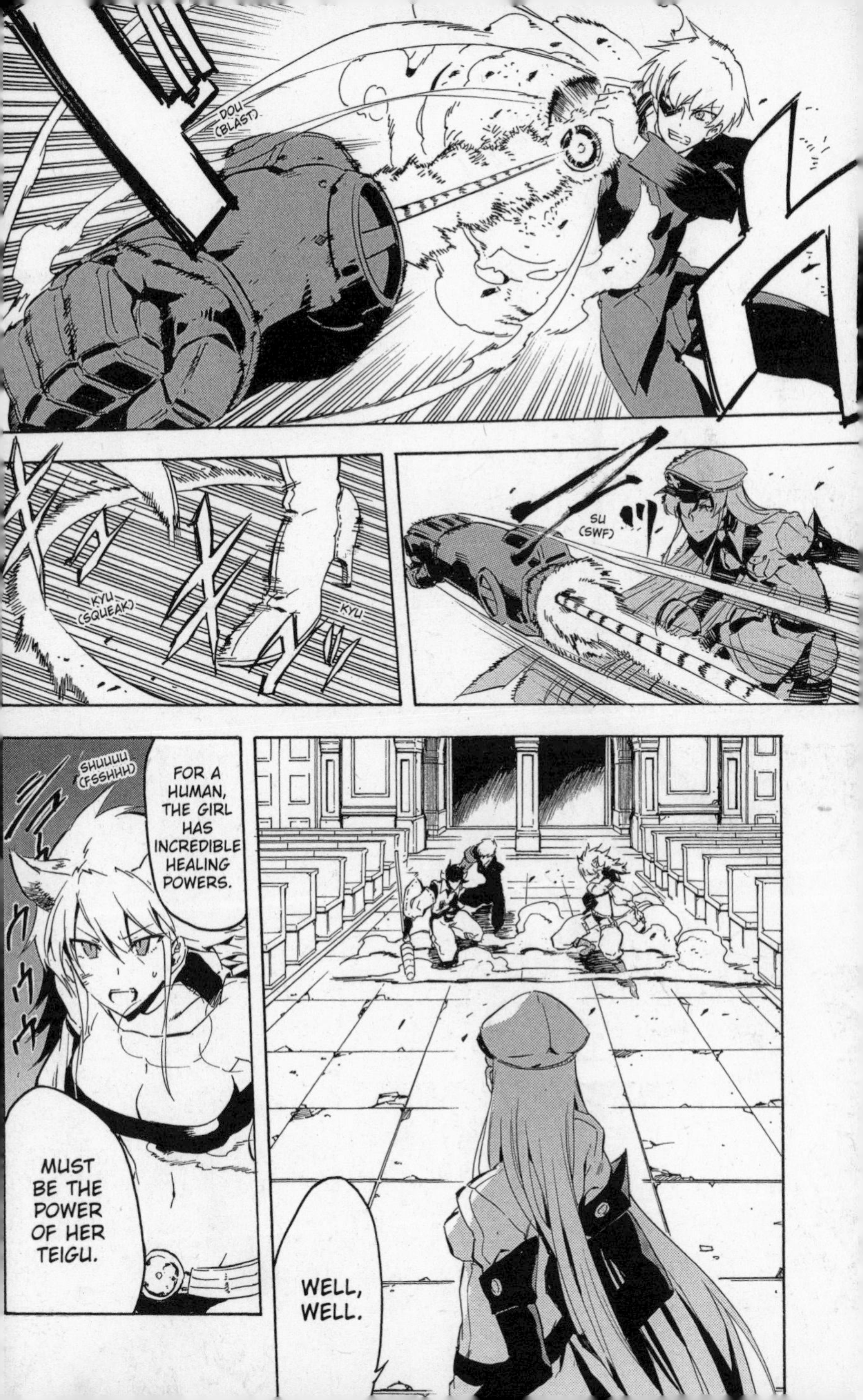
DOU (BLAST)
SU (SWF)
KYU (SQUEAK)
KYU
WELL, WELL.
SHUUUU (FSSHHH)
FOR A HUMAN, THE GIRL HAS INCREDIBLE HEALING POWERS.
MUST BE THE POWER OF HER TEIGU.

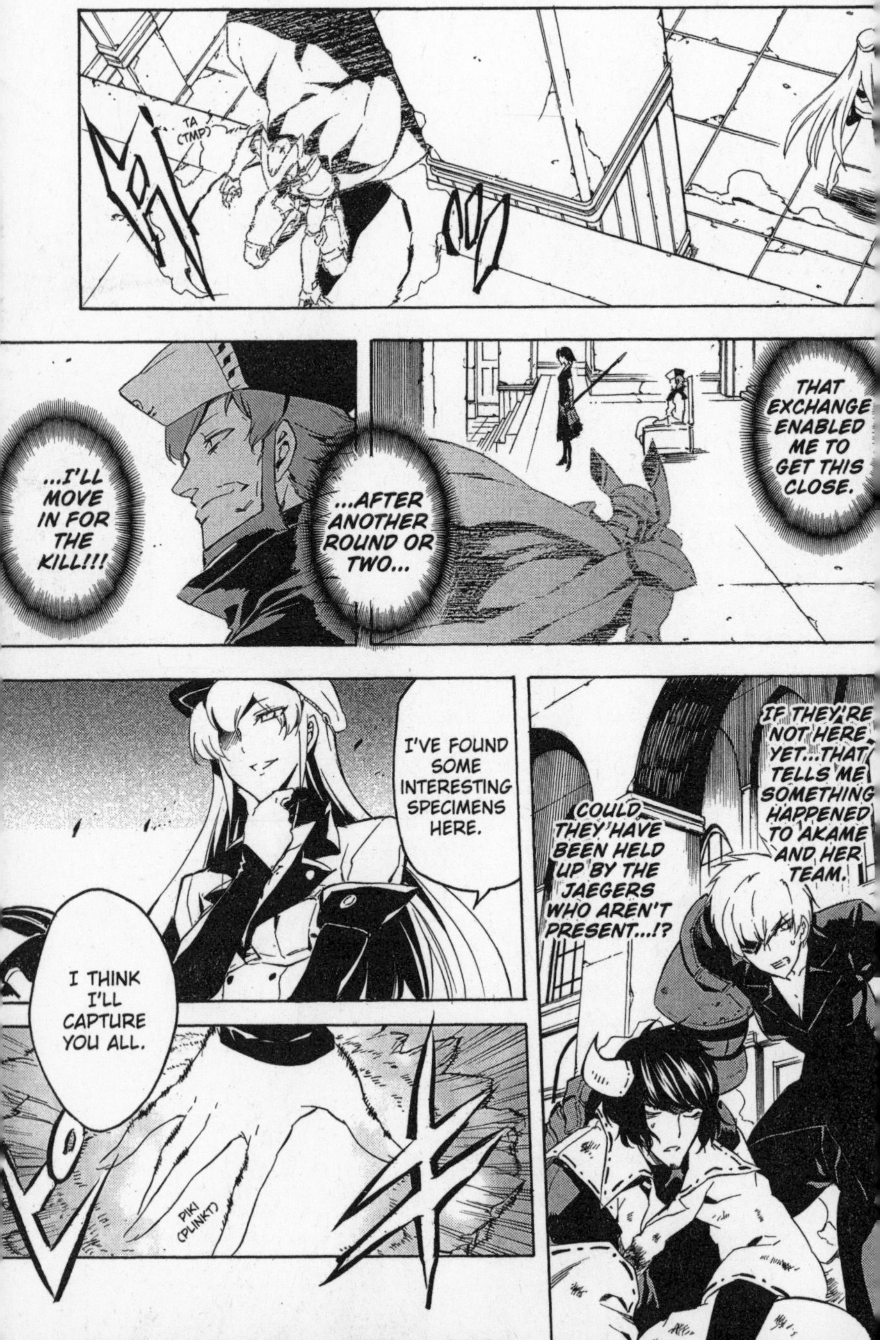
TA (TMP)
THAT EXCHANGE ENABLED ME TO GET THIS CLOSE.
...AFTER ANOTHER ROUND OR TWO...
...I'LL MOVE IN FOR THE KILL!!!
IF THEY'RE NOT HERE YET...THAT TELLS ME SOMETHING HAPPENED TO AKAME AND HER TEAM.
COULD THEY HAVE BEEN HELD UP BY THE JAEGERS WHO AREN'T PRESENT...!?
I'VE FOUND SOME INTERESTING SPECIMENS HERE.
I THINK I'LL CAPTURE YOU ALL.
PIKI (PLINK!)

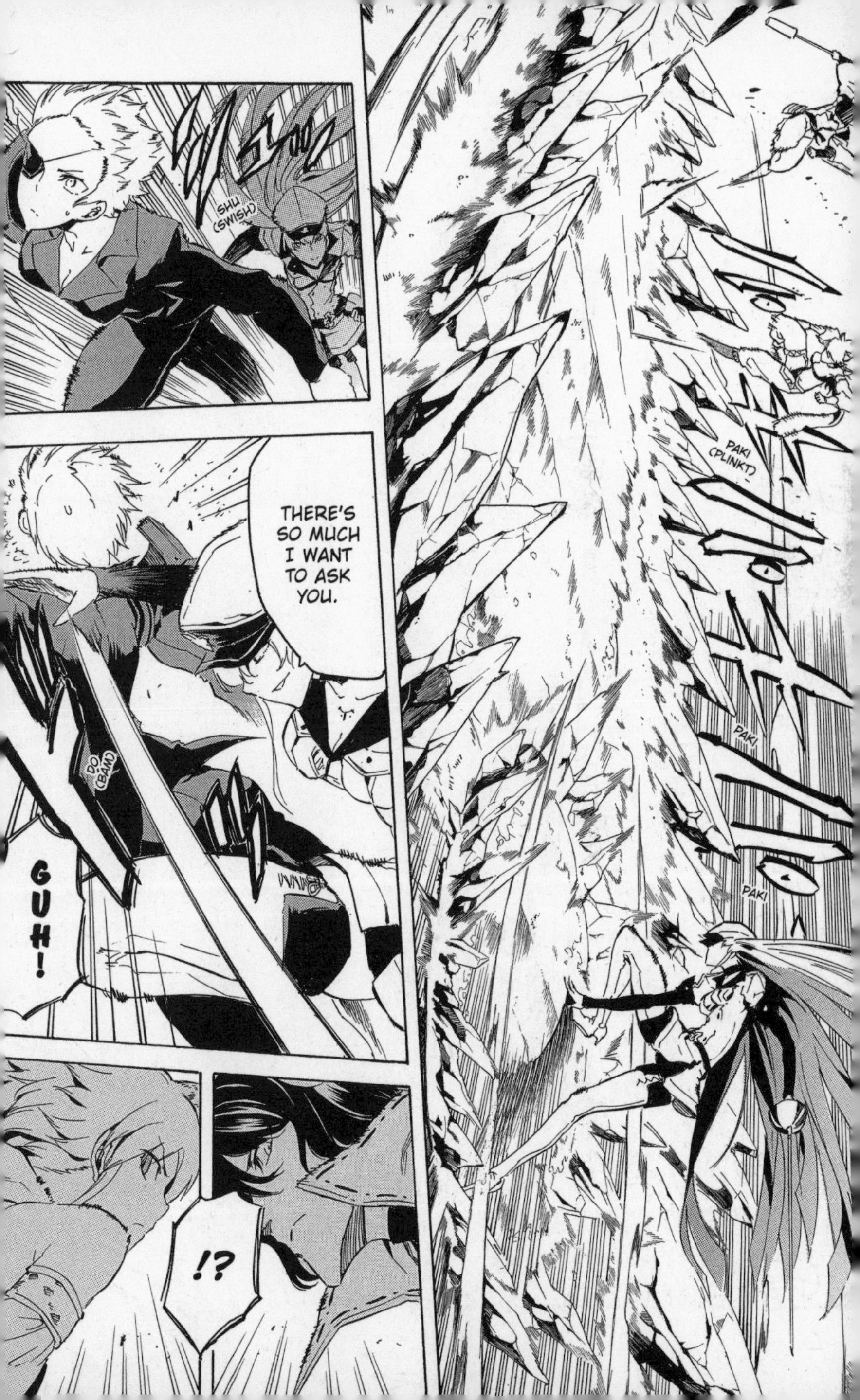
PAKI (PLINKT)
PAKI
PAKI
SHU (SWISH)
THERE'S SO MUCH I WANT TO ASK YOU.
DO (BAM)
GUH!
!?

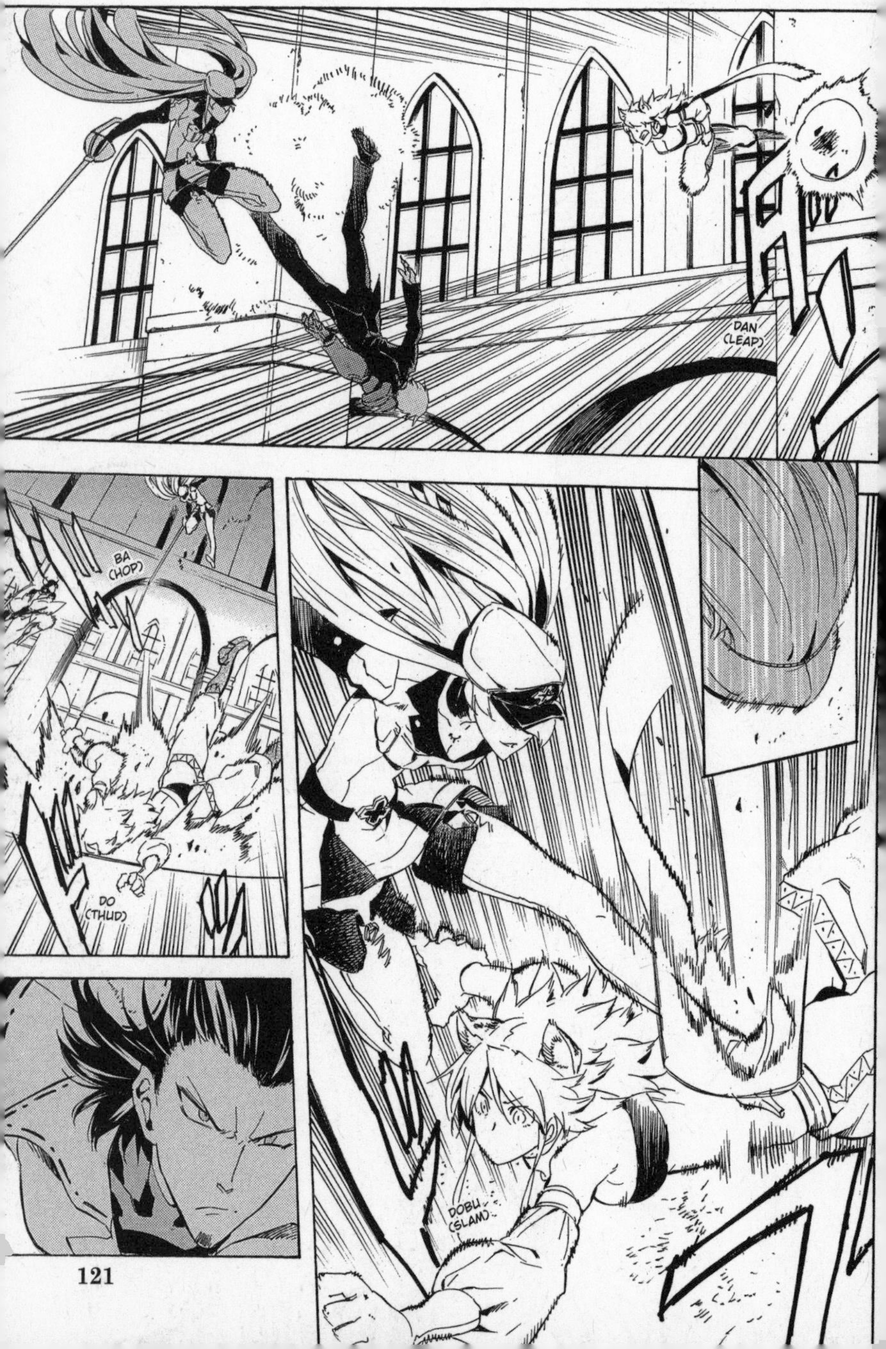
DAN
(LEAP)
DOBU
(SLAM)
BA
(HOP)
DO
(THUD)

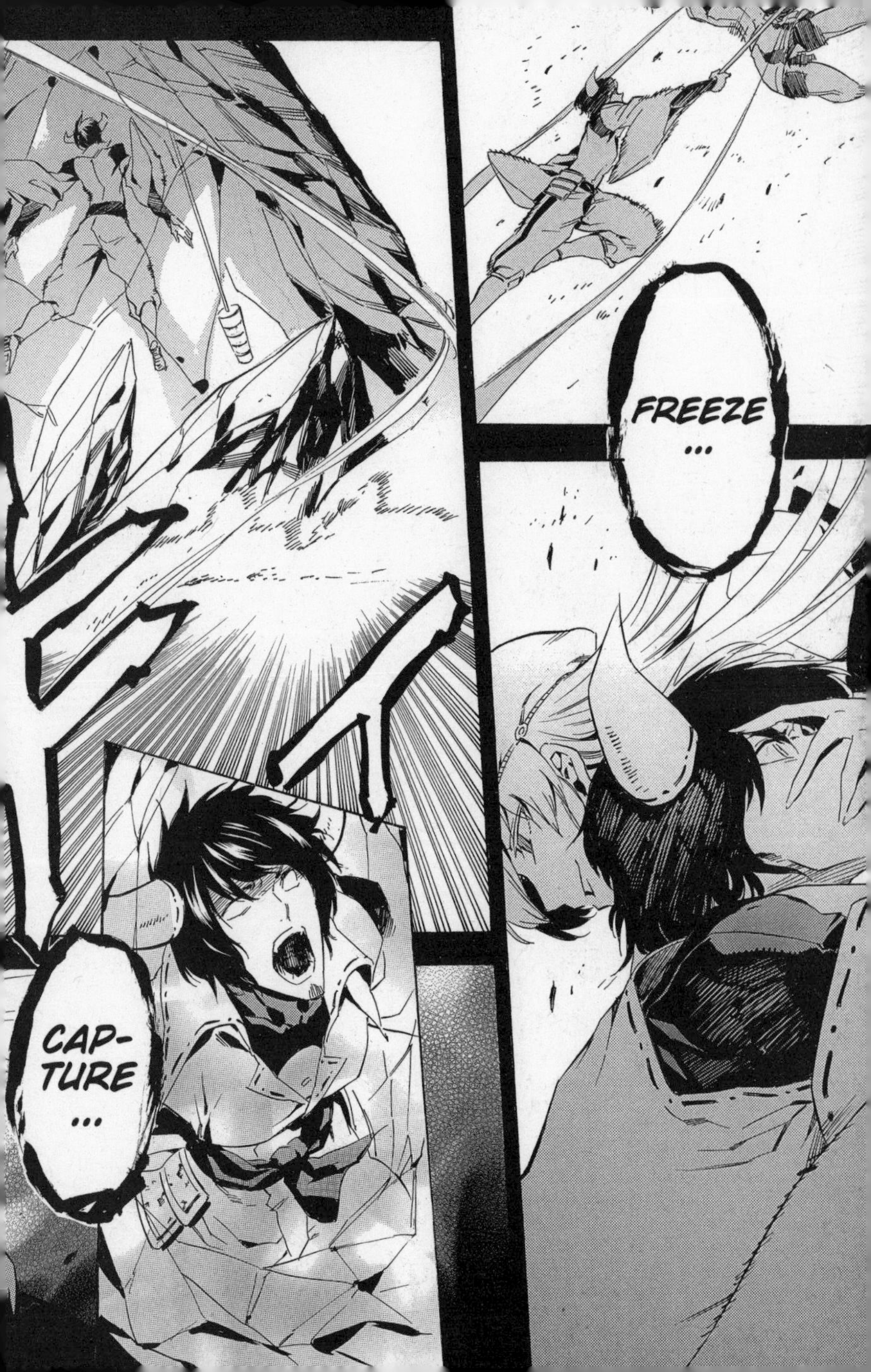
FREEZE ...
CAP-TURE ...

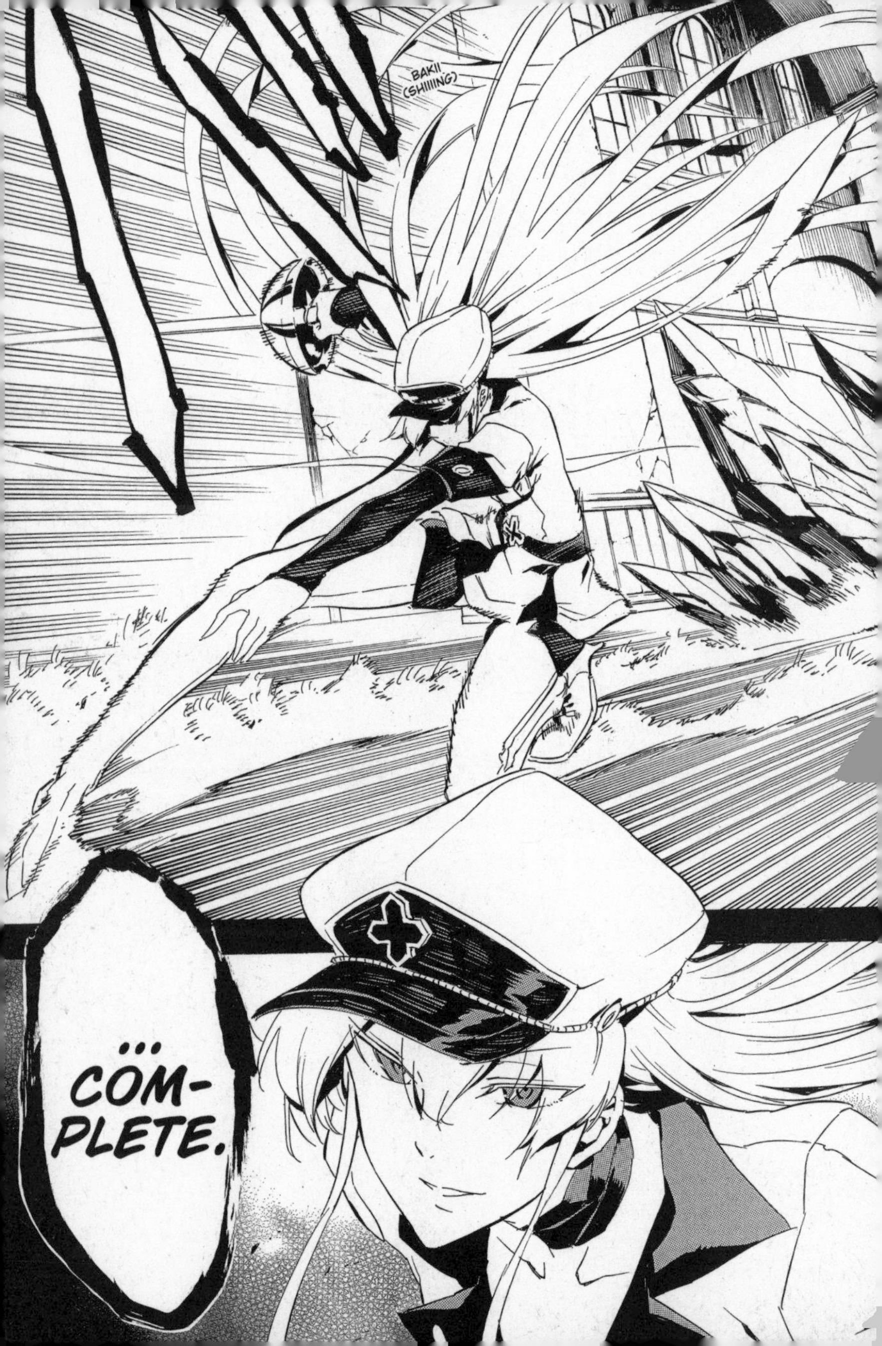
BAKII (SHIIIING)
... CÖM- PLETE.

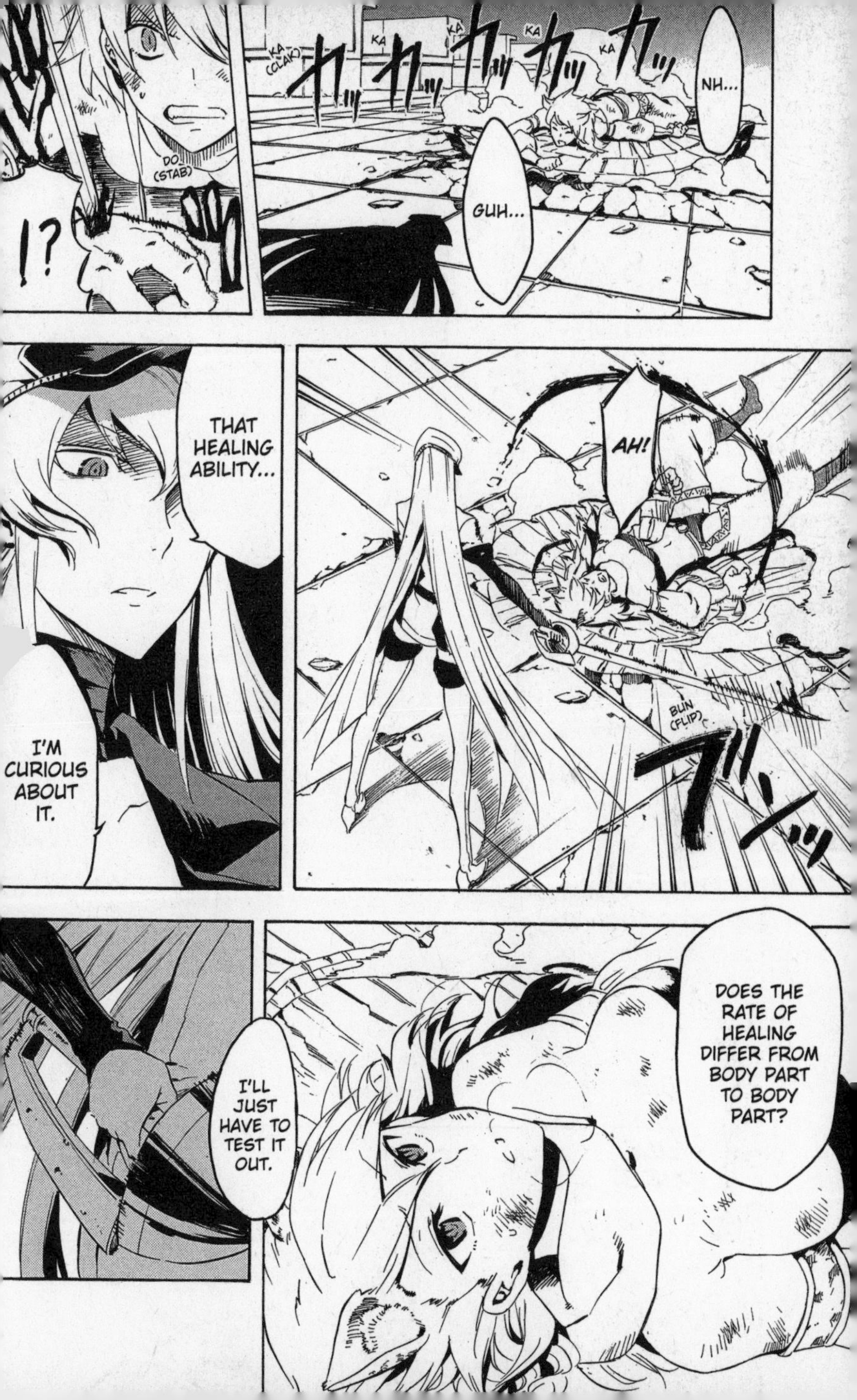
NH...
KA
KA
KA
KA (CLAK)
GUH...
DO (STAB)
!?
AH!
BUN (FLIP)
THAT HEALING ABILITY...
I'M CURIOUS ABOUT IT.
DOES THE RATE OF HEALING DIFFER FROM BODY PART TO BODY PART?
I'LL JUST HAVE TO TEST IT OUT.

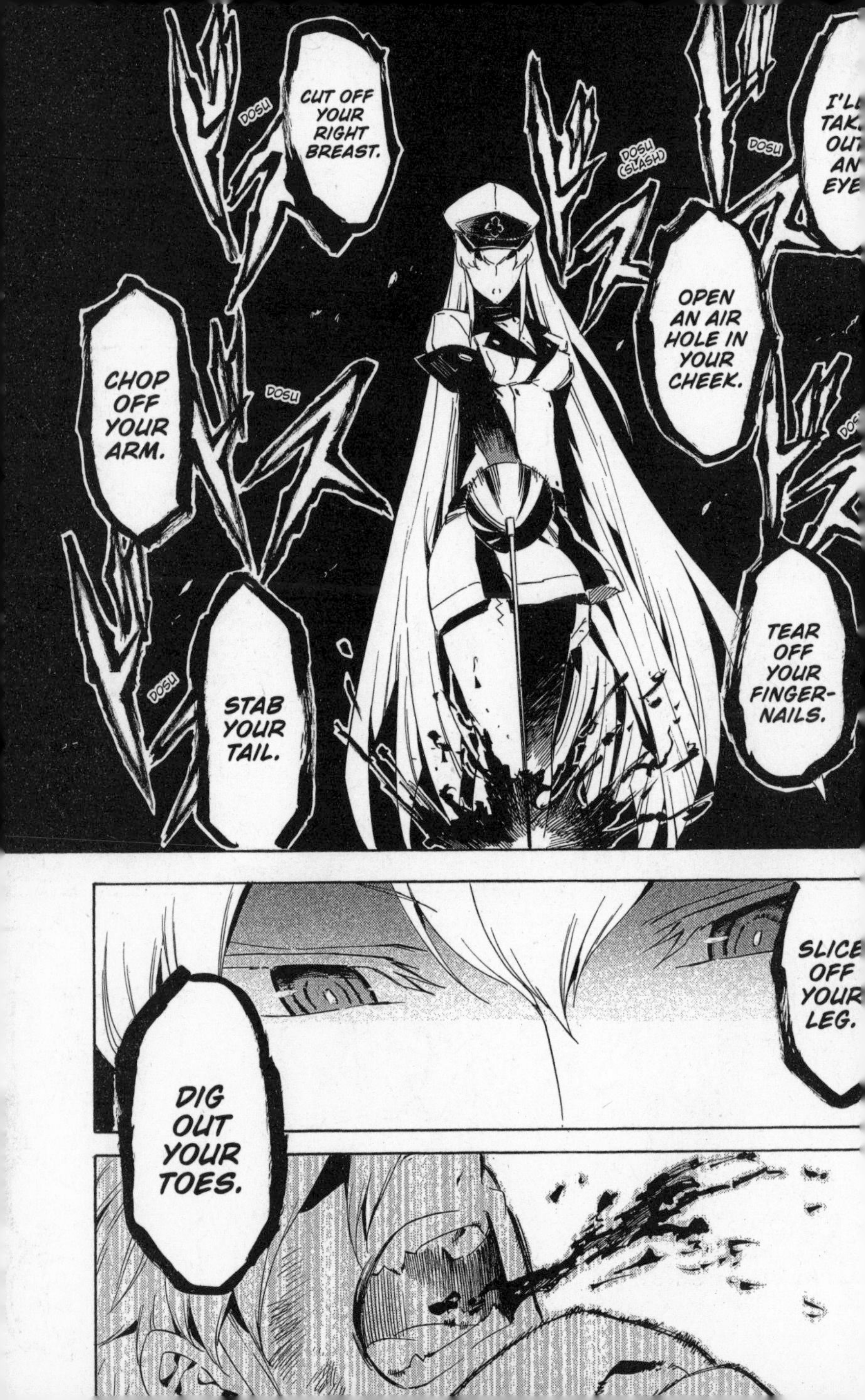

I'L TAK OUT AN EYE
DOSU
DOSU (SLASH)
OPEN AN AIR HOLE IN YOUR CHEEK.
CUT OFF YOUR RIGHT BREAST.
DOSU
TEAR OFF YOUR FINGER-NAILS.
DOSU
CHOP OFF YOUR ARM.
STAB YOUR TAIL.
DOSU
SLICE OFF YOUR LEG.
DIG OUT YOUR TOES.

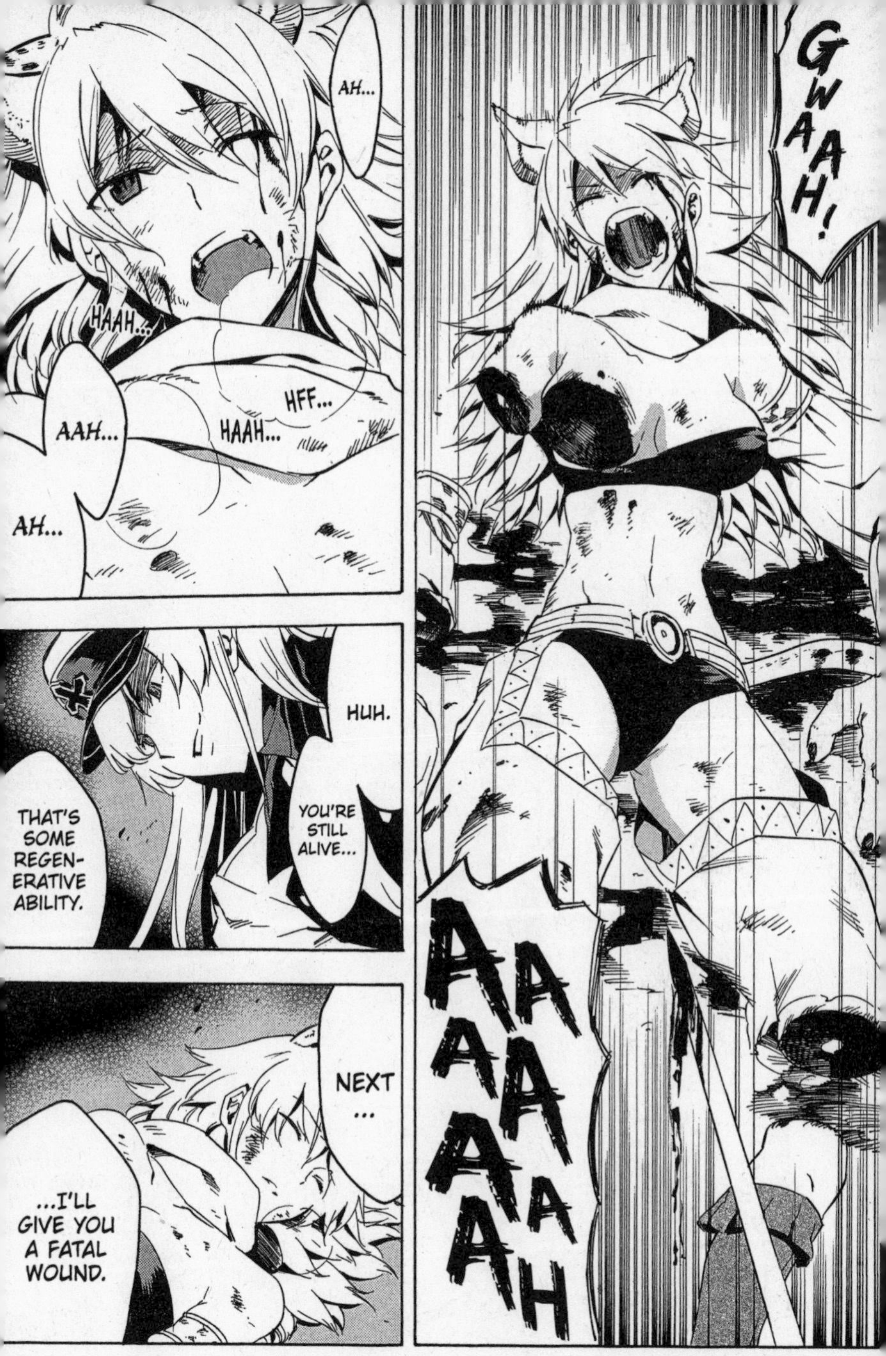
GWAH!
AAAAAAAAAH
AH...
HAAH...
HFF...
HAAH...
AAH...
AH...
HUH.
YOU'RE STILL ALIVE...
THAT'S SOME REGEN-ERATIVE ABILITY.
NEXT...
...I'LL GIVE YOU A FATAL WOUND.

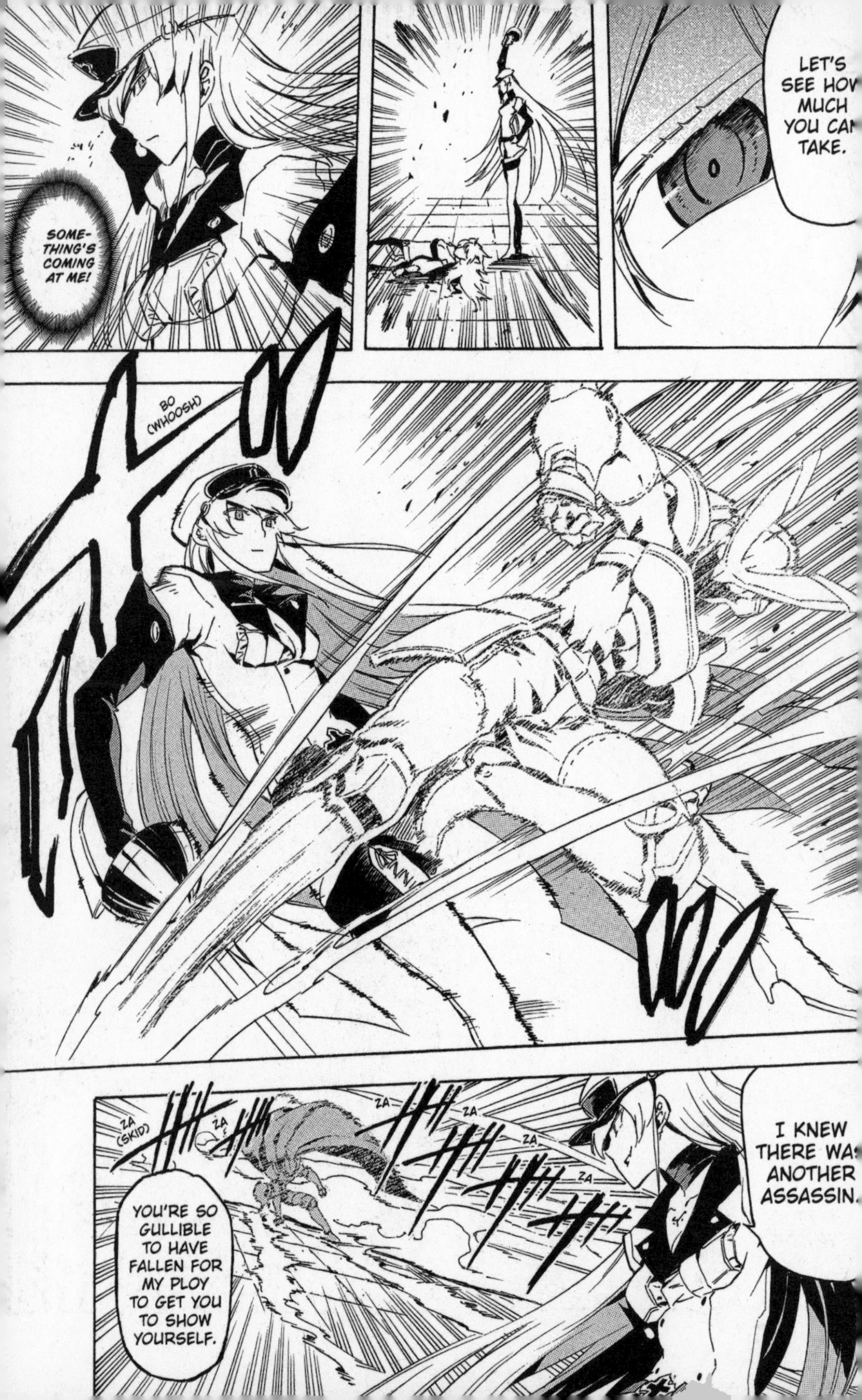
LET'S SEE HOW MUCH YOU CAN TAKE.
SOME-THING'S COMING AT ME!
BO (WHOOSH)
I KNEW THERE WAS ANOTHER ASSASSIN.
ZA
ZA
ZA
ZA
ZA
ZA
ZA (SKID)
YOU'RE SO GULLIBLE TO HAVE FALLEN FOR MY PLOY TO GET YOU TO SHOW YOURSELF.

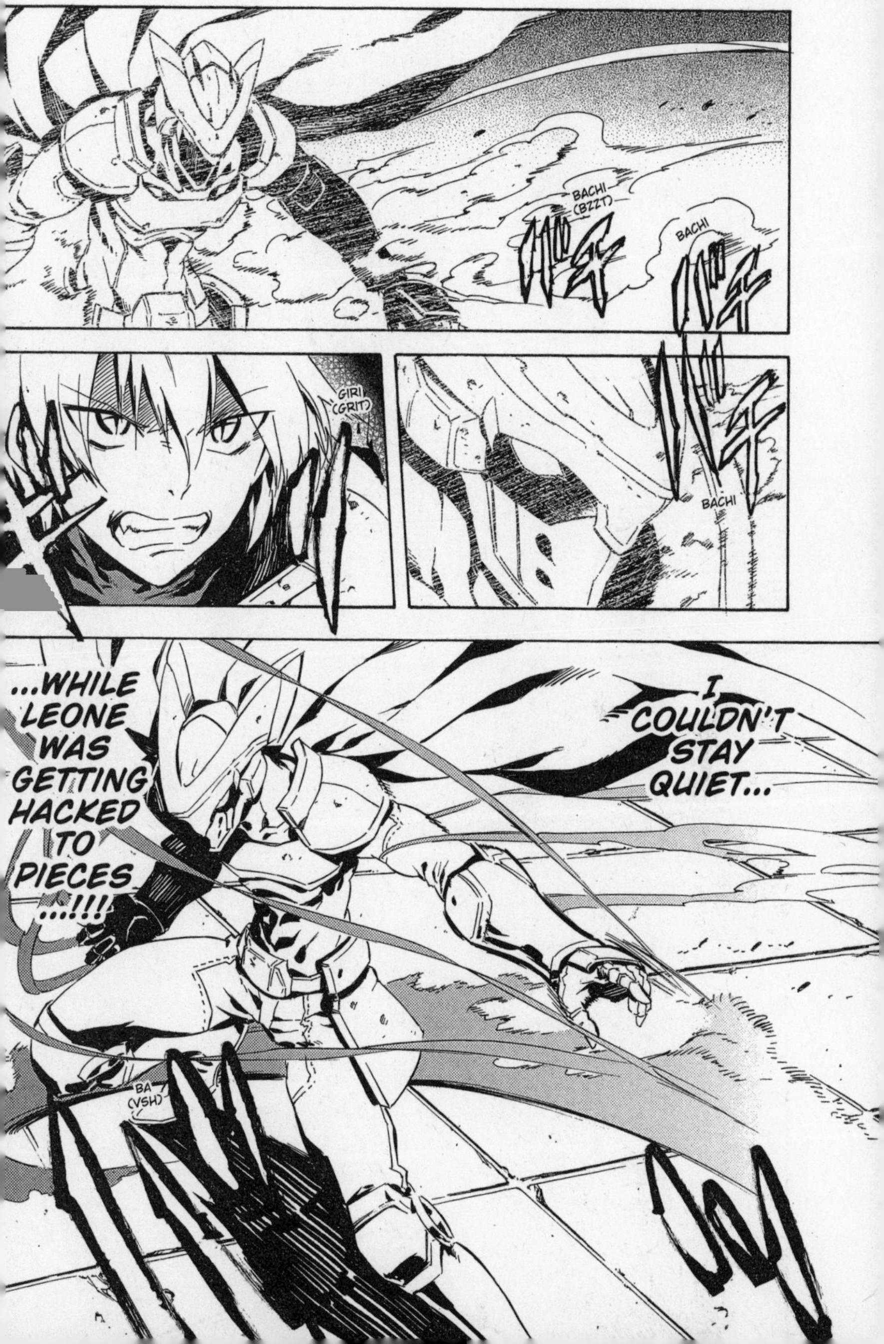
BACHI (BZZT)
BACHI
BACHI
GIRI (GRIT)
I COULDN'T STAY QUIET...
...WHILE LEONE WAS GETTING HACKED TO PIECES ...!!!
BA (VSH)

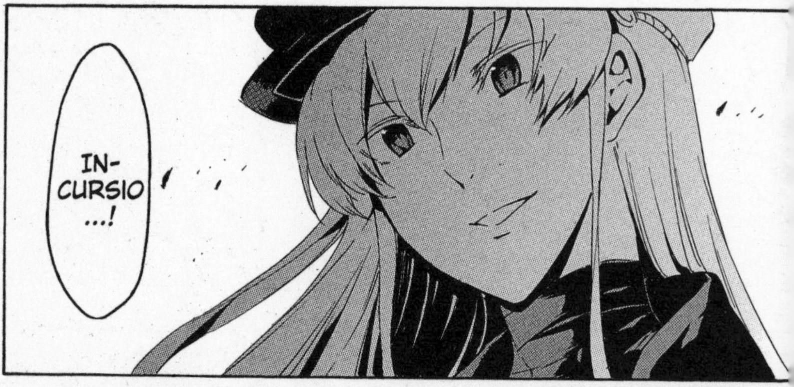
IN-
CURSIO
...!
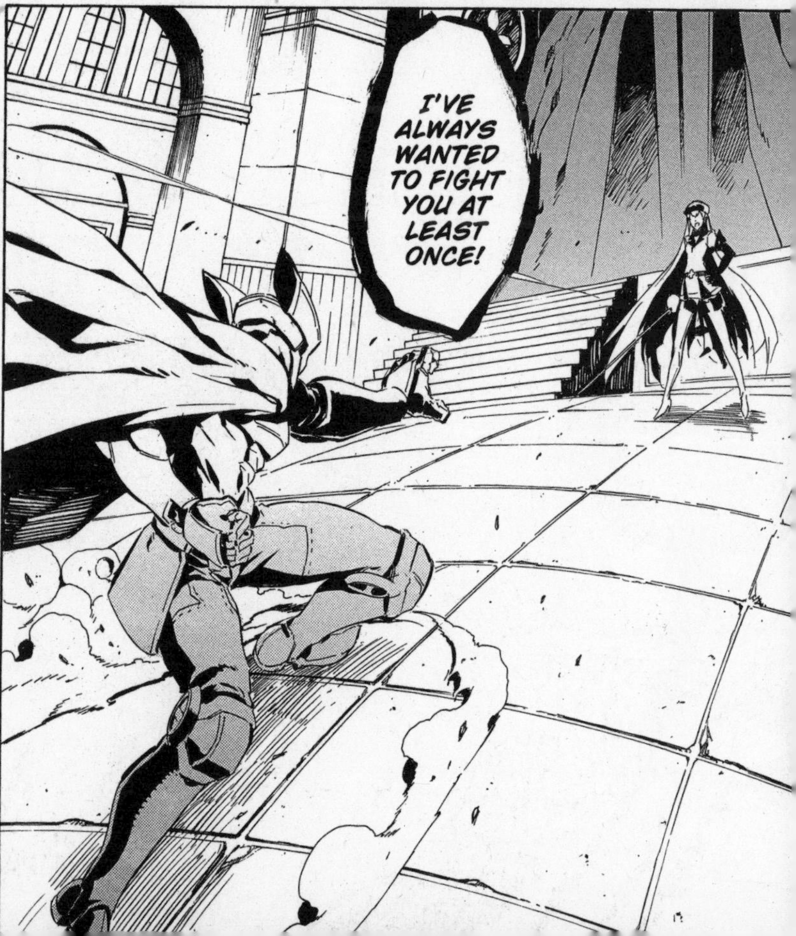
I'VE ALWAYS WANTED TO FIGHT YOU AT LEAST ONCE!

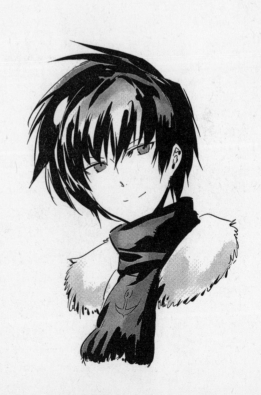

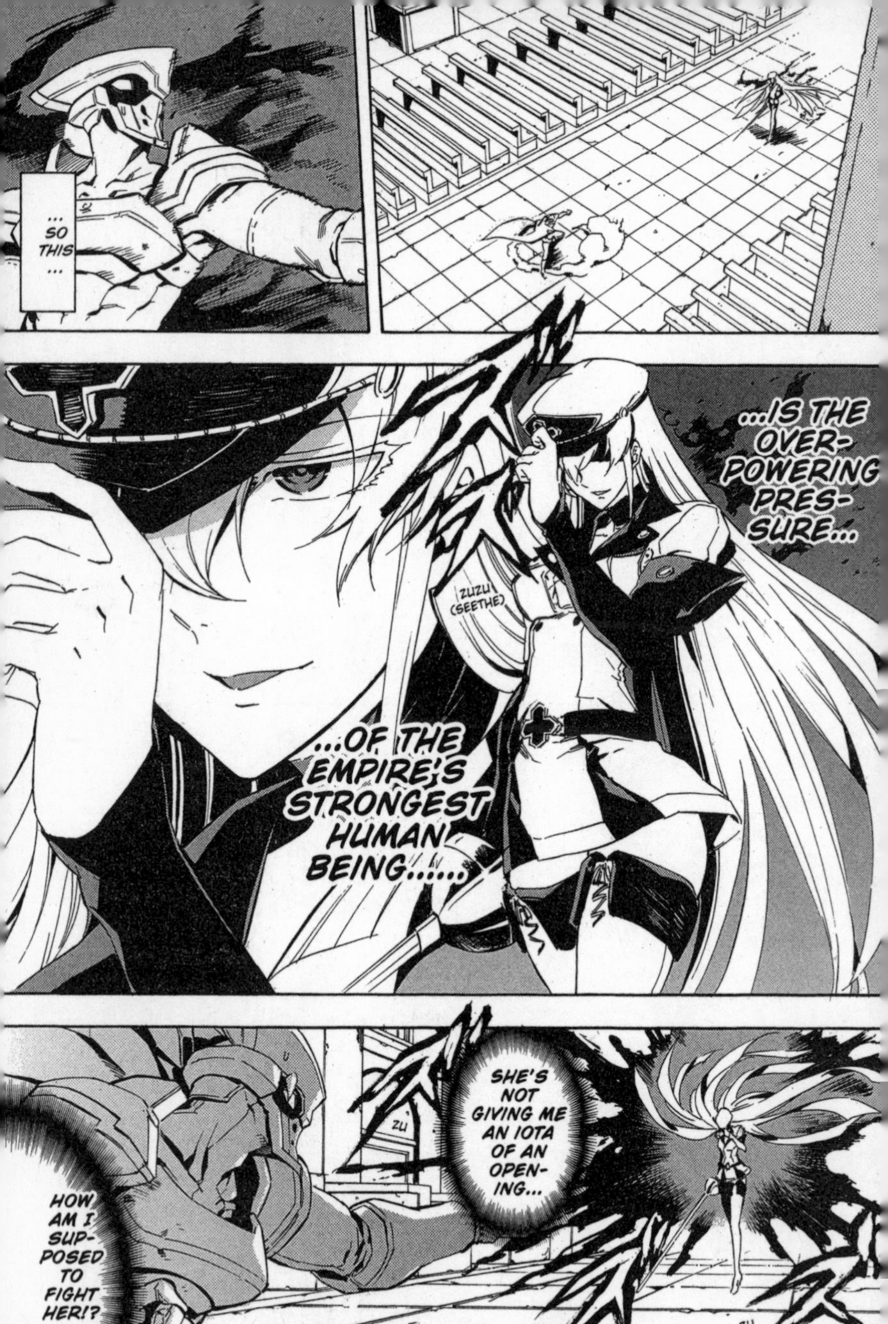
...SO THIS...
...IS THE OVER-POWERING PRES-SURE...
ZUZU (SEETHE)
...OF THE EMPIRE'S STRONGEST HUMAN BEING......
SHE'S NOT GIVING ME AN IOTA OF AN OPEN-ING...
ZU
ZU
ZU
HOW AM I SUP-POSED TO FIGHT HER!?

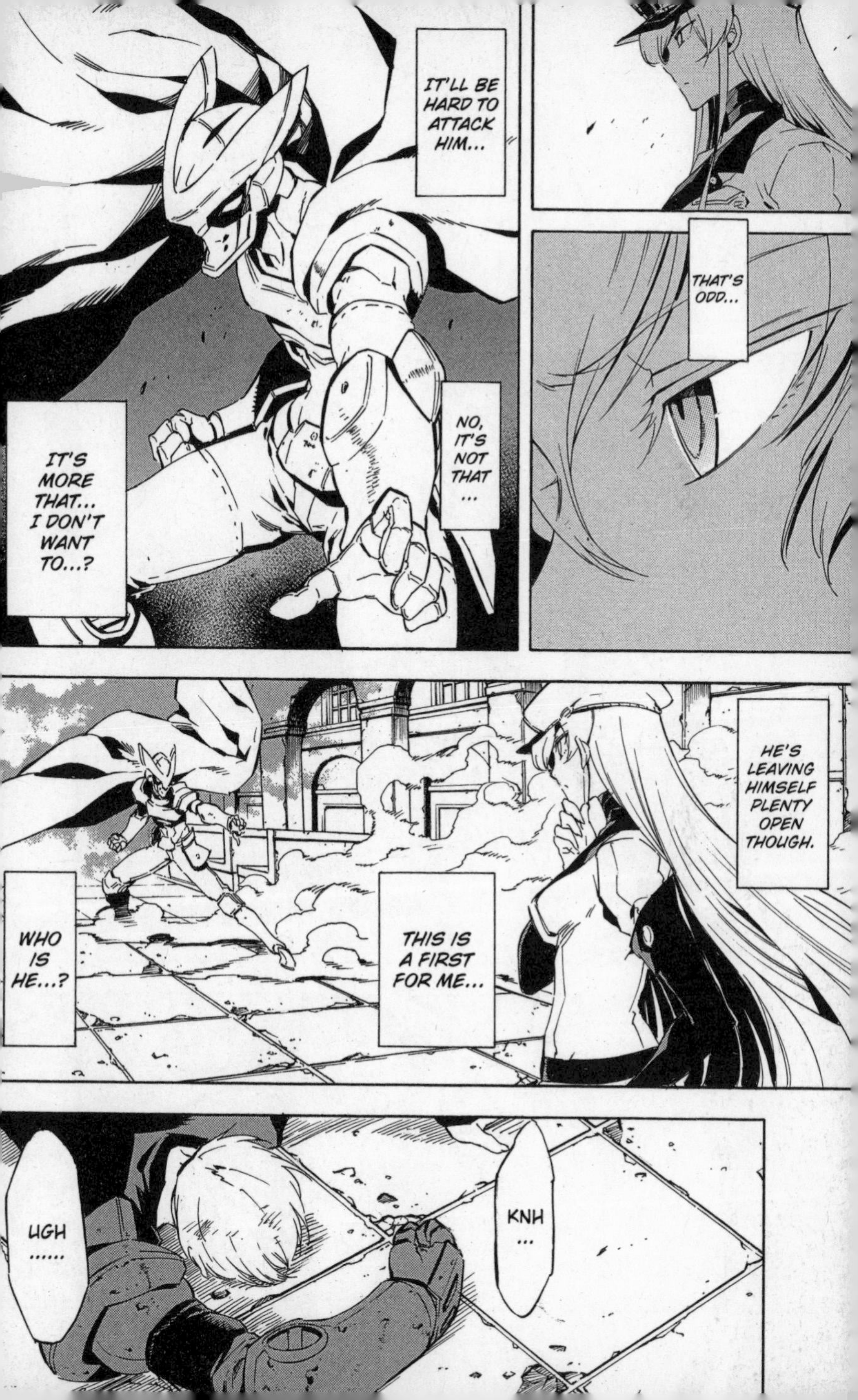
IT'LL BE HARD TO ATTACK HIM...
NO, IT'S NOT THAT...
IT'S MORE THAT... I DON'T WANT TO...?
THAT'S ODD...
HE'S LEAVING HIMSELF PLENTY OPEN THOUGH.
THIS IS A FIRST FOR ME...
WHO IS HE...?
KNH...
UGH......

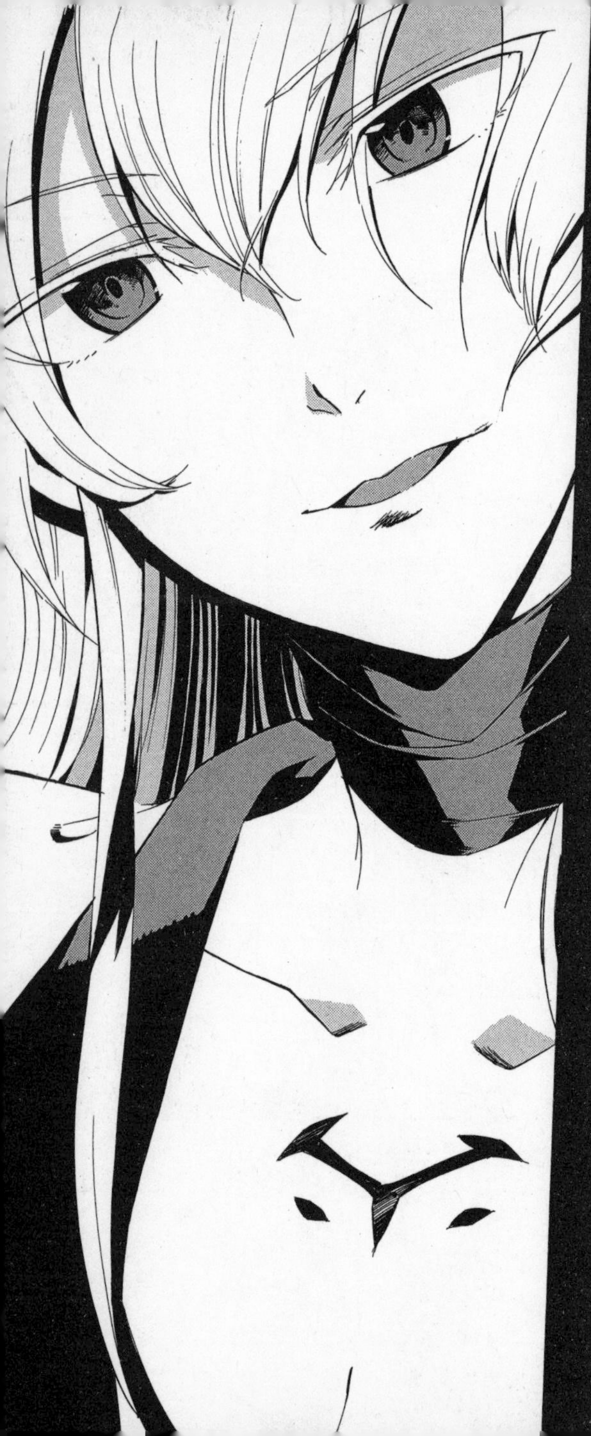

CHAPTER 42 - KILL THE DESPAIR (PART 1)

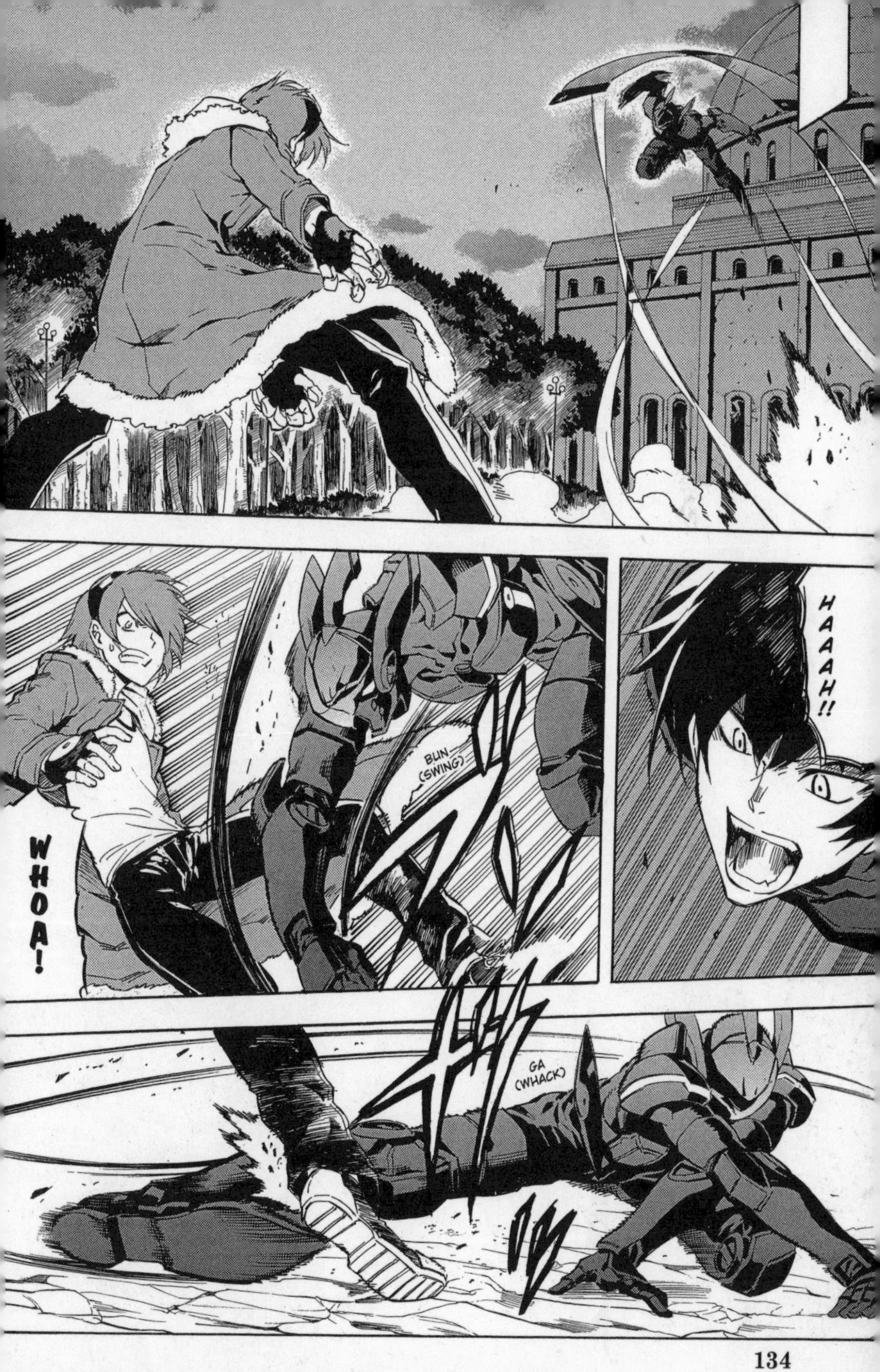
HAAAAH!!
BUN— (SWING)
WHOA!
GA (WHACK)

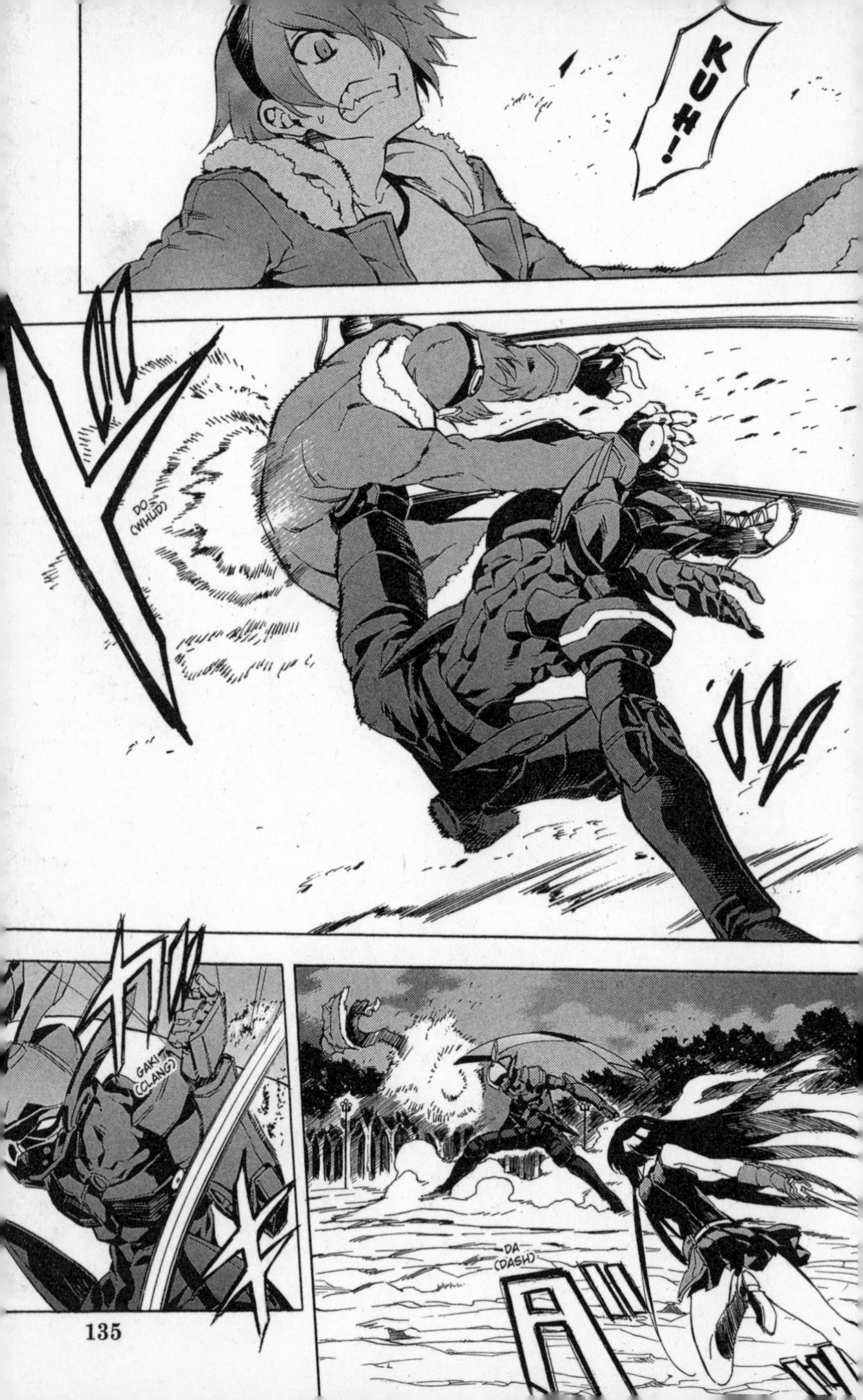
KUH!
DO (WHUD)
DA (DASH)
GAKI (CLANG)

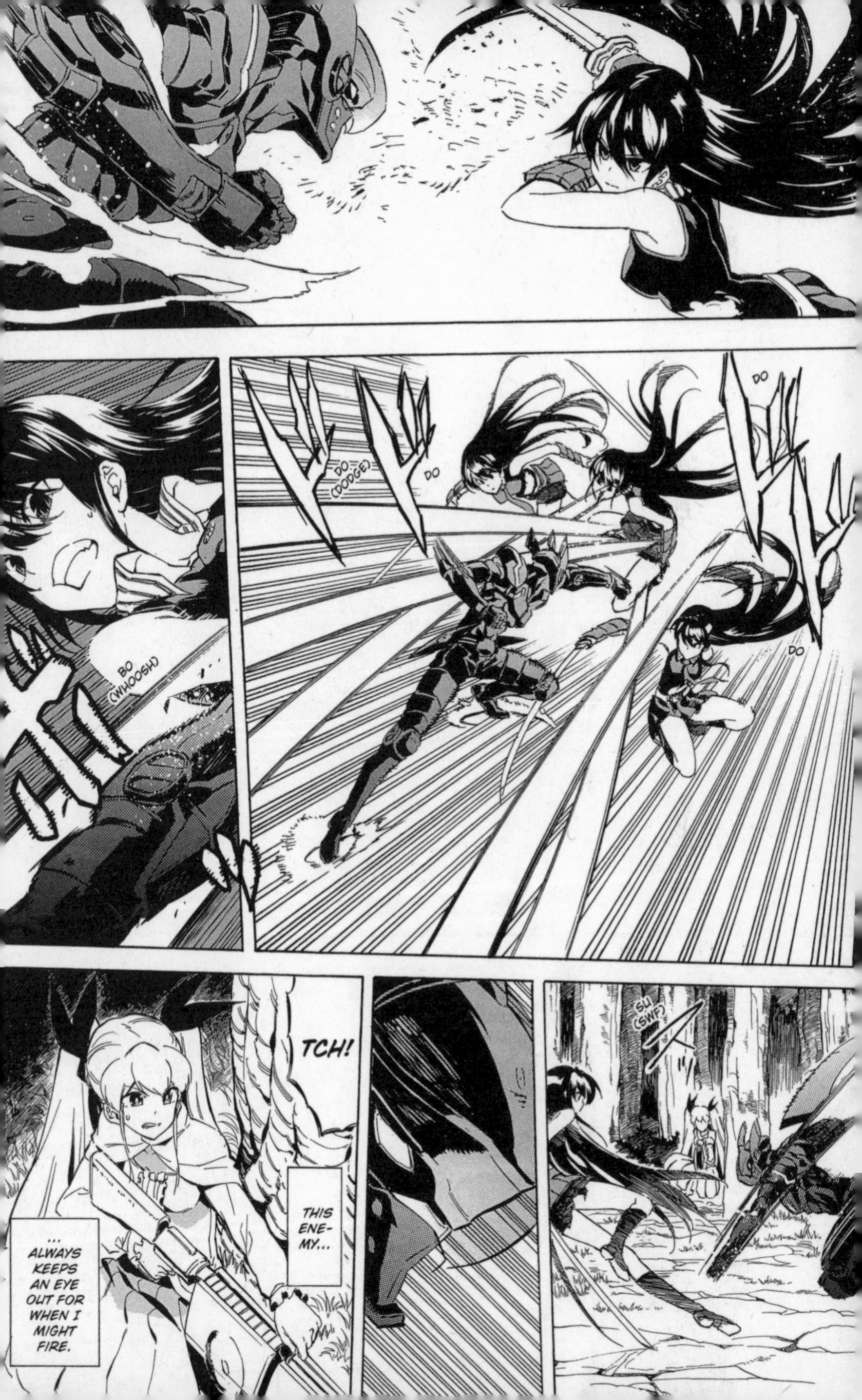
DO
DO (DODGE)
DO
DO
BO (WHOOSH)
SU (SWF)
TCH!
THIS ENEMY...
... ALWAYS KEEPS AN EYE OUT FOR WHEN I MIGHT FIRE.

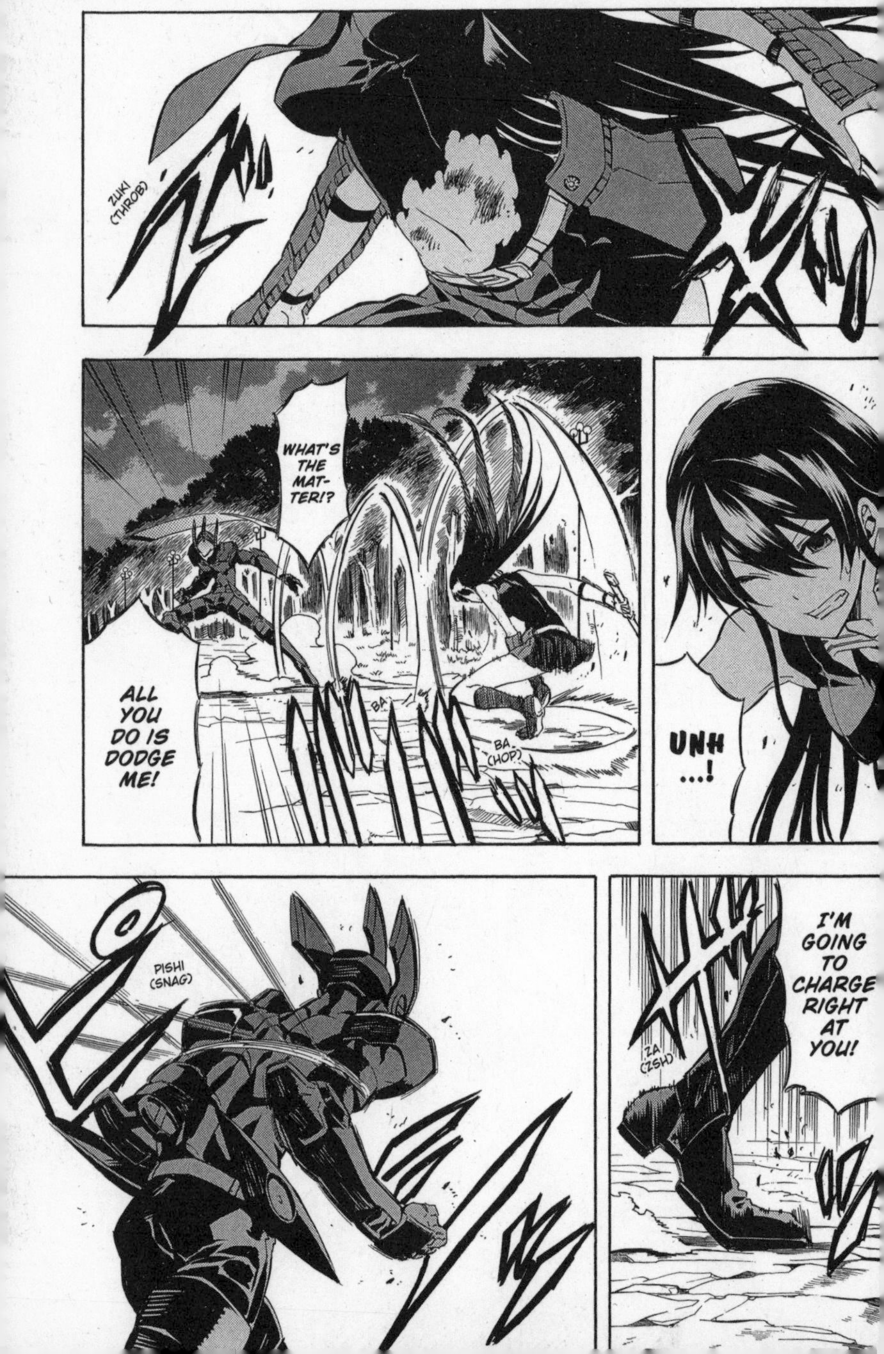
ZUKI (THROB)
UNH ...!
WHAT'S THE MAT-TER!?
ALL YOU DO IS DODGE ME!
BA
BA (HOP)
I'M GOING TO CHARGE RIGHT AT YOU!
ZA (ZSH)
PISHI (SNAG)

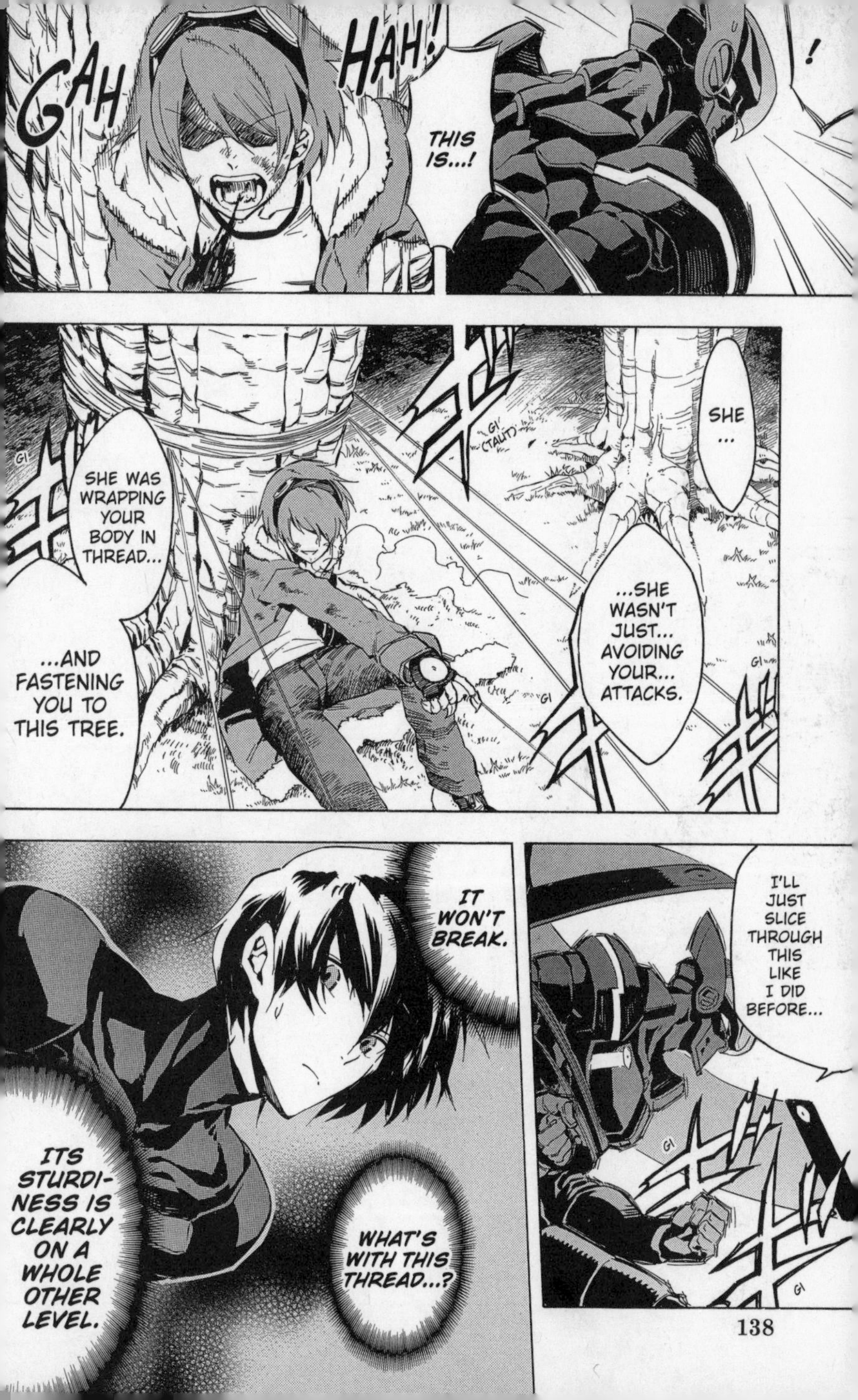
!
THIS IS...!
GAH
HAH!
SHE ...
...SHE WASN'T JUST... AVOIDING YOUR... ATTACKS.
GI
GI
GI (TAUT)
SHE WAS WRAPPING YOUR BODY IN THREAD...
GI
...AND FASTENING YOU TO THIS TREE.
I'LL JUST SLICE THROUGH THIS LIKE I DID BEFORE...
GI
GI
IT WON'T BREAK.
WHAT'S WITH THIS THREAD...?
ITS STURDINESS IS CLEARLY ON A WHOLE OTHER LEVEL.

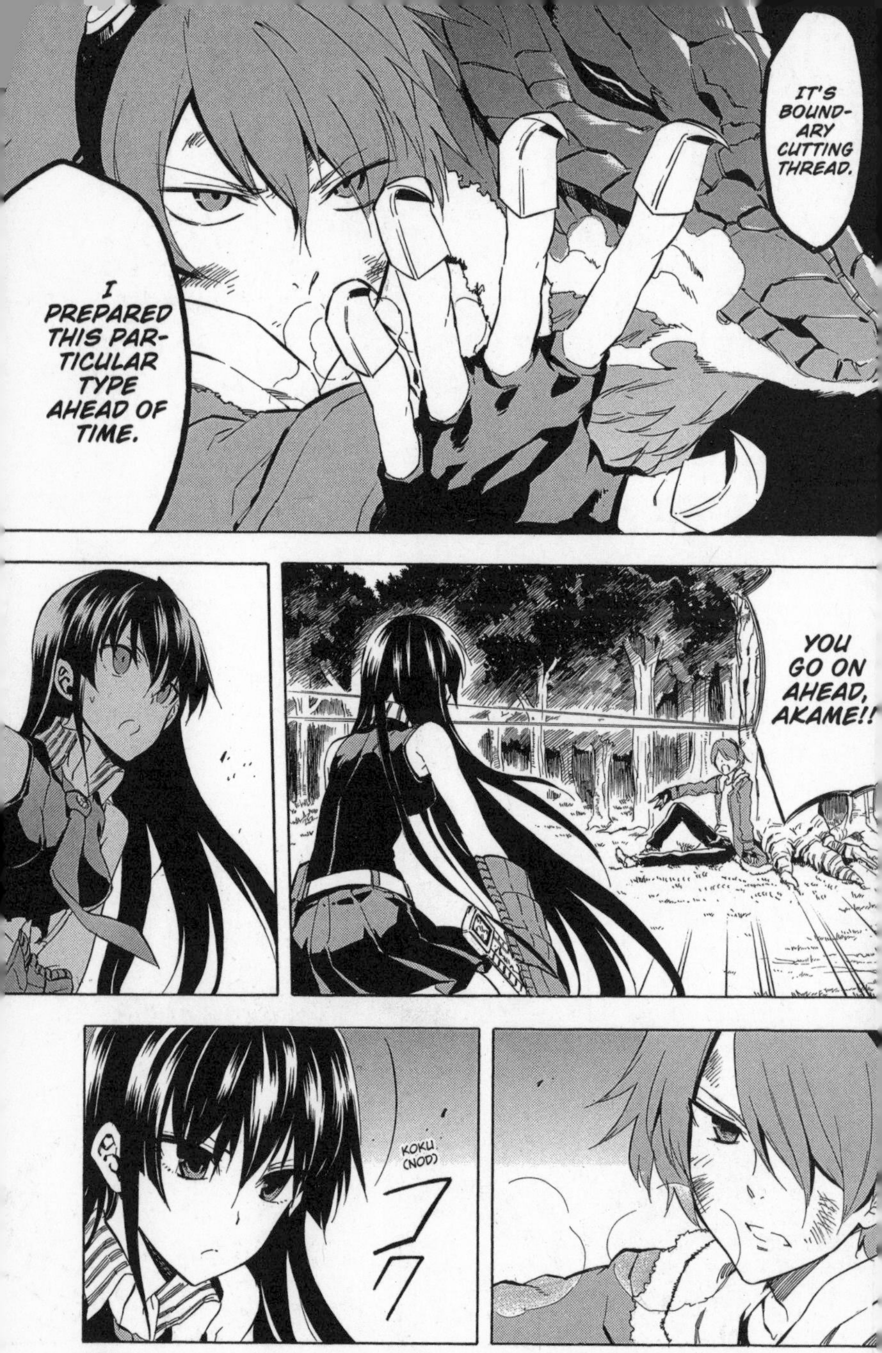
IT'S BOUNDARY-CUTTING THREAD.
I PREPARED THIS PARTICULAR TYPE AHEAD OF TIME.
YOU GO ON AHEAD, AKAME!!
KOKU (NOD)

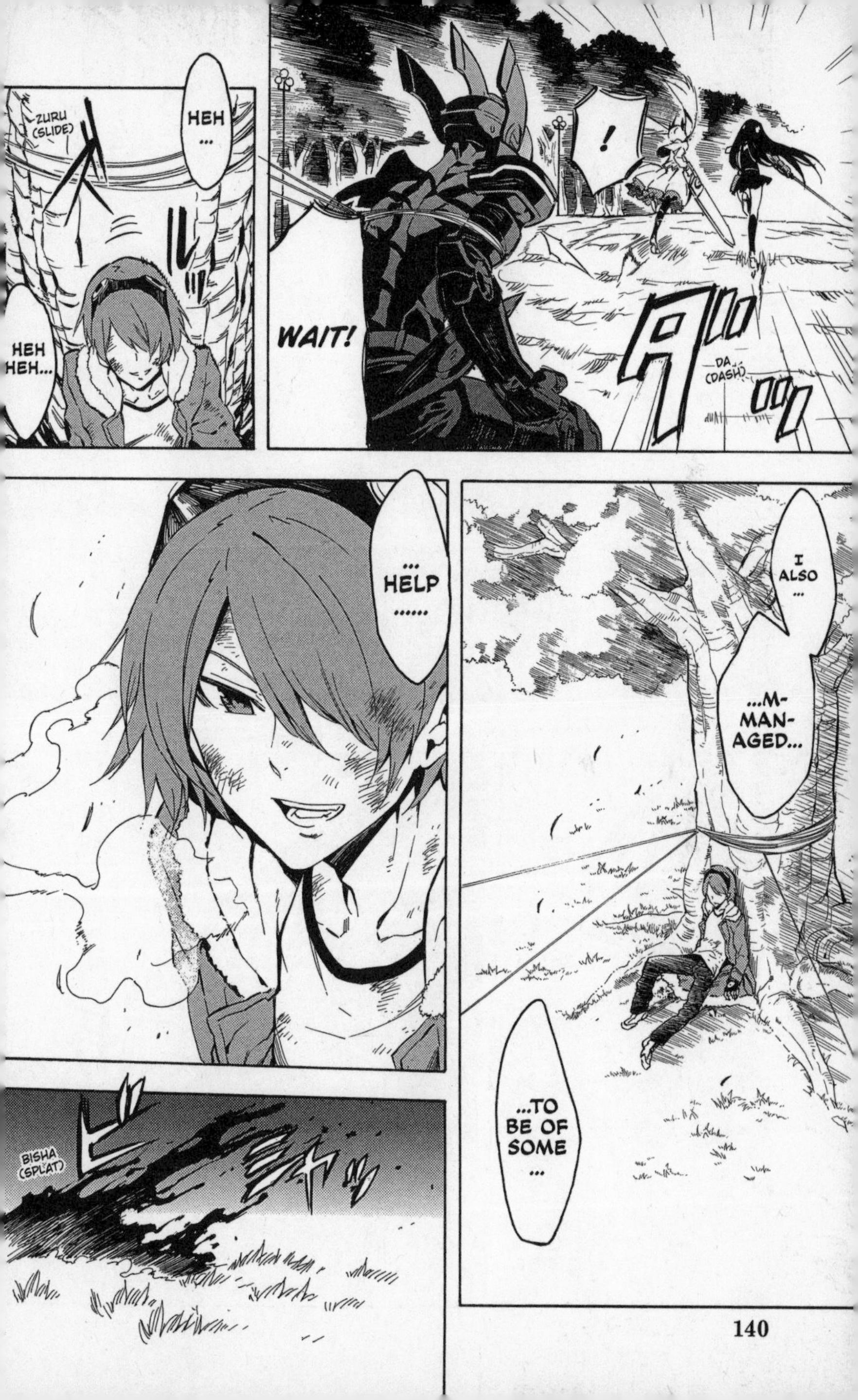
!
WAIT!
DA (DASH)
HEH ...
ZURU (SLIDE)
HEH HEH...
I ALSO ...
...M-MAN-AGED...
...TO BE OF SOME ...
... HELP ......
BISHA (SPLAT)

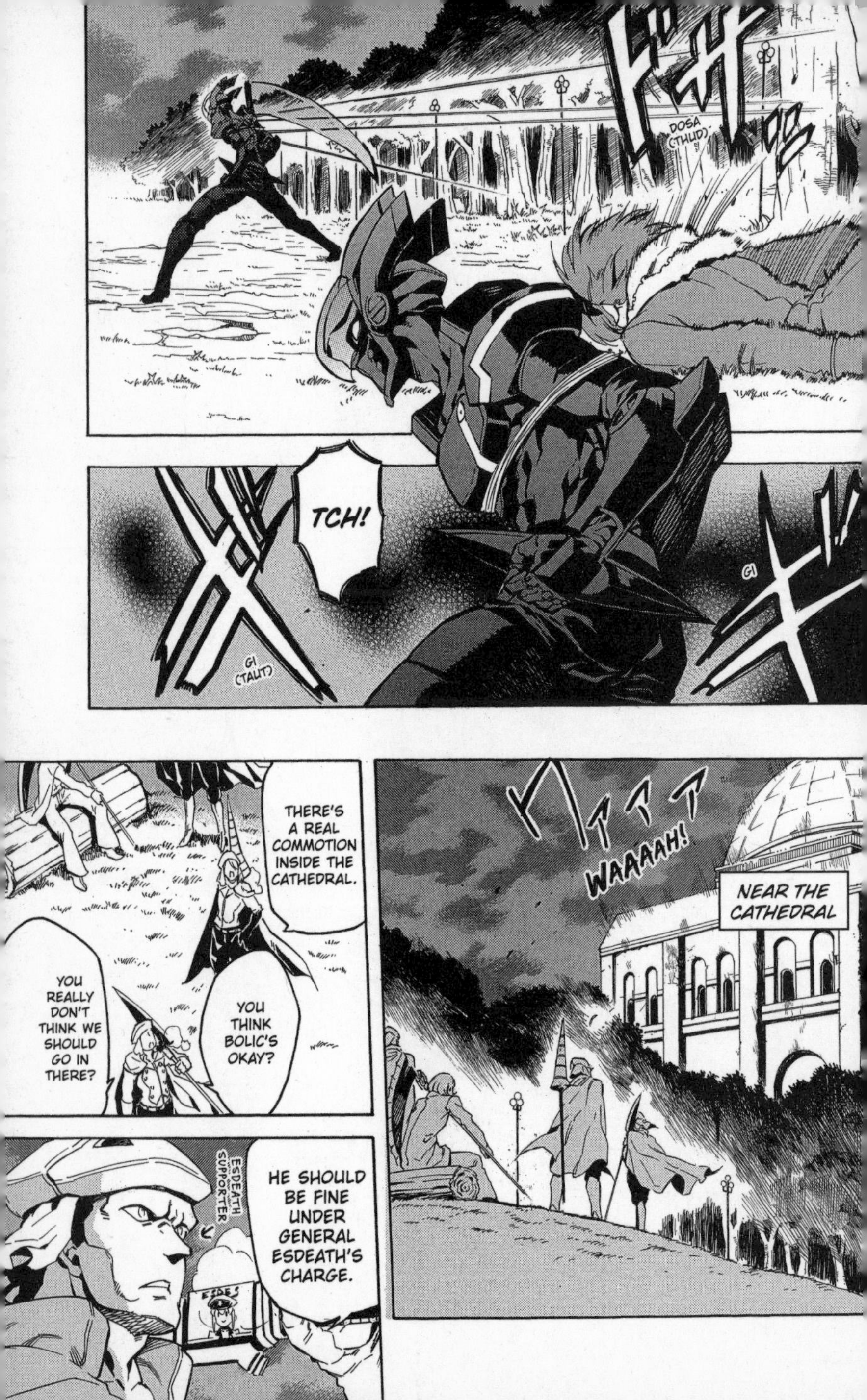
DOSA (THUD)
GI
TCH!
GI (TAUT)
WAAAAH!
NEAR THE CATHEDRAL
THERE'S A REAL COMMOTION INSIDE THE CATHEDRAL.
YOU THINK BOLIC'S OKAY?
YOU REALLY DON'T THINK WE SHOULD GO IN THERE?
ESDEATH SUPPORTER
HE SHOULD BE FINE UNDER GENERAL ESDEATH'S CHARGE.

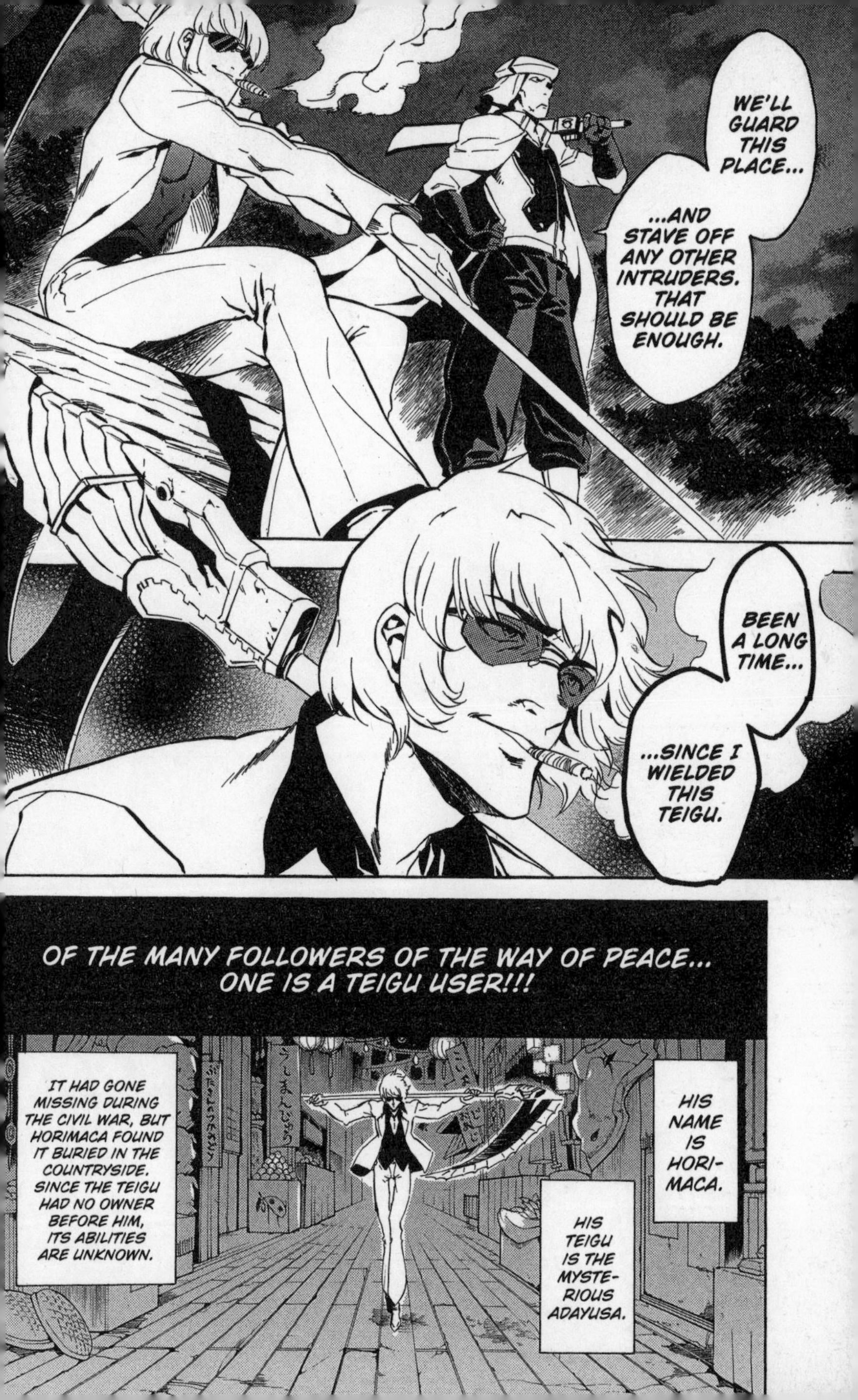
WE'LL GUARD THIS PLACE...
...AND STAVE OFF ANY OTHER INTRUDERS. THAT SHOULD BE ENOUGH.
BEEN A LONG TIME...
...SINCE I WIELDED THIS TEIGU.
OF THE MANY FOLLOWERS OF THE WAY OF PEACE... ONE IS A TEIGU USER!!!
HIS NAME IS HORI-MACA.
HIS TEIGU IS THE MYSTE-RIOUS ADAYUSA.
IT HAD GONE MISSING DURING THE CIVIL WAR, BUT HORIMACA FOUND IT BURIED IN THE COUNTRYSIDE. SINCE THE TEIGU HAD NO OWNER BEFORE HIM, ITS ABILITIES ARE UNKNOWN.

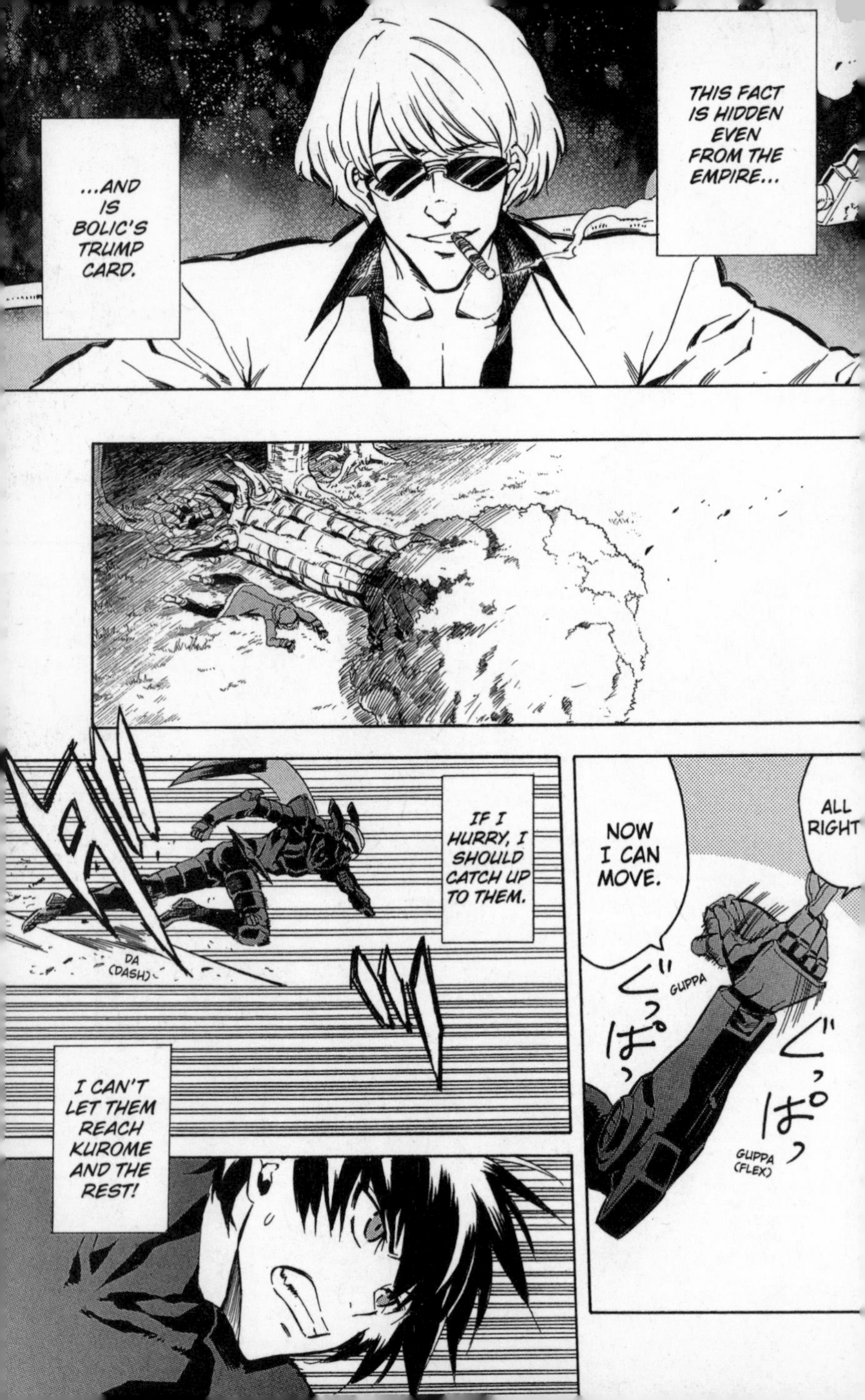
THIS FACT IS HIDDEN EVEN FROM THE EMPIRE...
...AND IS BOLIC'S TRUMP CARD.
ALL RIGHT
NOW I CAN MOVE.
ぐっぱっ
GUPPA
ぐっぱっ
GUPPA (FLEX)
IF I HURRY, I SHOULD CATCH UP TO THEM.
DA (DASH)
I CAN'T LET THEM REACH KUROME AND THE REST!

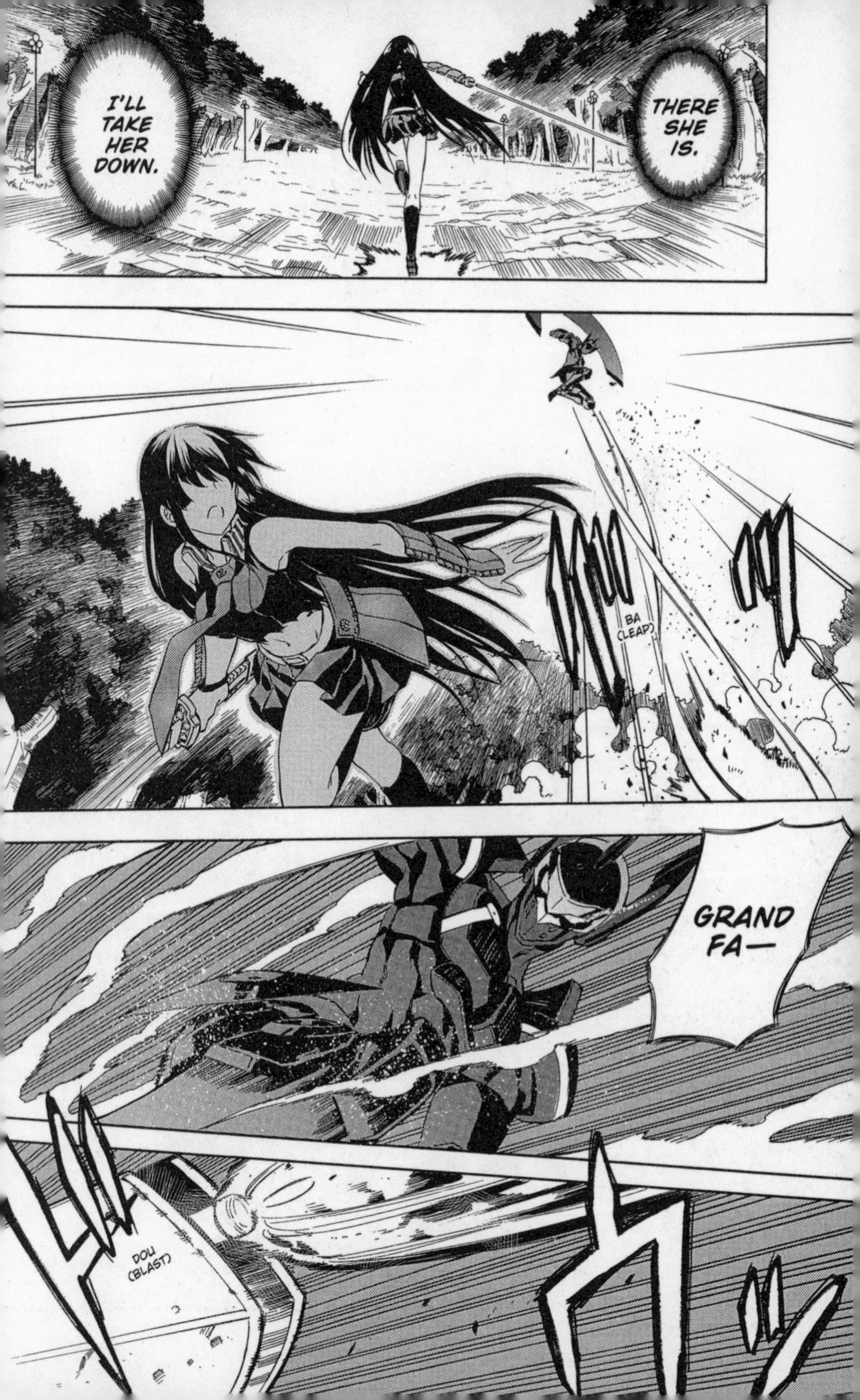
THERE SHE IS.
I'LL TAKE HER DOWN.
BA (LEAP)
GRAND FA—
DOU (BLAST)

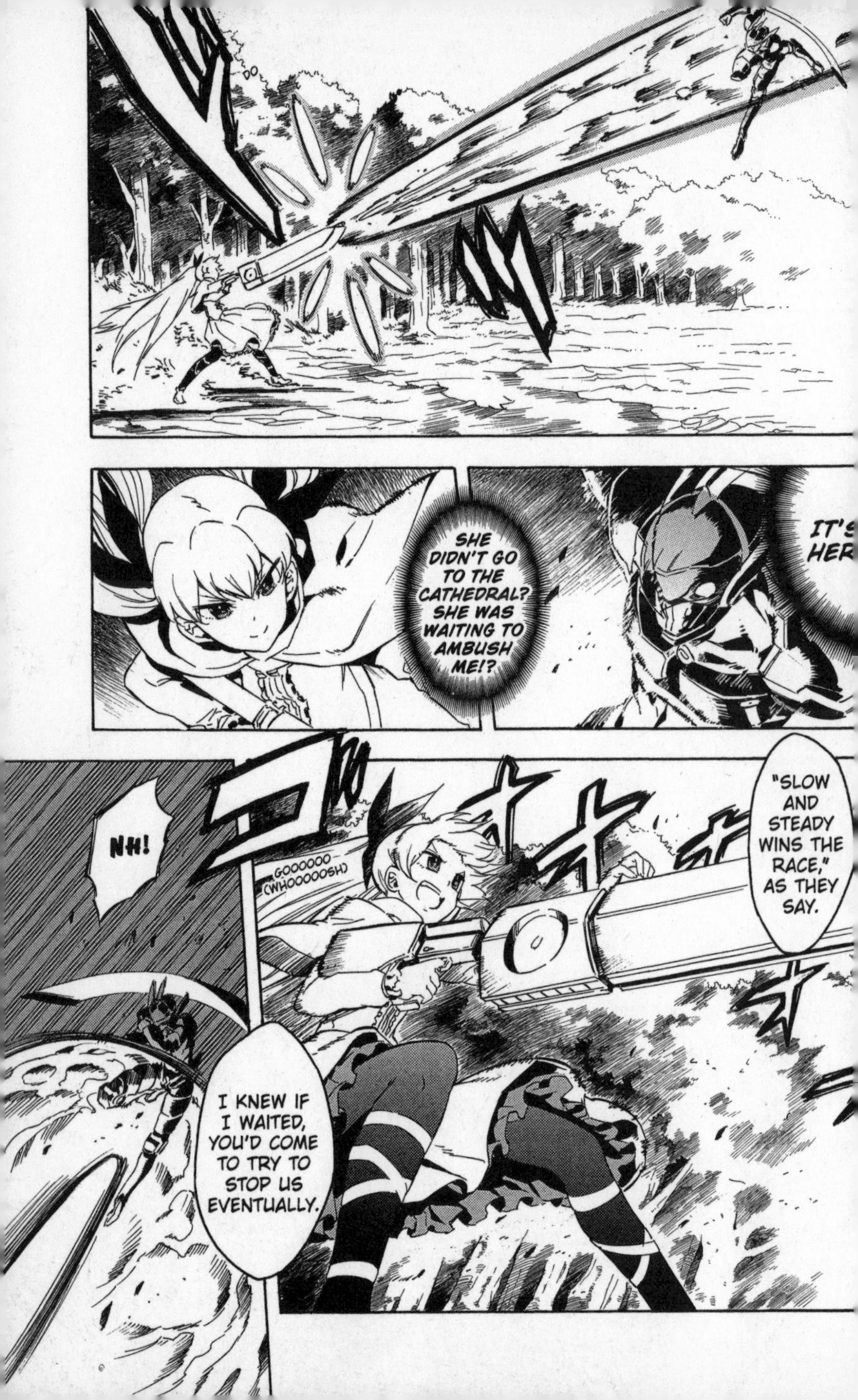
DO
IT'S HER
SHE DIDN'T GO TO THE CATHEDRAL? SHE WAS WAITING TO AMBUSH ME!?
"SLOW AND STEADY WINS THE RACE," AS THEY SAY.
NH!
GOOOOOO (WHOOOOOSH)
I KNEW IF I WAITED, YOU'D COME TO TRY TO STOP US EVENTUALLY.

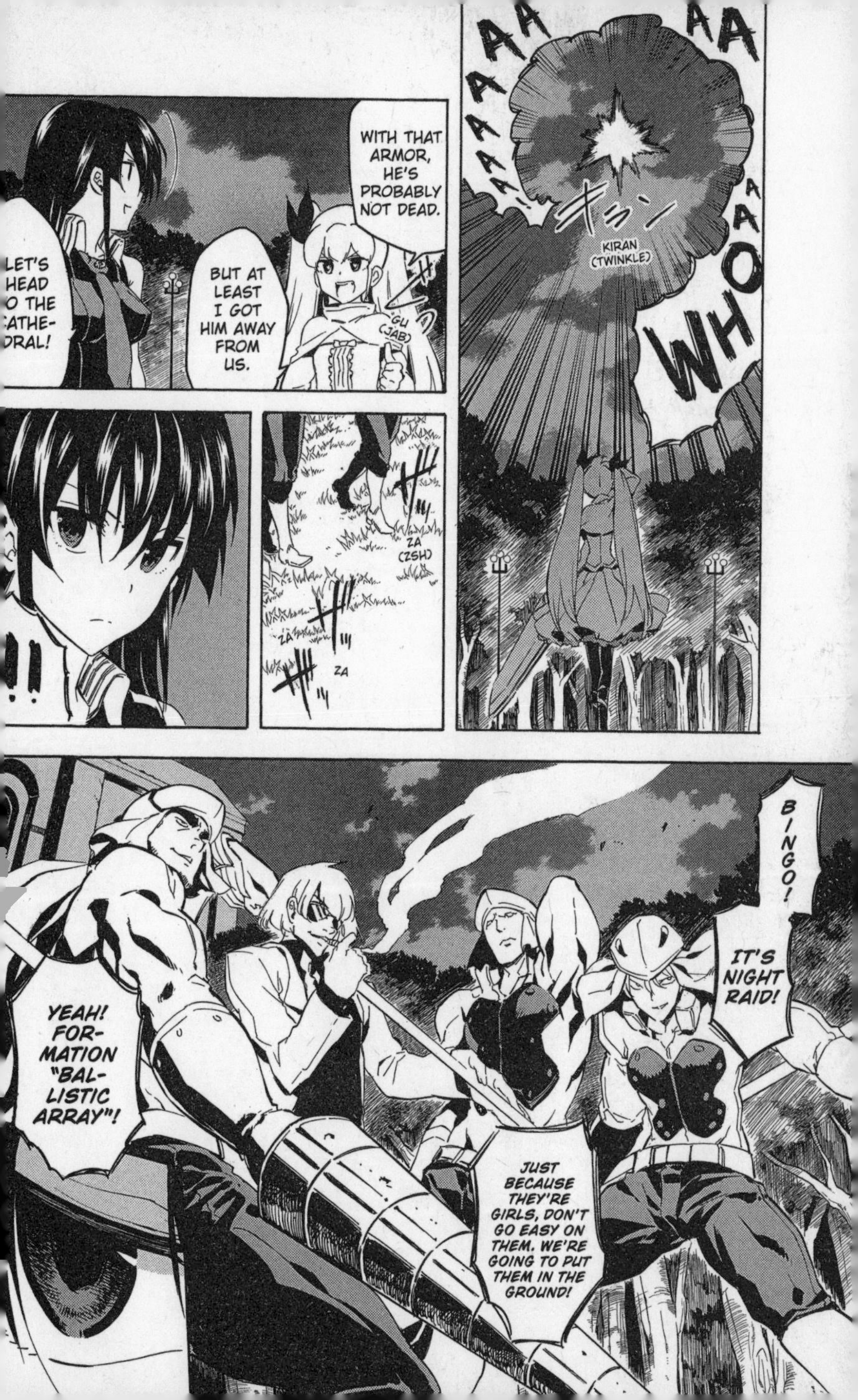
WHOAAAAAAAAAAAAA
KIRAN (TWINKLE)
WITH THAT ARMOR, HE'S PROBABLY NOT DEAD.
GU (JAB)
BUT AT LEAST I GOT HIM AWAY FROM US.
LET'S HEAD O THE ATHE-DRAL!
ZA (ZSH)
ZA
ZA
!!
BINGO!
IT'S NIGHT RAID!
JUST BECAUSE THEY'RE GIRLS, DON'T GO EASY ON THEM. WE'RE GOING TO PUT THEM IN THE GROUND!
YEAH! FORMATION "BALLISTIC ARRAY"!

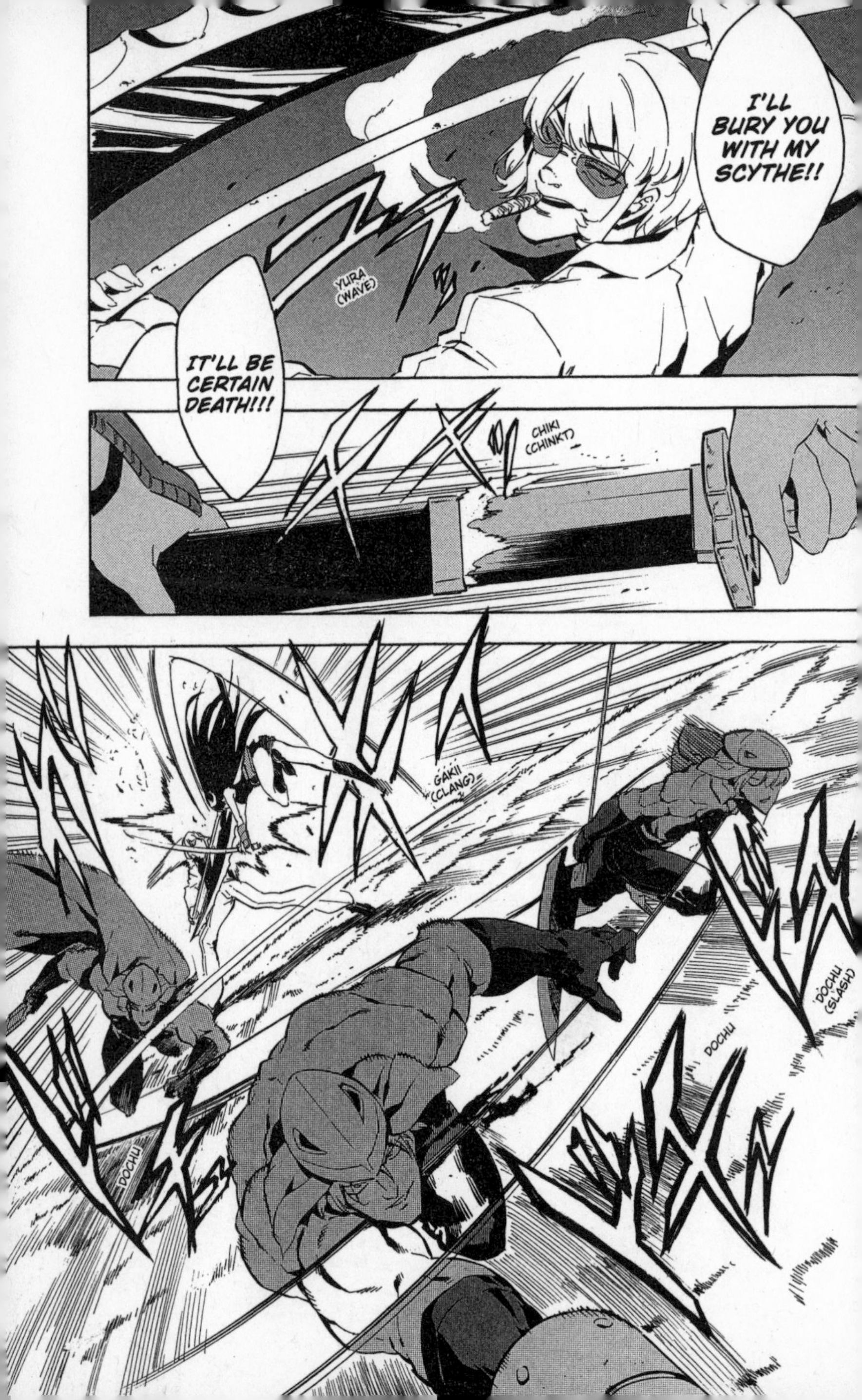
I'LL BURY YOU WITH MY SCYTHE!!
YURA (WAVE)
IT'LL BE CERTAIN DEATH!!!
CHIKI (CHINK!)
GAKII (CLANG)
DOCHU (SLASH)
DOCHU
DOCHU

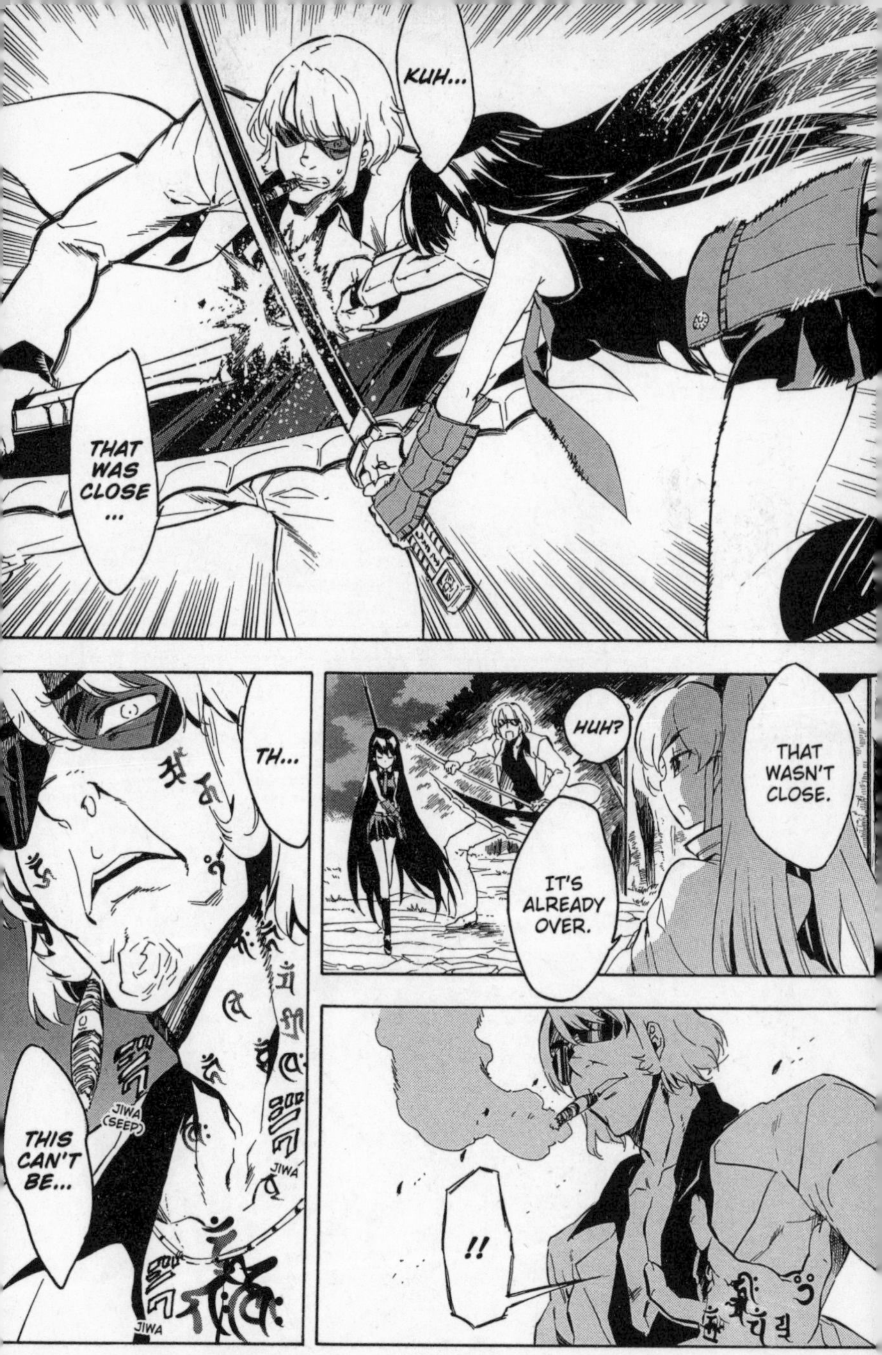
KUH...
THAT WAS CLOSE...
THAT WASN'T CLOSE.
HUH?
IT'S ALREADY OVER.
!!
TH...
JIWA (SEEP)
JIWA
THIS CAN'T BE...
JIWA

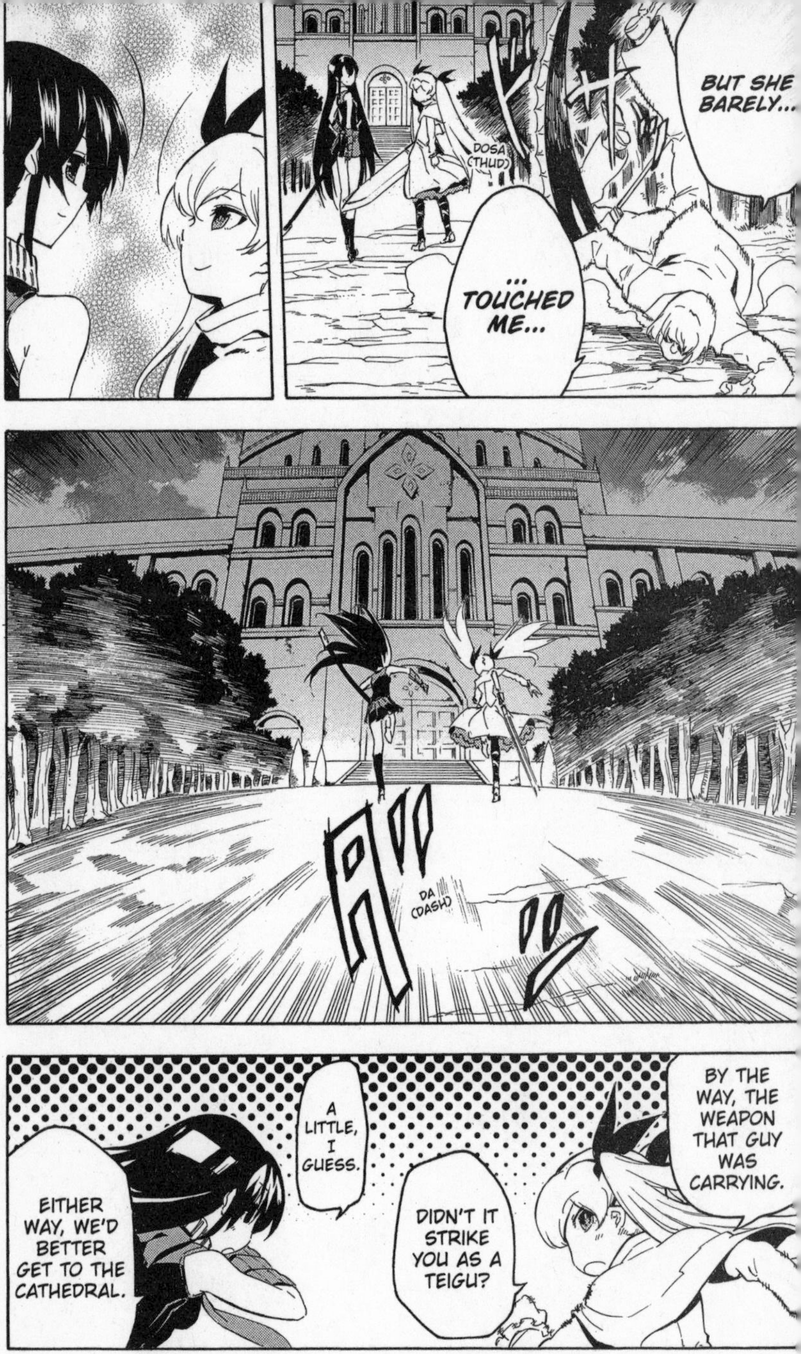
BUT SHE BARELY...
DOSA (THUD)
...TOUCHED ME...
DA (DASH)
BY THE WAY, THE WEAPON THAT GUY WAS CARRYING.
DIDN'T IT STRIKE YOU AS A TEIGU?
A LITTLE, I GUESS.
EITHER WAY, WE'D BETTER GET TO THE CATHEDRAL.

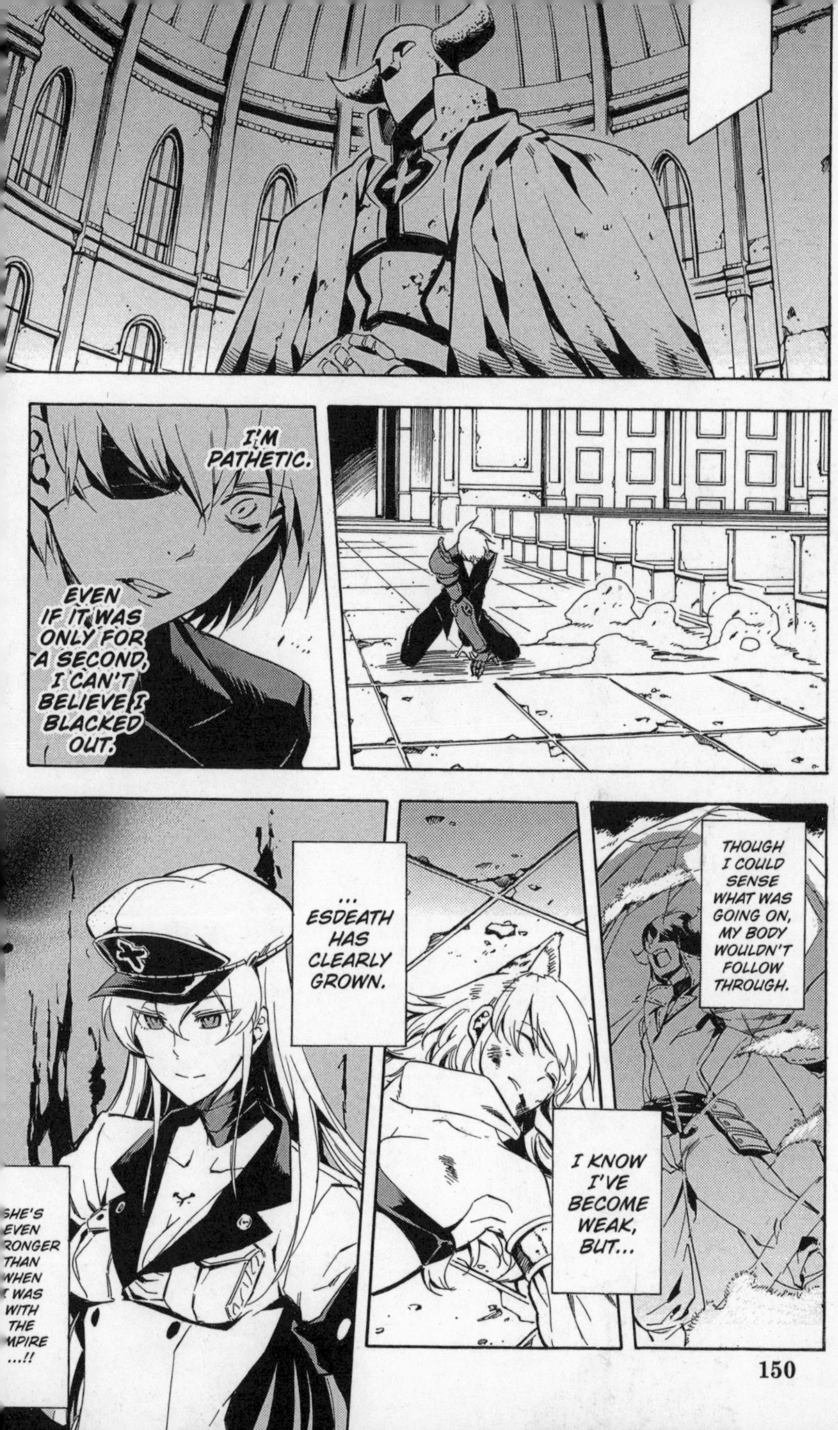
I'M PATHETIC.
EVEN IF IT WAS ONLY FOR A SECOND, I CAN'T BELIEVE I BLACKED OUT.
THOUGH I COULD SENSE WHAT WAS GOING ON, MY BODY WOULDN'T FOLLOW THROUGH.
I KNOW I'VE BECOME WEAK, BUT...
...ESDEATH HAS CLEARLY GROWN.
SHE'S EVEN RONGER THAN WHEN I WAS WITH THE MPIRE ...!!

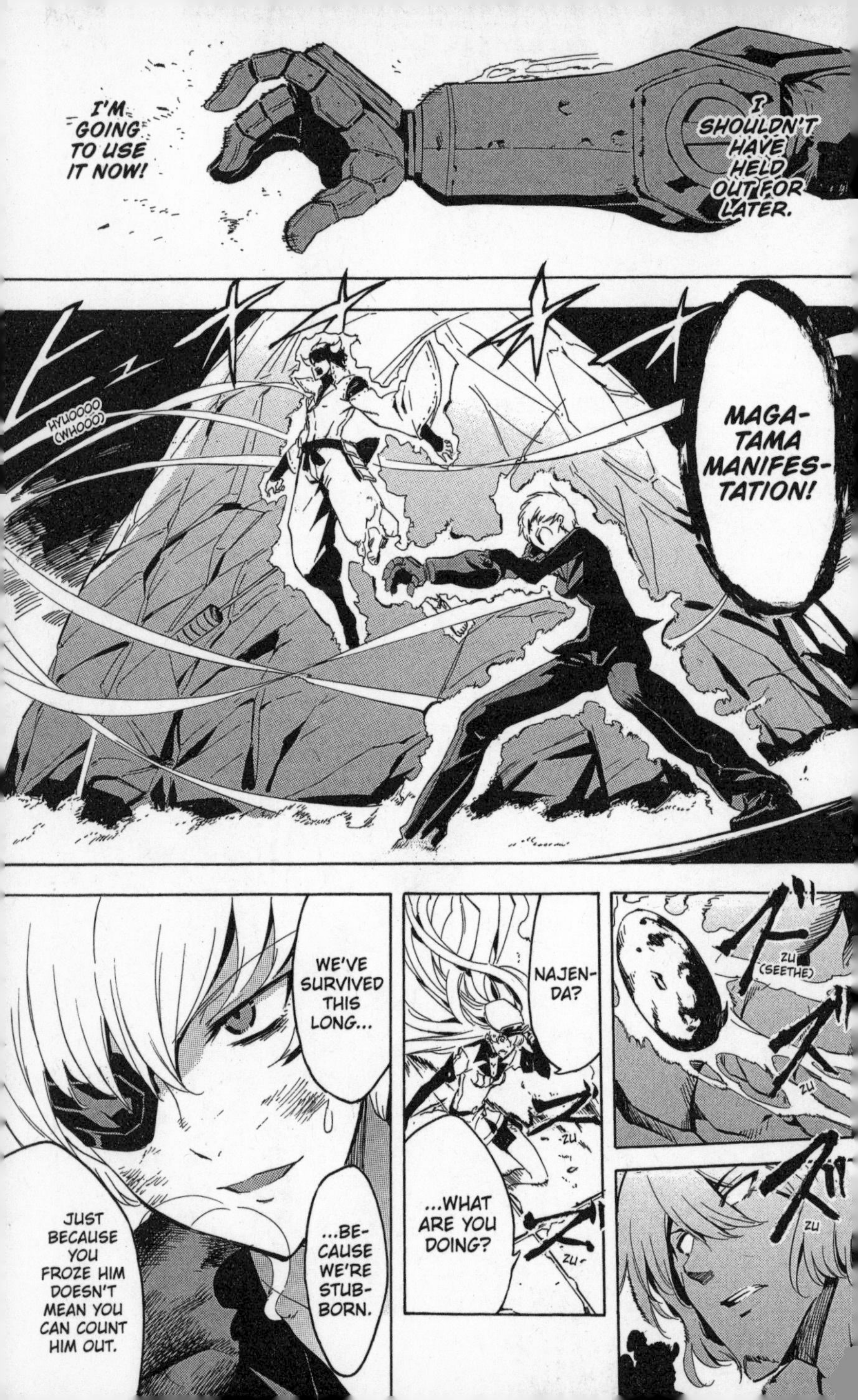
I SHOULDN'T HAVE HELD OUT FOR LATER.
I'M GOING TO USE IT NOW!
MAGA-TAMA MANIFES-TATION!
HYUOOOO (WHOOO)
ZU (SEETHE)
ZU
ZU
NAJEN-DA?
ZU
...WHAT ARE YOU DOING?
ZU
WE'VE SURVIVED THIS LONG...
...BE-CAUSE WE'RE STUB-BORN.
JUST BECAUSE YOU FROZE HIM DOESN'T MEAN YOU CAN COUNT HIM OUT.

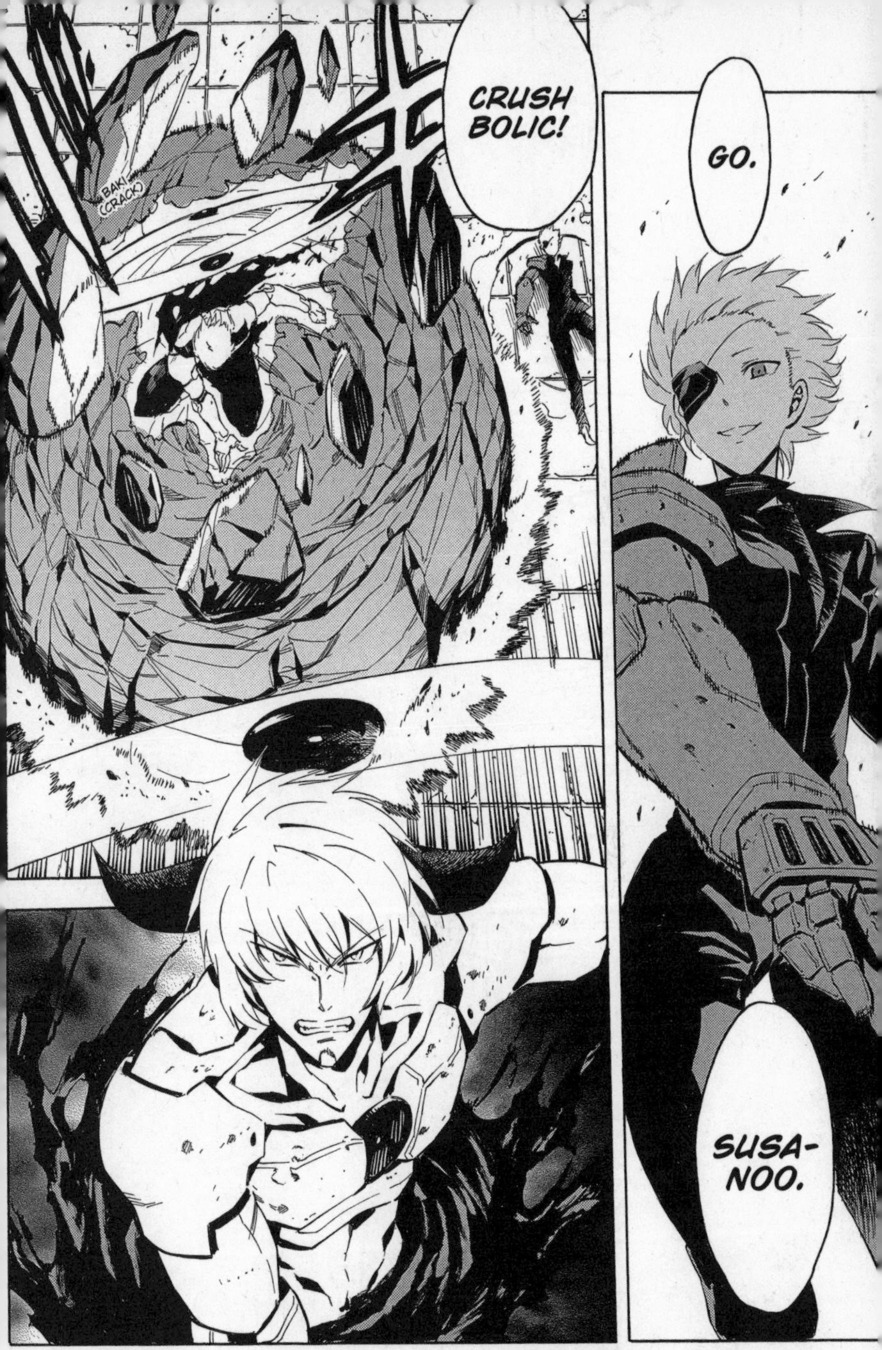
CRUSH BOLIC!
BAKI (CRACK)
GO.
SUSA-NOO.

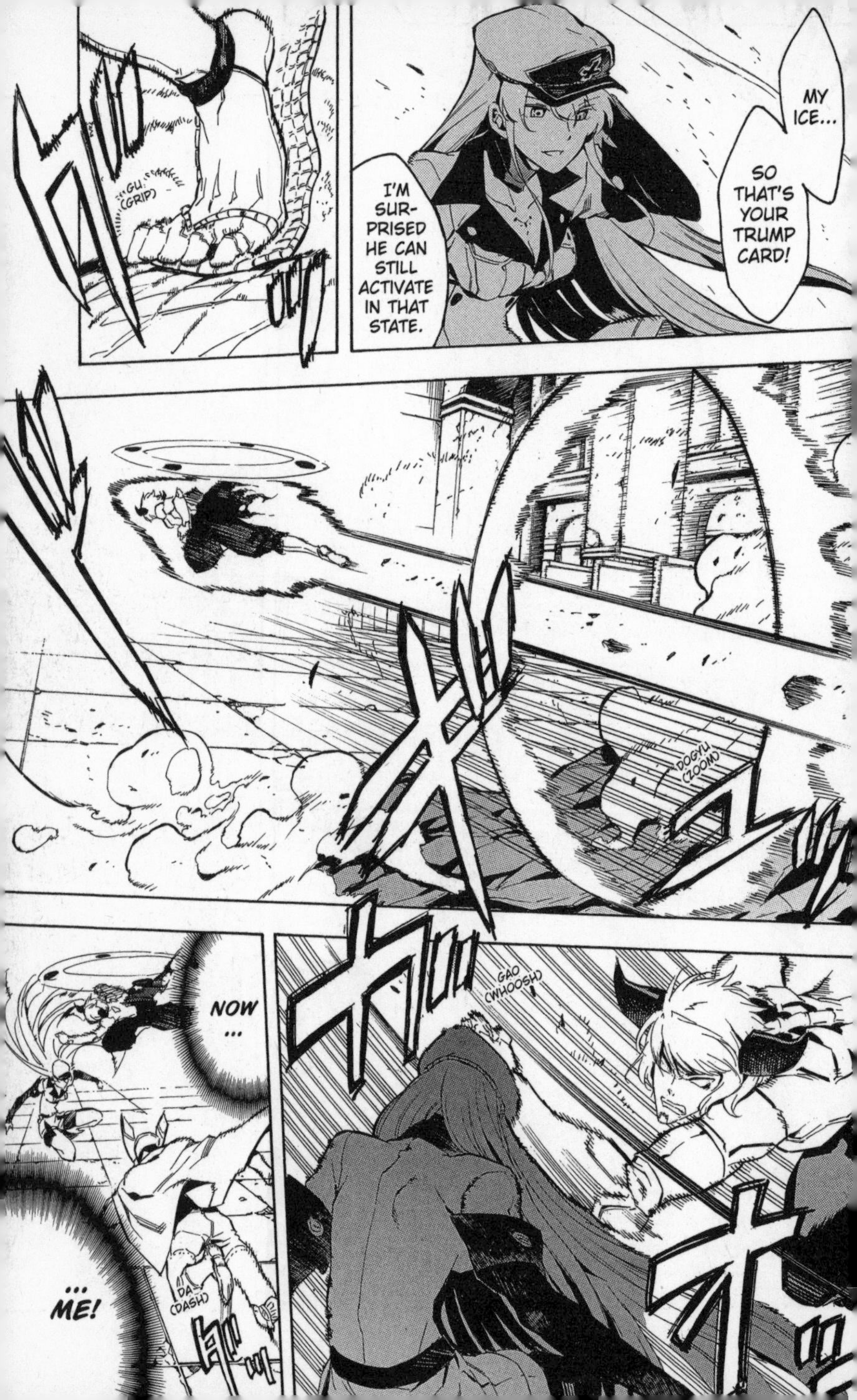
MY ICE...
SO THAT'S YOUR TRUMP CARD!
I'M SURPRISED HE CAN STILL ACTIVATE IN THAT STATE.
GU (GRIP)
DOGYU (ZOOM)
GAO (WHOOSH)
NOW ...
... ME!
DA (DASH)

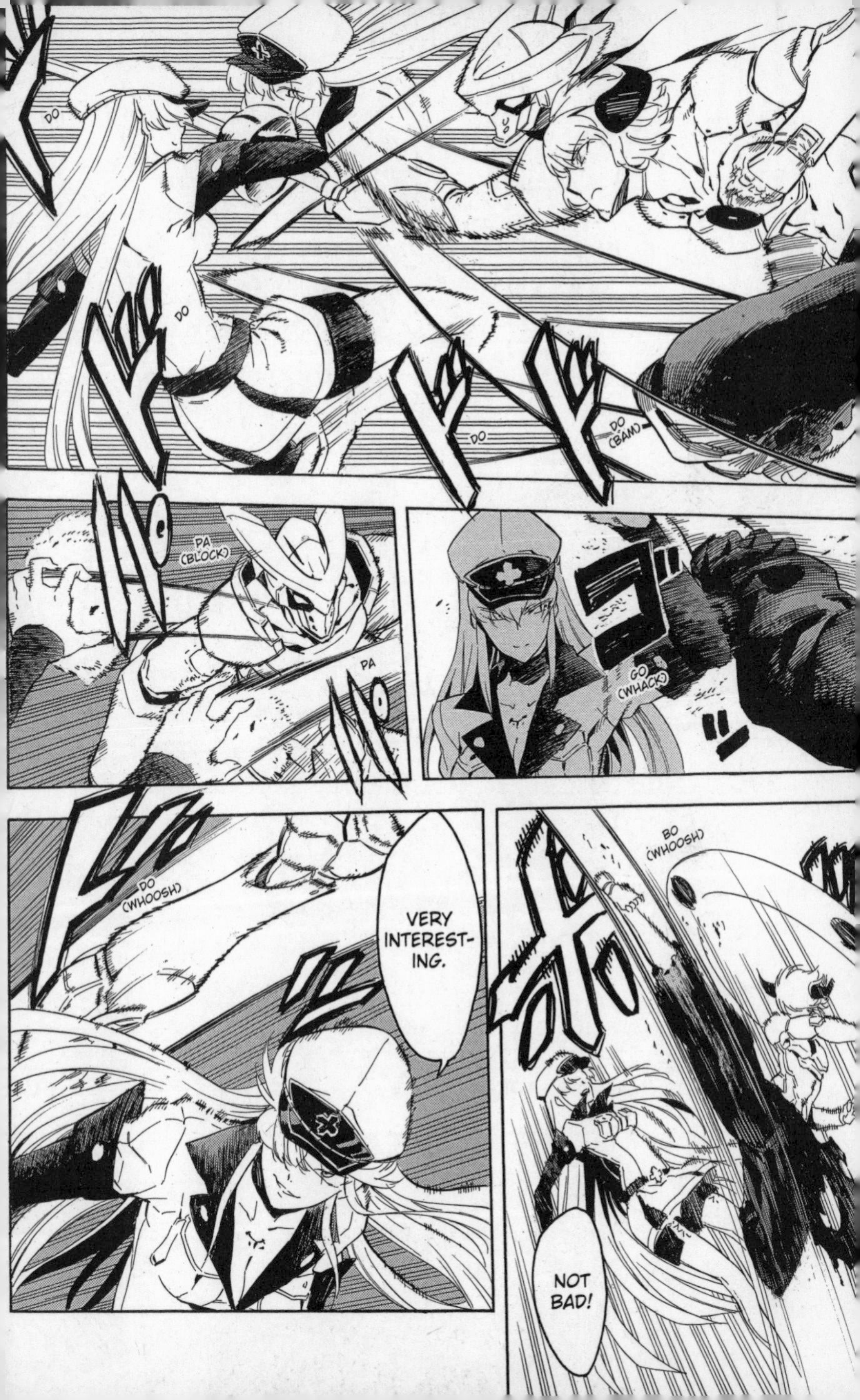
DO
(BAM)
DO
DO
DO
GO
(WHACK)
PA
(BLOCK)
PA
BO
(WHOOSH)
NOT BAD!
DO
(WHOOSH)
VERY INTEREST-ING.

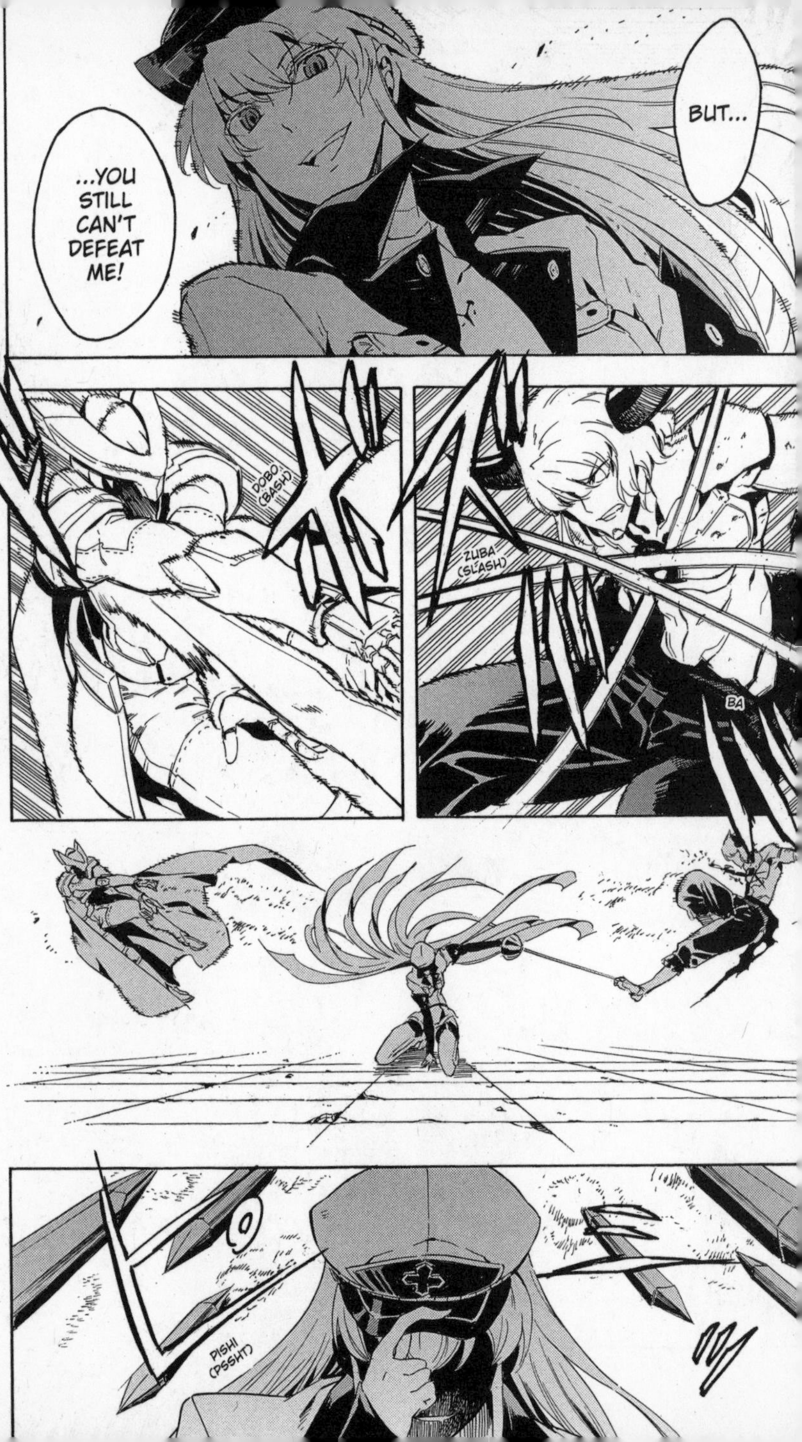
BUT...
...YOU STILL CAN'T DEFEAT ME!
ZUBA (SLASH)
BA
DOBO (BASH)
PISHI (PSSHT)

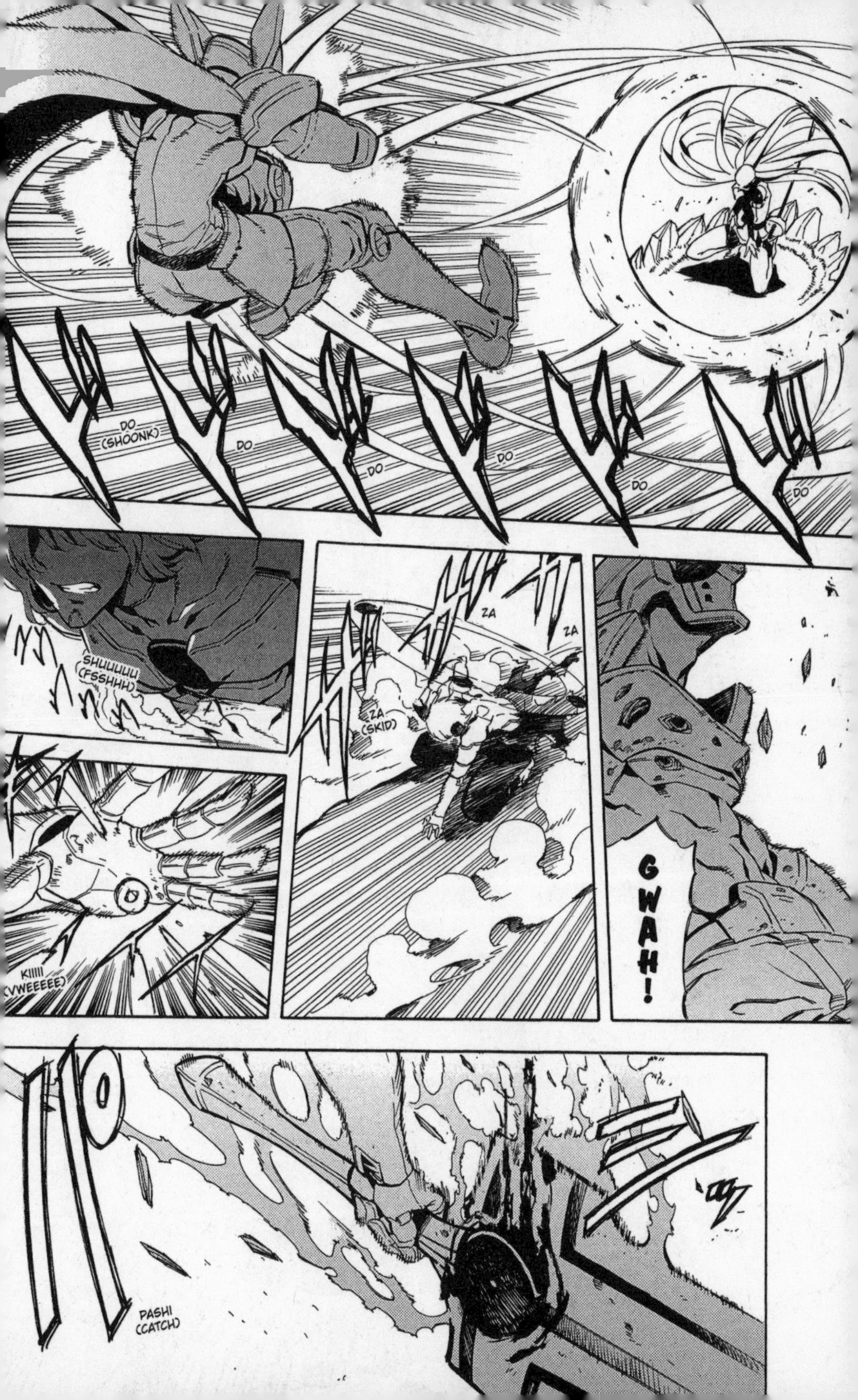
DO
DO
DO
DO
DO
DO (SHOONK)
GWAH!
ZA
ZA
ZA (SKID)
SHUUUUU (FSSHHH)
KIIIII (VWEEEEE)
PASHI (CATCH)

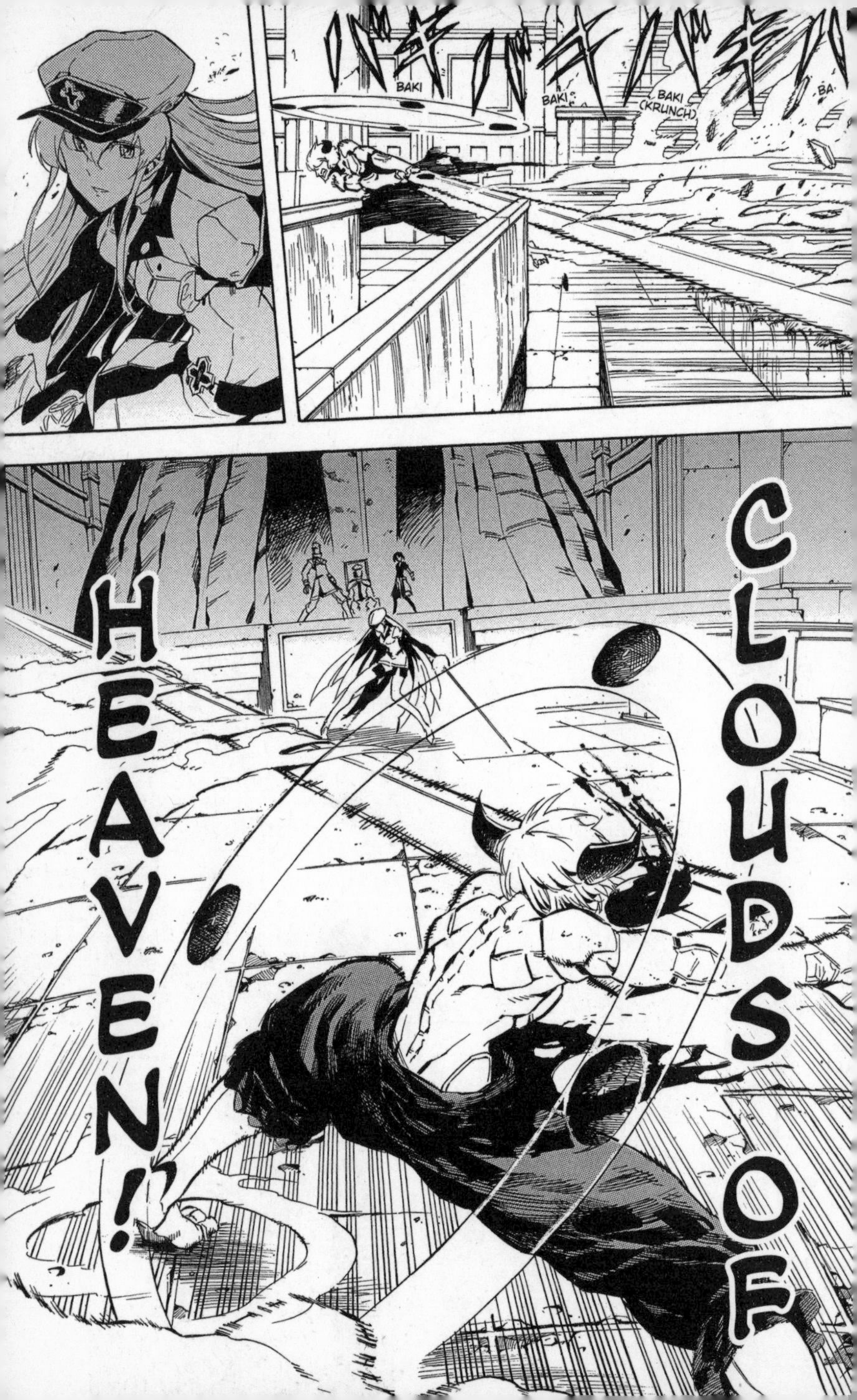
BAKI
BAKI
BAKI (KRUNCH)
BA
CLOUDS OF
HEAVEN!

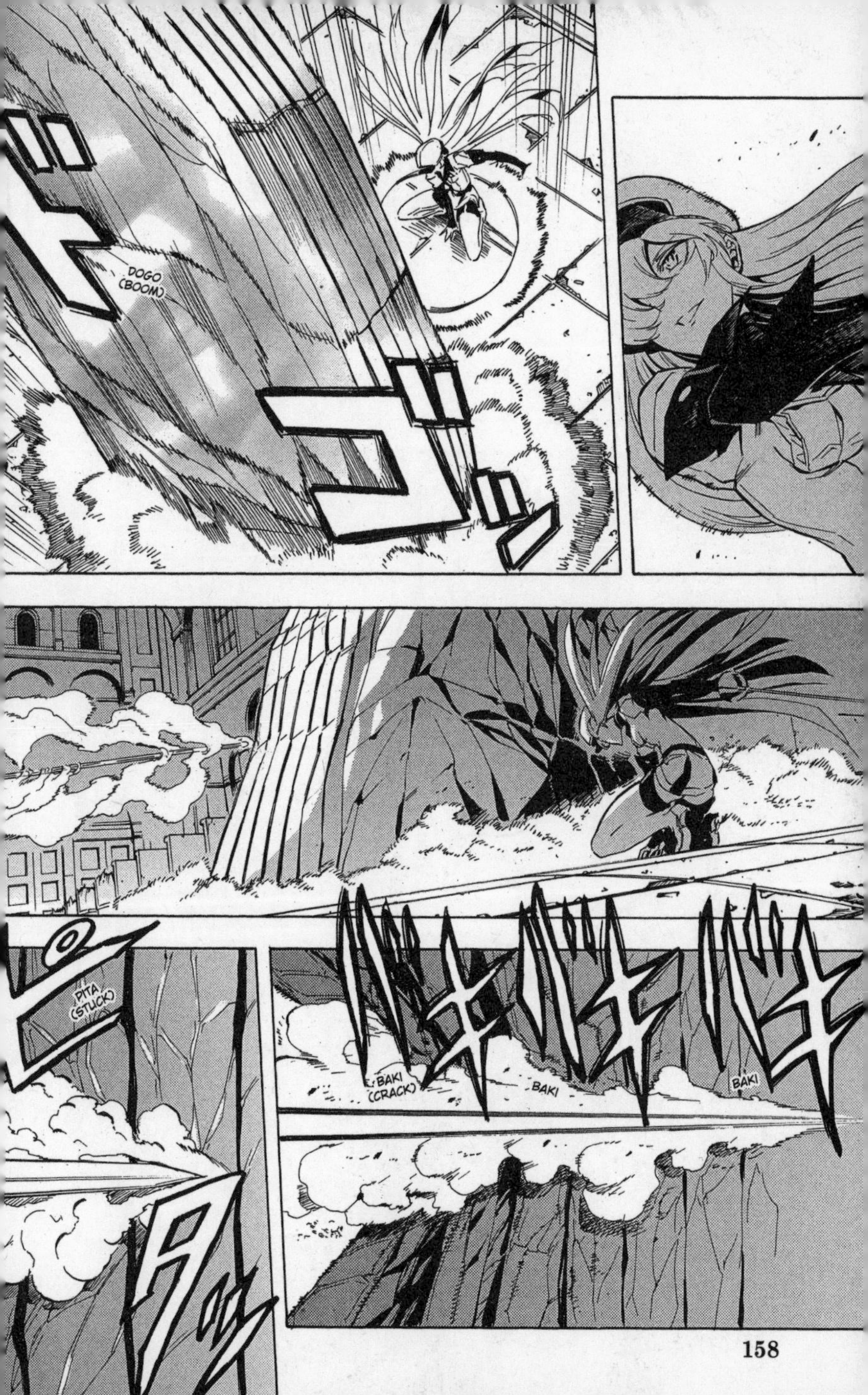
DOGO
(BOOM)
BAKI
(CRACK)
BAKI
BAKI
PITA
(STUCK)

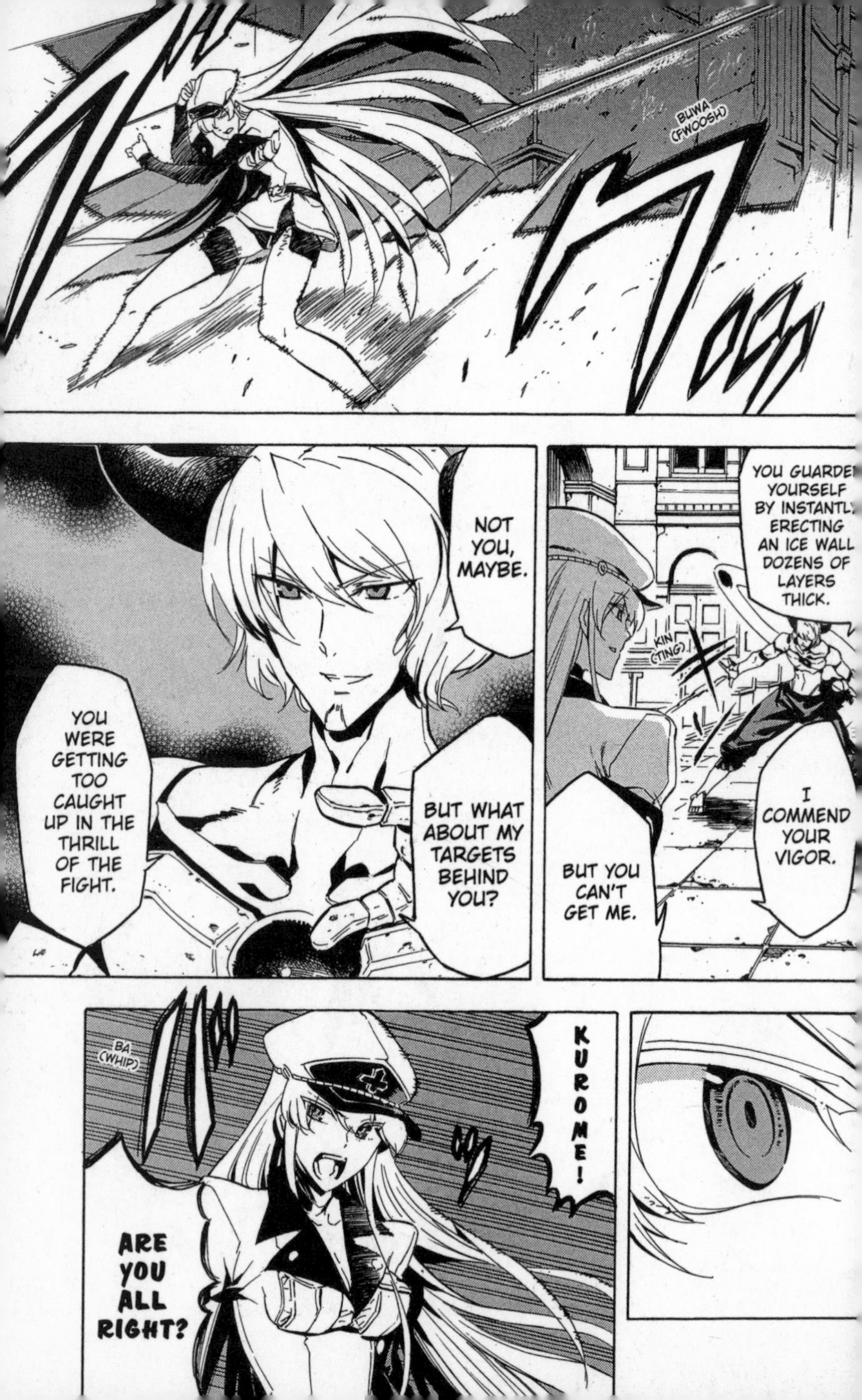
BUWA (FWOOSH)
YOU GUARDE YOURSELF BY INSTANTL ERECTING AN ICE WALL DOZENS OF LAYERS THICK.
KIN (TING)
I COMMEND YOUR VIGOR.
BUT YOU CAN'T GET ME.
NOT YOU, MAYBE.
BUT WHAT ABOUT MY TARGETS BEHIND YOU?
YOU WERE GETTING TOO CAUGHT UP IN THE THRILL OF THE FIGHT.
KUROME!
BA (WHIP)
ARE YOU ALL RIGHT?

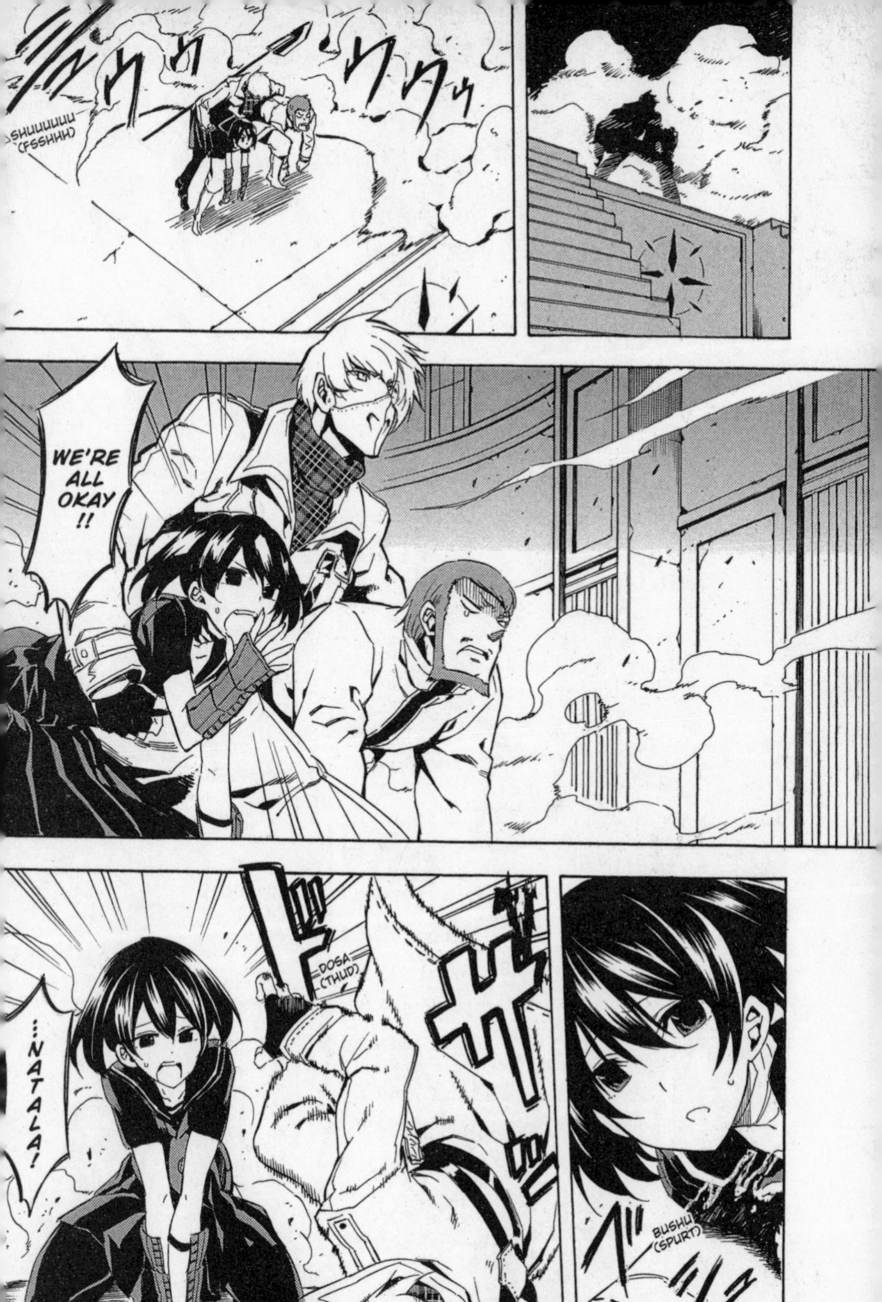
SHUUUUUUU (FSSHHH)
WE'RE ALL OKAY!!
BUSHU (SPURT)
DOSA (THUD)
...NATALA!

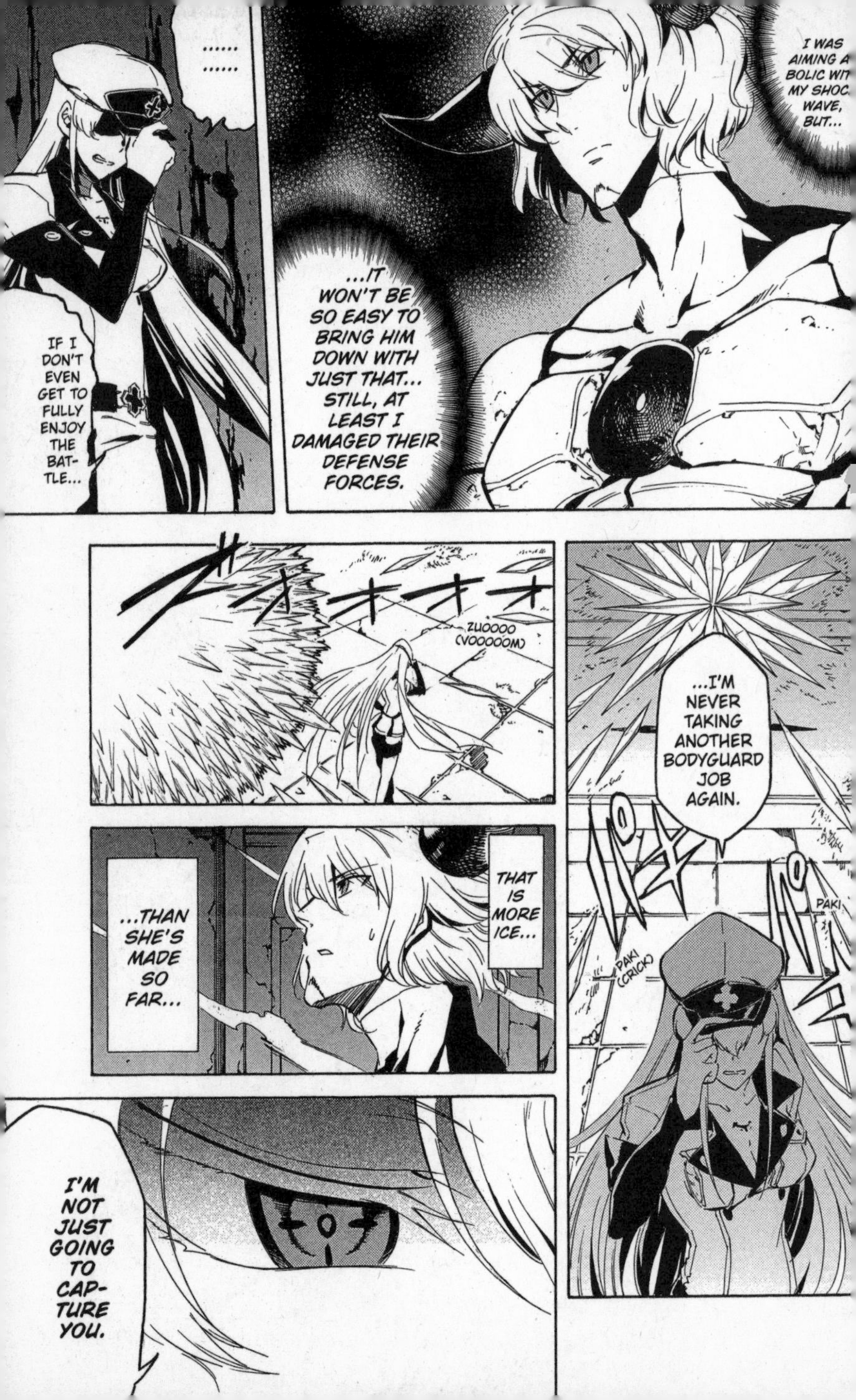
I WAS AIMING A BOLIC WIT MY SHOC WAVE, BUT...
...IT WON'T BE SO EASY TO BRING HIM DOWN WITH JUST THAT... STILL, AT LEAST I DAMAGED THEIR DEFENSE FORCES.
......
......
IF I DON'T EVEN GET TO FULLY ENJOY THE BAT-TLE...
...I'M NEVER TAKING ANOTHER BODYGUARD JOB AGAIN.
PAKI
PAKI (CRICK)
ZUOOOO (VOOOOOOM)
THAT IS MORE ICE...
...THAN SHE'S MADE SO FAR...
I'M NOT JUST GOING TO CAP-TURE YOU.

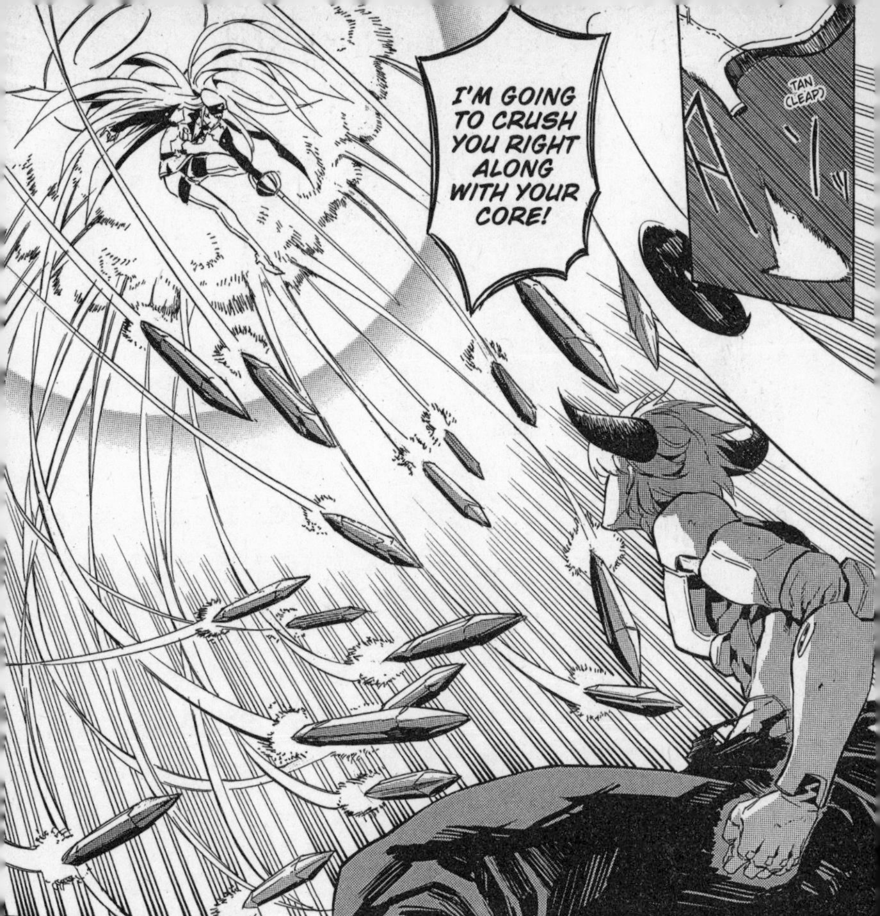
TAN (LEAP)
I'M GOING TO CRUSH YOU RIGHT ALONG WITH YOUR CORE!
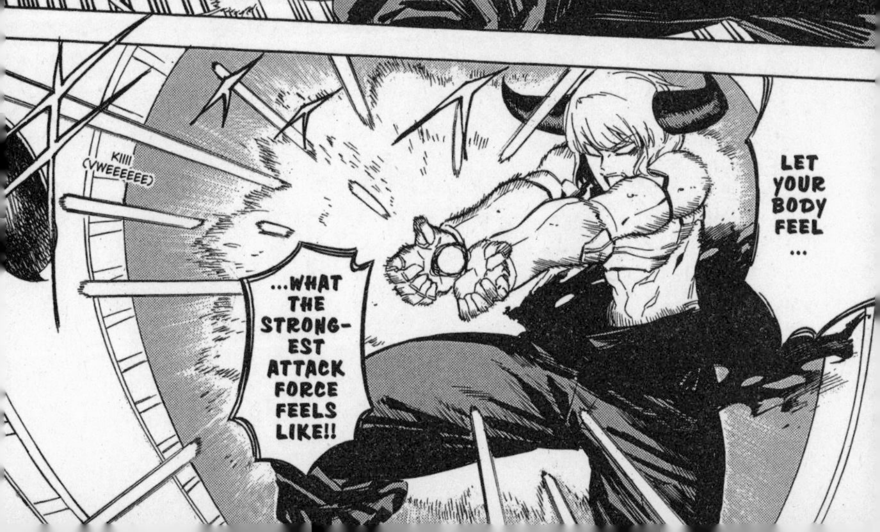
LET YOUR BODY FEEL...
KIIII (VWEEEEEE)
...WHAT THE STRONGEST ATTACK FORCE FEELS LIKE!!

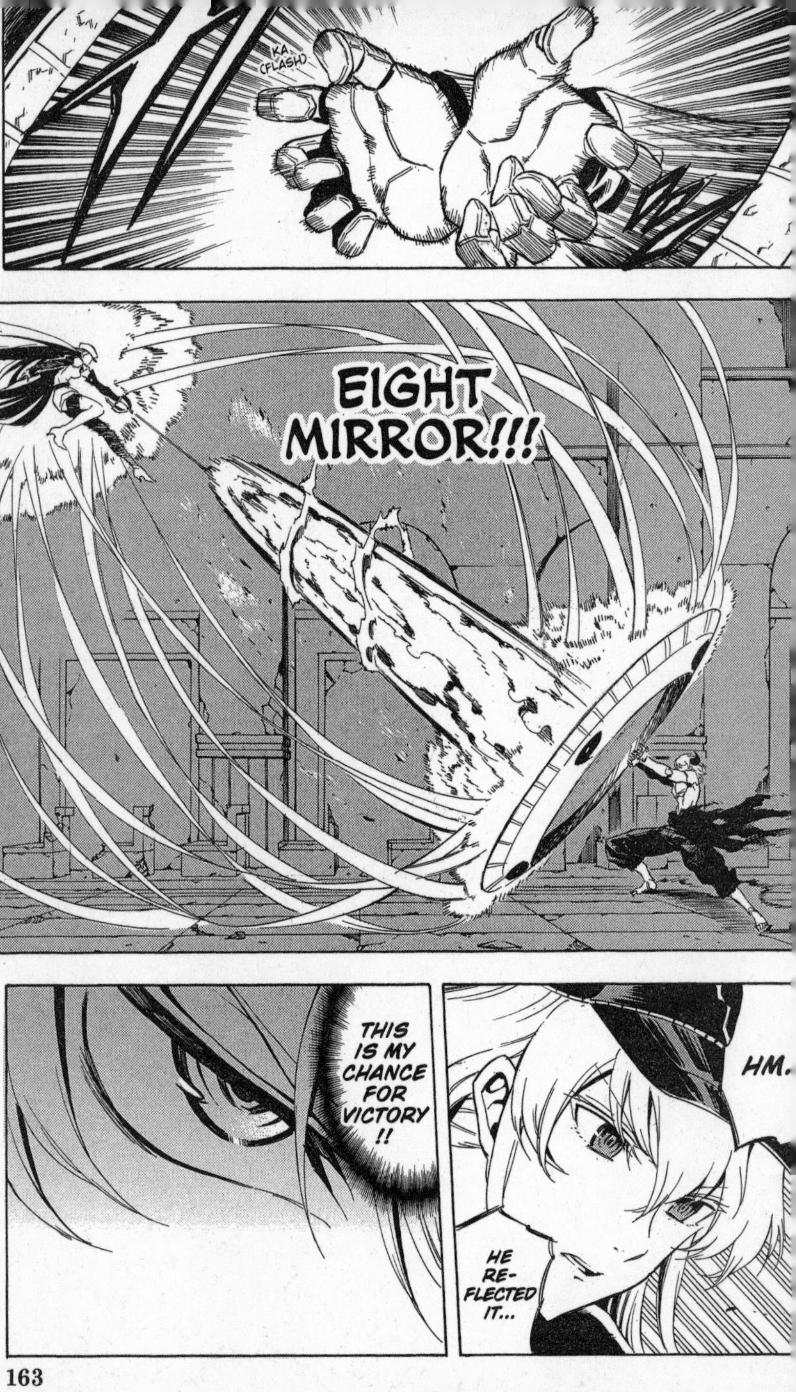
KA (FLASH)
EIGHT MIRROR!!!
HM.
HE RE-FLECTED IT...
THIS IS MY CHANCE FOR VICTORY !!

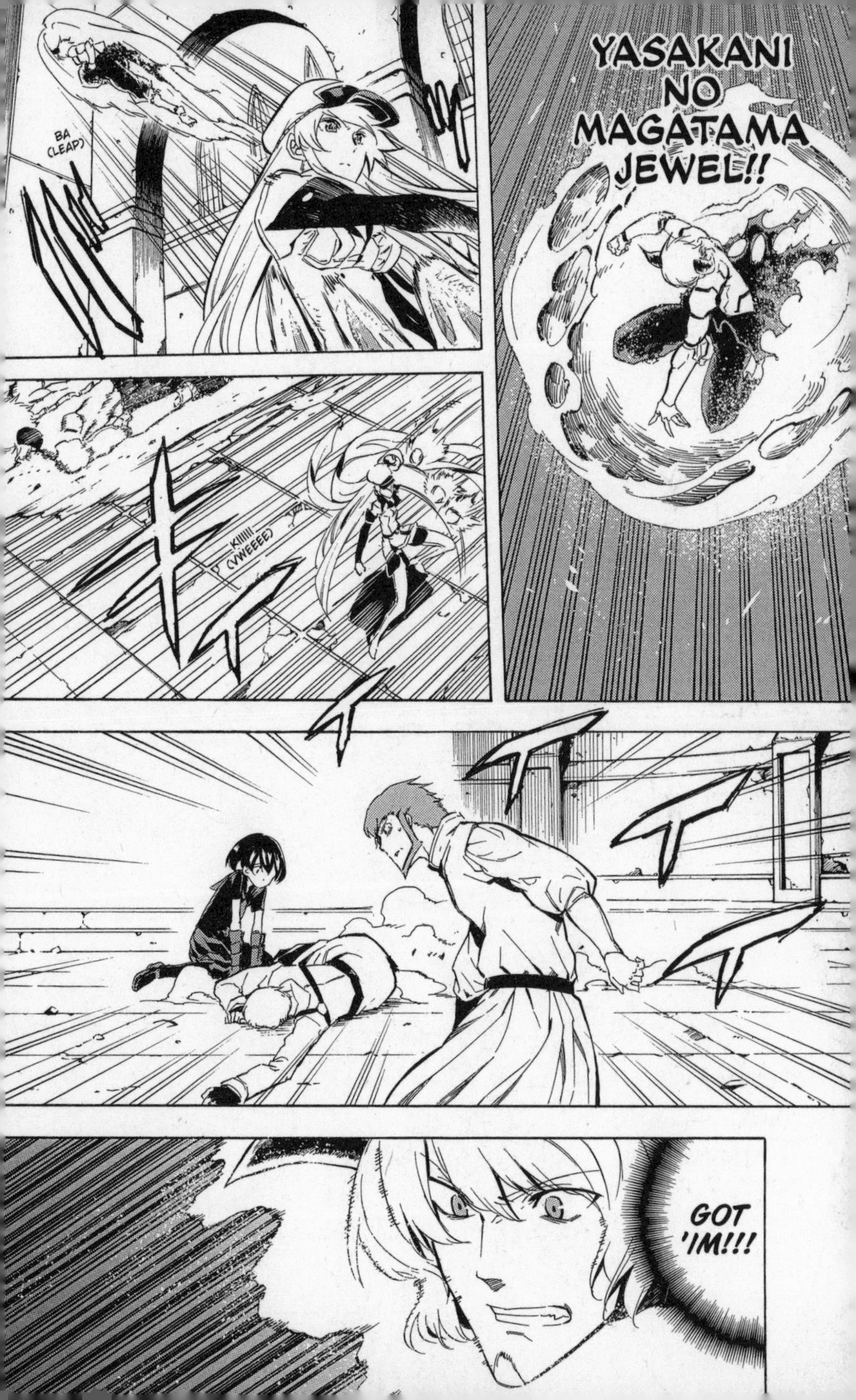
YASAKANI NO MAGATAMA JEWEL!!
BA (LEAP)
KIIIIII (VWEEEE)
GOT 'IM!!!

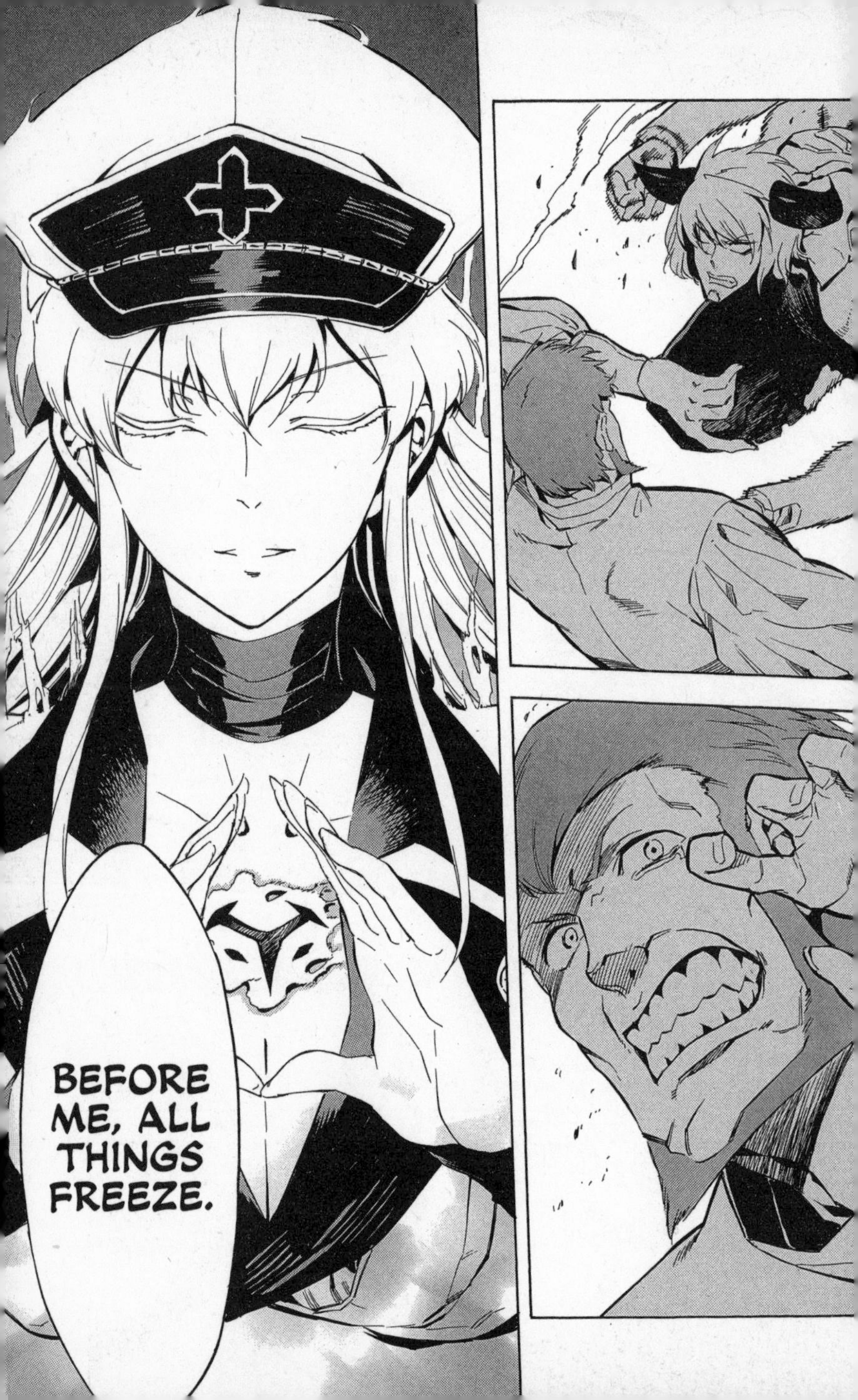
BEFORE ME, ALL THINGS FREEZE.

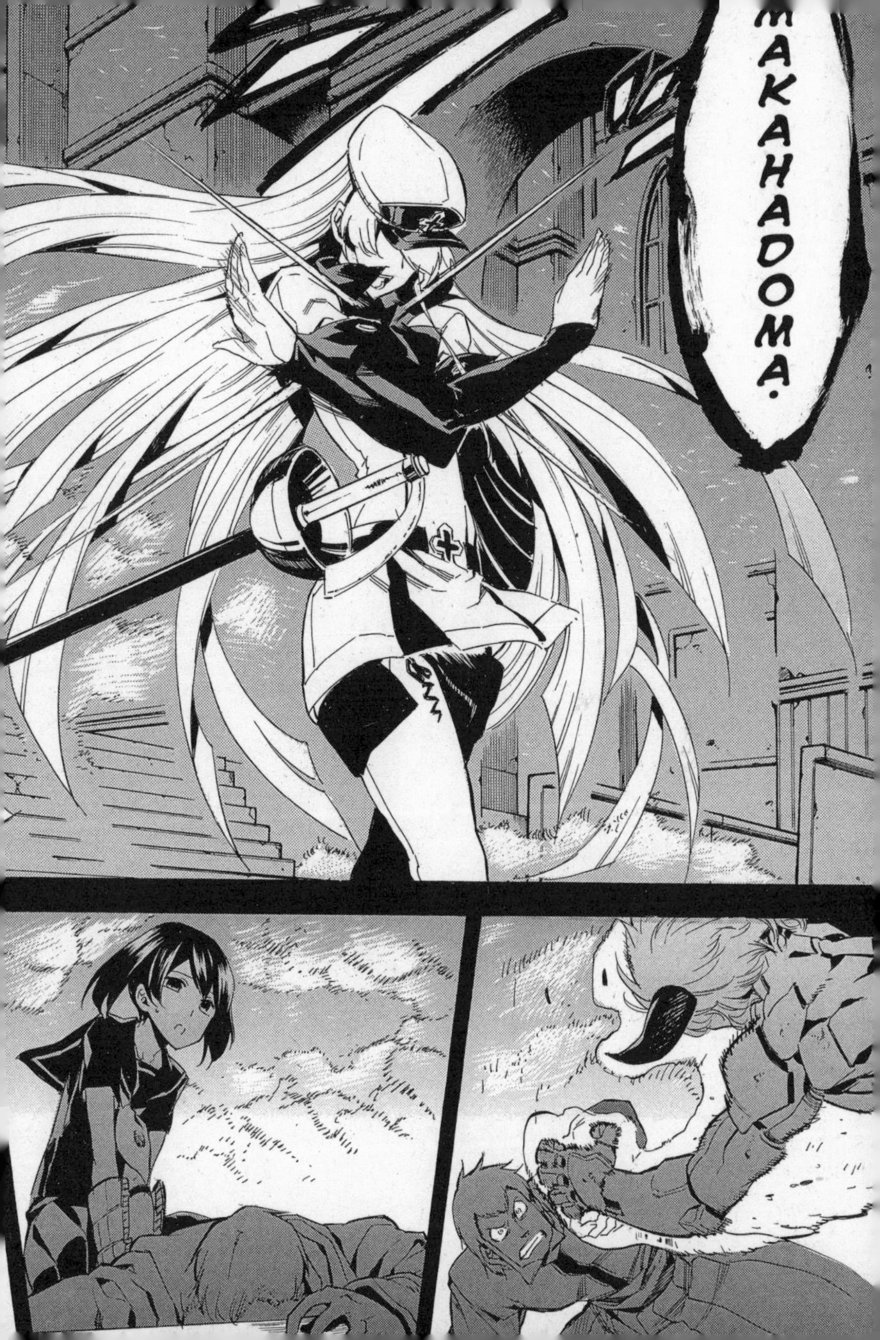
MAKAHADOOMA.

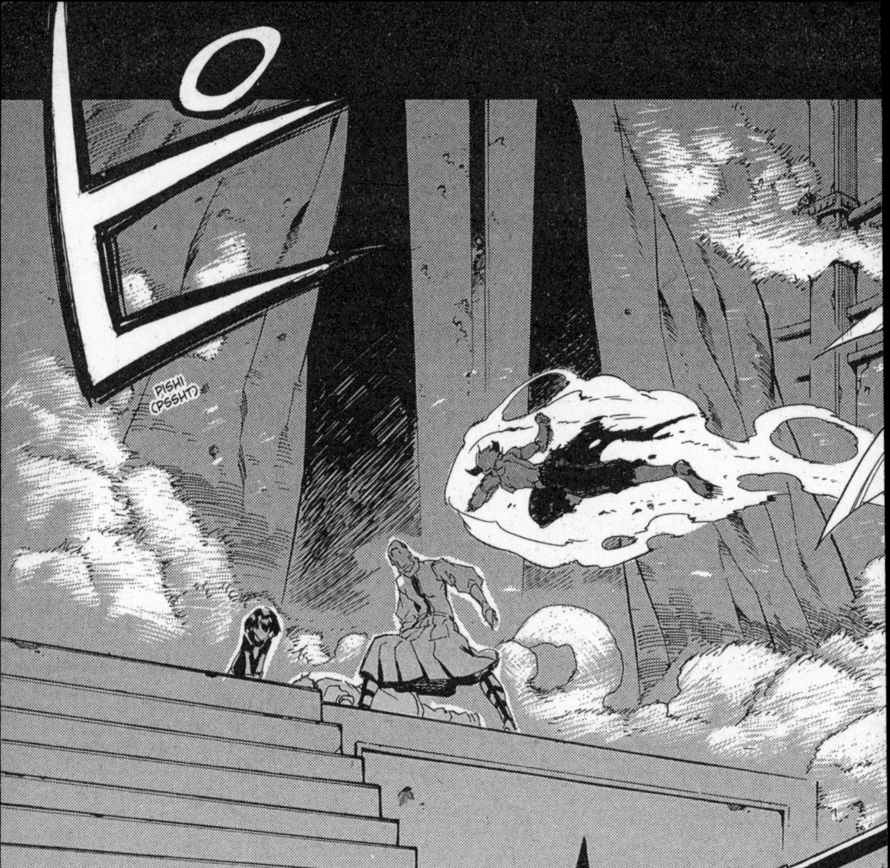
PISHI (PSSHT)

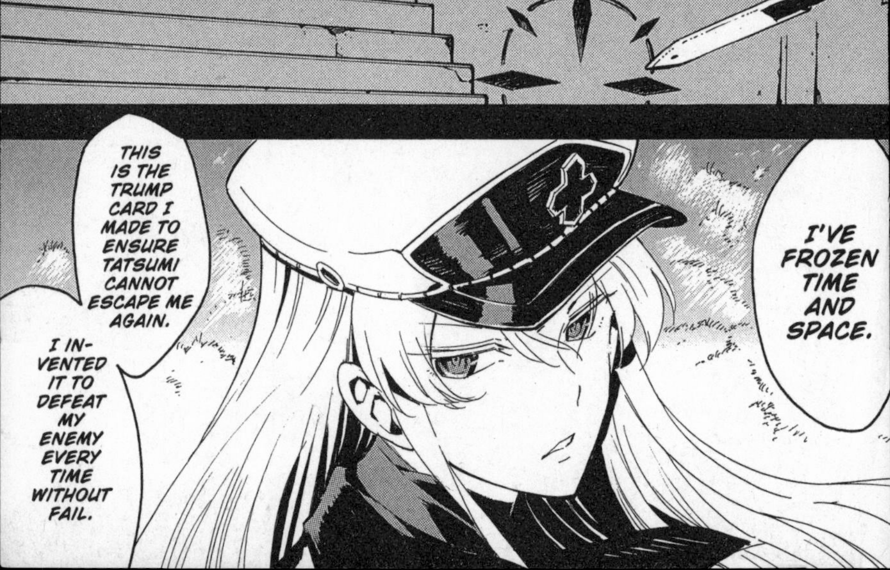
I'VE FROZEN TIME AND SPACE.
THIS IS THE TRUMP CARD I MADE TO ENSURE TATSUMI CANNOT ESCAPE ME AGAIN.
I IN-VENTED IT TO DEFEAT MY ENEMY EVERY TIME WITHOUT FAIL.

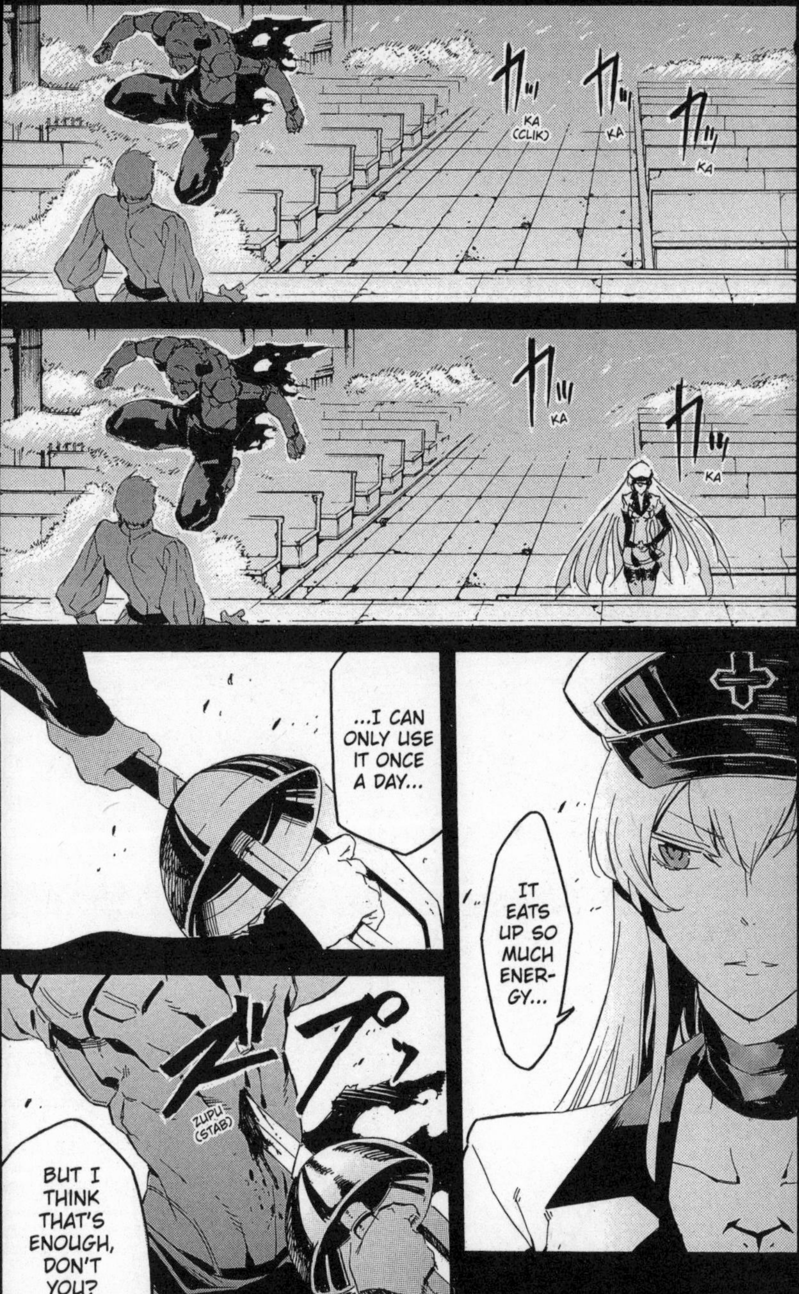
KA
KA
KA (CLIK)
KA
KA
IT EATS UP SO MUCH ENERGY...
...I CAN ONLY USE IT ONCE A DAY...
ZUPU (STAB)
BUT I THINK THAT'S ENOUGH, DON'T YOU?

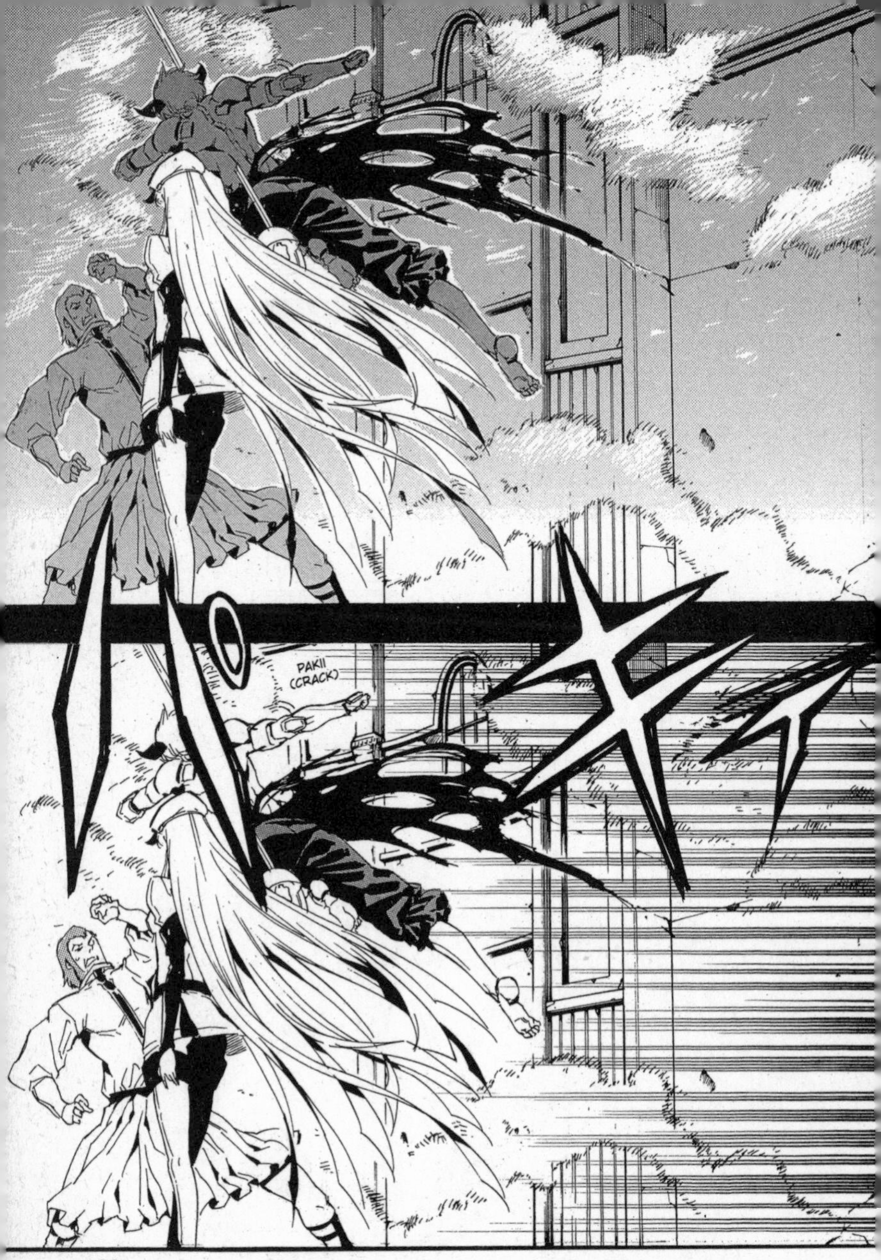
PAKII
(CRACK)

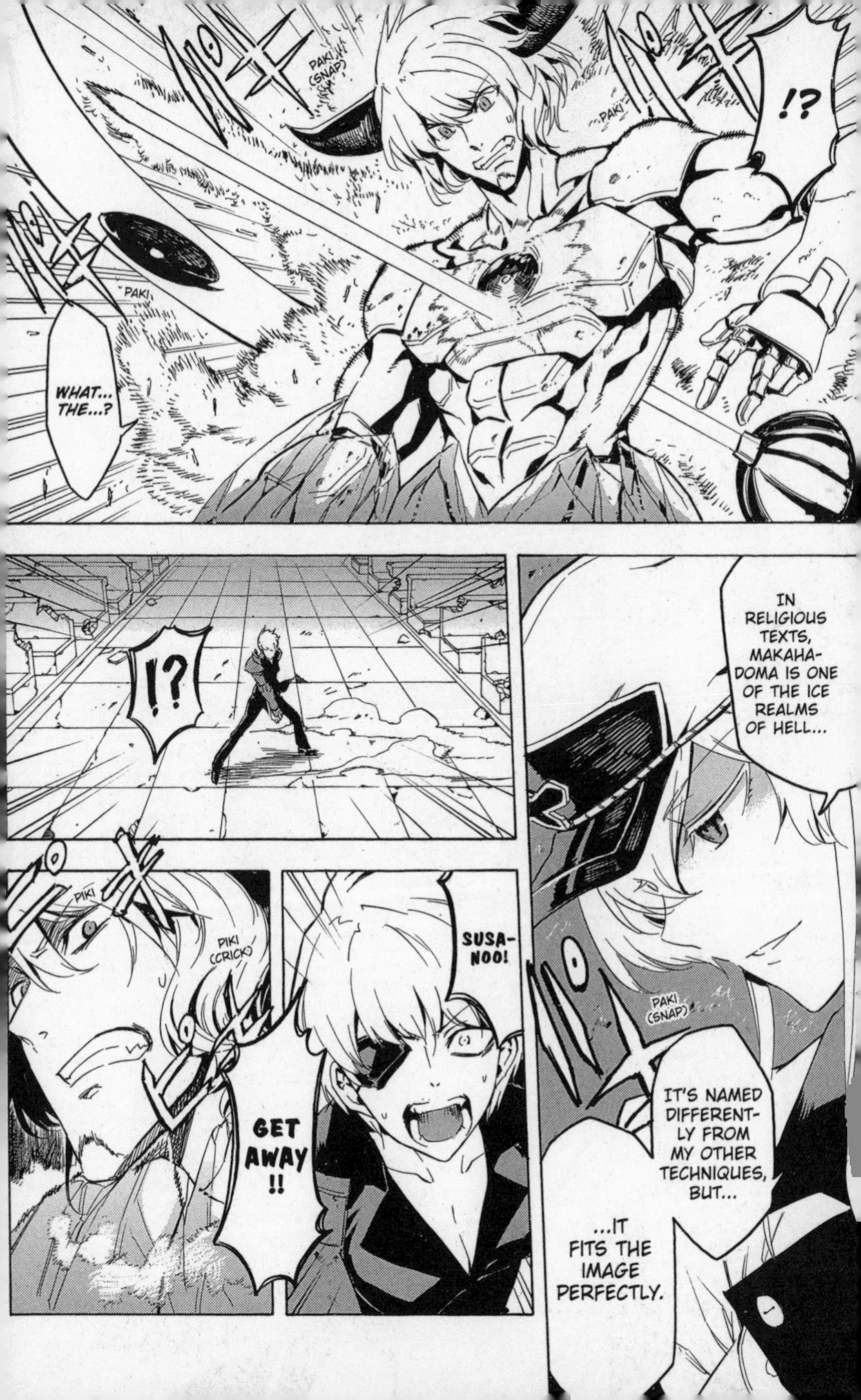
!?
PAKI
PAKI (SNAP)
PAKI
WHAT... THE...?
IN RELIGIOUS TEXTS, MAKAHA-DOMA IS ONE OF THE ICE REALMS OF HELL...
PAKI (SNAP)
IT'S NAMED DIFFERENT-LY FROM MY OTHER TECHNIQUES, BUT...
...IT FITS THE IMAGE PERFECTLY.
!?
SUSA-NOO!
GET AWAY !!
PIKI
PIKI (CRICK)

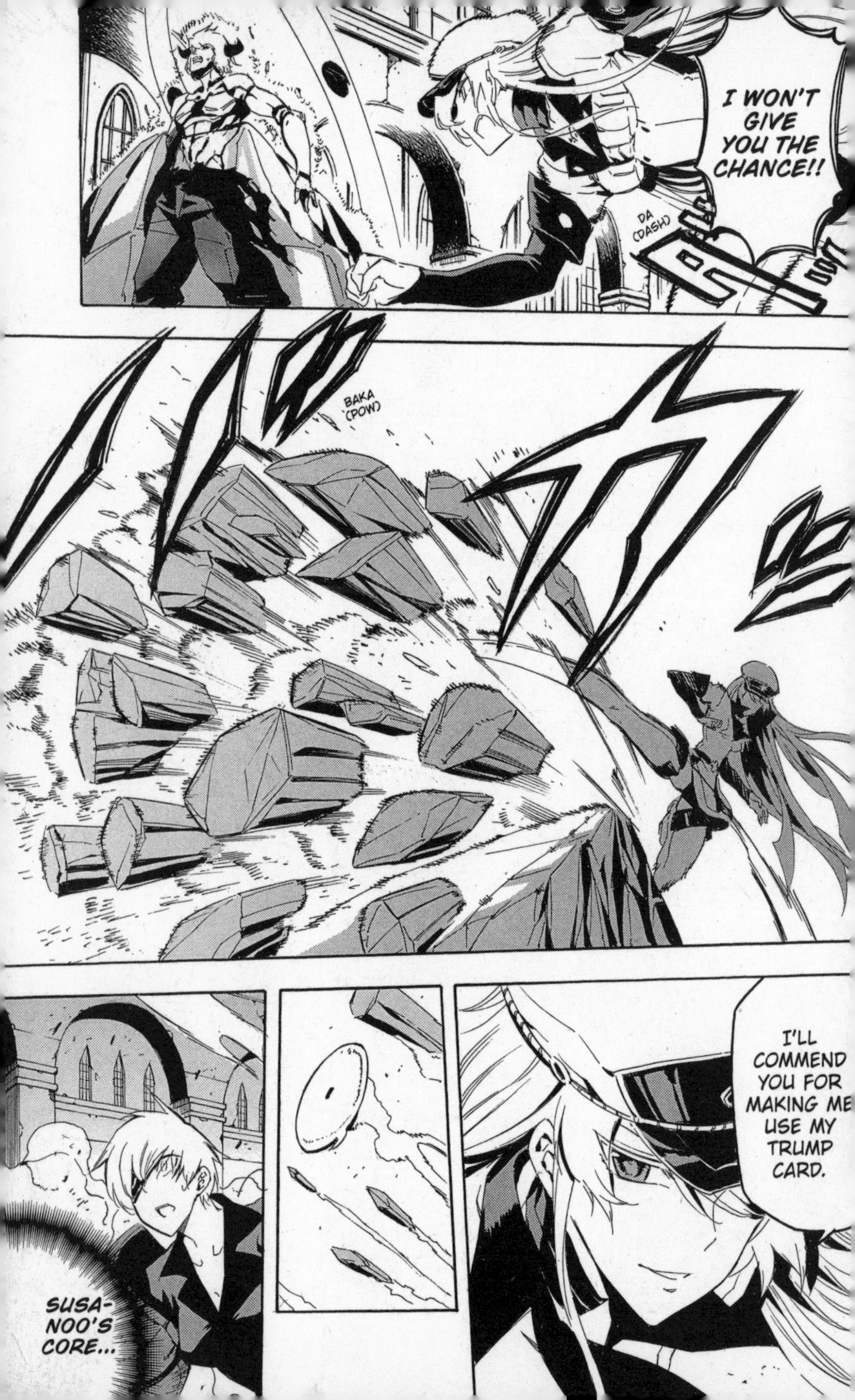
I WON'T GIVE YOU THE CHANCE!!
DA (DASH)
BAKA (POW)
I'LL COMMEND YOU FOR MAKING ME USE MY TRUMP CARD.
SUSA-NOO'S CORE...

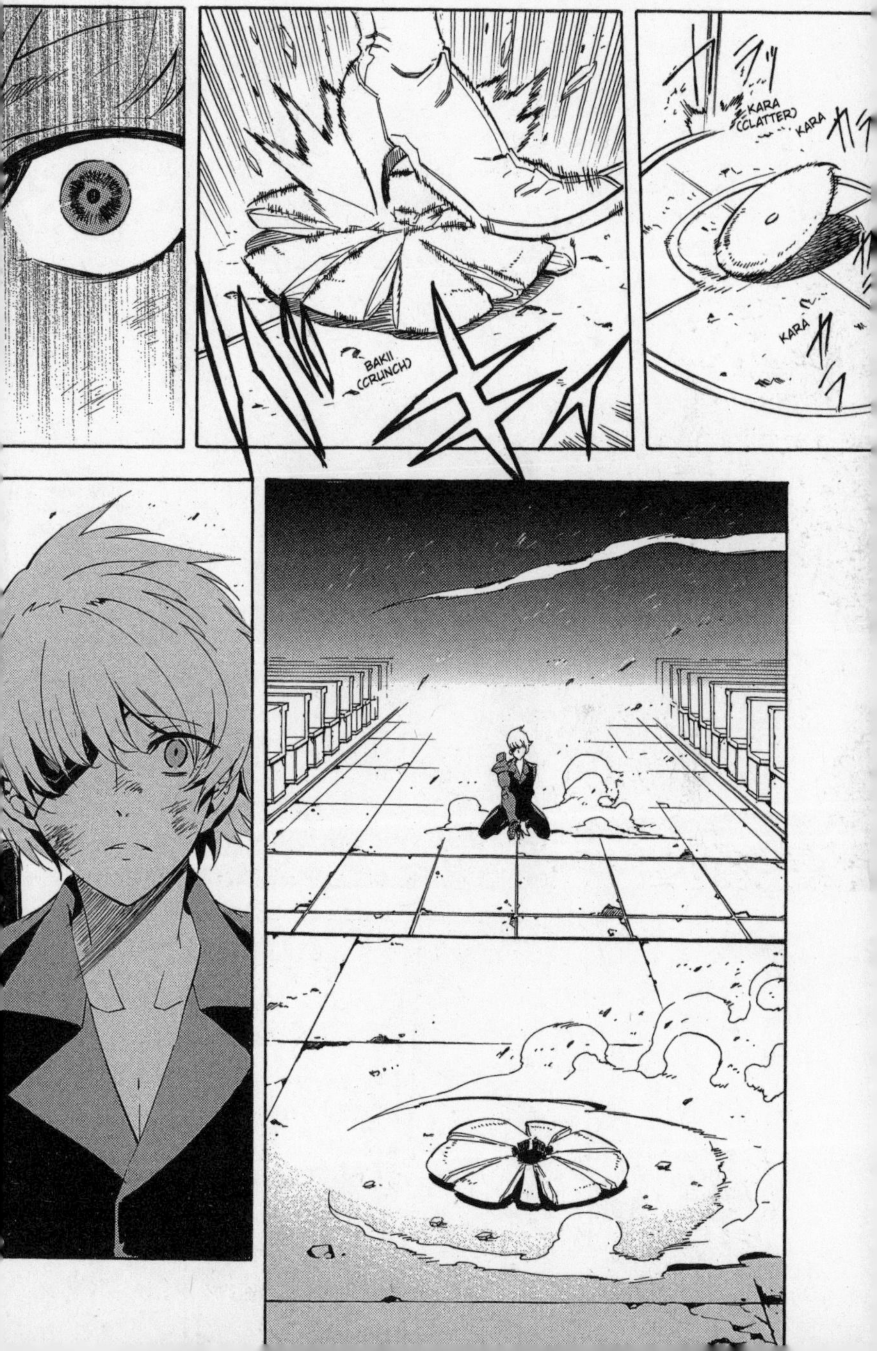
KARA (CLATTER)
KARA
KARA
BAKII (CRUNCH)

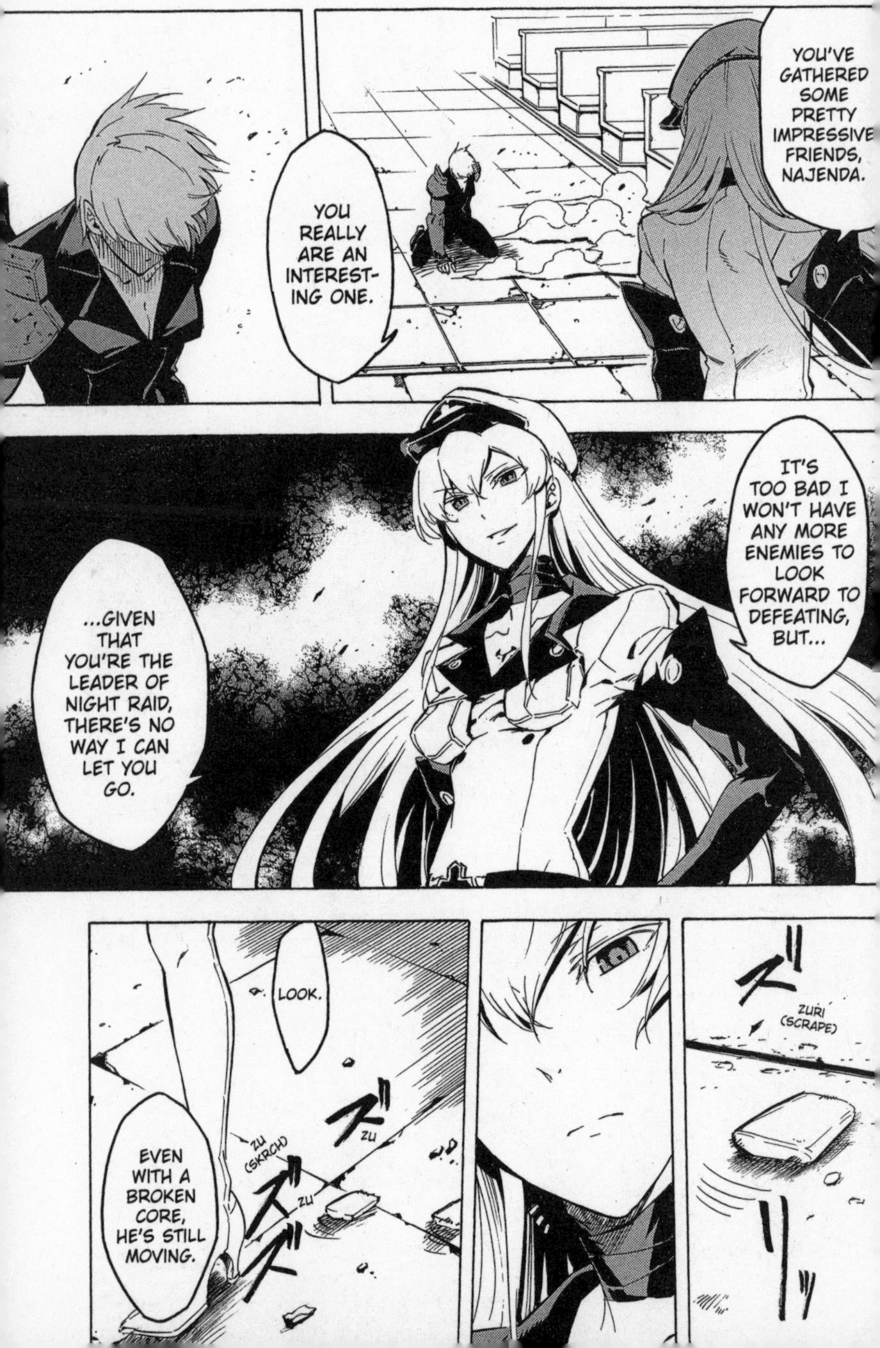
YOU'VE GATHERED SOME PRETTY IMPRESSIVE FRIENDS, NAJENDA.
YOU REALLY ARE AN INTEREST-ING ONE.
IT'S TOO BAD I WON'T HAVE ANY MORE ENEMIES TO LOOK FORWARD TO DEFEATING, BUT...
...GIVEN THAT YOU'RE THE LEADER OF NIGHT RAID, THERE'S NO WAY I CAN LET YOU GO.
ZURI (SCRAPE)
LOOK.
ZU
ZU (SKRCH)
ZU
EVEN WITH A BROKEN CORE, HE'S STILL MOVING.

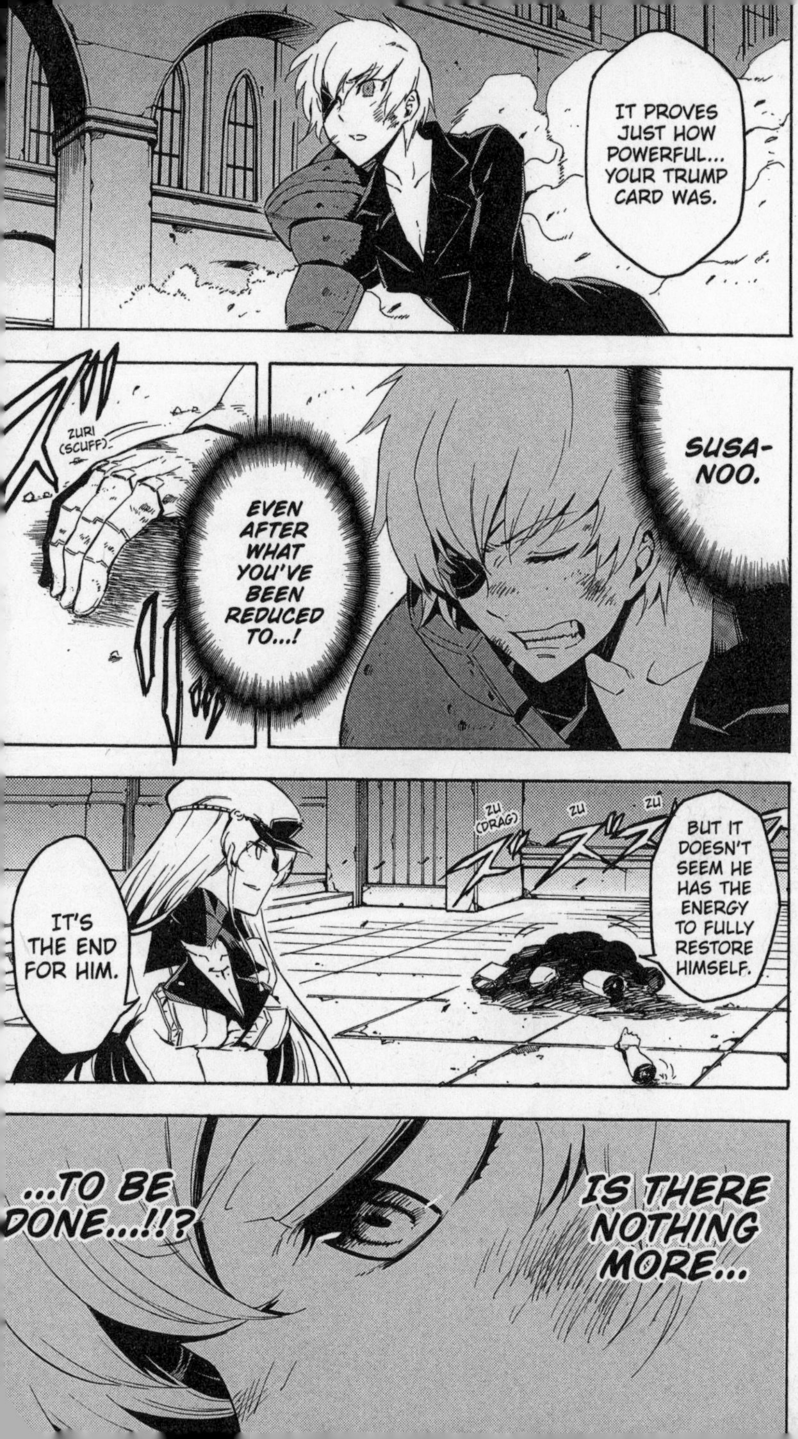
IT PROVES JUST HOW POWERFUL... YOUR TRUMP CARD WAS.
SUSA-NOO.
EVEN AFTER WHAT YOU'VE BEEN REDUCED TO...!
ZURI (SCUFF)
ZU ZU ZU (DRAG)
BUT IT DOESN'T SEEM HE HAS THE ENERGY TO FULLY RESTORE HIMSELF.
IT'S THE END FOR HIM.
IS THERE NOTHING MORE...
...TO BE DONE...!!?

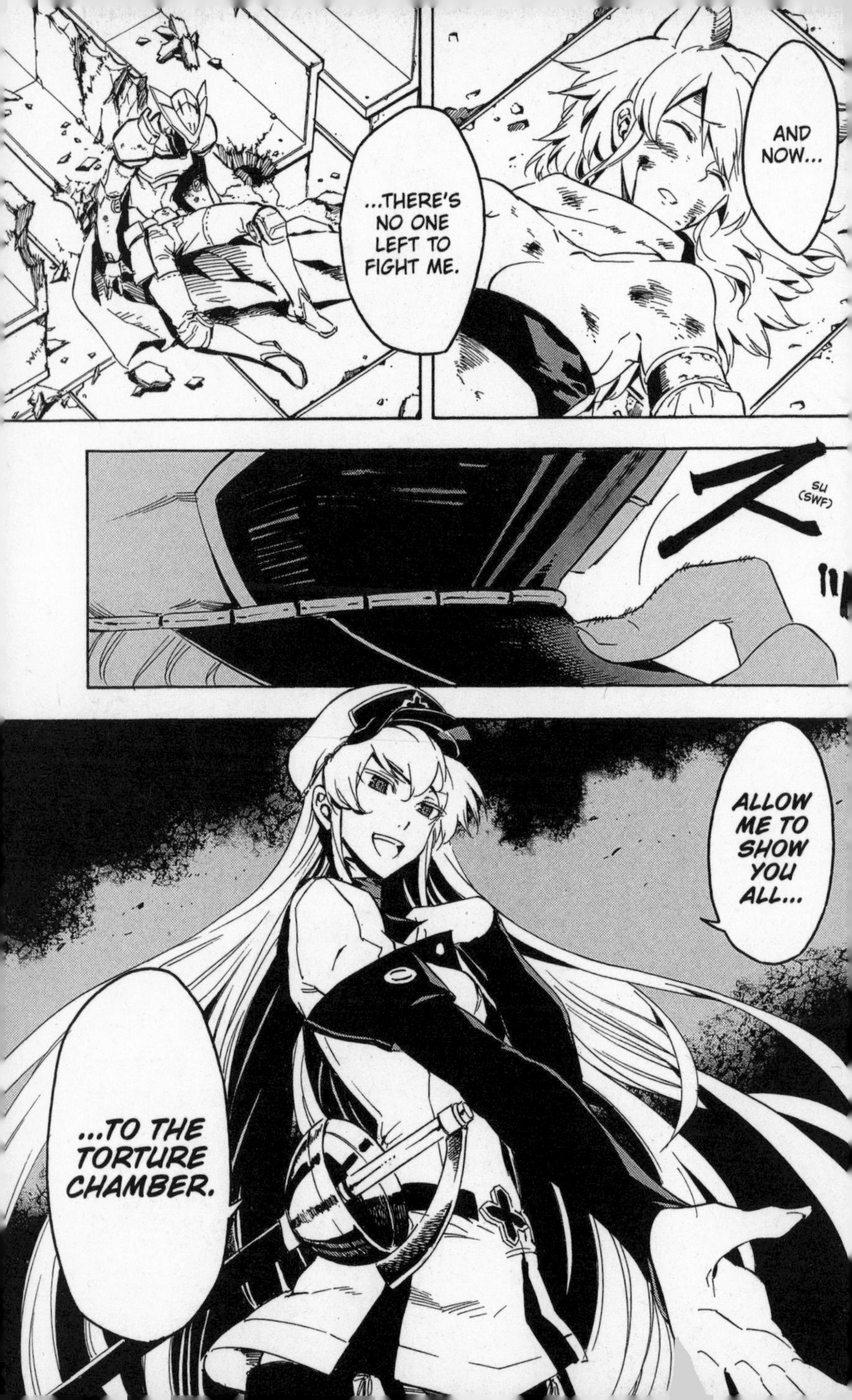
AND NOW...
...THERE'S NO ONE LEFT TO FIGHT ME.
SU (SWF)
ALLOW ME TO SHOW YOU ALL...
...TO THE TORTURE CHAMBER.

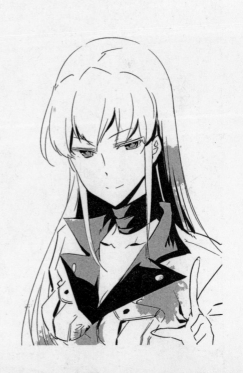

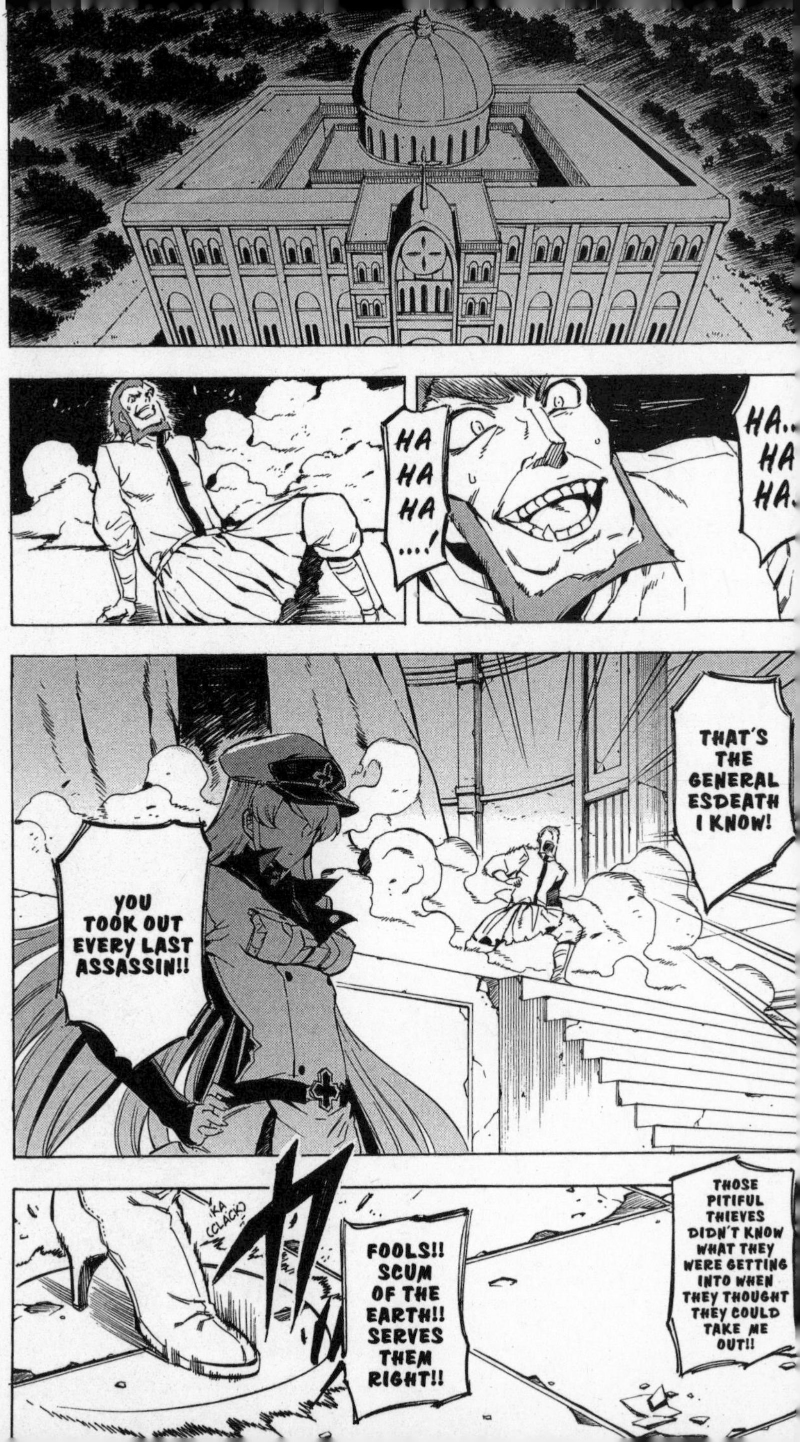
HA... HA HA...
HA HA HA ....!
THAT'S THE GENERAL ESDEATH I KNOW!
YOU TOOK OUT EVERY LAST ASSASSIN!!
THOSE PITIFUL THIEVES DIDN'T KNOW WHAT THEY WERE GETTING INTO WHEN THEY THOUGHT THEY COULD TAKE ME OUT!!
FOOLS!! SCUM OF THE EARTH!! SERVES THEM RIGHT!!
KA CLACK

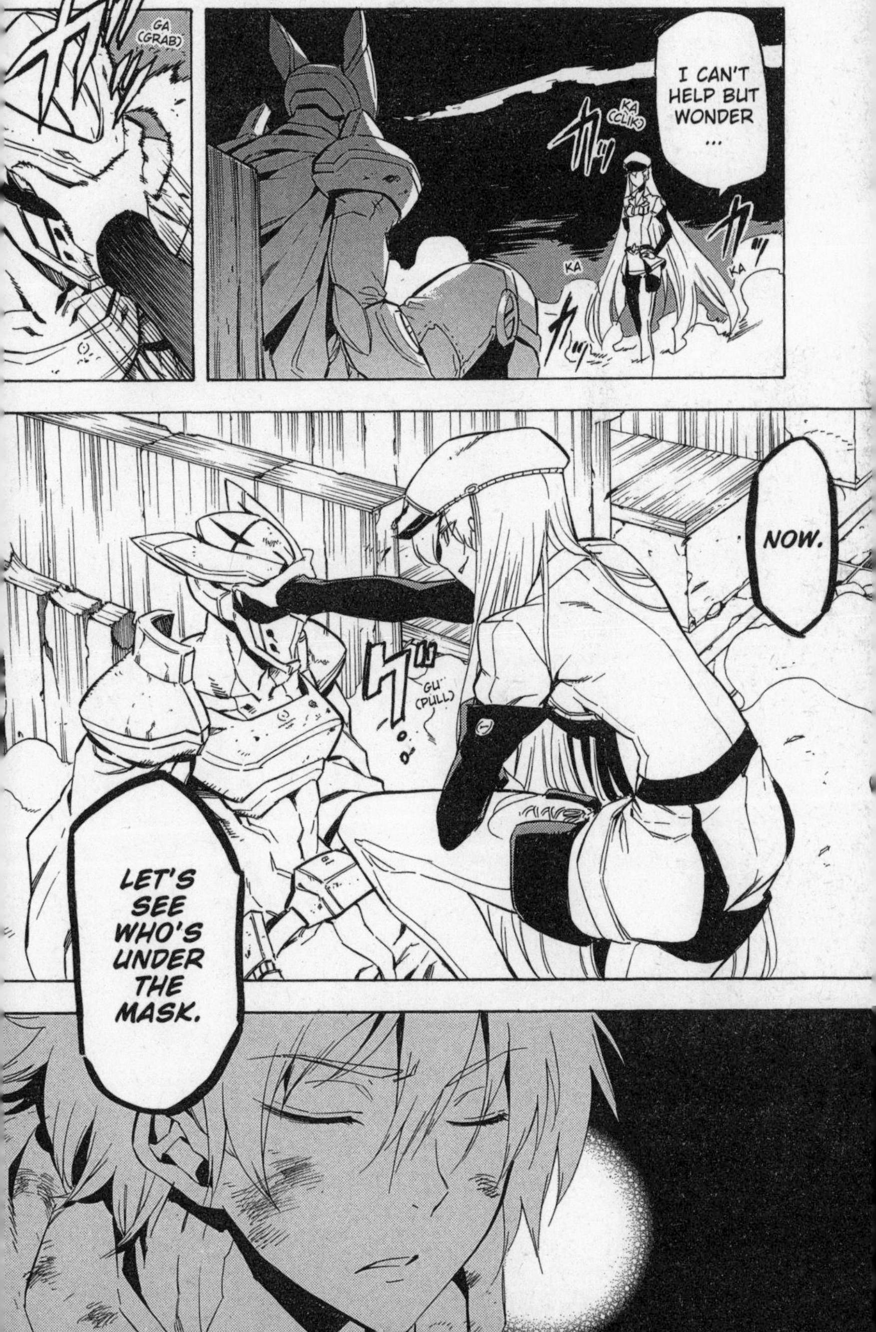
I CAN'T HELP BUT WONDER ...
KA (CLIK)
KA
KA
GA (GRAB)
NOW.
GU (PULL)
LET'S SEE WHO'S UNDER THE MASK.

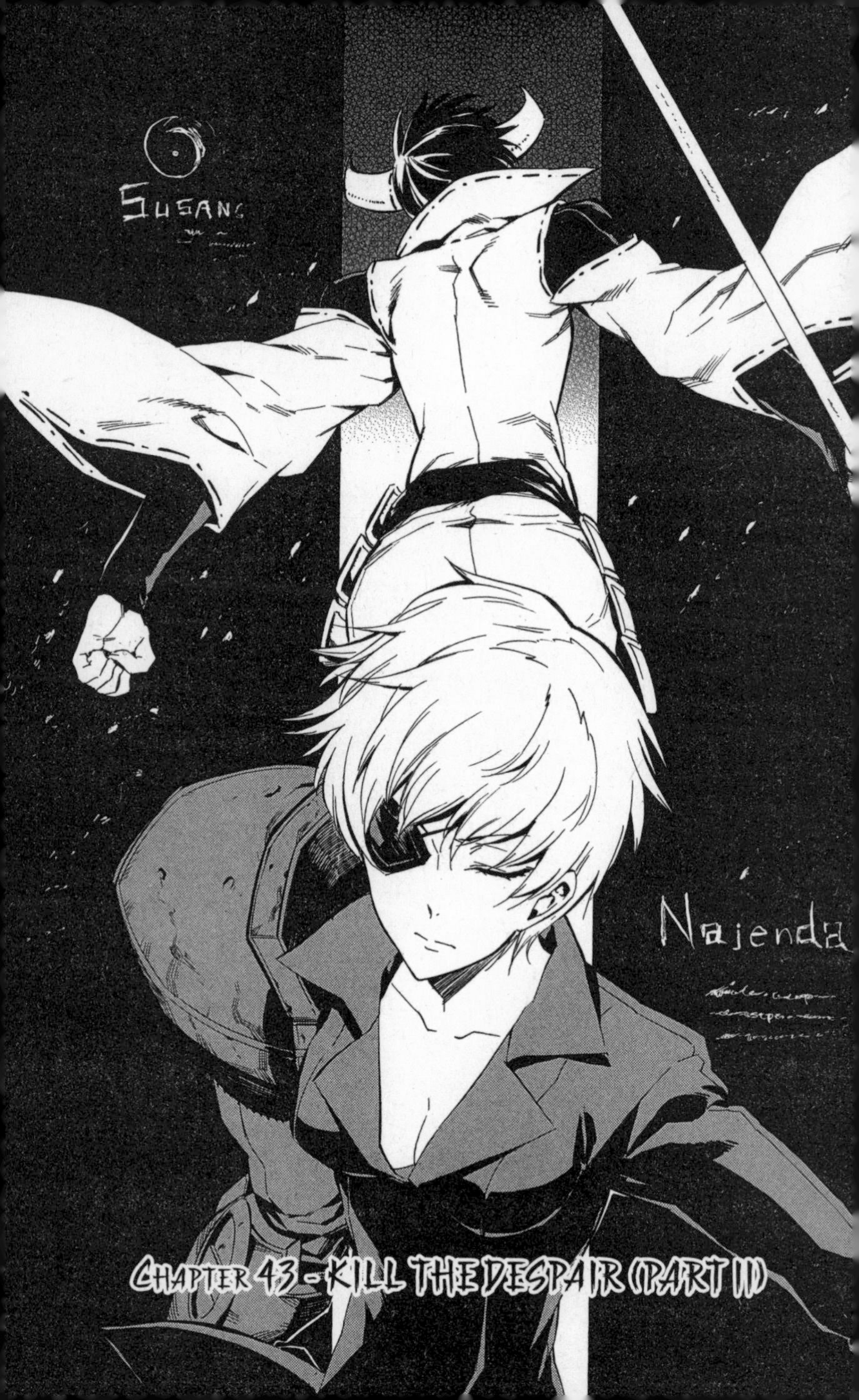
Susano
Najenda
Chapter 43 - Kill the Despair (Part II)

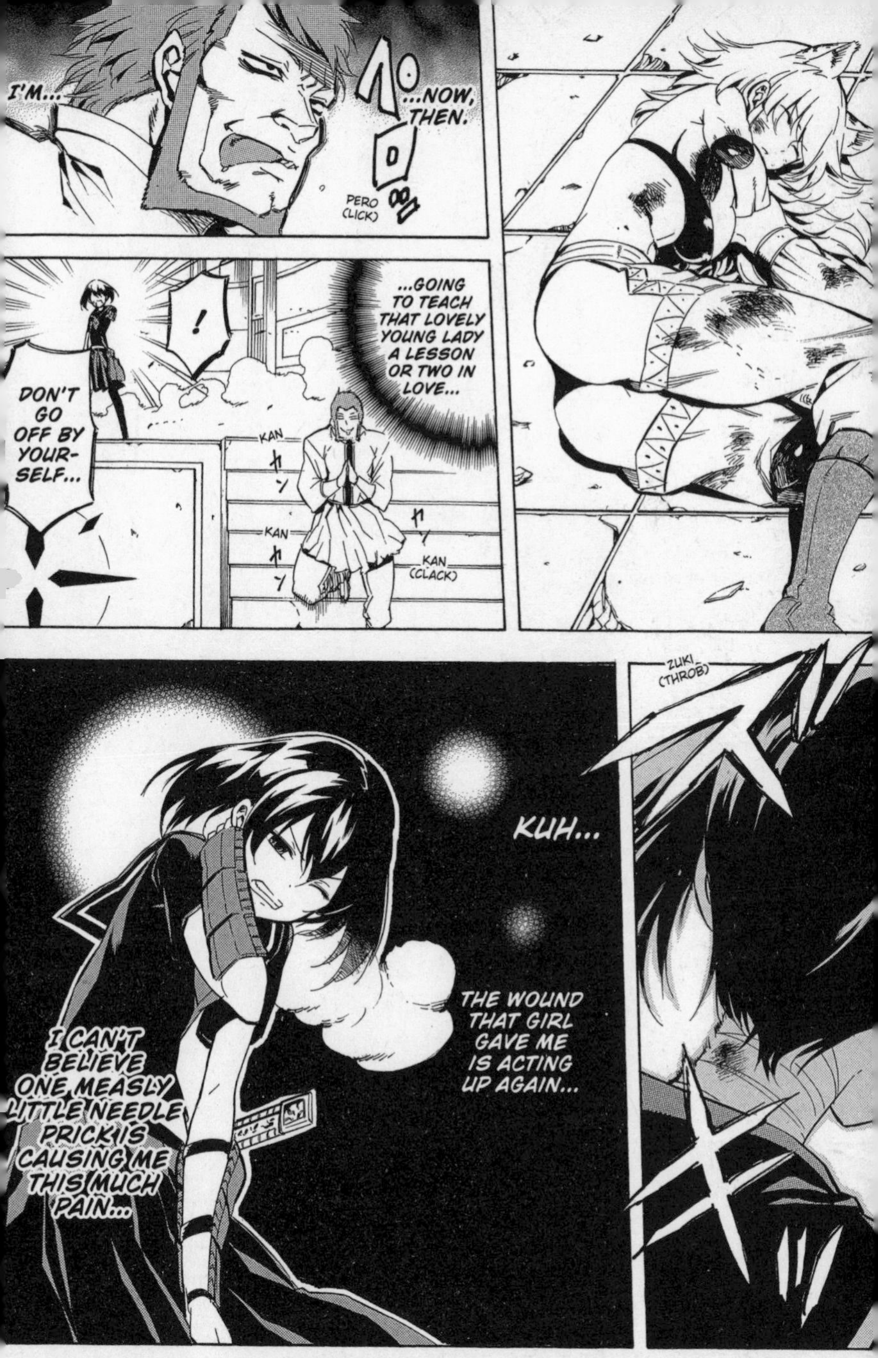
...NOW, THEN.
I'M...
PERO (LICK)
...GOING TO TEACH THAT LOVELY YOUNG LADY A LESSON OR TWO IN LOVE...
!
DON'T GO OFF BY YOURSELF...
KAN
KAN
KAN (CLACK)
ZUKI (THROB)
KUH...
THE WOUND THAT GIRL GAVE ME IS ACTING UP AGAIN...
I CAN'T BELIEVE ONE MEASLY LITTLE NEEDLE PRICK IS CAUSING ME THIS MUCH PAIN...

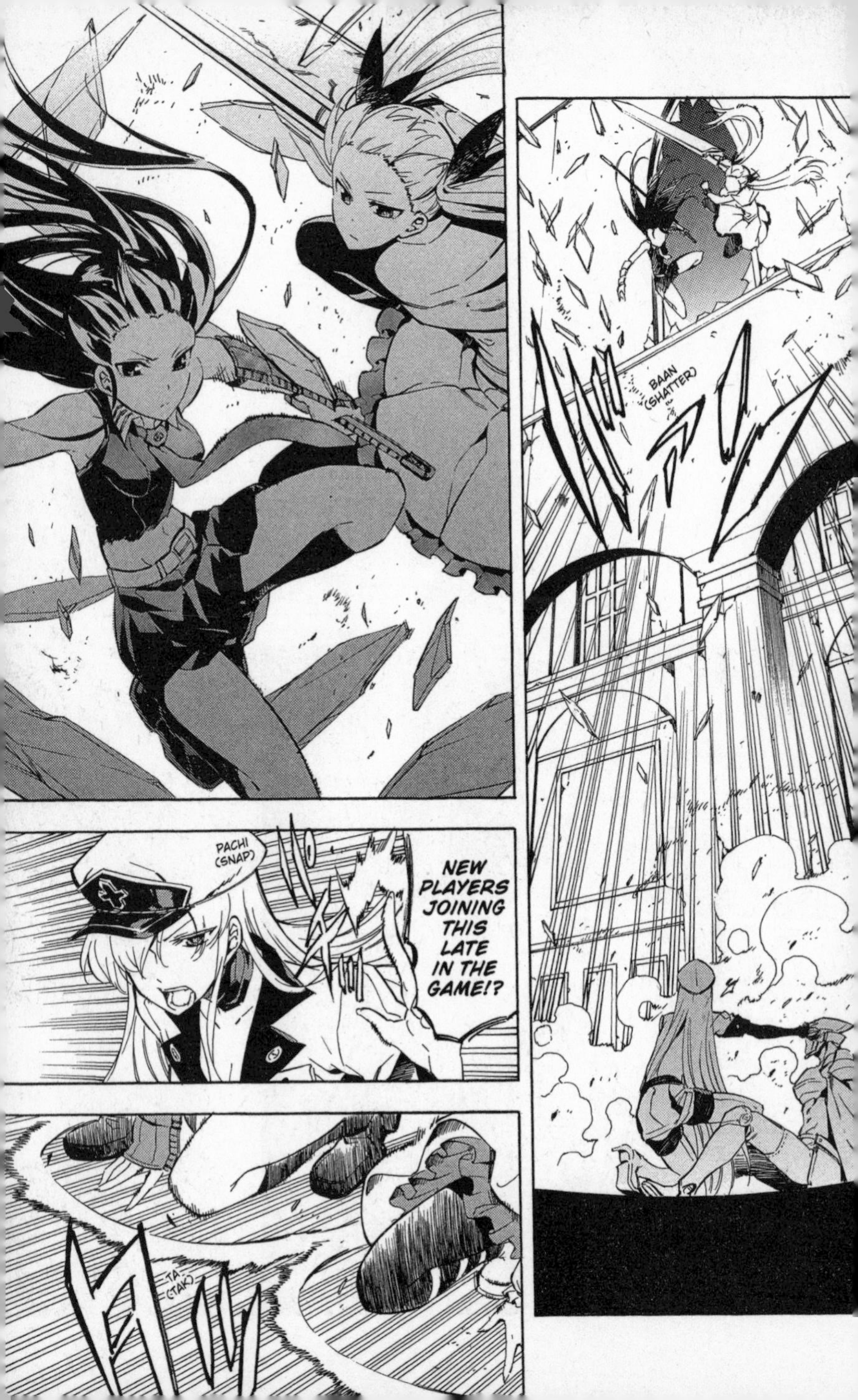
BAAN (SHATTER)
PACHI (SNAP)
NEW PLAYERS JOINING THIS LATE IN THE GAME!?
TA (TAK)

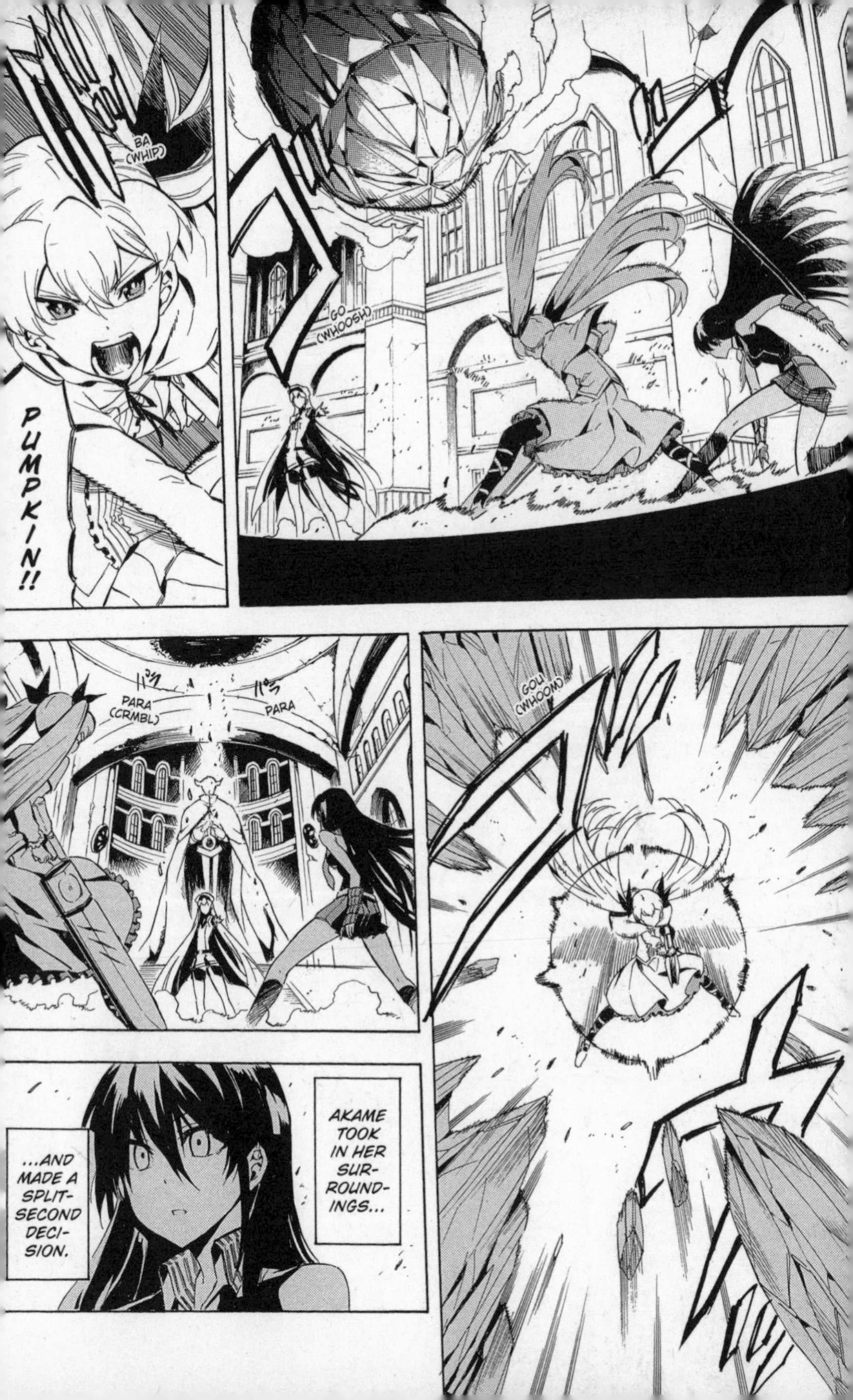
GO (WHOOSH)
BA (WHIP)
PUMPKIN!!
GOU (WHOOM)
PARA
PARA (CRMBL)
AKAME TOOK IN HER SURROUNDINGS...
...AND MADE A SPLIT-SECOND DECISION.

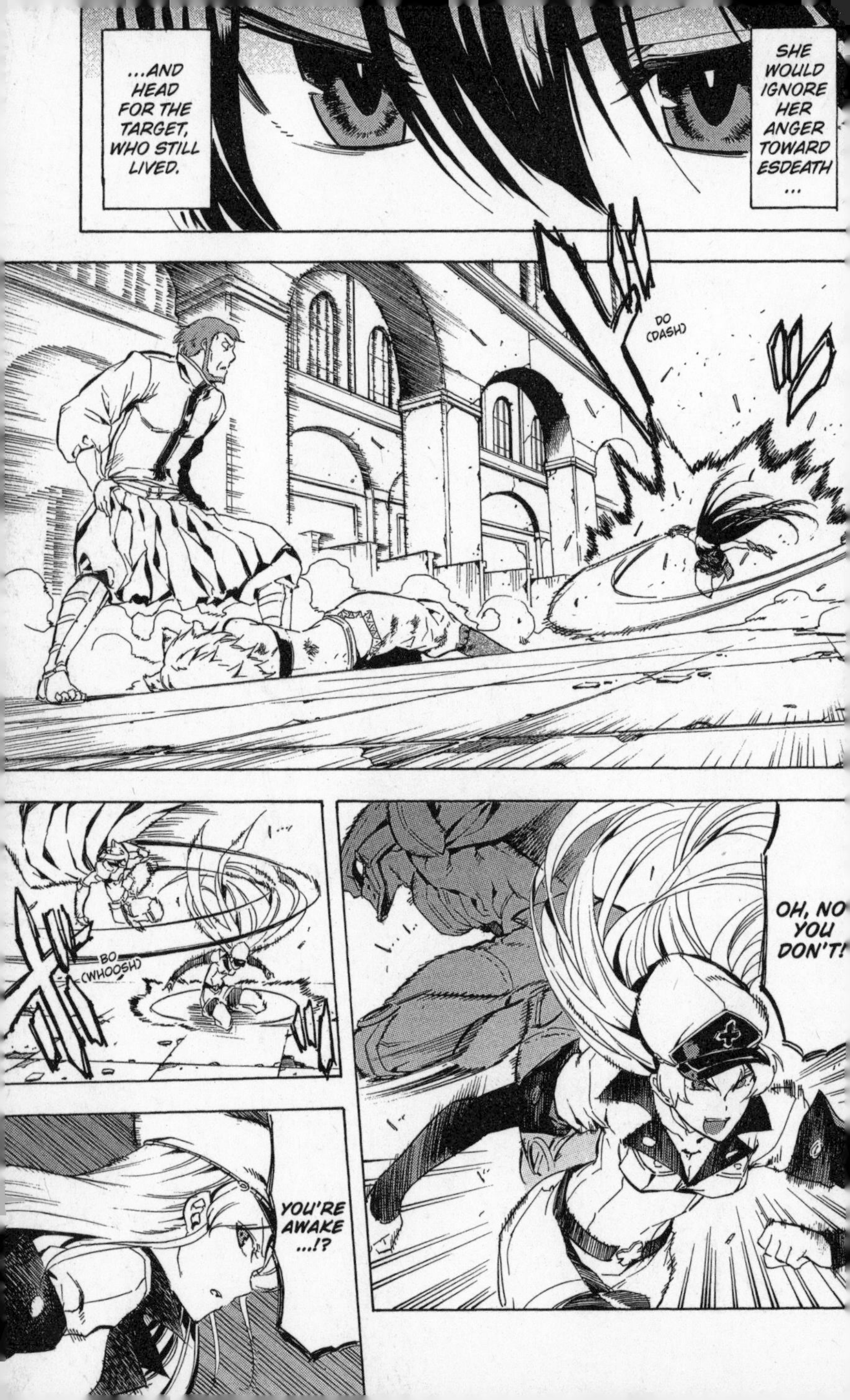
SHE WOULD IGNORE HER ANGER TOWARD ESDEATH ...
...AND HEAD FOR THE TARGET, WHO STILL LIVED.
DO (DASH)
OH, NO YOU DON'T!
BO (WHOOSH)
YOU'RE AWAKE ...!?

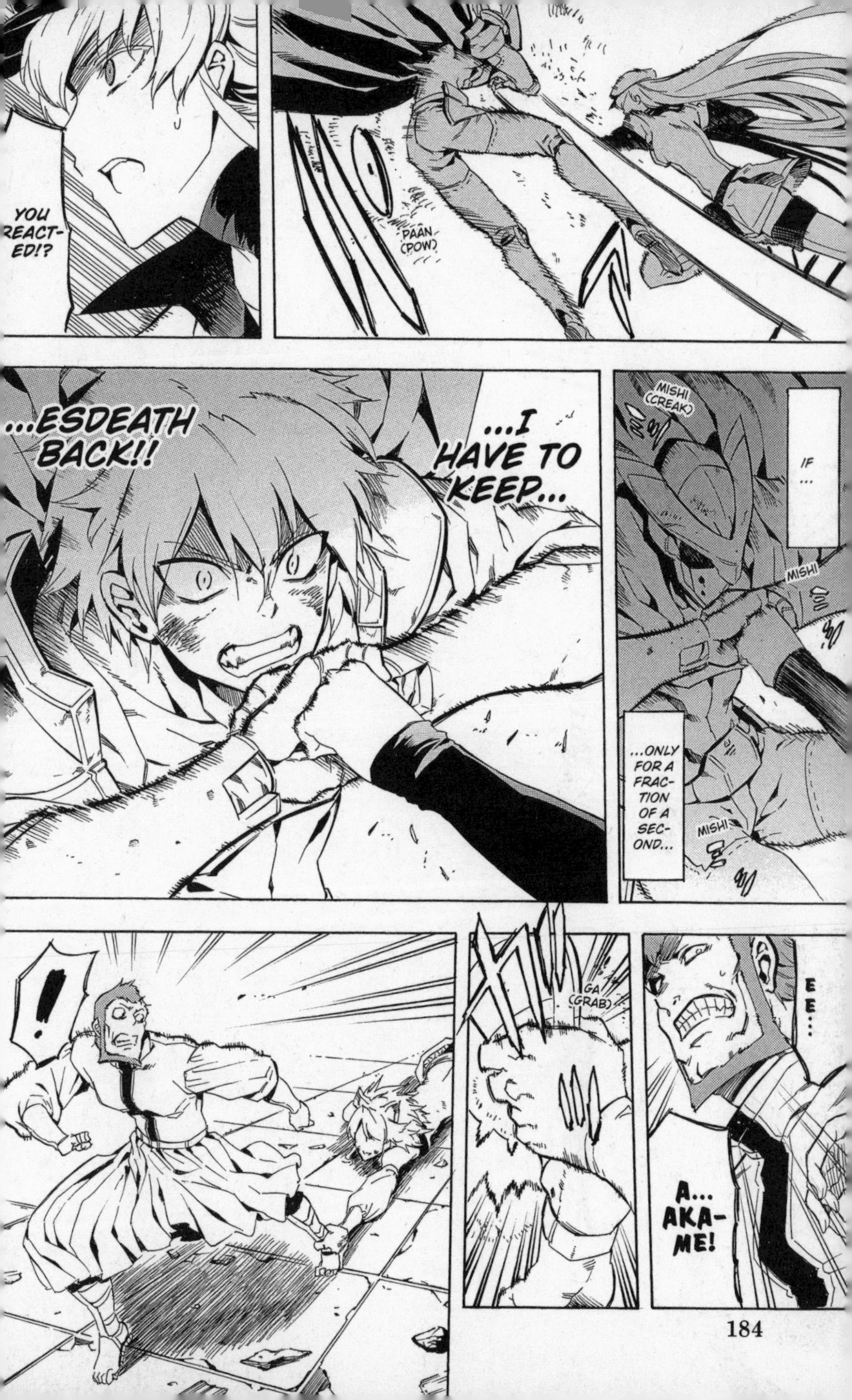
PAAN (POW)
YOU REACTED!?
MISHI (CREAK)
IF...
MISHI
...ONLY FOR A FRACTION OF A SECOND...
MISHI
...I HAVE TO KEEP...
...ESDEATH BACK!!
EE...
A... AKAME!
GA (GRAB)
!

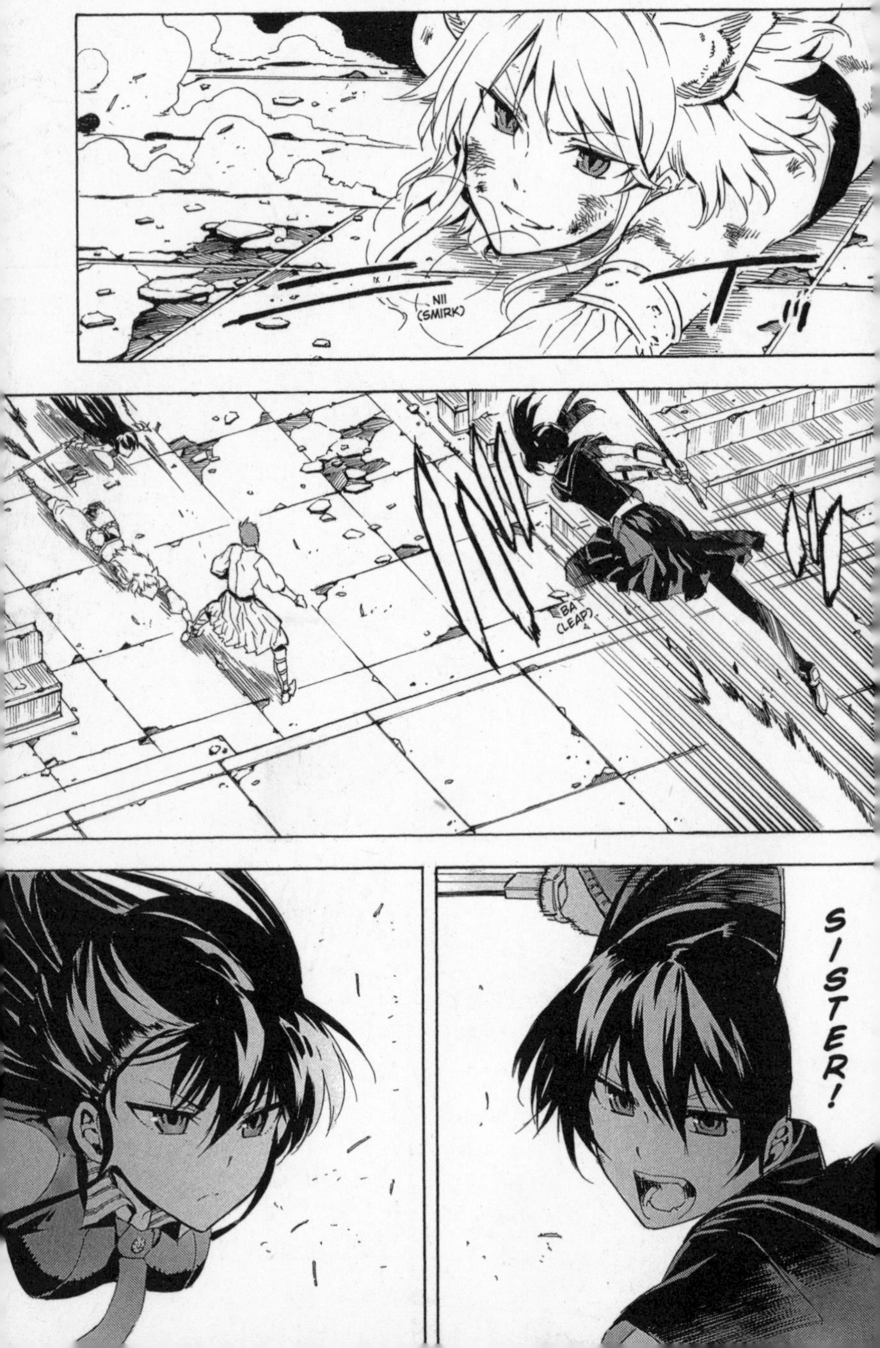
NII (SMIRK)
BA (LEAP)
SISTER!

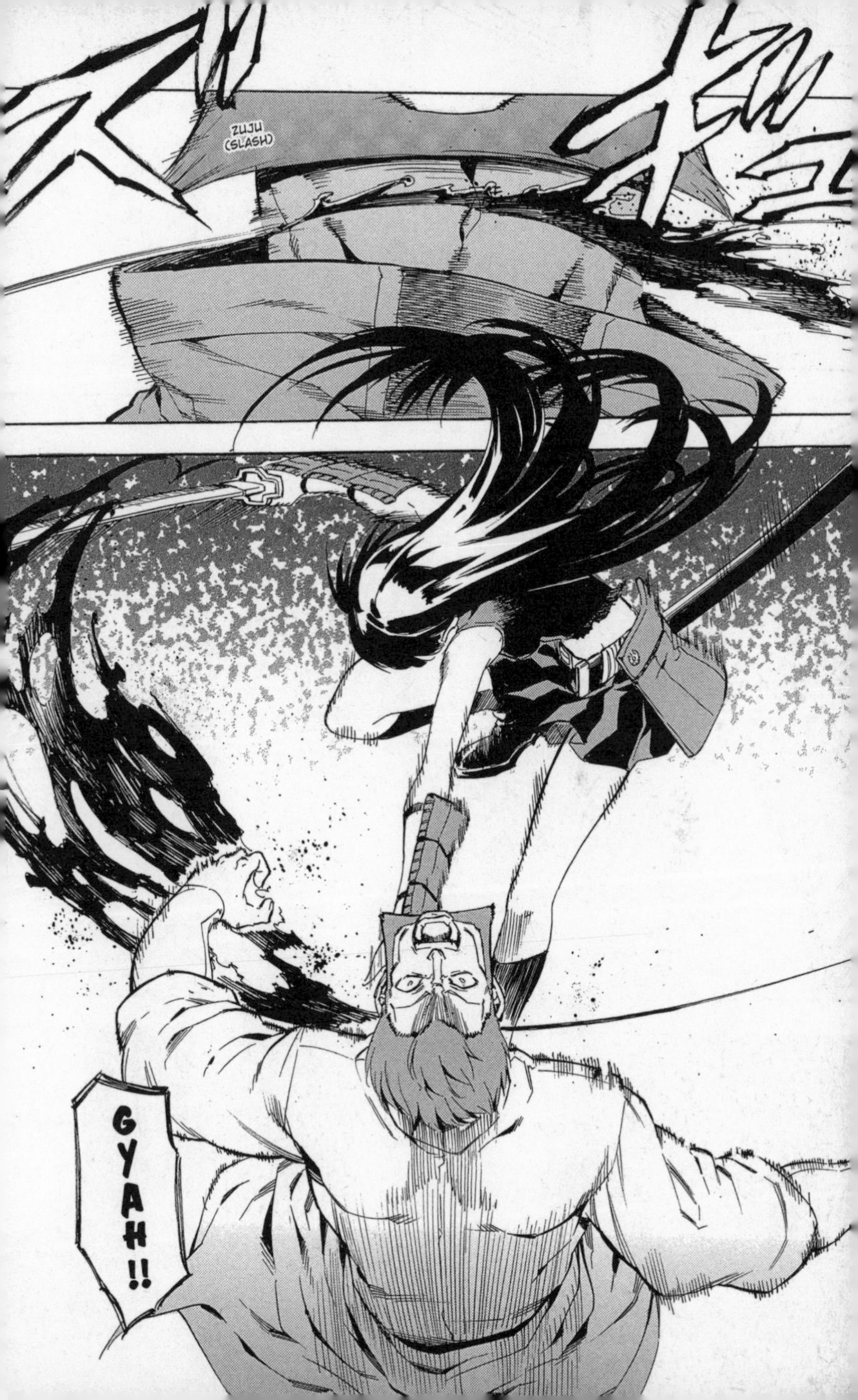
ZUJU (SLASH)
GYAH!!

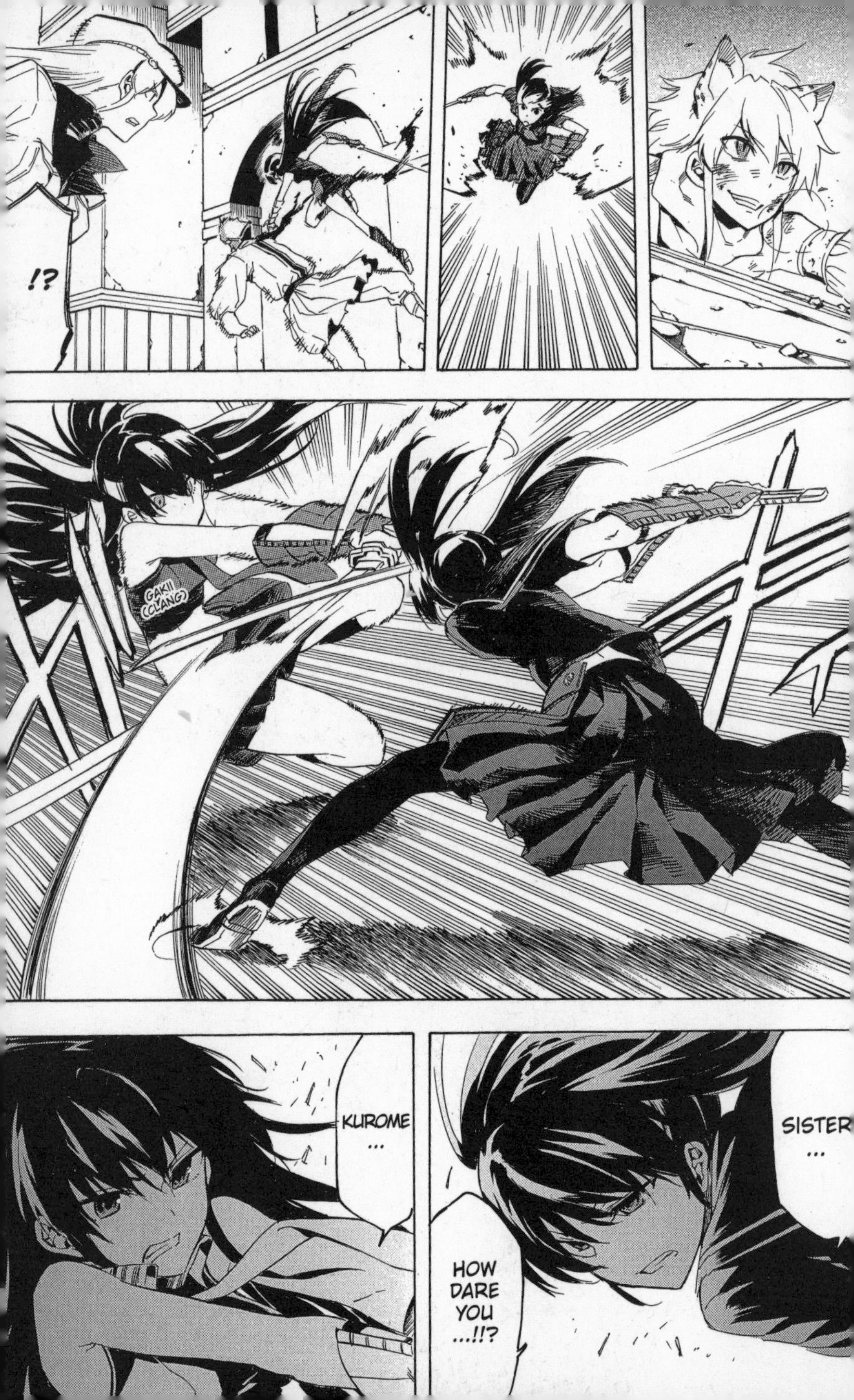
!?
GAKII (CLANG)
SISTER ...
HOW DARE YOU ...!!?
KUROME ...

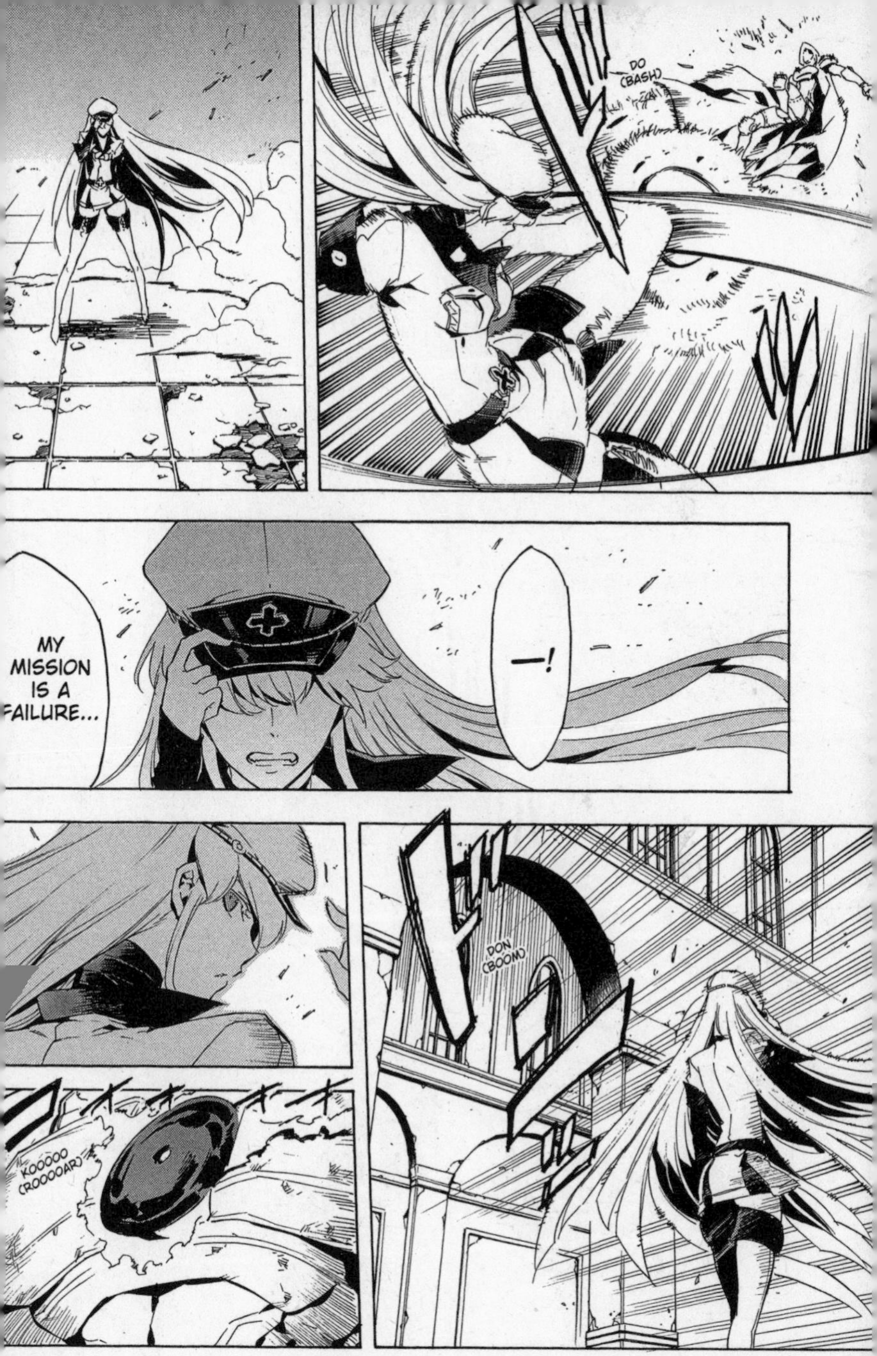
DO
(BASH)
—!
MY MISSION IS A FAILURE...
DON
(BOOM)
KOOOOO
(ROOOOAR)

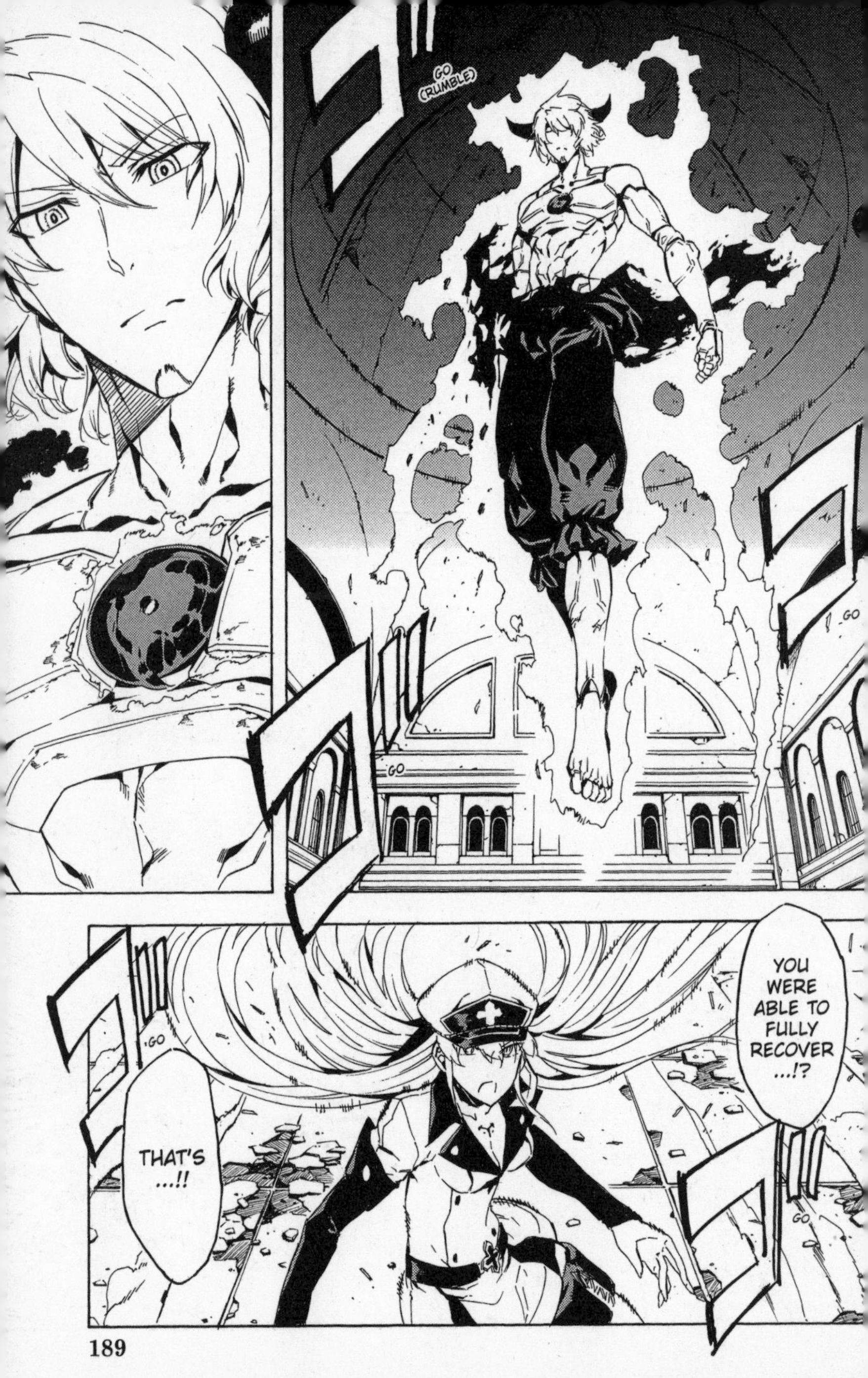
GO (RUMBLE)
GO
GO
YOU WERE ABLE TO FULLY RECOVER ...!?
GO
THAT'S ...!!
GO

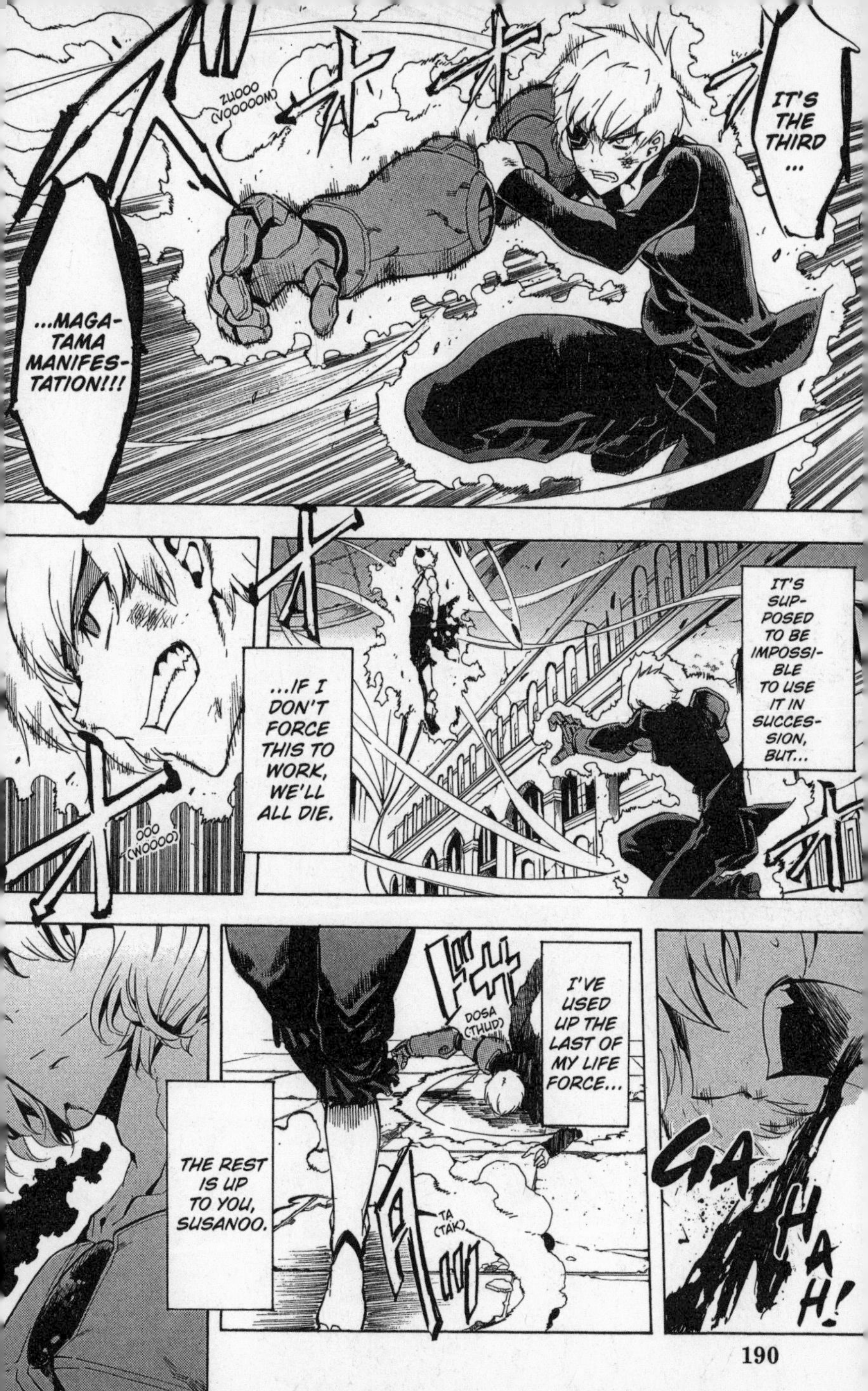
IT'S THE THIRD...
ZUOOO (VOOOOOM)
...MAGATAMA MANIFESTATION!!!
IT'S SUPPOSED TO BE IMPOSSIBLE TO USE IT IN SUCCESSION, BUT...
...IF I DON'T FORCE THIS TO WORK, WE'LL ALL DIE.
OOO (WOOOO)
GAHAH!
I'VE USED UP THE LAST OF MY LIFE FORCE...
DOSA (THUD)
TA (TAK)
THE REST IS UP TO YOU, SUSANOO.

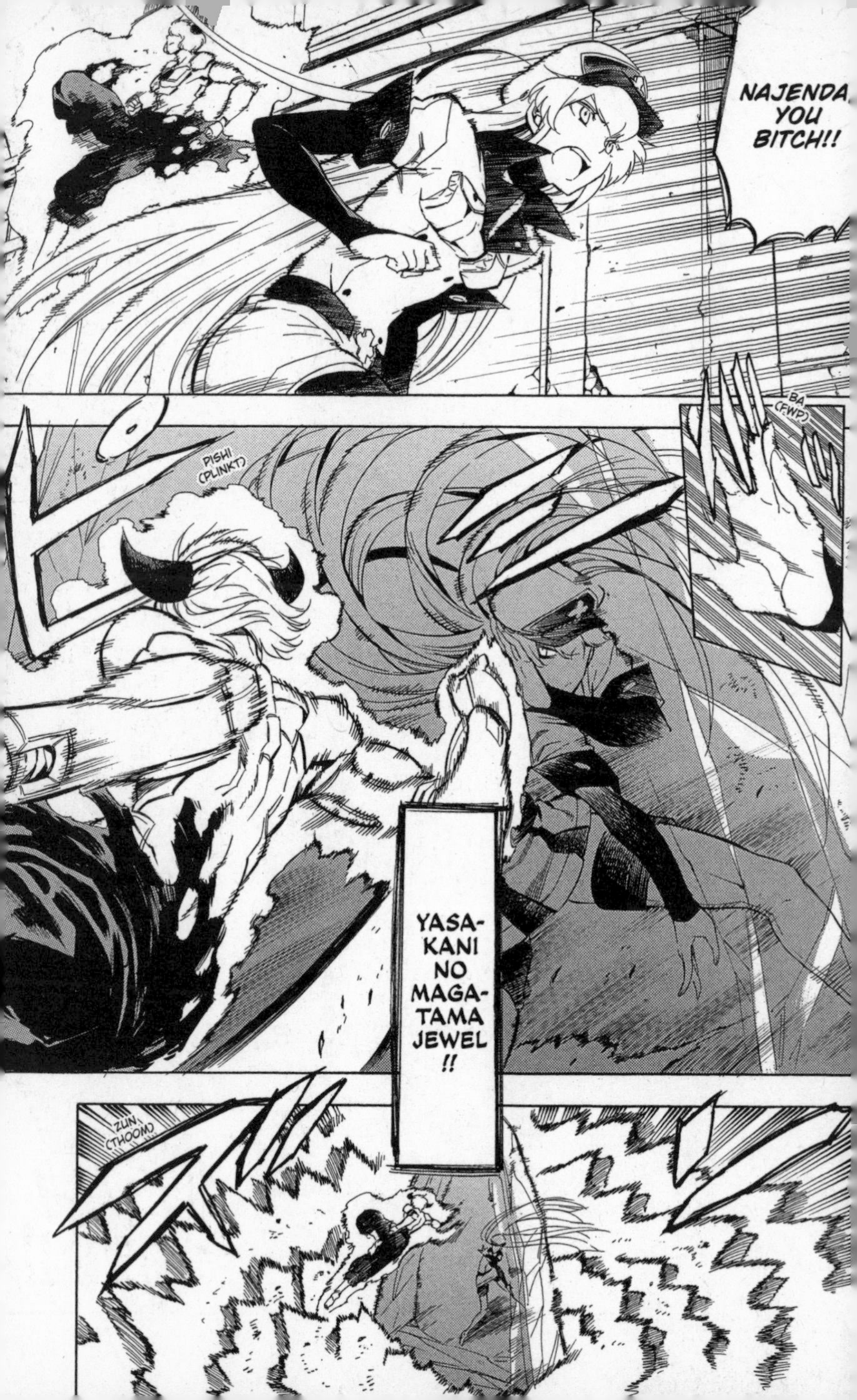
NAJENDA, YOU BITCH!!
BA (FWP)
PISHI (PLINKT)
YASA-KANI NO MAGA-TAMA JEWEL !!
ZUN (THOOM)

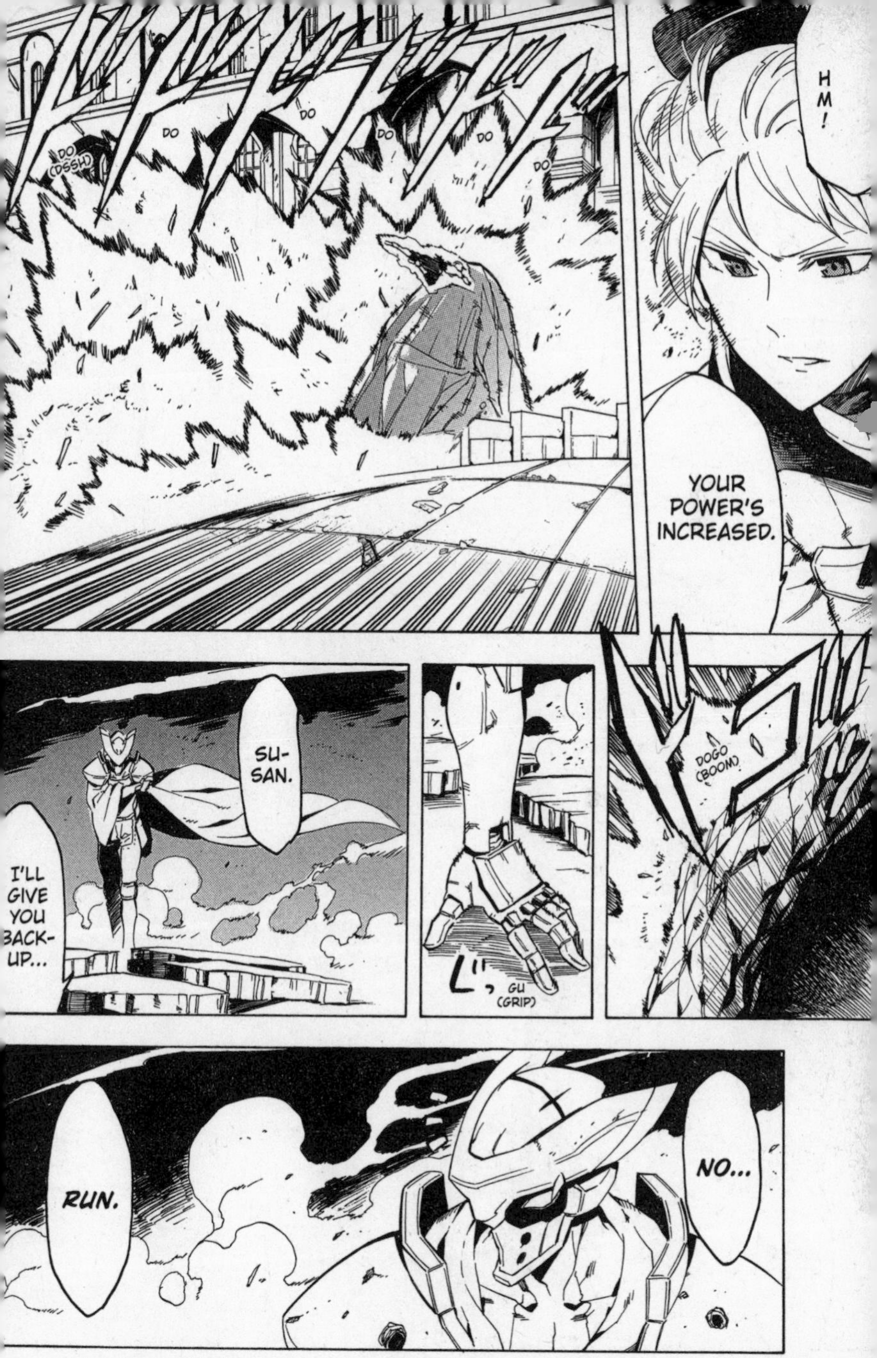
HM!
YOUR POWER'S INCREASED.
DO (DSSH)
DO
DO
DO
DO
DO
DOGO (BOOM)
GU (GRIP)
SU-SAN.
I'LL GIVE YOU BACK-UP...
NO...
RUN.

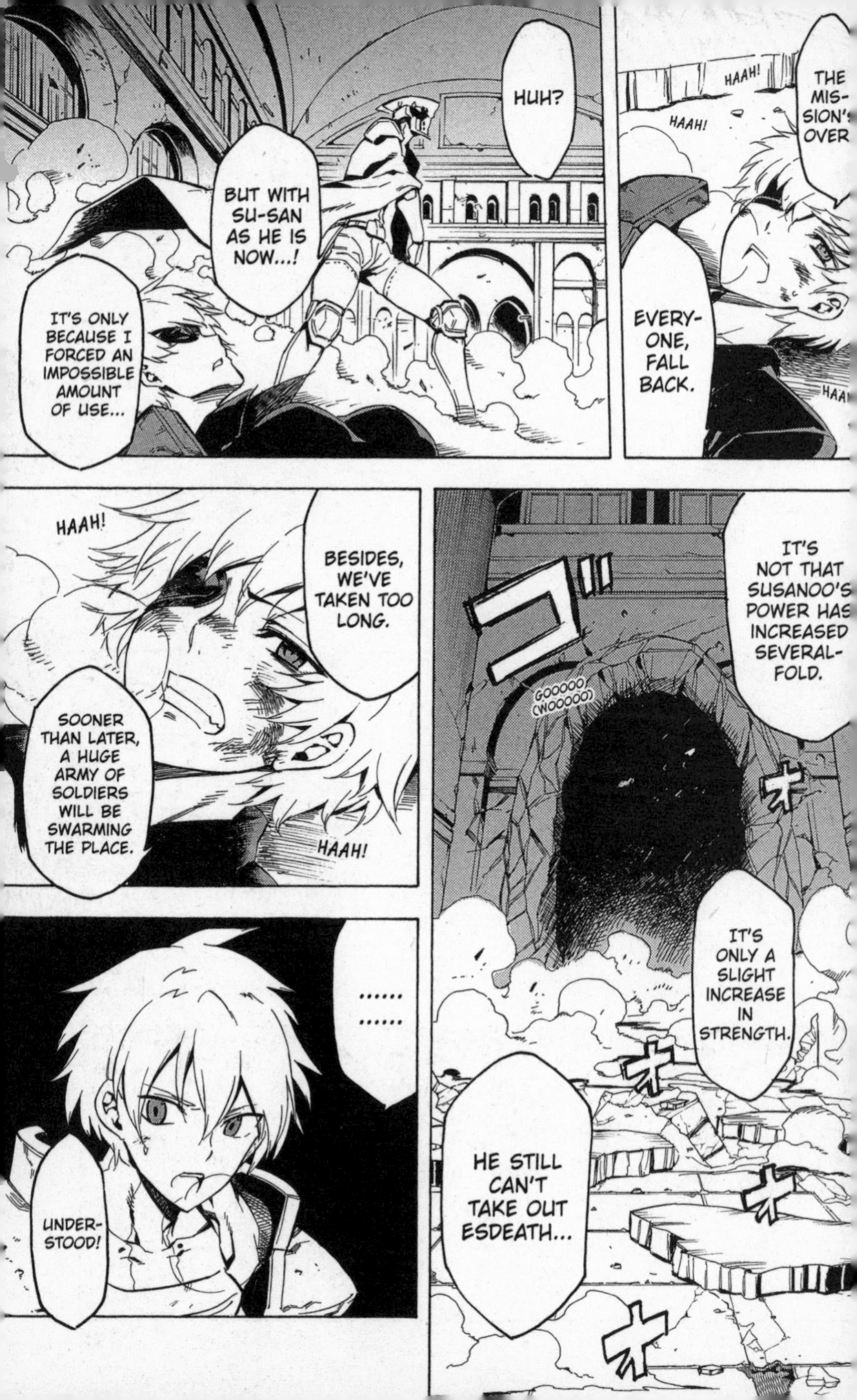
HAAH!
THE MIS-SION'S OVER
HAAH!
EVERY-ONE, FALL BACK.
HUH?
BUT WITH SU-SAN AS HE IS NOW...!
IT'S ONLY BECAUSE I FORCED AN IMPOSSIBLE AMOUNT OF USE...
IT'S NOT THAT SUSANOO'S POWER HAS INCREASED SEVERAL-FOLD.
GOOOOO (WOOOOO)
IT'S ONLY A SLIGHT INCREASE IN STRENGTH.
HE STILL CAN'T TAKE OUT ESDEATH...
HAAH!
BESIDES, WE'VE TAKEN TOO LONG.
SOONER THAN LATER, A HUGE ARMY OF SOLDIERS WILL BE SWARMING THE PLACE.
HAAH!
......
......
UNDER-STOOD!

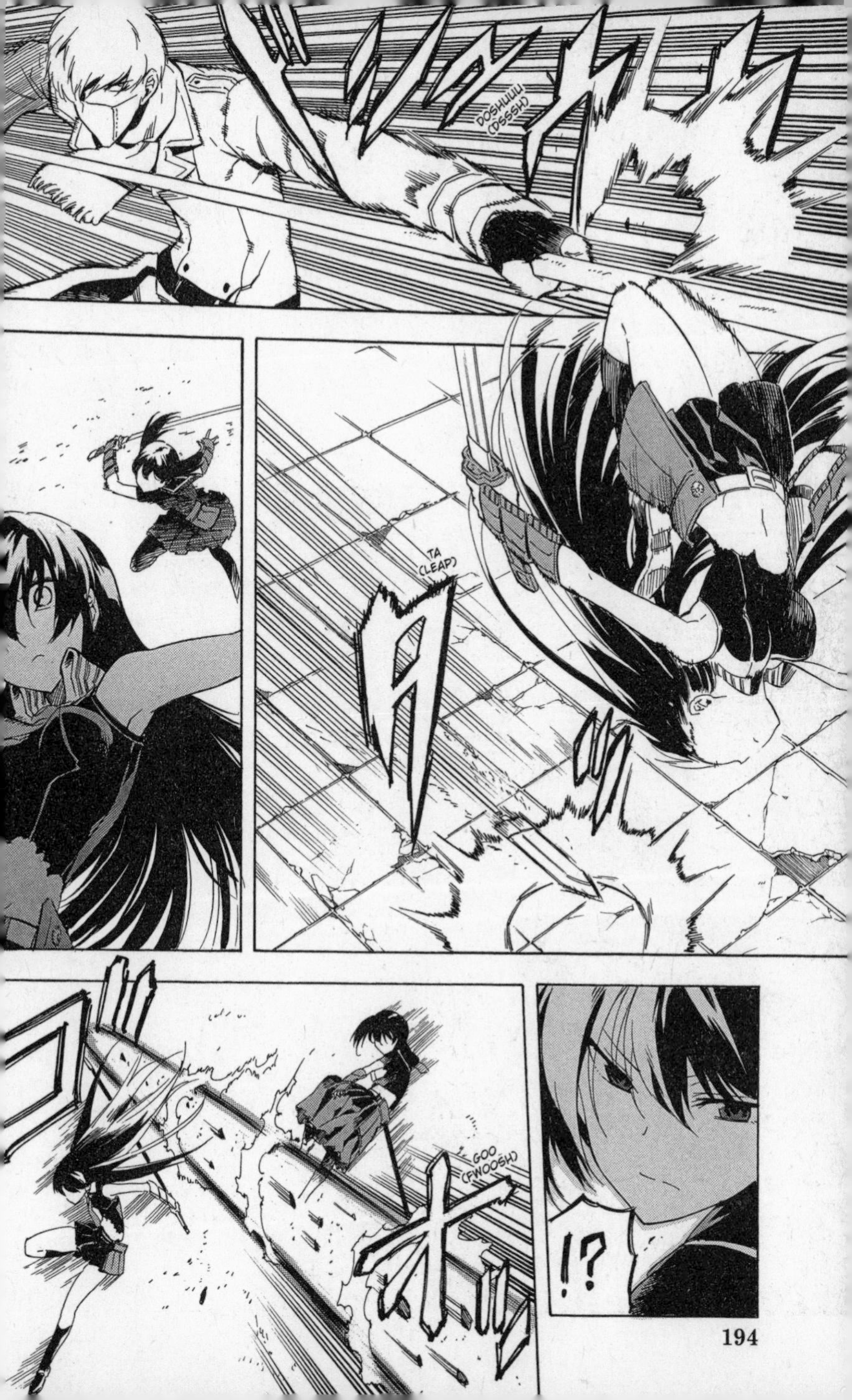
DOSHUUUN
(DSSSH)
TA
(LEAP)
!?
GOO
(FWOOSH)

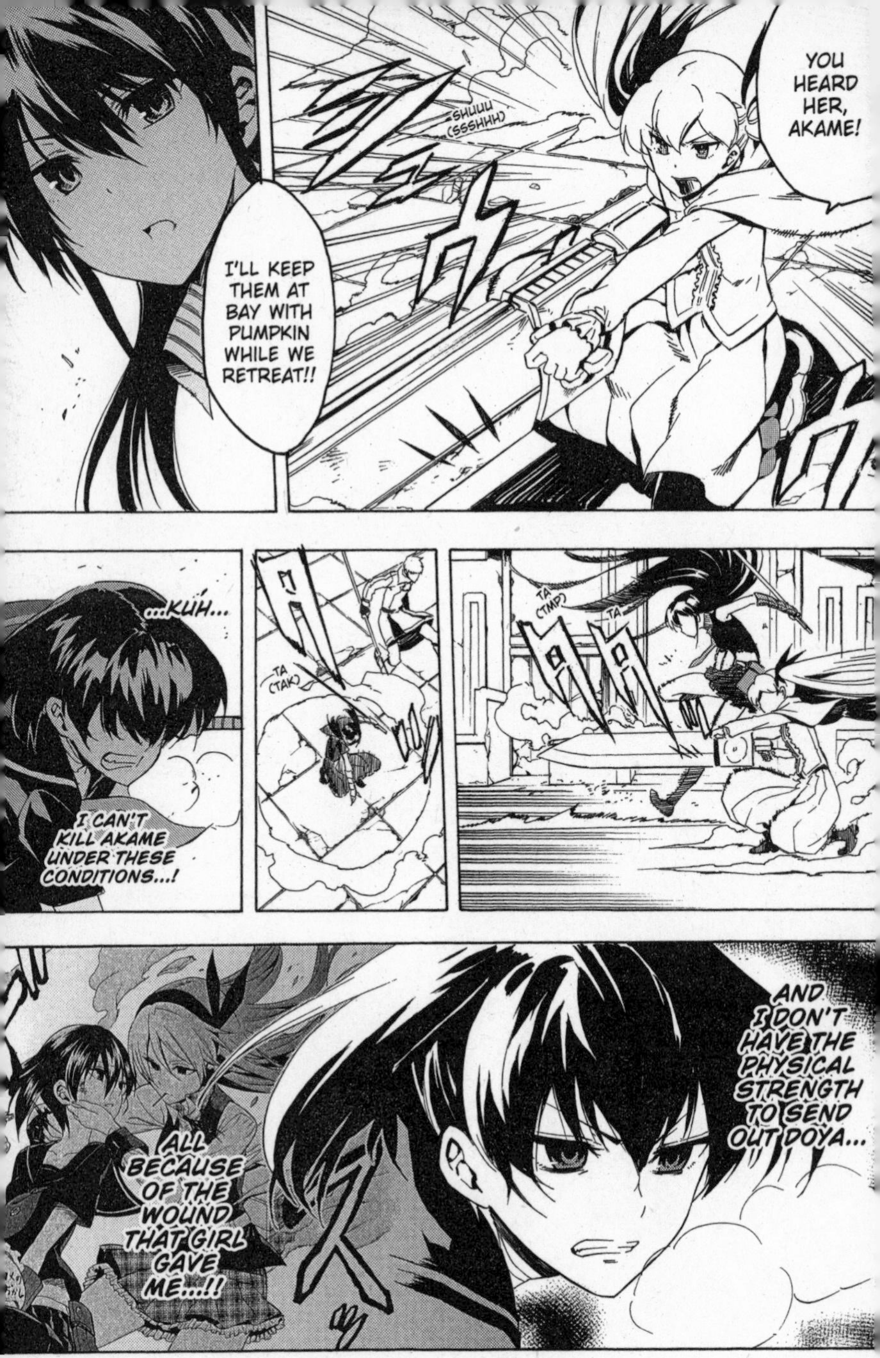
YOU HEARD HER, AKAME!
SHUUU (SSSHHH)
I'LL KEEP THEM AT BAY WITH PUMPKIN WHILE WE RETREAT!!
TA (TMP)
TA
TA (TAK)
...KUH...
I CAN'T KILL AKAME UNDER THESE CONDITIONS...!
AND I DON'T HAVE THE PHYSICAL STRENGTH TO SEND OUT DOYA...
ALL BECAUSE OF THE WOUND THAT GIRL GAVE ME...!!

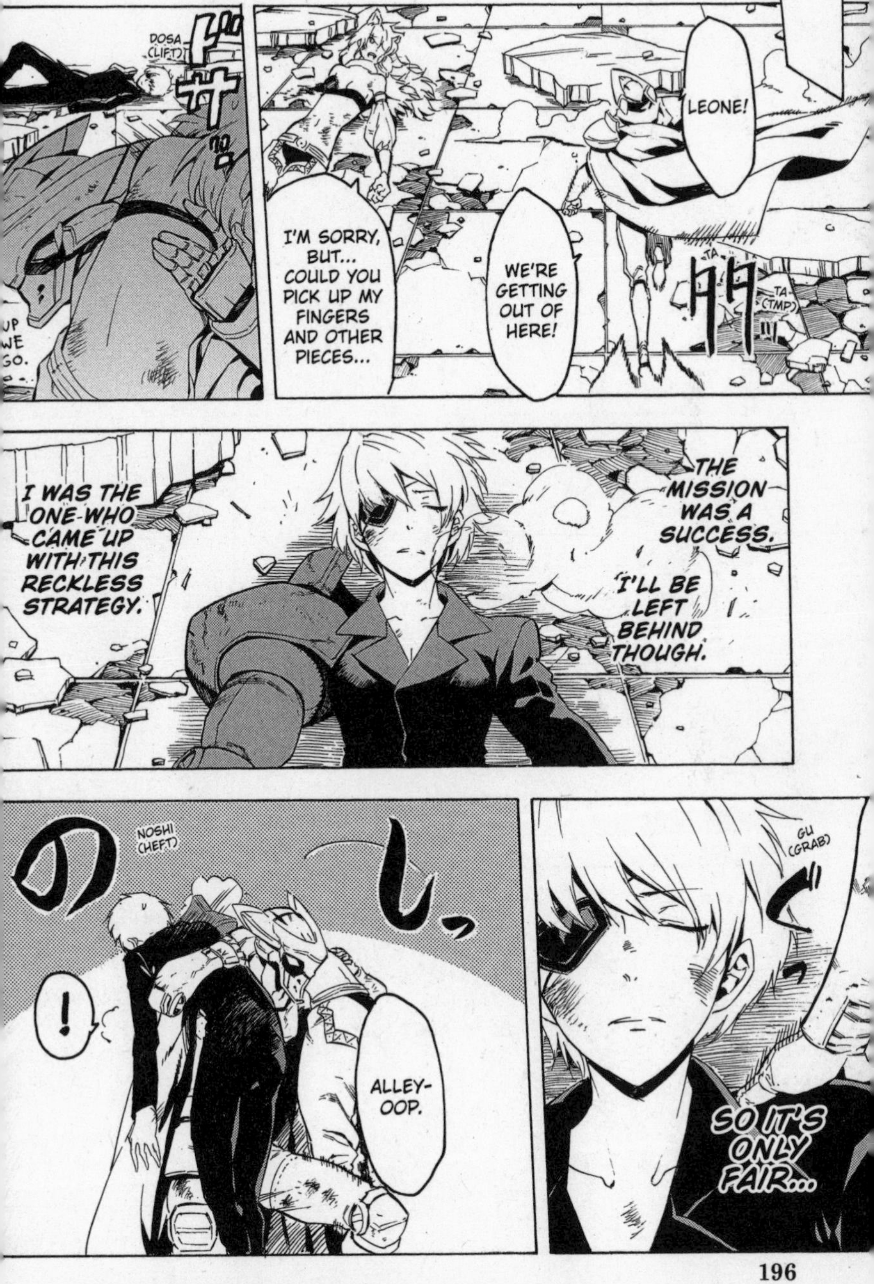
LEONE!
TA TA (TMP)
WE'RE GETTING OUT OF HERE!
I'M SORRY, BUT... COULD YOU PICK UP MY FINGERS AND OTHER PIECES...
DOSA (LIFT)
UP WE GO.
THE MISSION WAS A SUCCESS.
I'LL BE LEFT BEHIND THOUGH.
I WAS THE ONE WHO CAME UP WITH THIS RECKLESS STRATEGY.
GU (GRAB)
SO IT'S ONLY FAIR...
NOSHI (HEFT)
!
ALLEY-OOP.

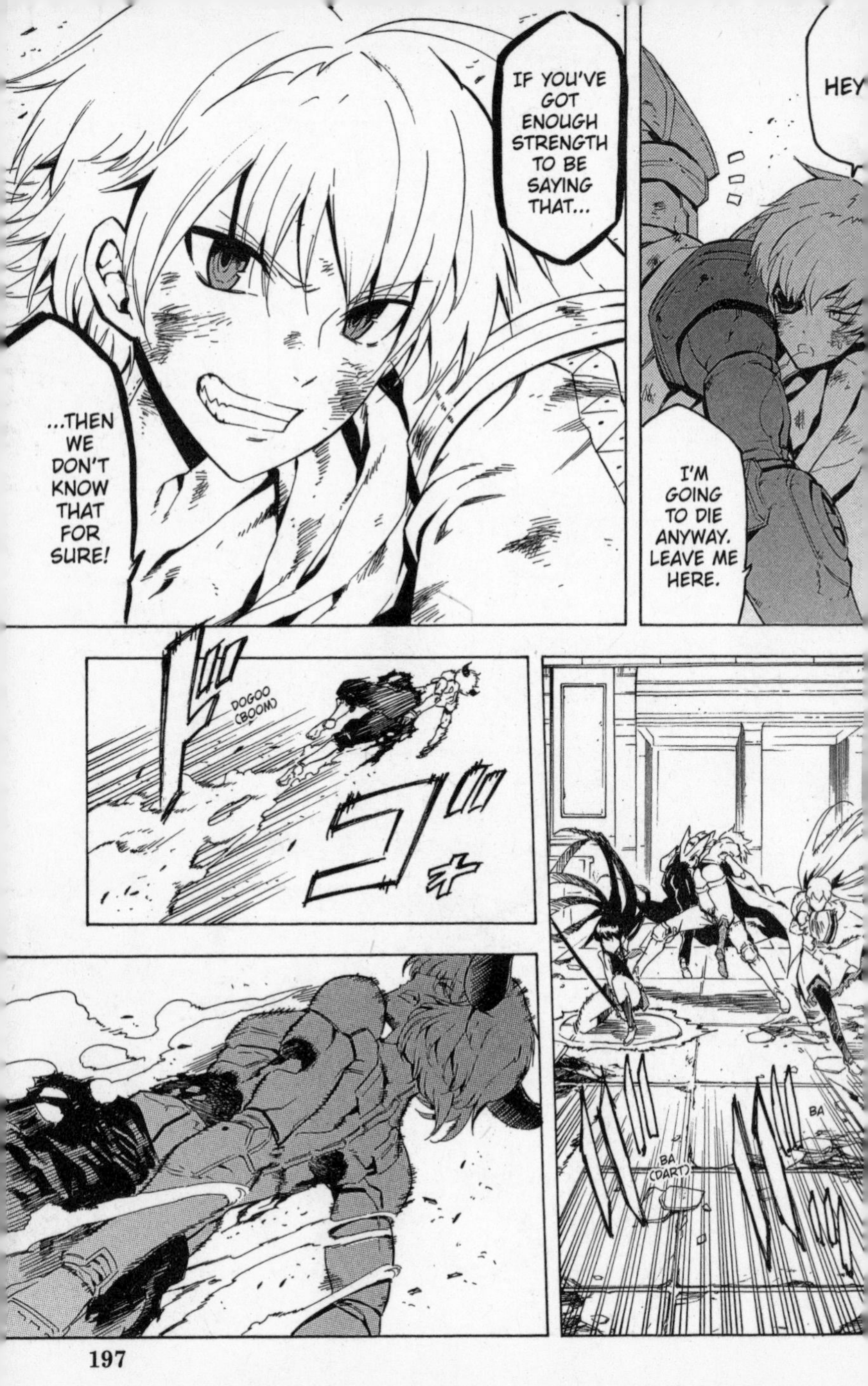
HEY
I'M GOING TO DIE ANYWAY. LEAVE ME HERE.
IF YOU'VE GOT ENOUGH STRENGTH TO BE SAYING THAT...
...THEN WE DON'T KNOW THAT FOR SURE!
BA
BA (DART)
DOGOO (BOOM)

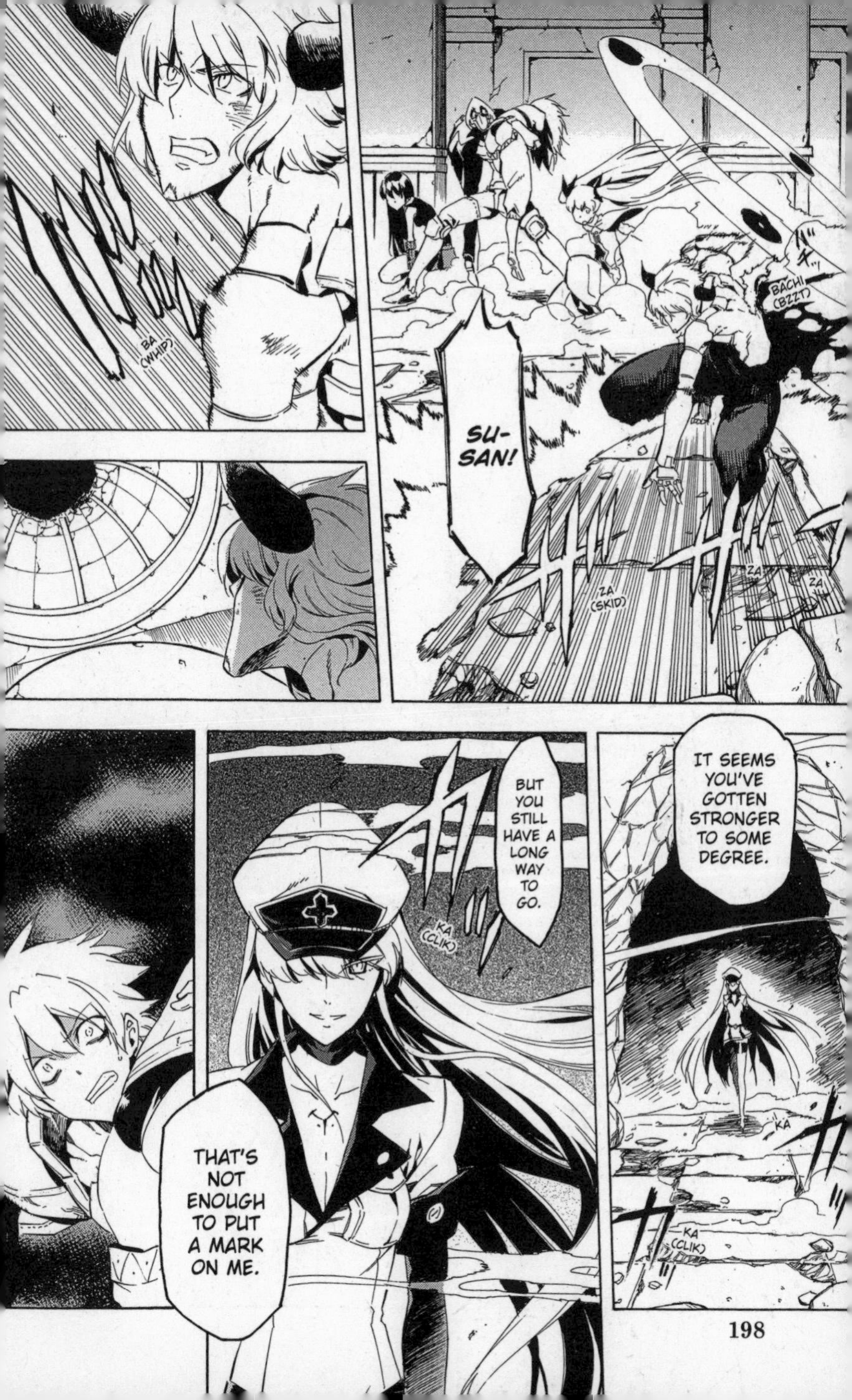
BACHI (BZZT)
SU-SAN!
ZA (SKID)
ZA
ZA
BA (WHIP)
IT SEEMS YOU'VE GOTTEN STRONGER TO SOME DEGREE.
KA
KA (CLIK)
BUT YOU STILL HAVE A LONG WAY TO GO.
KA (CLIK)
THAT'S NOT ENOUGH TO PUT A MARK ON ME.

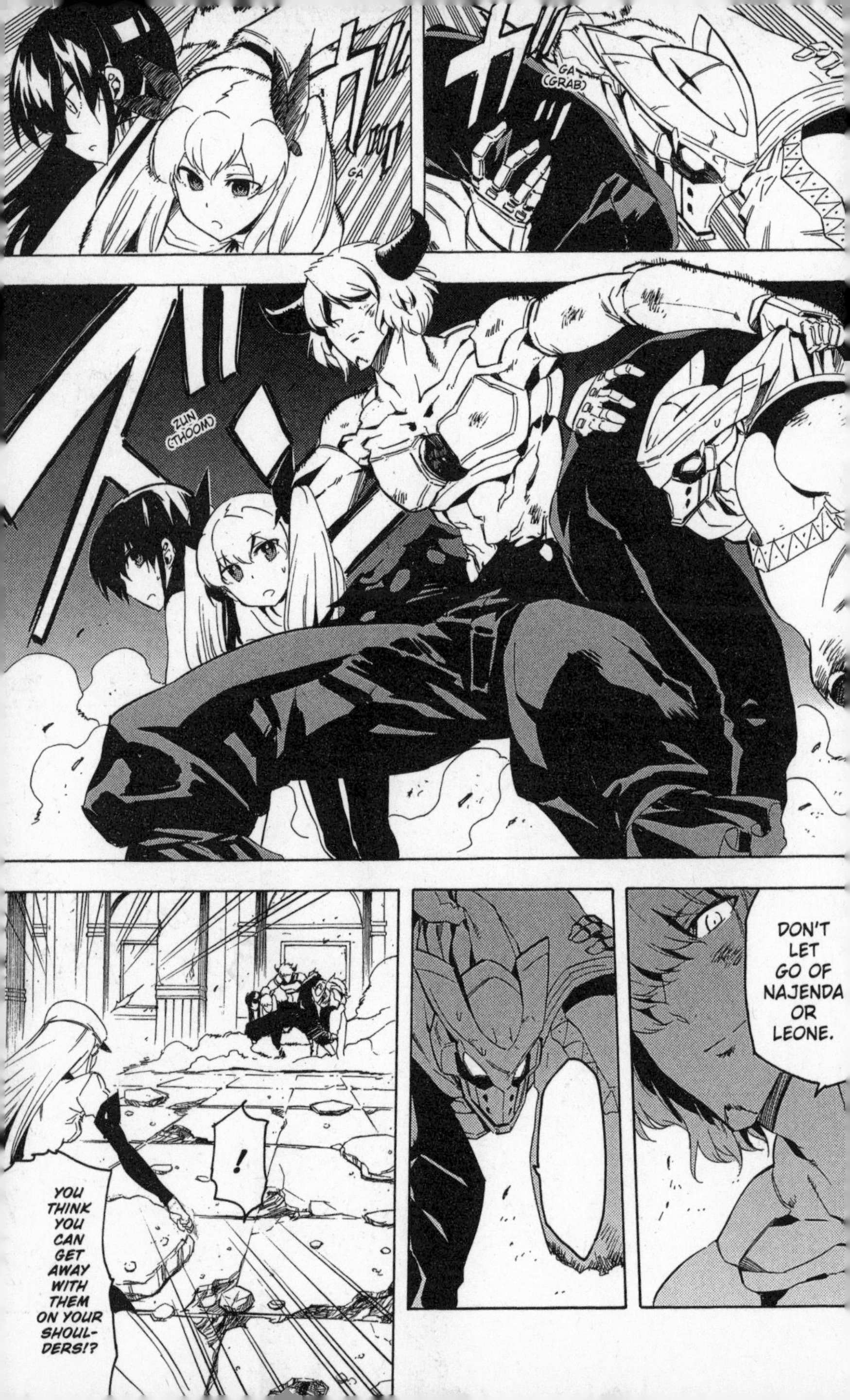
GA (GRAB)
GA
ZUN (THOOM)
DON'T LET GO OF NAJENDA OR LEONE.
!
YOU THINK YOU CAN GET AWAY WITH THEM ON YOUR SHOULDERS!?

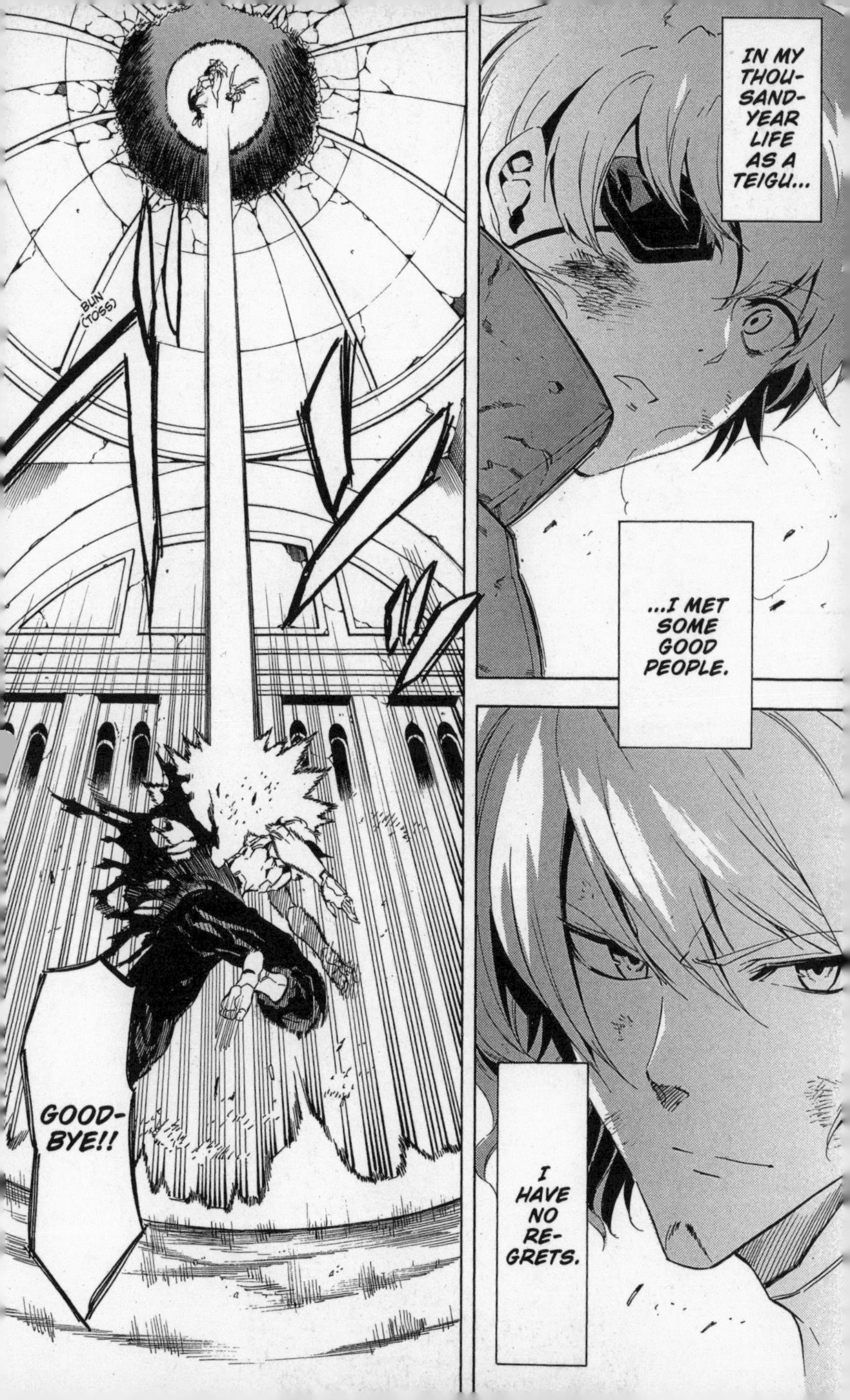
IN MY THOUSAND-YEAR LIFE AS A TEIGU...
...I MET SOME GOOD PEOPLE.
I HAVE NO REGRETS.
BUN (TOSS)
GOODBYE!!

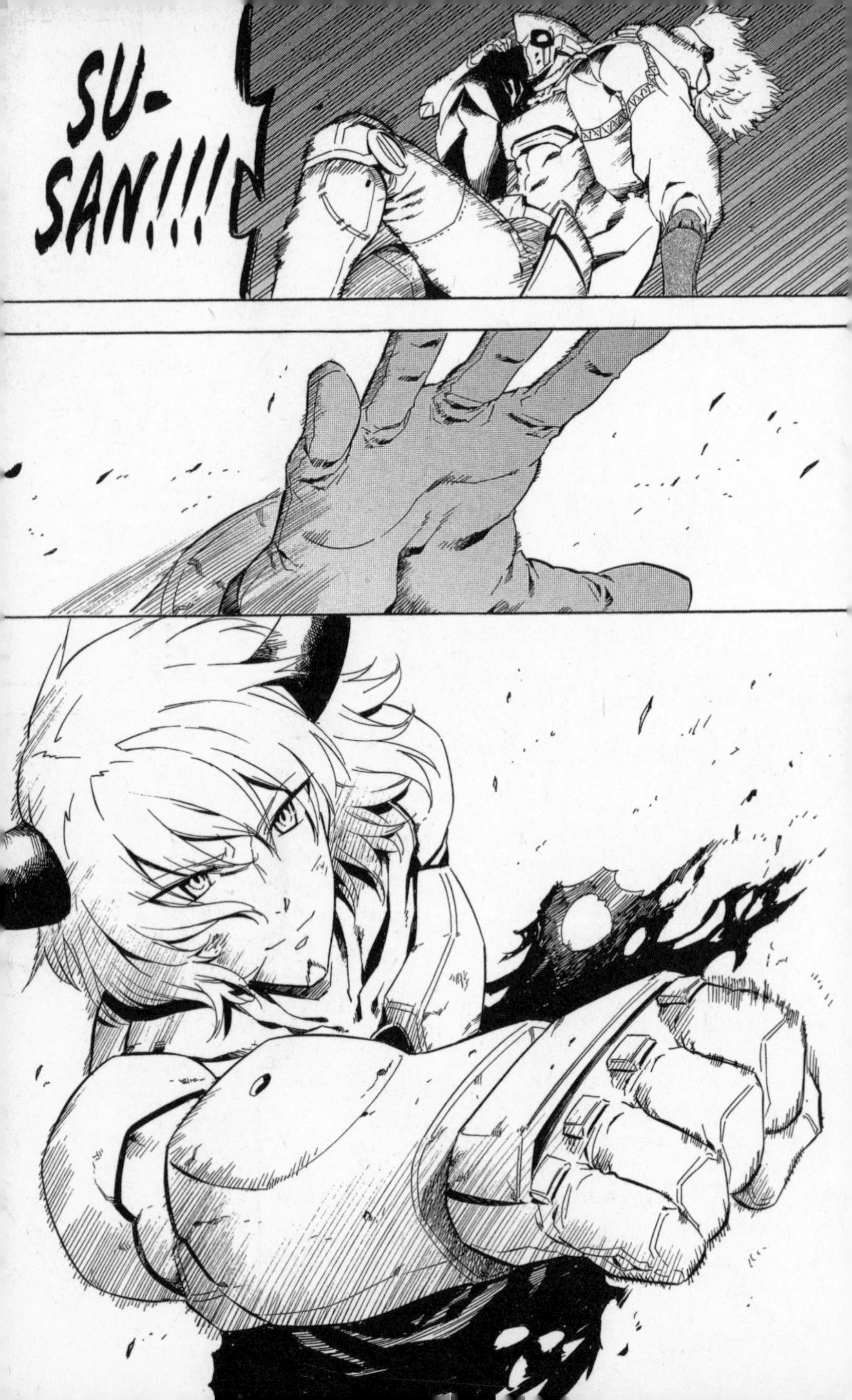
SU-SAN!!!

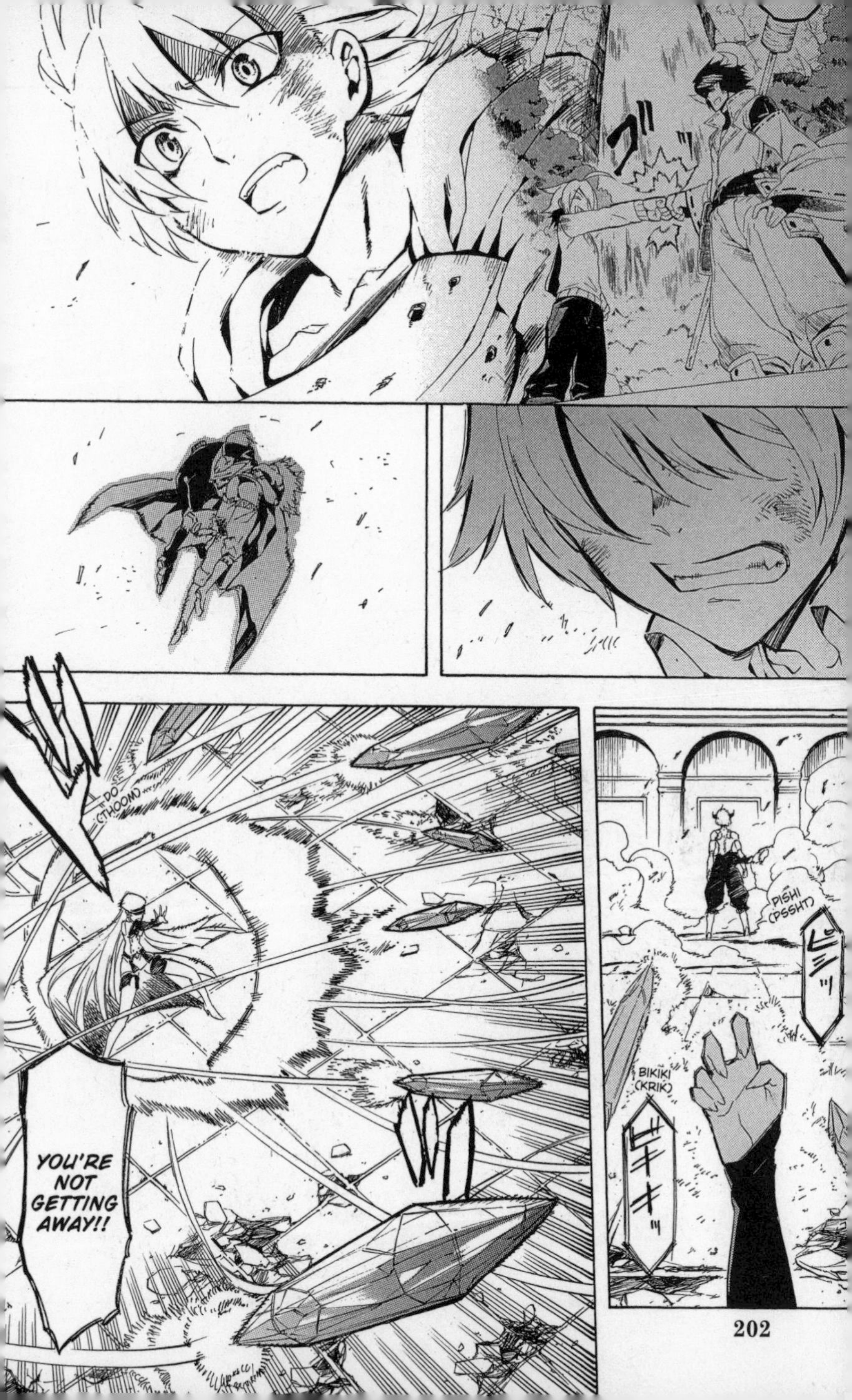
PISHI (PSSHT)
BIKIKI (KRIK)
DO (THOOM)
YOU'RE NOT GETTING AWAY!!

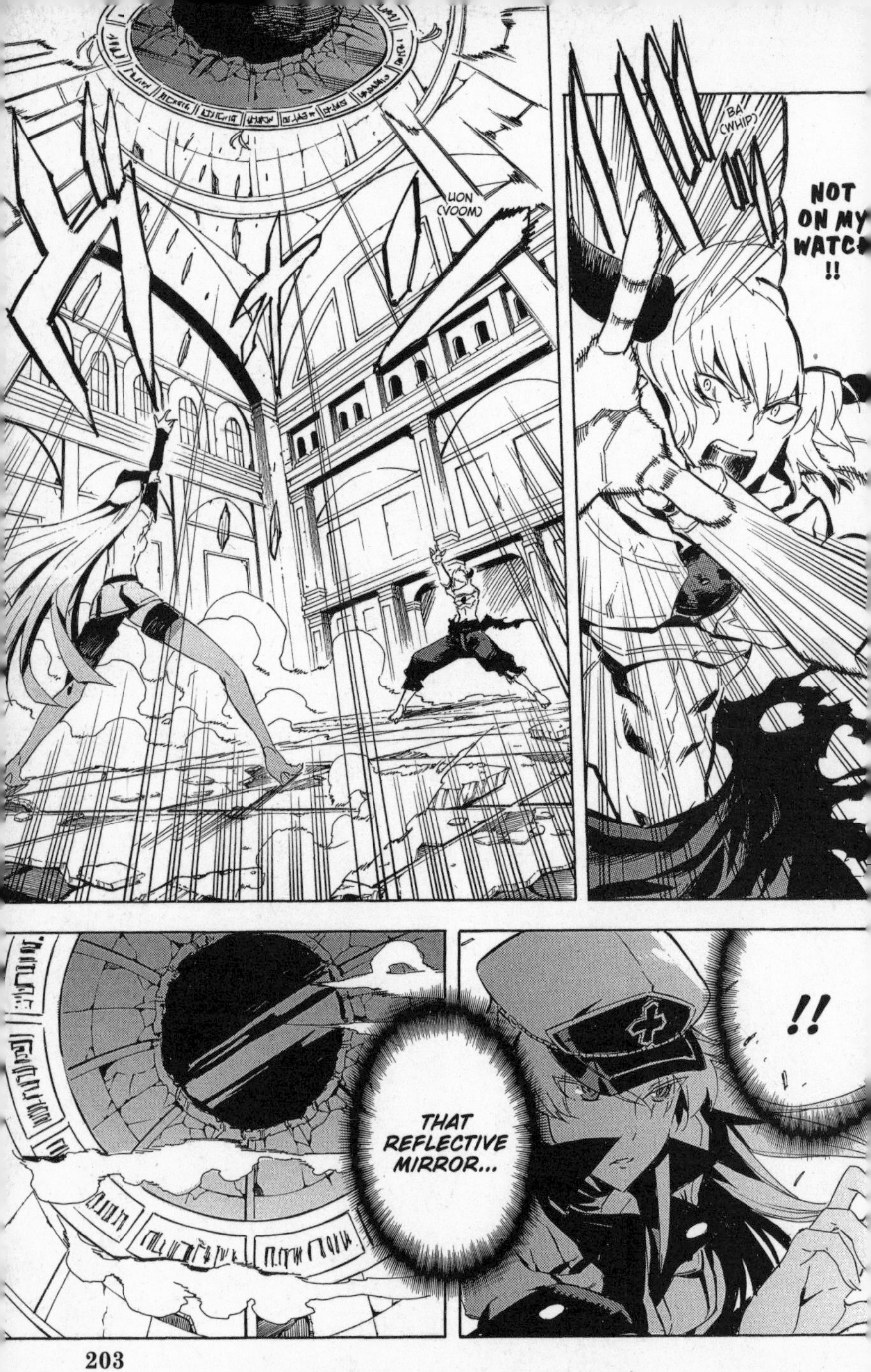
BA (WHIP)
NOT ON MY WATCH !!
UON (VOOM)
!!
THAT REFLECTIVE MIRROR...

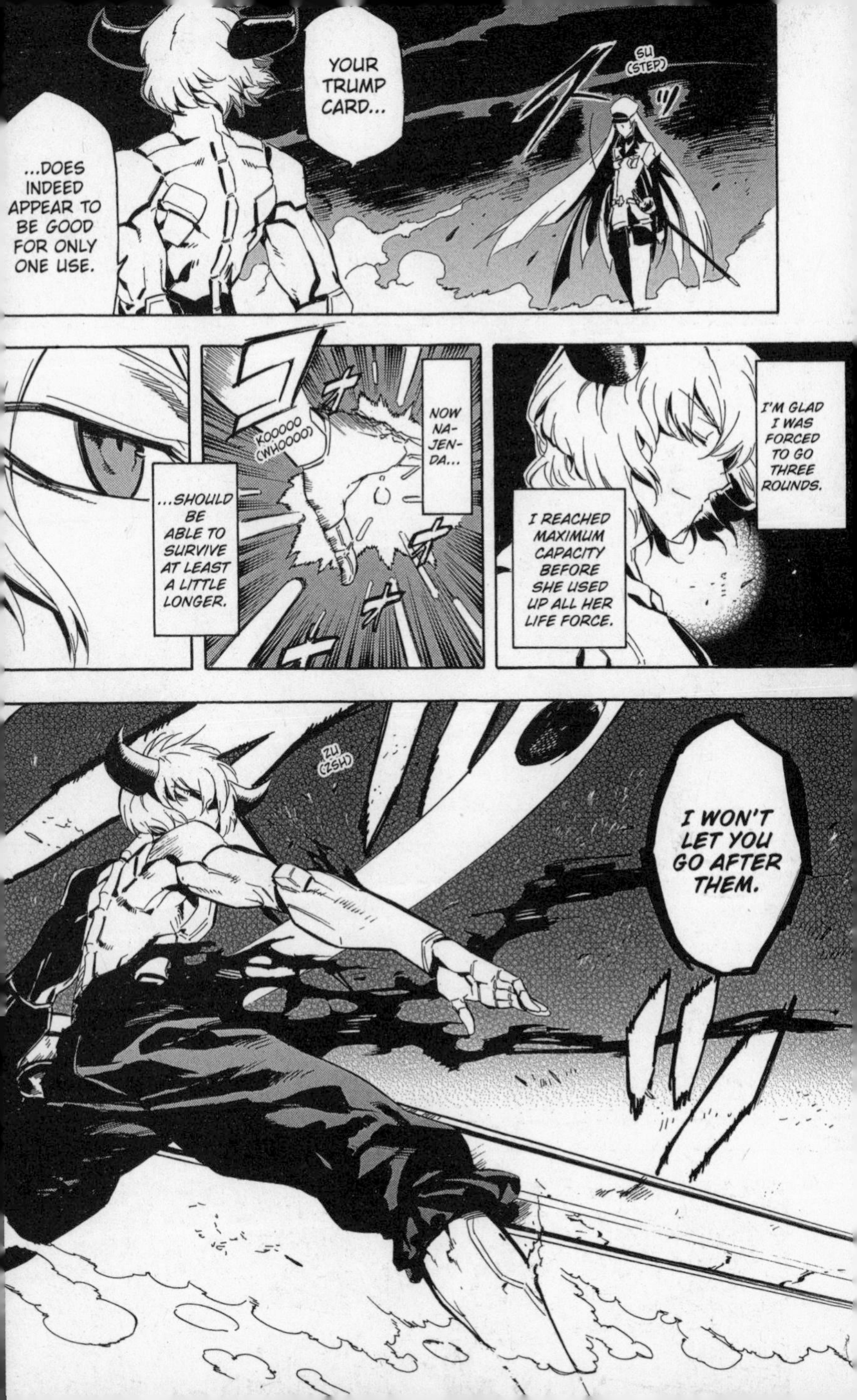
SU (STEP)
YOUR TRUMP CARD...
...DOES INDEED APPEAR TO BE GOOD FOR ONLY ONE USE.
I'M GLAD I WAS FORCED TO GO THREE ROUNDS.
I REACHED MAXIMUM CAPACITY BEFORE SHE USED UP ALL HER LIFE FORCE.
NOW NAJENDA...
KOOOOO (WHOOOO)
...SHOULD BE ABLE TO SURVIVE AT LEAST A LITTLE LONGER.
I WON'T LET YOU GO AFTER THEM.
ZU (ZSH)

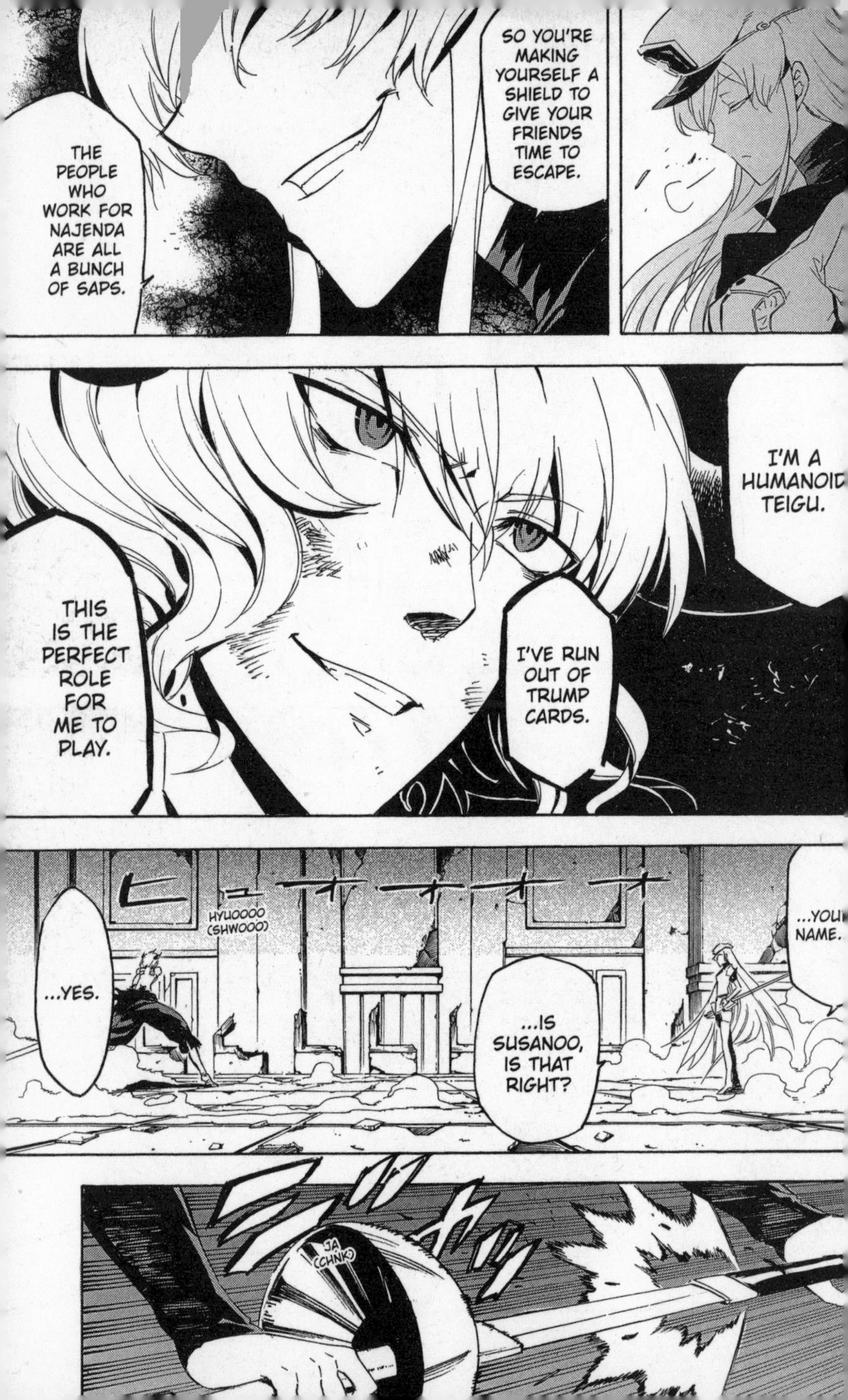
SO YOU'RE MAKING YOURSELF A SHIELD TO GIVE YOUR FRIENDS TIME TO ESCAPE.
THE PEOPLE WHO WORK FOR NAJENDA ARE ALL A BUNCH OF SAPS.
I'M A HUMANOID TEIGU.
I'VE RUN OUT OF TRUMP CARDS.
THIS IS THE PERFECT ROLE FOR ME TO PLAY.
...YOUR NAME.
...IS SUSANOO, IS THAT RIGHT?
HYUOOOO (SHWOOO)
...YES.
JA (CHNK)

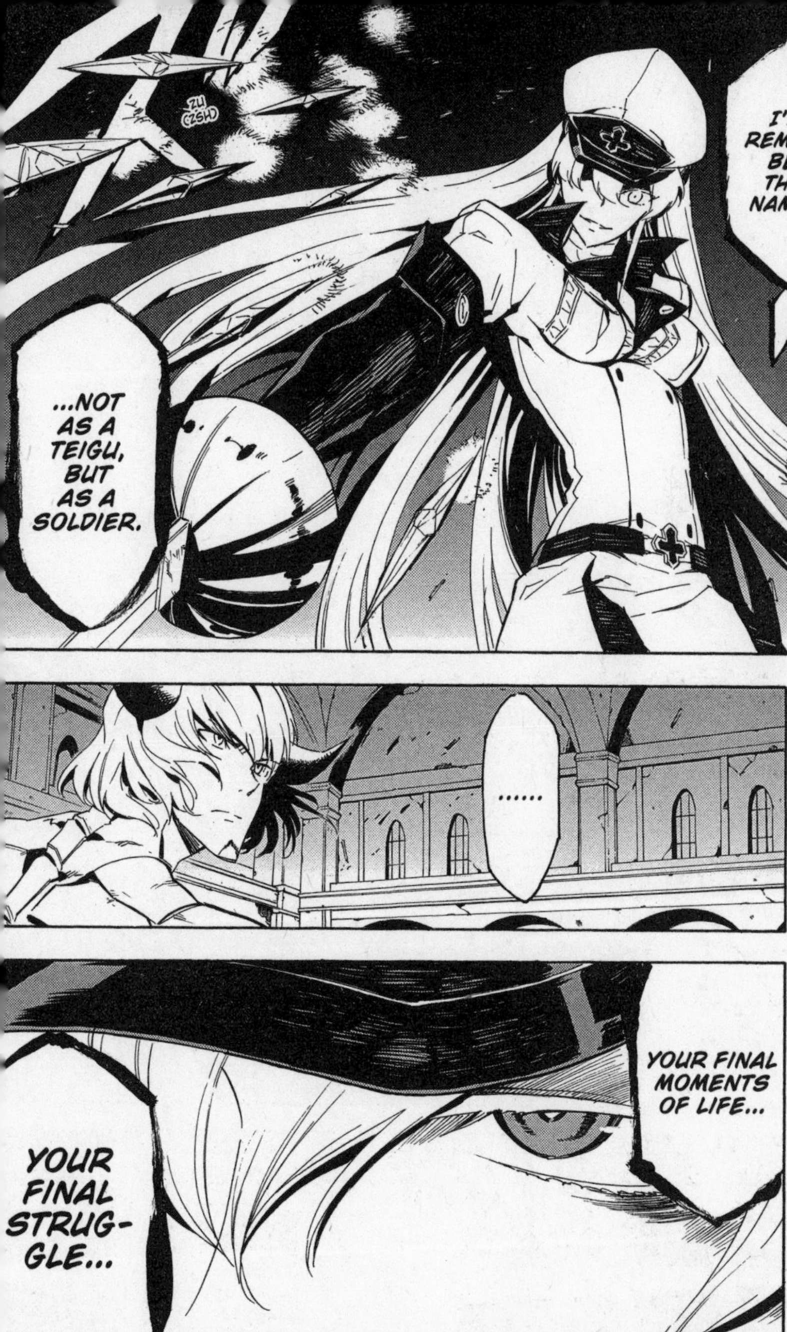
I'LL REMEMBER THAT NAME...
...NOT AS A TEIGU, BUT AS A SOLDIER.
......
YOUR FINAL MOMENTS OF LIFE...
YOUR FINAL STRUGGLE...

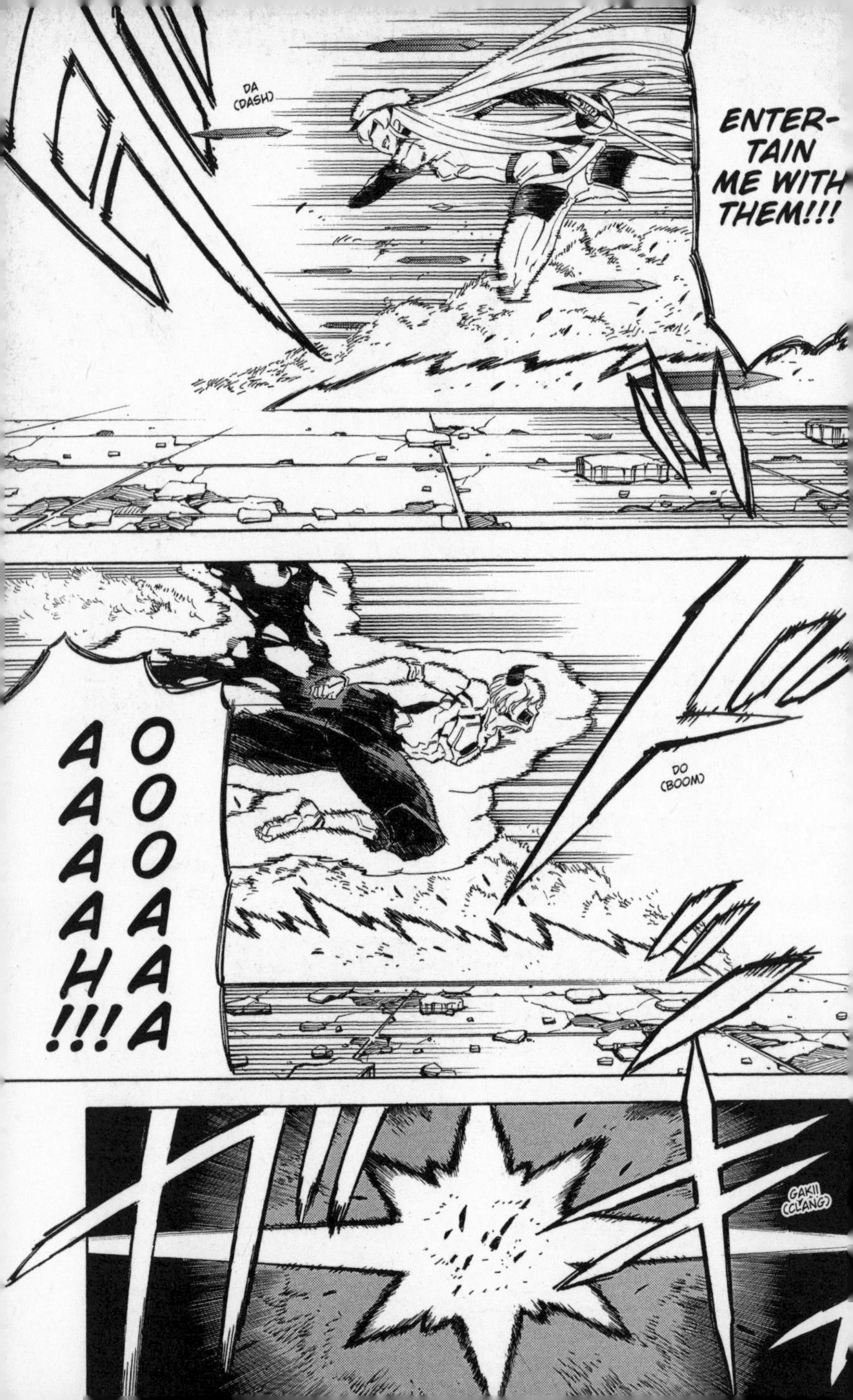
ENTER-TAIN ME WITH THEM!!!
DA (DASH)
DO (BOOM)
OOOAAAA
AAAAH!!!
GAKII (CLANG)

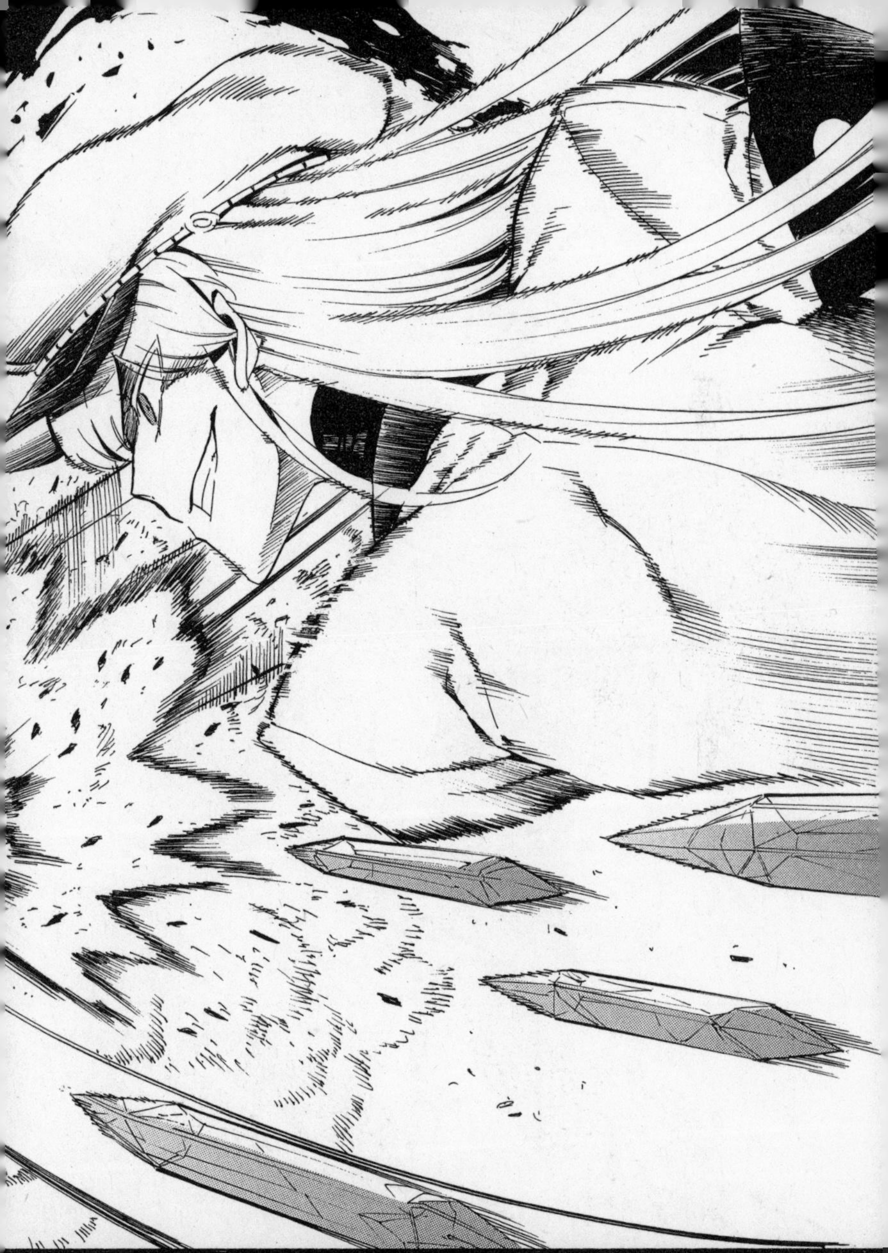

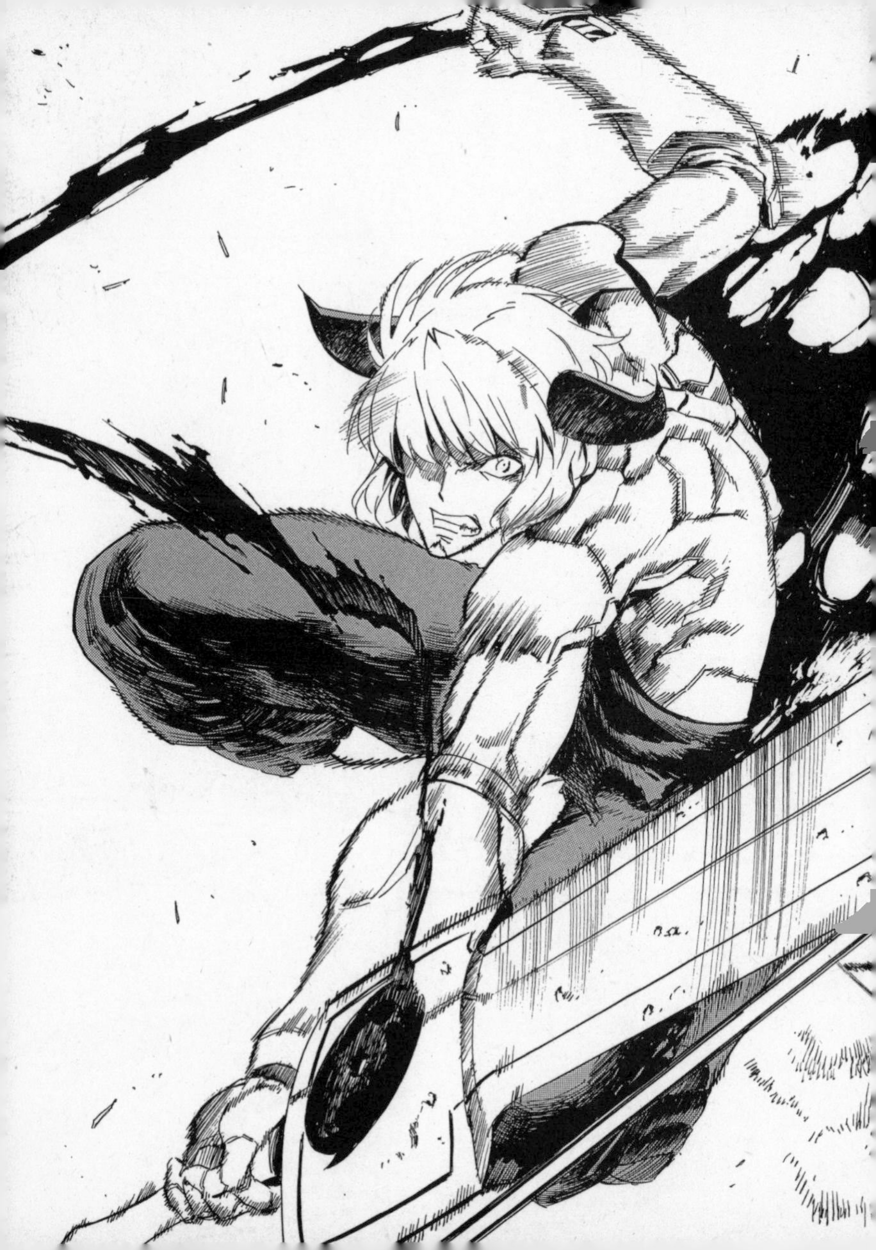

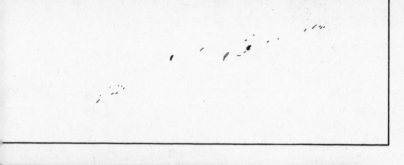

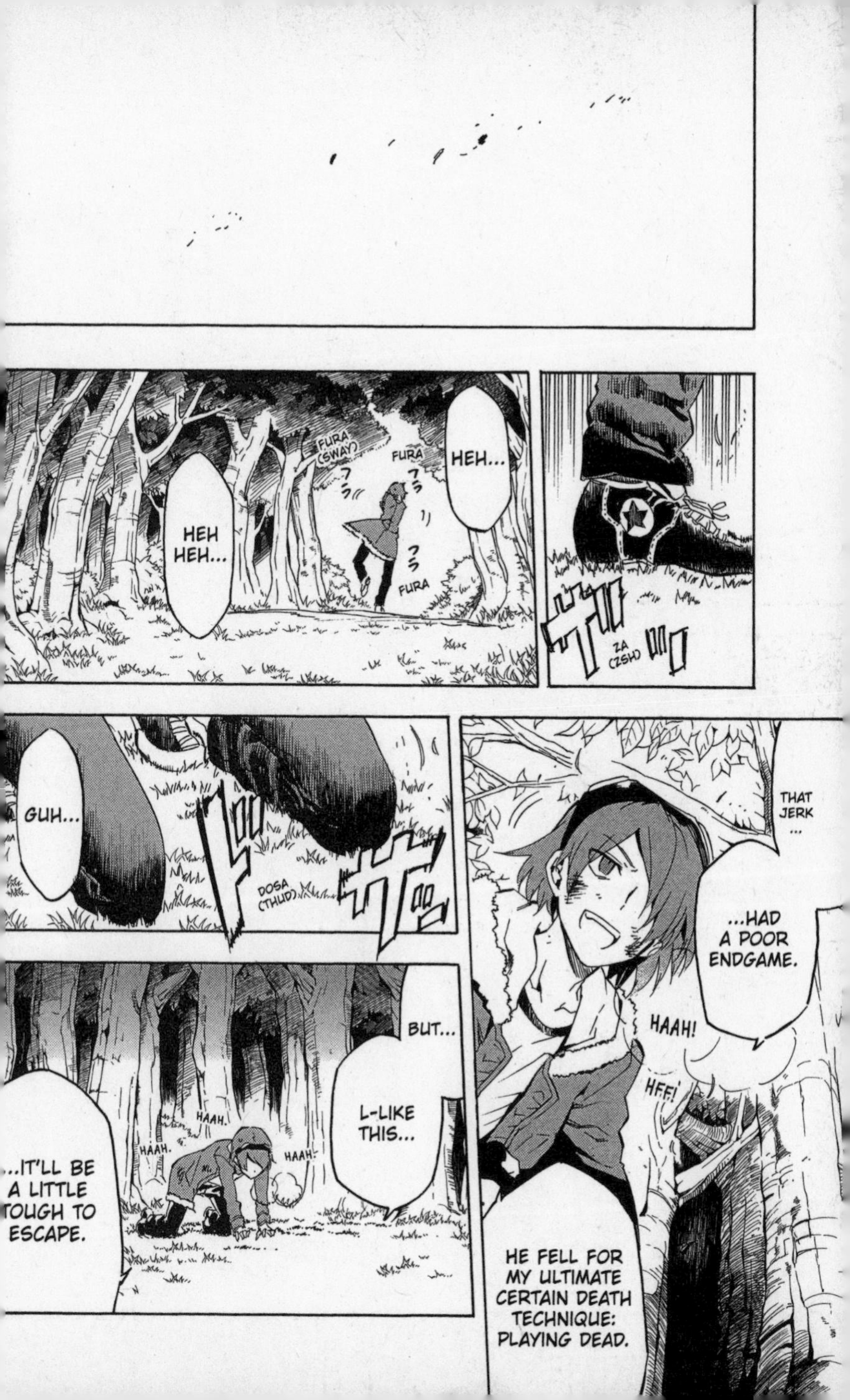
ZA
(ZSH)
HEH...
FURA
(SWAY)
FURA
HEH
HEH...
FURA
THAT
JERK
...
...HAD
A POOR
ENDGAME.
HAAH!
HFF!
HE FELL FOR
MY ULTIMATE
CERTAIN DEATH
TECHNIQUE:
PLAYING DEAD.
DOSA
(THUD)
GUH...
BUT...
L-LIKE
THIS...
HAAH.
HAAH.
HAAH.
...IT'LL BE
A LITTLE
TOUGH TO
ESCAPE.

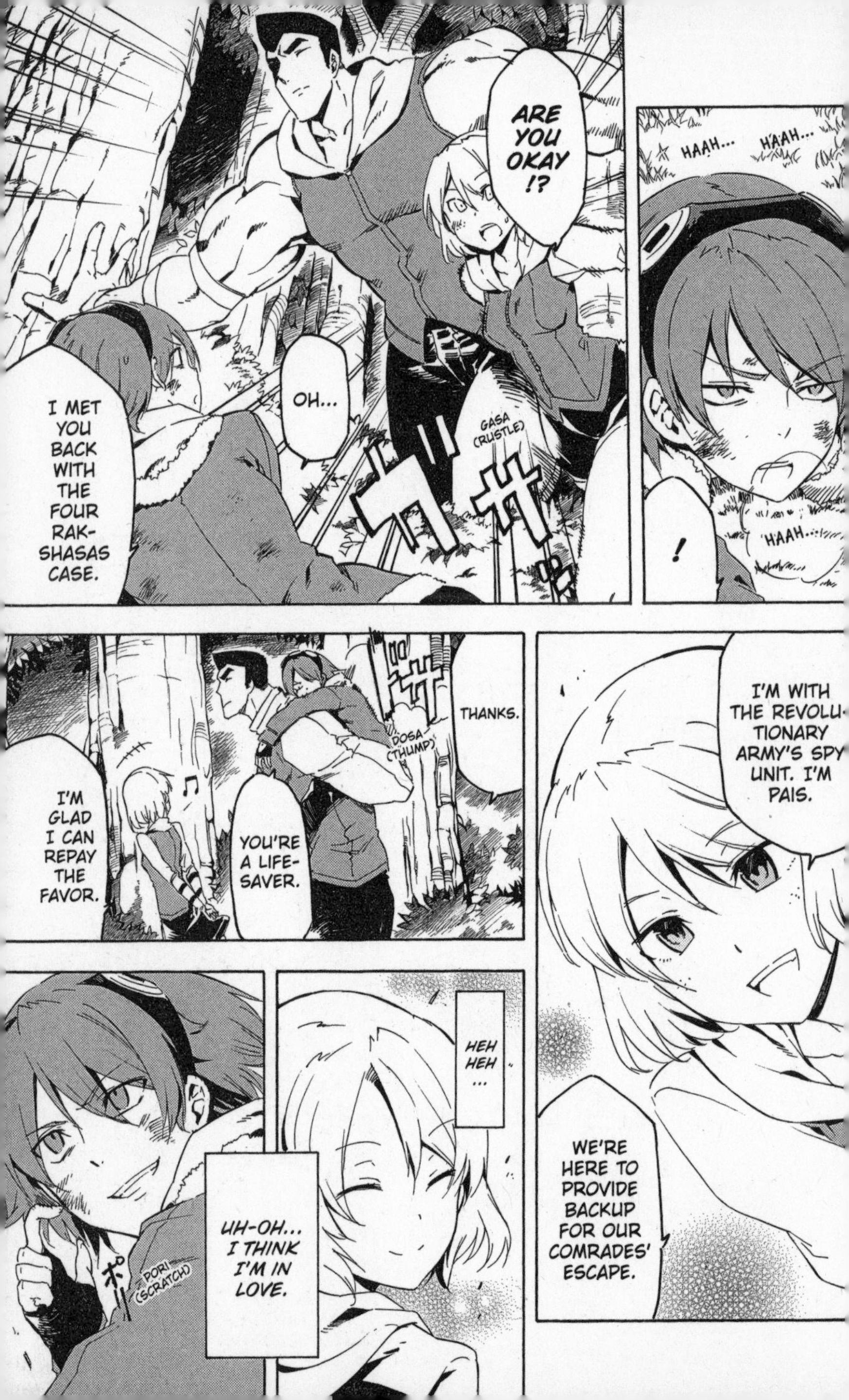
HAAH... HAAH...
!
HAAH...
ARE YOU OKAY!?
GASA (RUSTLE)
OH...
I MET YOU BACK WITH THE FOUR RAKSHASAS CASE.
I'M WITH THE REVOLUTIONARY ARMY'S SPY UNIT. I'M PAIS.
WE'RE HERE TO PROVIDE BACKUP FOR OUR COMRADES' ESCAPE.
THANKS.
DOSA (THUMP)
YOU'RE A LIFE-SAVER.
I'M GLAD I CAN REPAY THE FAVOR.
HEH HEH...
UH-OH... I THINK I'M IN LOVE.
PORI (SCRATCH)

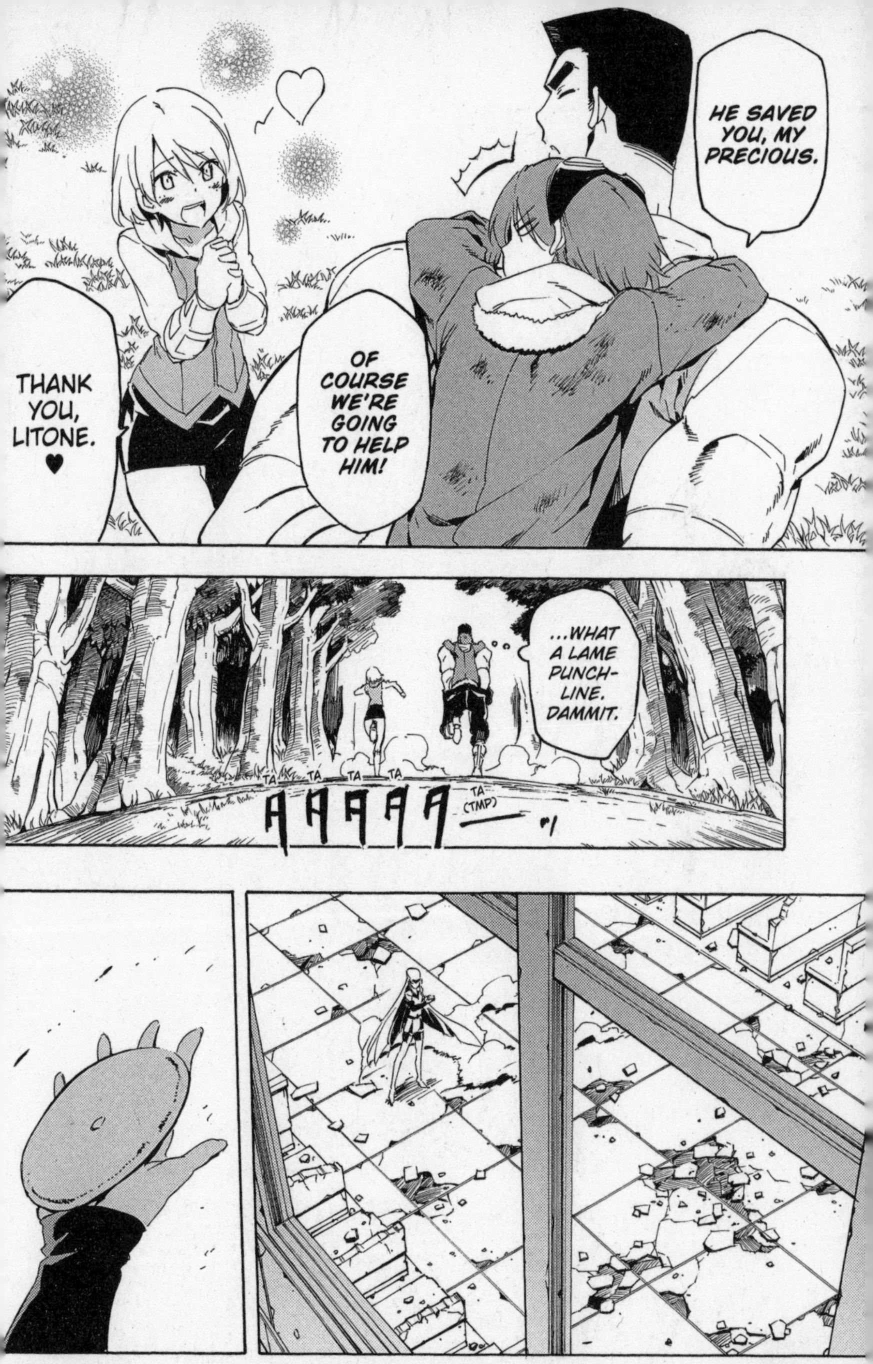
HE SAVED YOU, MY PRECIOUS.
OF COURSE WE'RE GOING TO HELP HIM!
THANK YOU, LITONE. ♥
...WHAT A LAME PUNCH-LINE. DAMMIT.
TA TA TA TA TA (TMP)

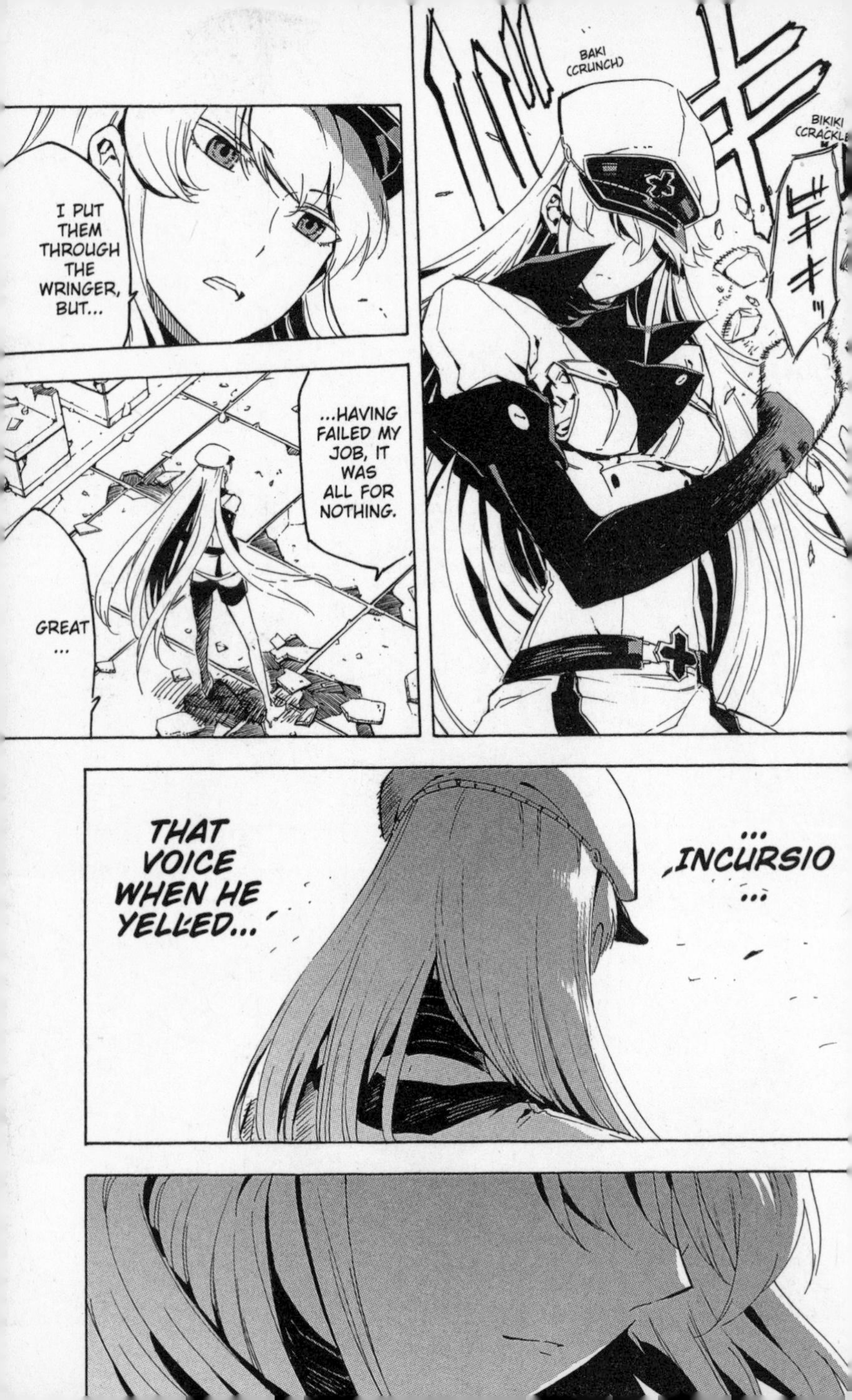

BAKI (CRUNCH)
BIKIKI (CRACKLE)
ビキキッ
I PUT THEM THROUGH THE WRINGER, BUT...
...HAVING FAILED MY JOB, IT WAS ALL FOR NOTHING.
GREAT ...
...INCURSIO ...
THAT VOICE WHEN HE YELLED...

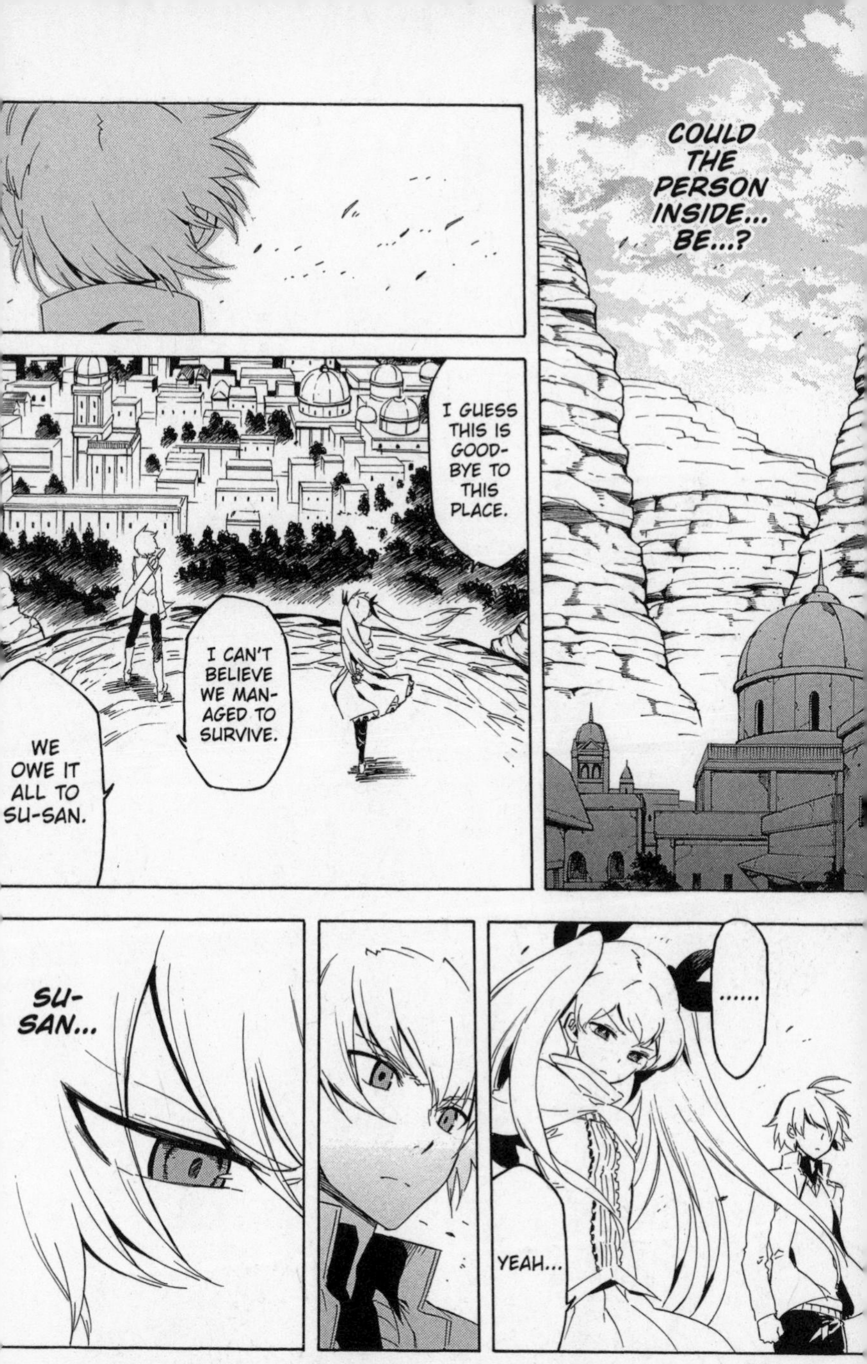
COULD THE PERSON INSIDE... BE...?
I GUESS THIS IS GOOD-BYE TO THIS PLACE.
I CAN'T BELIEVE WE MAN-AGED TO SURVIVE.
WE OWE IT ALL TO SU-SAN.
......
YEAH...
SU-SAN...

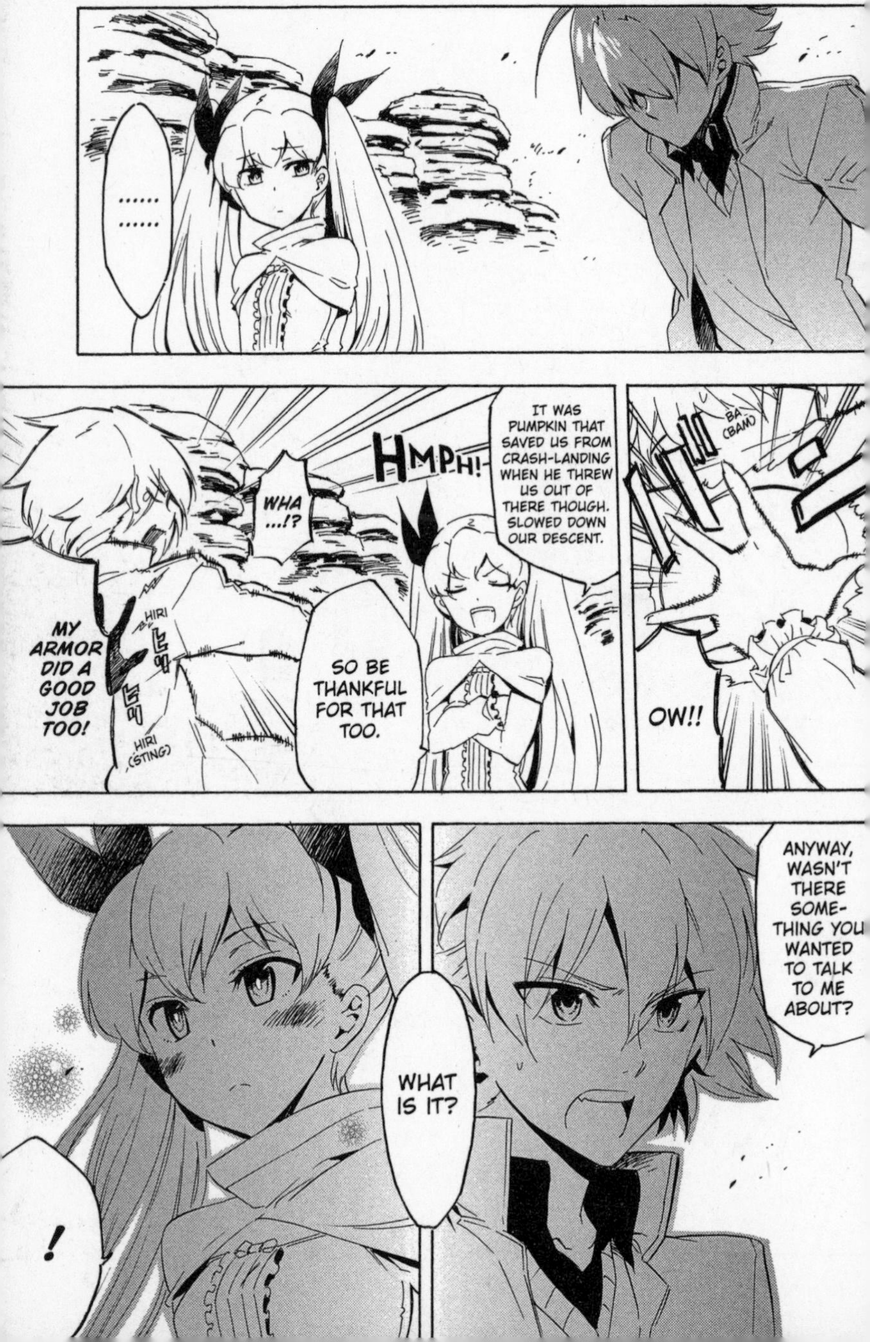
......
......
BA (BAM)
OW!!
IT WAS PUMPKIN THAT SAVED US FROM CRASH-LANDING WHEN HE THREW US OUT OF THERE THOUGH. SLOWED DOWN OUR DESCENT.
HMPH!
SO BE THANKFUL FOR THAT TOO.
WHA ...!?
MY ARMOR DID A GOOD JOB TOO!
HIRI
HIRI (STING)
ANYWAY, WASN'T THERE SOME-THING YOU WANTED TO TALK TO ME ABOUT?
WHAT IS IT?
!

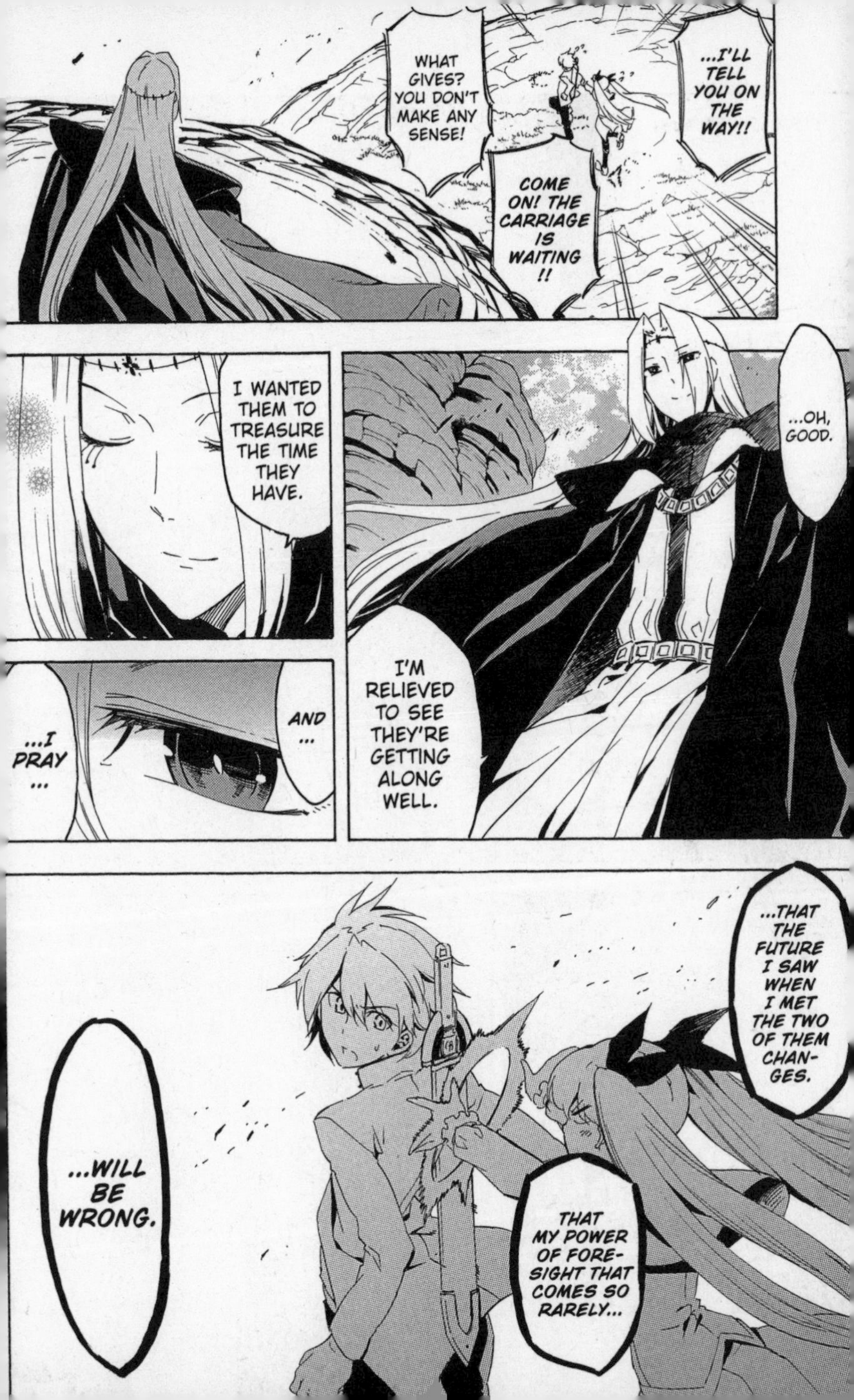
COME ON! THE CARRIAGE IS WAITING!!
WHAT GIVES? YOU DON'T MAKE ANY SENSE!
...I'LL TELL YOU ON THE WAY!!
...OH, GOOD.
I'M RELIEVED TO SEE THEY'RE GETTING ALONG WELL.
I WANTED THEM TO TREASURE THE TIME THEY HAVE.
AND ...
...I PRAY ...
...THAT THE FUTURE I SAW WHEN I MET THE TWO OF THEM CHANGES.
THAT MY POWER OF FORESIGHT THAT COMES SO RARELY...
...WILL BE WRONG.

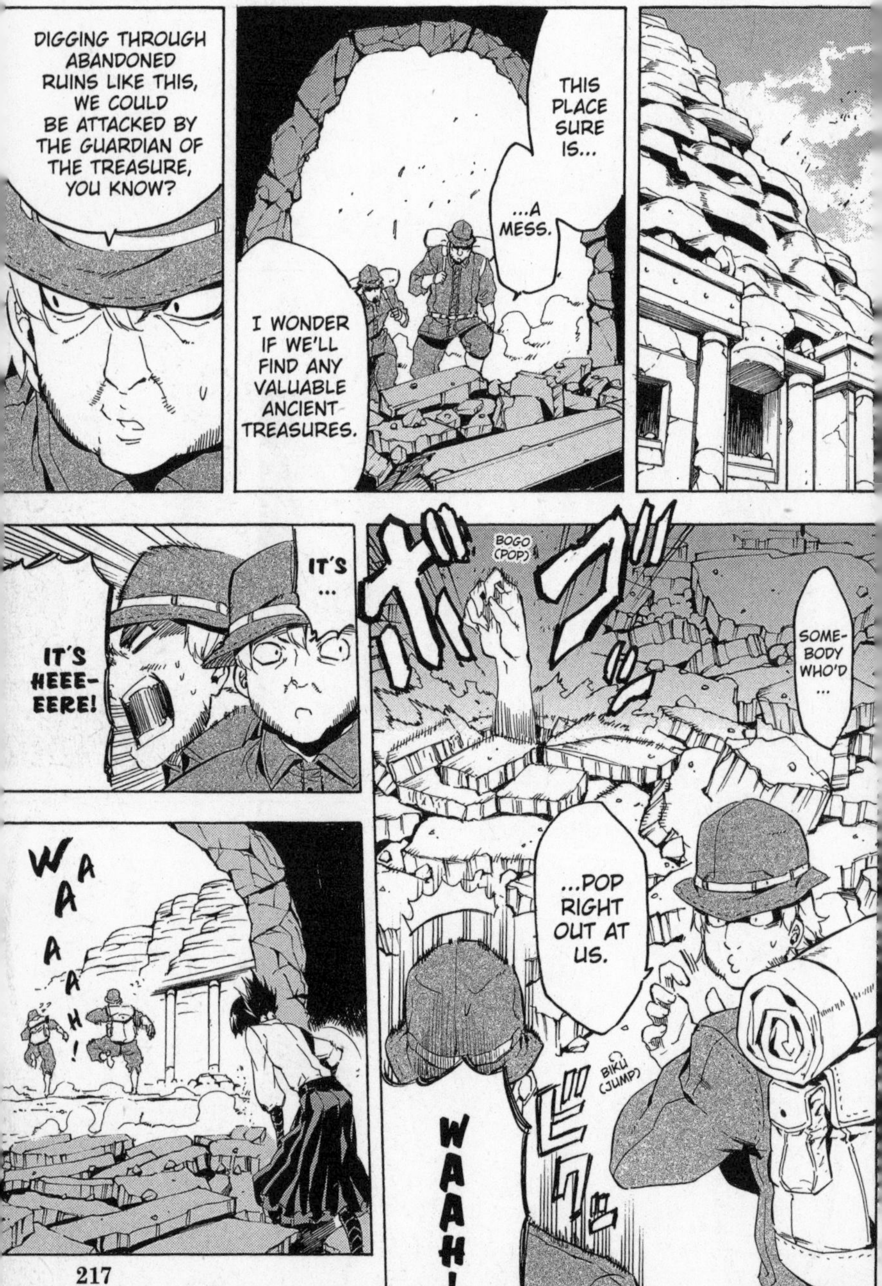
THIS PLACE SURE IS...
...A MESS.
I WONDER IF WE'LL FIND ANY VALUABLE ANCIENT TREASURES.
DIGGING THROUGH ABANDONED RUINS LIKE THIS, WE COULD BE ATTACKED BY THE GUARDIAN OF THE TREASURE, YOU KNOW?
BOGO (POP)
SOME-BODY WHO'D...
...POP RIGHT OUT AT US.
BIKU (JUMP)
WAAH!
IT'S...
IT'S HEEE-EERE!
WAAAAAH!

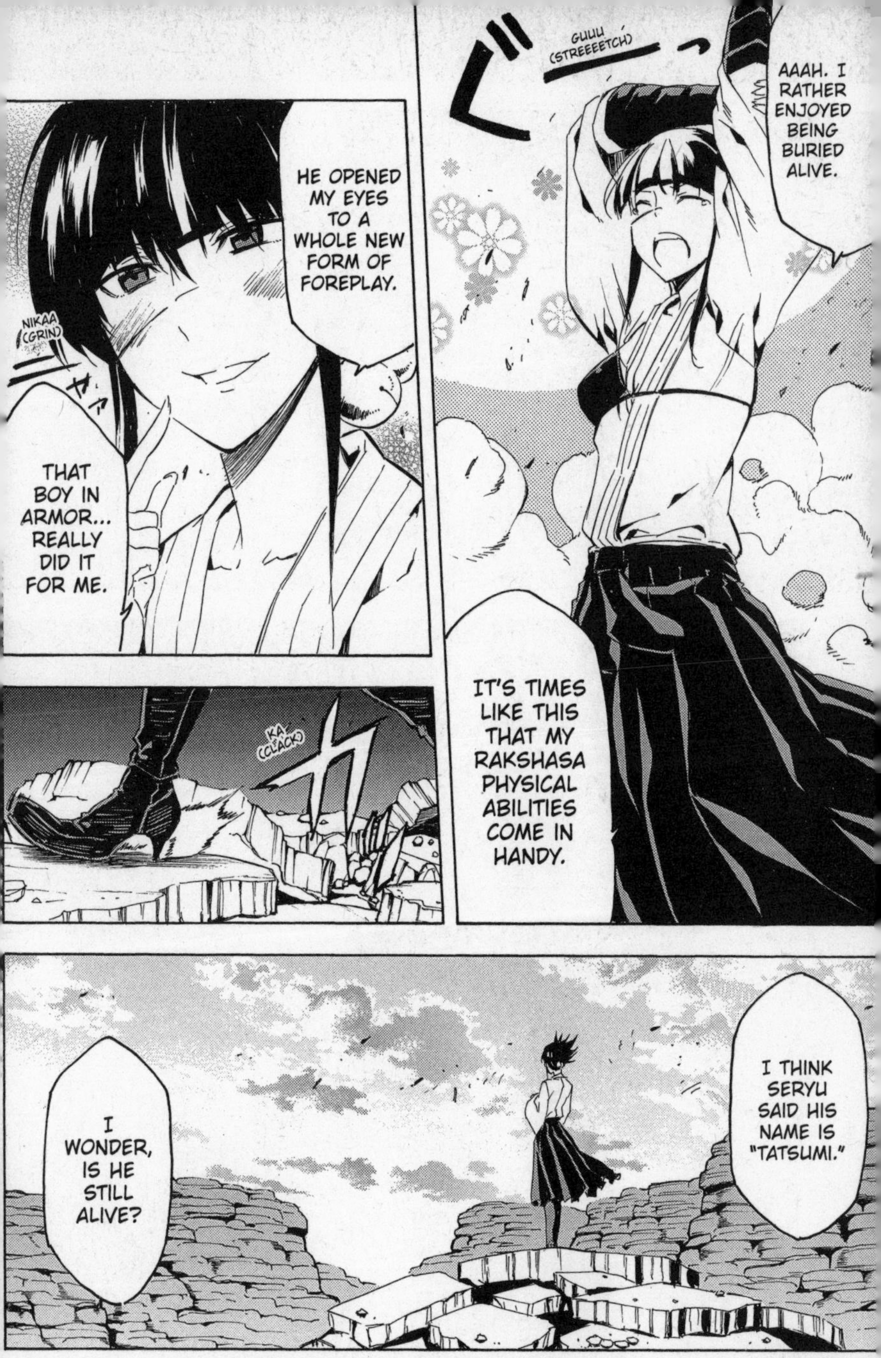
GUUU (STREEEETCH)
AAAH. I RATHER ENJOYED BEING BURIED ALIVE.
IT'S TIMES LIKE THIS THAT MY RAKSHASA PHYSICAL ABILITIES COME IN HANDY.
HE OPENED MY EYES TO A WHOLE NEW FORM OF FOREPLAY.
NIKAA (GRIN)
THAT BOY IN ARMOR... REALLY DID IT FOR ME.
KA (CLACK)
I THINK SERYU SAID HIS NAME IS "TATSUMI."
I WONDER, IS HE STILL ALIVE?

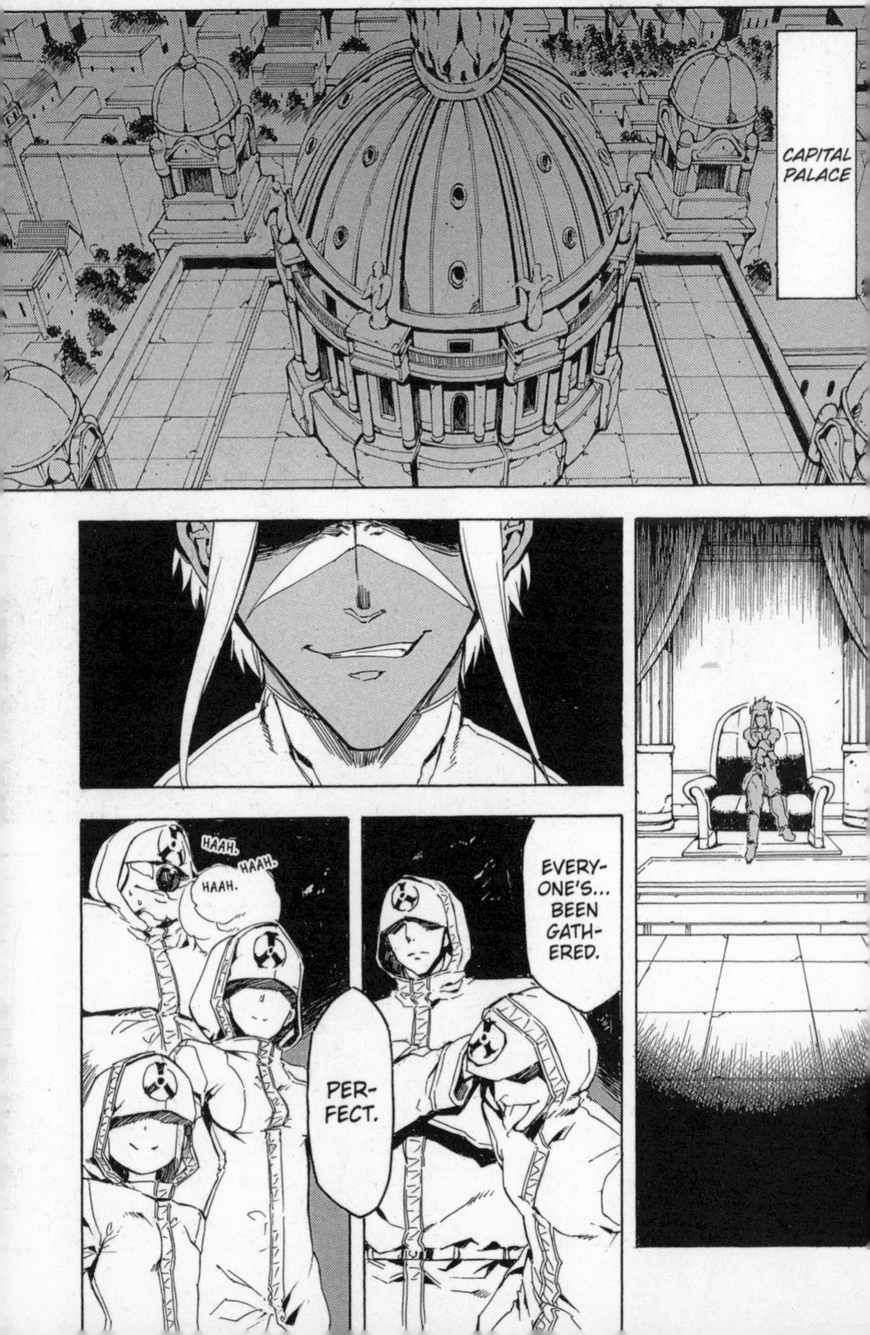
CAPITAL PALACE
EVERY-ONE'S... BEEN GATH-ERED.
PER-FECT.
HAAH.
HAAH.
HAAH.

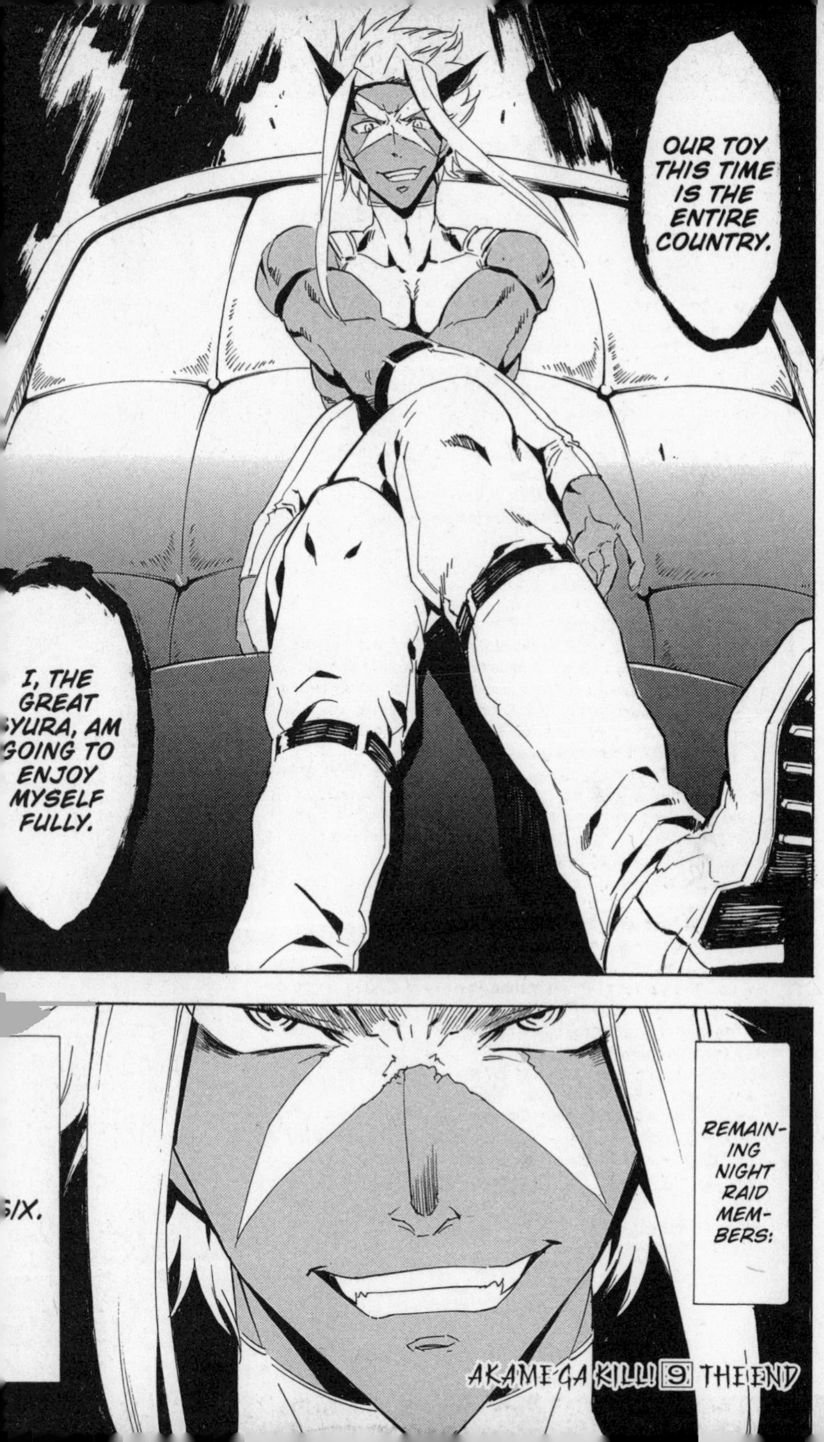
OUR TOY THIS TIME IS THE ENTIRE COUNTRY.
I, THE GREAT SYURA, AM GOING TO ENJOY MYSELF FULLY.
REMAIN-ING NIGHT RAID MEM-BERS:
SIX.
AKAME GA KILL! 9 THE END

TAKAHIRO's POSTSCRIPT

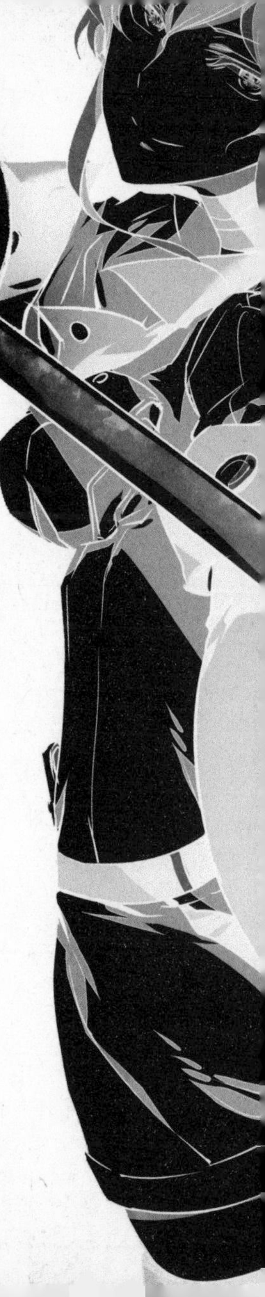

Hello, this is Takahiro from Minato Soft. This time around, I have Wave holding an interview with Esdeath to talk about the new technique she unleashed this volume and fill us in on how she invented it, the origins of its name, and more.

[W → Wave E → Esdeath]

W: General, thank you for taking the time to come out here and speak with me.

E: Certainly, though I know I don't look very good at the moment, having just failed at my job and all... Anyway, this is a fresh start, so let's begin.

W: General, that trump card you pulled was pretty incredible. Freezing time and space...

E: But I can only use it once a day, and it takes a few seconds for it to work.

W: Still, it's wicked strong. How did you come up with it?

E: It's the result of my search for an attack that would defeat any enemy. And there's another reason: Tatsumi. On my return home from the deserted island, Tatsumi fled ahead of me in just a few seconds. If only I'd had this technique, he couldn't have gotten away. Next time, I'm going to make him live with me.

W: (*Okay, I get the reason, but we've gotten a little off track...*)

E: I hear that the way to a man's heart is through his stomach. So I'm going to have Tatsumi try my one-pot stew.

W: Your cooking certainly is delicious, if I remember correctly. But what men really like to eat is, well, somthing a little more...homey? Like meat and potatoes? General, you specialize in one-pot recipes and BBQ...That's the kind of food you'd feed an army with, but...

E: Hmm...But that's all I know how to do.

W: Anyway, General, about that Makahadoma technique...

E: Ah, yes. The secret to freezing time and space is all in the pose.

W: The pose? Is that really the key?

E: It's important to get into it. And coming up with the right name is critical too.

W: Oh, I understand. I always shout out the name when I deliver a kick.

E: I was torn between naming it "Cocytus" and "Makahadoma." I also threw around the idea of "Ice Age," but...I abandoned it.

W: (*You do so many amazing things, General, it blows my mind. Getting into it... I think I can understand that.*)

And there you have Wave showing a little more of his friendly side. Well, see you in the next volume!

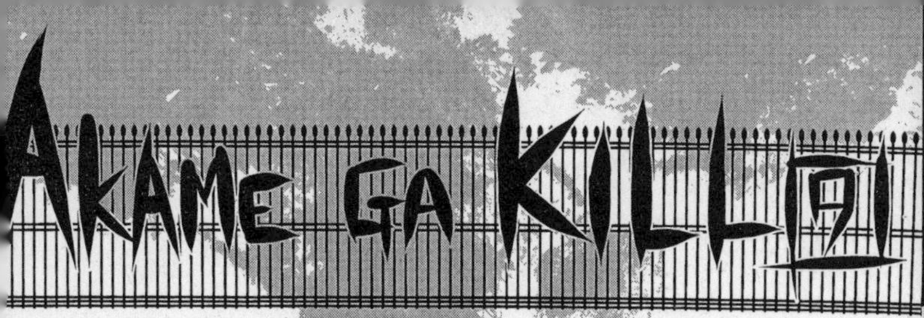
AKAME GA KILL!

MAIN STAFF

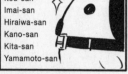

Itou-san
Imai-san
Hiraiwa-san
Kano-san
Kita-san
Yamamoto-san

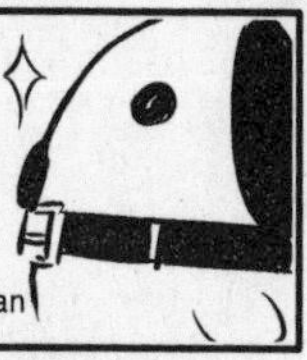

Original Writer
Takahiro-san

Editor
Koizumi-san

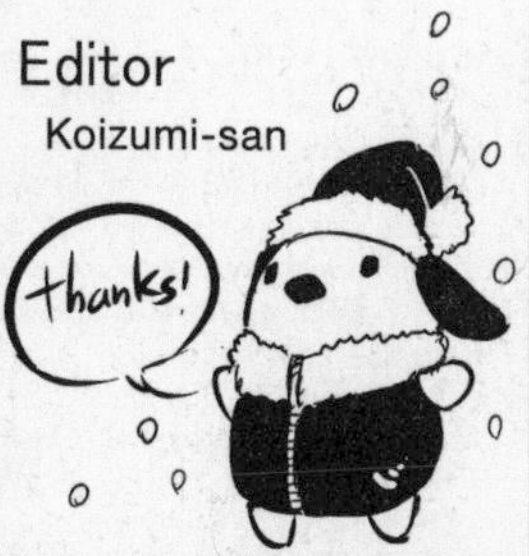
thanks!

COMMENTS

I drew this story feeling as hurried and fidgety as ever. A lot was going on so I was pretty frazzled, but now that I've somehow managed to get it all down, what a relief!
Thank you always to all of you who bought this!
And apparently it's being adapted into an anime! Yahoo!

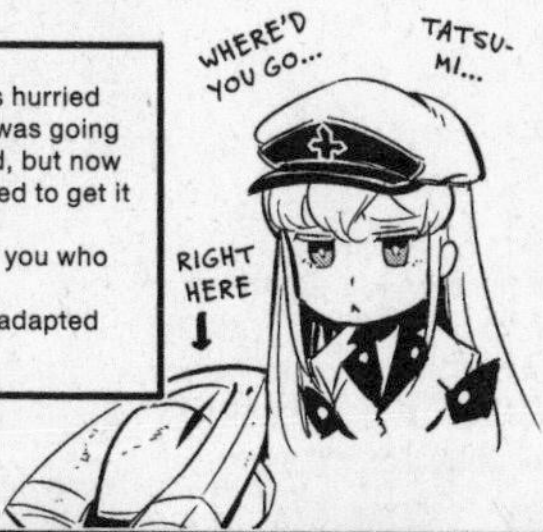
TATSU-MI...
WHERE'D YOU GO...
RIGHT HERE

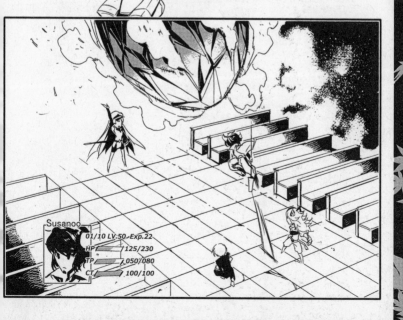

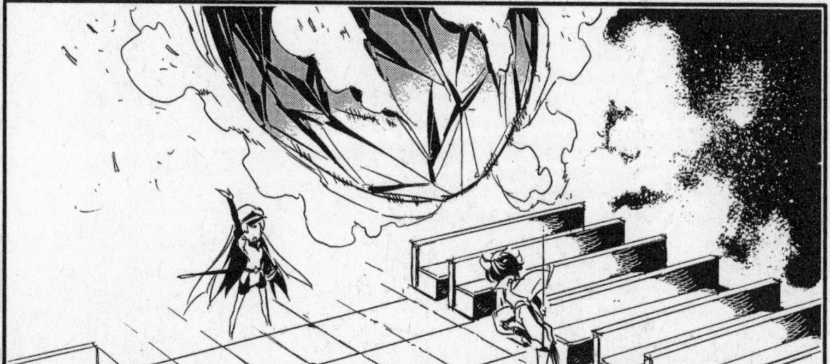
Susanoo
01/10 LV.50 Exp.22
HP 125/230
TP 050/080
CT 100/100

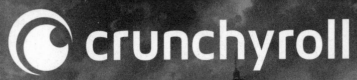

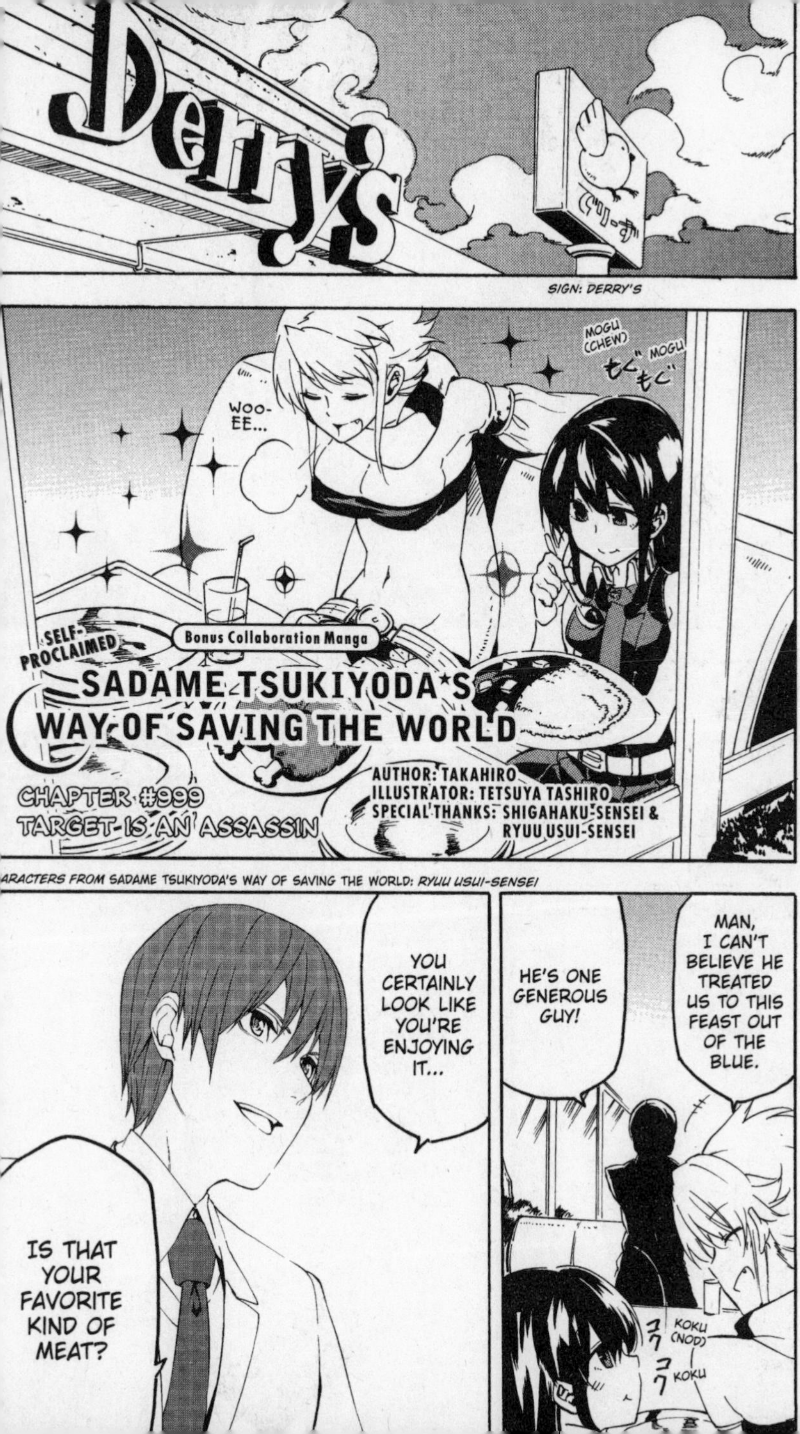
SIGN: DERRY'S
Derry's
MOGU (CHEW) MOGU
もぐ もぐ
WOO-EE...
SELF-PROCLAIMED
Bonus Collaboration Manga
SADAME TSUKIYODA'S WAY OF SAVING THE WORLD
CHAPTER #999
TARGET IS AN ASSASSIN
AUTHOR: TAKAHIRO
ILLUSTRATOR: TETSUYA TASHIRO
SPECIAL THANKS: SHIGAHAKU-SENSEI & RYUU USUI-SENSEI
ARACTERS FROM SADAME TSUKIYODA'S WAY OF SAVING THE WORLD: RYUU USUI-SENSEI
MAN, I CAN'T BELIEVE HE TREATED US TO THIS FEAST OUT OF THE BLUE.
HE'S ONE GENEROUS GUY!
KOKU (NOD) KOKU
YOU CERTAINLY LOOK LIKE YOU'RE ENJOYING IT...
IS THAT YOUR FAVORITE KIND OF MEAT?

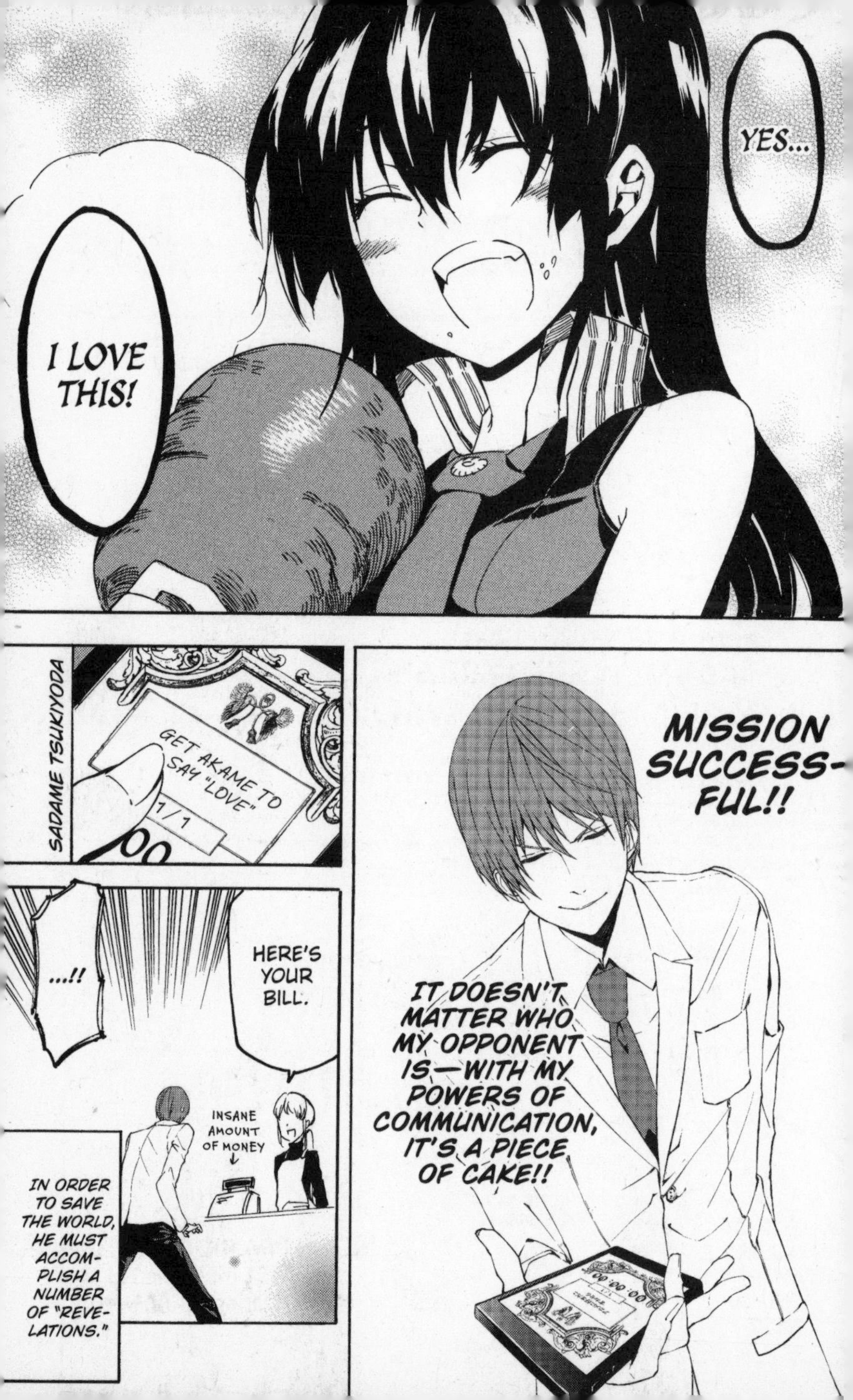
YES...
I LOVE THIS!
MISSION SUCCESS-FUL!!
IT DOESN'T MATTER WHO MY OPPONENT IS—WITH MY POWERS OF COMMUNICATION, IT'S A PIECE OF CAKE!!
SADAME TSUKIYODA
GET AKAME TO SAY "LOVE"
1/1
HERE'S YOUR BILL.
...!!
INSANE AMOUNT OF MONEY
IN ORDER TO SAVE THE WORLD, HE MUST ACCOMPLISH A NUMBER OF "REVELATIONS."

AKAME GA KILL!

Takahiro
Tetsuya Tashiro

Translation: Christine Dashiell
Lettering: Erin Hickman

AKAME GA KILL! Vol. 9
© 2014 Takahiro, Tetsuya Tashiro / SQUARE ENIX CO., LTD. First published in Japan in 2014 by SQUARE ENIX CO., LTD. English translation rights arranged with SQUARE ENIX CO., LTD. and Yen Press, LLC through Tuttle-Mori Agency, Inc., Tokyo.

English translation © 2017 by SQUARE ENIX CO., LTD.

Yen Press
1290 Avenue of the Americas
New York, NY 10104

Visit us at yenpress.com
facebook.com/yenpress
twitter.com/yenpress
yenpress.tumblr.com
instagram.com/yenpress

Yen Press is an imprint of Yen Press, LLC.
The Yen Press name and logo are trademarks of Yen Press, LLC.

The publisher is not responsible for websites (or their content) that are not owned by the publisher.

Library of Congress Control Number: 2015373812

First Yen Press Edition: January 2017

ISBNs: 978-0-316-34012-0 (paperback)
       978-0-316-30596-9 (ebook)

10 9 8 7 6 5 4 3 2 1

BVG

Printed in the United States of America